# Political Approaches to Educational Administration and Leadership

# Routledge Research in Education

# Political Approaches to Educational Administration and Leadership

Eugénie A. Samier
with Adam G. Stanley

Routledge
Taylor & Francis Group
New York   London

First published 2008
by Routledge
711 Third Avenue, New York, NY 10017

Simultaneously published in the UK
by Routledge
2 Park Square, Milton Park, Abingdon, Oxfordshire OX14 4RN

*Routledge is an imprint of the Taylor & Francis Group, an informa business*

First issued in paperback 2010

© 2008 Taylor & Francis

Typeset in Sabon by IBT Global

*Library of Congress Cataloging-in-Publication Data*

Samier, Eugénie Angèle, 1954–
Political approaches to educational administration and leadership / Eugénie A. Samier
   with Adam G. Stanley.
      p. cm. — (Routledge research in education ; 14)
   Includes bibliographical references and index.
   ISBN-13: 978-0-415-96207-0 (hbk)
   ISBN-10: 0-415-96207-2 (hbk)
   ISBN-13: 978-0-203-92867-7 (ebk)
   ISBN-10: 0-203-92867-9 (ebk)
1. School management and organization—Political aspects.  2. Educational
leadership—Political aspects.  I. Stanley, Adam.  II. Title.

LB2806.S325 2008
371.2—dc22                                                               2007041682

ISBN13: 978-0-415-96207-0 (hbk)
ISBN13: 978-0-415-89740-2 (pbk)
ISBN13: 978-0-203-92867-7 (ebk)

# Contents

# List of Figures

# List of Tables

# 1 Introduction

*Eugénie A. Samier*

Politics is ubiquitous in administration and leadership, on all levels from the macroglobal to individual units of an organisation and interpersonal relations. As the distribution of power, and therefore decision-making, it necessarily involves administration and leadership. Pollitt and Bouckaert's recent *Public Management Reform* takes a political approach to administrative studies that is equally relevant to educational administration, examining several levels of political influence: socioeconomic forces within which jurisdictions are embedded (including international politics); the political system, consisting of party political ideas, pressure from citizens, and new management ideas; chance events, like scandals and disasters, that require political action; and to some extent the 'elite decision-makers' who determine what is desirable and feasible, which would include cabinet ministers and mandarins who occupy a quasipolitical and quasiadministrative role (2004: 25). To these can be added micropolitics and the correlatives of authority, consent and obedience. The importance of politics to administration and leadership is emphasised in their characterisation of regimes as 'politico-administrative' (2004: 39). Not only is politics endemic to administration, and intensified when leadership is added, but it comprises a necessary foundational dimension to the political character of nations, upon which their administrative systems, political roles, and patterns of political behaviour and conceptions are built. One of the most influential systems, neoliberalism and the New Public Management ideology (referred to sometimes in education as the corporatisation and commercialisation of education), has had a significant effect on the public sector internationally since the early 1980s. This collection explores how politics relates to education in as many aspects as one volume can hope to cover.

Designing a book collection always presents a number of problems. Additionally, exploring the complex and far-ranging topic of politics, given the many dimensions and effects of formal and informal, exogenous and endogenous political activity, greatly increases those challenges. Such an exploration crosses over many disciplinary boundaries involving political culture, sociology of politics, political ethics, psychology and psychopathology of power, political economy, and political aesthetics. It also implicates a broad range

of topics in administration and leadership: values, professionalism, authority and power, governance, management ideologies, legitimacy, policy, interest group goals, conflict, control and consent, and micropolitical formations
(coalitions, factions, cliques, and so forth). Politics underlies many current
concerns and issues in the social justice area, such as gender equity, pluralism,
democratisation, organisational change and innovation, and conceptions of
civil society, as well as internationalisation and globalisation. It was necessary, therefore, to select representative topics for this project.

The politics of education all too often consists of war stories, still largely
dominated by the old boys' network with little discussion of historical,
sociocultural, economic, and other dimensions. Like the two previous collections, on ethics (Samier 2003) and on aesthetics (Samier and Bates 2006),
this volume is oriented toward a philosophical and theoretical foundation
for educational administration and leadership. It is intended to demonstrate
the relevance of this foundation to practical issues and problems internationally, both within the organisational context and extraorganisationally.
As such, the book focuses on a complex and comprehensive application
of political principles as they affect our understanding of, and practice in,
educational organisations. It also provides a framework for philosophical
foundations courses. Relying on the 'philosophical foundations' courses traditionally provided by the curriculum division is a common practice. While
conceptions of a good education are important to educational administration and leadership, equally important are philosophical writings on the
state, government, and leadership from social and political perspectives.

Even though it has become common practice in the English-speaking
world to use the terms 'leadership' and 'administration' synonymously in
education to denote formal positions of authority, the title of this collection
indicates a distinction between the two terms (although all the contributors might not share this view). Following to some extent in the Weberian
tradition, and in the public administration tradition, I interpret the distinction as follows: administrative roles are those that are formally structured
and whose legitimacy and authority are sanctioned through policy regimes
that do not require acceptance of the person but the responsibilities of the
office; leadership roles, on the other hand, are constructed in interpersonal
relationships that are not necessarily formally sanctioned, whose legitimacy is conferred by followers on individuals for their personal qualities,
and whose value is not bound by existing organisational or institutional
purpose, design, and policy regimes. In other words, administration is an
organisationally constituted formal category, and leadership is a personally
constructed political category. This view is taken by authors like Edwards
(1998: 557) and Gronn (1999: 3–7) who define the difference as roles that
are distinguishable by relation to the status quo and risk aversion on the
part of administration and management, and risk taking on the part of
leadership. One could also surmise, as Weber did, that people desire to
subordinate themselves to a leader rather than an administrator because

they can make a personal connection with the former, while the latter carries connotations of a bureaucratically dehumanised environment.

This collection conceptualises politics on three level: the political philosophy and theory that provide conceptions and values, the political structures that shape formal institutions and informal constructions, and the political processes that characterise everyday political life.

## POLITICAL PHILOSOPHY, STRUCTURES, AND PROCESSES

Politics has been a perennial problem for all sociocultural structures, recognised as long as philosophy has existed and consisting of the intellectual history of the field. Classical political philosophy includes the pre-Socratics, such as Xenophanes and Heraclitus, who wrote about the state and its relationship to bureaucracy, and Democritus, who examined concepts of the polis and its leadership (see Gadamer 1998). The two major authors from this period are Plato and Aristotle. Plato emphasised the roles of knowledge, rationality and ethics in *The Republic* and *The Laws*. A number of minor dialogues examined related concepts: for example, bravery in *Laches;* self-control leading to wisdom, courage, and justice in *Charmides;* obedience, duty, and honour in the *Apology;* and statesmanship in *Politicus.* Aristotle, more empirically oriented, analysed types of political community in *Politics* in relation to how well they contribute to citizen virtue and allow for citizen participation in the political process, as well as the causes and preventions of revolution. He established an early classification system of six state types: the good types, including monarchy, aristocracy, polity, and the corrupt, consisting of tyranny, oligarchy, and democracy. Complementing *Politics* is the *Nicomachean Ethics* in which Aristotle classified knowledge into three categories: theoretical knowledge, aiming at contemplation necessary to determine eternal truths, including the principles of logic and mathematics; practical knowledge, aiming at action for the good life; and productive knowledge, aiming at creative activities in both artisan and artistic endeavours.

Plato regarded those competent to lead to be wise, that is, those with the knowledge and skill to morally wield power and authority (e.g., see *The Republic*). Aristotle's conceptions of leadership are expressed as forms of rulership, typical for most premodern authors. He distinguished six types in *Politics,* the first three of moral character, kingship, aristocracy, and polity, and the other three being deviant, tyranny, oligarchy, and democracy. His discussion of justice relevant to these is in the *Nicomachean Ethics,* a text that needs to be read alongside the *Politics.*

One of the most relevant Roman authors on politics and government is Cicero, whose *De Officiis, De Legibus,* and *Pro Milone,* contain discussions of the proper role of government and leadership and an early model of a pragmatic approach, which is guided largely by moral principle but flexible

enough in realpolitik to appreciate the compromises that might be necessary to form alliances and respond to unusual or pressing circumstances. A
medieval thinker, whose discussion of government still holds relevant principles is Thomas Aquinas in the *Summa Theologica*, covering various governmental topics and political ethics, some of which are carried in modern
international law (in the just use of force).

A tradition that spans centuries is the strategic and tactical. This includes
Sun Tzu's *Art of War*, Machiavelli's *The Prince* and *Art of War*, and, to
a lesser extent, von Clausewitz' *On War*. These works are important for
administration and leadership, covering formal state decisions as well as
strategies and tactics relevant to formal administrative activities and the
more informal day-to-day organisational politics.

Early modern philosophy includes Machiavelli's *Discourses* on the state
and politics, including its implications for administration, as well as one of
his exemplars, 'The Life of Castruccio Castracani of Lucca,' a man who 'is
armed, proud, cruel, and fearsome' (see Macfarland 1999). Social contract
theory, most important for modern democratic states, was developed by
John Locke, who envisioned the state as a structure created by mankind
within a world created by God. Locke was followed by Jean-Jacques Rousseau, who regarded the state as a social structure created to replace the state
of nature to ensure the rights of justice, laws, and morality for the individual, and for whom the state has the responsibility to maintain education
whereby intelligence and enlightenment are cultivated. Charles de Secondat
Montesquieu, in *The Spirit of the Laws*, contributed to fundamental political and administrative theory in his separation of powers, the sovereign
from the administration, and further division of the latter into the legislative, executive, and judicial, reflected in modern constitutions.

Also influential in continental European political philosophy are many
figures rarely explored in English-language theory. For example, Johann
Oldendorp (1487–1567), a lawyer, professor, Reformationist, and city
counsellor, wrote on the relationship of the law and state, laying a foundation for the modern principles upon which administration is built. Johann
Ulrich von Cramer (1706–1772), a judge, legal scholar, and Enlightenment
philosopher, also influenced the development of modern law and administration. And, despite their fame, Kant and Hegel's political writings are
relatively little used, particularly in administrative studies. Kant contributed
to classical liberal theory, constitutional republicanism, and a democratic
peace theory. Hegel developed conceptions of civil society and the appropriate role of government, influential educational principles for what became
known later as the Humboldt model for the university, and a more radical
liberalism from which Marx drew inspiration.

For Anglo-Saxon countries, inclined towards a pragmatic administration
tradition, instead of the legal-administrative tradition of much of Western continental Europe, utilitarianism provided fundamental societal and governmental principles. This includes the work of Francis Hutcheson, Jeremy Bentham,

in *Principles of the Civil Code,* and John Stuart Mill, in *On Liberty.* Their influence contributed to American pragmatism and social choice theory.

The modern tradition of realpolitik, to some extent reflective of Machiavelli but aimed at creating balances of power (unlike the usual English meaning of power politics), begins with Cardinal Richelieu of France, followed by Frederick the Great of Prussia, the Austrian Foreign Minister Metternich, and Otto von Bismarck of Prussia. It is in this tradition particularly that strategic and tactical practice is condoned, evident in modern practitioners like Henry Kissinger.

Political schools derive from philosophy. The long-standing and influential school of Marxism brings a critique of capitalism and bureaucracy to the field, along with a broader notion of democracy. Representative authors include Bowles and Gintis (1976), Freire (1973), Apple (1982a), Giroux (1981), and Smyth (1989). Marxist theory also heavily influenced the later development of feminism and pluralism, race-related critique, postcolonialism, and a school that has superseded Marxism recently, Critical Theory. The Frankfurt School first entered educational discussion in the 1960s, largely popularised by Marcuse, but since then Jürgen Habermas has dominated the field primarily through his theory of communicative action. Two early essays, 'The University in a Democracy—Democratization of the University' and 'Student Protest in the Federal Republic of Germany' (1970), give some indication of the direction he was taking regarding the politics of education. As a continuation of the Enlightenment tradition, Critical Theory provides a contrast to postmodern writers who have also been influential in educational thinking, primarily Foucault on the relationship between power and knowledge.

Democratisation has taken on two opposed forms: a range of 'left' views from neo-Marxism (see Smyth 1989), Critical Theory, and left-liberalism; and a neoliberal or conservative form, inspired by Hayek (1994) and primarily oriented toward a market model. Both have profound implications for governance and the entire character of educational organisations since they affect the distribution of power, resources, and decision-making. The ascendancy of neoliberalism internationally, in the form of the New Public Management ideology, has altered the public sector in most countries, occasioning in educational critique a rapidly increasing body of literature on the corporatisation and commercialisation of education, an early important text being Sheila Slaughter and Larry Leslie's *Academic Capitalism: Politics, Policies, and the Entrepreneurial University* (1997).

Political analysis extends also to structures of administration, those institutional configurations derived from political values and relationships in different kinds of political systems, such as democracy, oligarchy, and dictatorship. The most dominant is the politics of bureaucracy, found in Child's study of 'Organizational Structure and Strategies of Control' (1972), Holden's '"Imperialism" in Bureaucracy' (1966), Moe's 'The Politics of Bureaucratic Structure' (1989), and carried into education through Meyer,

Scott and Deal's 'Institutional and Technical Sources of Organizational Structure' (1981). An important related political concept is legitimacy, found in Habermas' *Legitimation Crisis* (1975) and Della Fave (1986). Recently, political neoinstitutionalism has emerged, prompted by DiMaggio and Powell's 'The Iron Cage Revisited' (1983), examining the institutional context within which each institution resides (Peters 1998). Another structure that has played a large role internationally in the development of educational systems is colonialism, critiqued in postcolonial literature, following the lead of Edward Said (1978), but in education emerging earlier with the writing of Friere.

An important type of structure, especially for leadership studies, but greatly underrepresented is elitism. This approach has a long history, beginning with Pareto (*The Rise and Fall of the Elites*, 1901), Mosca (*The Ruling Class*, 1896), Michels (*Political Parties*, 1911), Gramsci (*Prison Notebooks*, 1949–1953), C. Wright Mills (*The Power Elite*, 1956), Bukharin (*The Economic Theory of the Leisure Class*, 1914), Bottomore (*Elites and Society*, 1964), and neo-Marxist scholars like Poulantzas (*Political Power and Social Classes*, 1968), and Miliband (*The State in Capitalist Society*, 1969). More recent scholars are Domhoff and Dye (*Power Elites and Organizations*, 1987), and Domhoff (*Who Rules America?*, 1967). Elite theory is not only important in examining administrative structures and roles, but leadership roles in their formal and informal construction. Related structures of importance to education are the iron triangle, a term initially coined by McConnell (1966), and patriarchy, explored in education by Lerner (1986) and Luke and Gore (1992), as well as a broad range of differential rankings through social stratification.

Formal political processes range from relationships between social institutions, such as the economic, religious and political systems with the educational sector, to formal internal politics of an organisation in the form of governance structures, collective bargaining, negotiation and arbitration, as well as advisory bodies representing interest groups such as equity groups (in Canada, women, aboriginal peoples, visible minorities, and people with disabilities). A number of influential studies appeared in the 1980s, including Mastenbroek (1980), Fisher (1983), and Rubin (1983).

As important as formal politics is in understanding institutional structures and practices, the informal rules, or 'rules of the game,' derived from bureaucratic norms to clientelism and patrimonialism are equally important, 'created, communicated, and enforced outside of officially sanctioned channels' (Helmke and Levitsky 2004: 725). Two influential books departing politically from the 'rational' discussion were Tullock's *The Politics of Bureaucracy* (1965) and Peters' *The Politics of Bureaucracy* (1978). Referred to often as 'micropolitics' (Ball 1987), or Realpolitik, this area examines the coalitions, alliances, and factions that form in an organisation (e.g., Hoyle 1982; Pfeffer 1978), potentially affecting all aspects of organisational life in positive and negative ways, and implicated in ethics and psychology as academic bullying and mobbing in some of its most pernicious forms. Contributors to this dimension of politics have included Clegg (1989) on resistance and complicity, Mintzberg (1983) on internal and external coalitions, Porter et al. (1983) on the politics of influence, and Storey (1985) on labour complicity in management control. Pettigrew (1973) explored the politics of decision-making.

Helmke and Levitsky (2004) have recently proposed a four-part theory for classifying and analysing informal institutional practices, or the types of informal rules by which influence and decision-making operate. This includes various relationships of informal practices with effective and ineffective formal institutions; in some cases, effective practices are substituted where the formal are weak or compete through incentives to violate formal rules, and in others, practices are complemented by filling in gaps or accommodating through creating incentives to alter rules. The 1999 Special Issue of *School Leadership & Management* made a notable contribution to micropolitics. In the introductory paper, Mawhinney provides a thorough overview of micropolitical writings in educational administration and leadership, an approach that has been developing since Iannaccone's early foray in 1975 in *Educational Policy Systems*.

Ledeneva (2006) employs a large range of informal practices in her analysis of contemporary Russia to determine how politics and economics are conducted in a state in which formal rules are dysfunctional, impractical or lacking, that is, using the strategies and 'navigation' between formal rules and informal norms used by individuals and groups to get things done. These include: 'black PR' to damage the reputation of rivals; the use of compromising information; solidarity of a group whose fate is interdependent; the barter 'market' or shadow barter; a lack of transparency in the forms of insufficient accountability leading to corruption; and the use of informal punishment and manipulative use of the disciplinary system. These may become much more important to education as neoliberalism forces public education to entrepreneurialise and enter the competitive marketplace. Informal politics also includes the manipulation of policies, procedures, and rules whether through 'working to rule' or treating the application of rules differentially to organisational friends and foes (West 1985). Change, reform, and innovation also generate micropolitics, explored in some detail by Frost and Egri (1991), Meyerson and Scully (1995), and Weiler (1985).

The analysis of power has been a major feature of political analysis since early in the history of administrative studies, and, arguably, the most important feature for leadership roles. One of the earliest studies is French and Raven's 'The Bases of Social Power' (1959), followed by Bachrach and Baratz' 'The Two Faces of Power' (1962), and several authors exploring in greater detail how power functions in the administrative setting, such as Blau (1964), Zaleznik (1970), Clegg (1975), Bacharach and Lawler (1980), and Pfeffer (1981; 1992). In educational administration, power has also been regarded as an important political feature (Apple 1982b; Nyberg

1981). Related to studies of power are conflict theories, focussed primarily in intraorganisational conflict, such as Raven and Knuglenski (1970) and Kolb and Bartunek (1992), with a strong representation from educational administration, in Baldridge (1971), Bennet and Wilkie (1973) and Richardson (1973). Examination of power plays has led to a strong subfield of strategy and tactics. Mintzberg was one of the earliest, with 'Patterns in Strategy Formation' (1978), followed by Kipnis et al. (1980), Gray and Ariss (1985), Knights and Morgan (1991), and Fairholm (1993). Postmodern theory has also contributed heavily to this field, most notably Foucault (1980).

Organisational culture is another source of political analysis, involving the effect of politics on organisations producing toxic cultures or culture being used as a medium for political activity. Key authors in this area have been Deal and Kennedy (1982), Lucas (1987), Meyer and Rowan (1992), and Van Maanen and Barley (1984), as well as Galtung (1981) in education. Topics of interest include: political myths (Edelman 1971), rituals of intimidation (O'Day 1974), and degradation ceremonies (Garfinkel 1956).

One approach that has again gained credence is the psychology and psychopathology of power. In the 1970s, Karen Horney and Bruno Bettelheim examined the underlying psychological processes that influence behaviour contributing to organisational conflict. Most recently, Manfred Kets de Vries (2006) has applied neo-Freudian theory to the 'inner theatre' of those with power who have a negative effect on organisational culture and abuse their authority over individuals. This behaviour derives from the irrational rather than the rational, the 'deeply submerged' part of the iceberg of the informal organisation. In other words, he credits the 'rot at the top,' that is, personality disorders, for an undue share in creating neurotic organisational cultures (Kets de Vries and Miller 1984). Others have explored the emotional costs of power for a number of decades, such as Lasswell (1962), McClelland (1975), Ouchi and Johnson (1978), and Baum (1983).

A little-examined aspect of educational politics is clandestine activity, such as intelligence gathering, surveillance, sabotage, misrepresentation, resistance, and disinformation against members of the organisation and of other organisations. It is the covert side of the organisation that is arguably the most difficult challenge for leadership, both in overcoming its negative effects and in avoiding these practices themselves in a highly politicised and changing environment. Secrecy and 'tradecraft' include many of the activities involved in formal negotiations, as well as sabotage (Brown 1977; Jermier, Knights and Nord 1994) and strategic decision-making and communication (Hancock and Hellawell 2003).

The politics of an organisation are affected by all sociocultural factors, producing many multidimensional critiques, too extensive to cover in an overview. However, there are three more factors that deserve mention here, given their importance and development in sociopolitical scholarship. One is communication, examined by Morley and Shockley-Zalabak (1986) for its role in conflict and by Mumby (1988) for discourse in power relations. Another is ideology, a phenomenon examined by Althusser (1971) and Eagleton (1991) and applied in organisational theory by Meyer (1984), as a legitimation problem by Brown (1978), and in the educational world by Grace (1978).

One way to approach the politics of leadership is through a typology of styles based upon the degree of leader and followership orientation to organisational norms and power structures, ranging from a close adherence to a radical rejection. The first, affirmational or 'reconciler,' in which leaders and followers conform to existing organisational tasks and socioemotional goals, is aimed at renewal and regeneration that preserve or recreate the original goals and ethos. Individuals are oriented toward maintaining consensus and group cohesion by building alliances, using teamwork, and often using counseling techniques to diffuse problems, as well as sacrificing policy goals through compromise to satisfy diverse interests. Opposition remains diffused over a broad range of internal and external constituencies. Bennis (1989) and Meier (1989) are examples of this form.

A second style, in an escalating opposition, is reform or 'mobiliser' leadership, in which there is ambivalence to organisational goals: A discrepancy exists between organisational principles and ideals, or sustaining myth, and customary practices (e.g., principle of equality or equity). This style is characterised by a sociopolitical movement arising from opposition to constituted authority not providing leadership on targeted issues, and a receptivity to changes that exist in the broad community of the organization. Change is advocated through relatively gradual and peaceful tactics emphasising persuasion and nonviolent confrontation and alliance with and cooperation from extraorganisational sources and movements (e.g., research institutes). Kavanagh (1987) and Turner (1981) discuss this style.

An intermediary style is the subversive, driven primarily by extraorganisational considerations and aimed at introducing new principles (e.g., equality, equity) or replacing one legitimate executive structure with another (removing an illegitimate power elite) without altering the fundamental ethos of the organization. This requires well-developed strategic and tactical skills, not always characterised by violence, but more often conspiracy. This is often the first stage of revolutionary movements. Lukes (1985) provides an analysis of this form.

The penultimate style involves the transitional leader who brings about the dismantling of a system or structure but is unable to create a new and successful replacement. The leader generally originates within the elite power structure, positioned to create the alliances, and has the knowledge to 'bring the system down,' possibly beginning as a reformer type, however, typically developing into a 'reactionary' leader as the dismantling process grows out of control. This form is characterised by well-developed factions and political polarization, seen in the case of Gorbachev (Kaiser 1992).

The final style is revolutionary, aimed at replacing existing structures, which are viewed as irremediably wrong. The community is alienated from the sustaining myth to the degree that a fundamental reconstitution is deemed necessary both in terms of vision (philosophy) and new type of structure. It is characterised by tactics of violence, willingness to sacrifice, and power struggle at the top (leadership elite), eventually evolving into a reign of terror. The leader often arises from a constituted role (e.g., Lenin, Robespierre), often from the intelligentsia and professional class, thereby having administrative ability, a high level of task ability, and strong management of the socioemotional dimension. The two classic texts on revolutionary process and roles are Brinton (1965) and Skocpol (1979).

## CHAPTER OVERVIEWS

Part One, 'Political Philosophy: The Foundations,' begins with a figure probably most often maligned and misused in management studies, but little dealt with in detail in educational administration and leadership: Machiavelli. In Chapter Two, 'Beyond Foxes and Lions,' Andrea Migone reconciles two of the most polarised views, the Machiavelli of the 'wily, cruel princes' and that of the 'hopeful herald of republican virtue,' concentrating his analysis on *The Prince* and the *Discourses*. His reading views Machiavelli predominantly as a theorist of sociopolitical change who regarded societies as going through cyclical changes between the corrupt, as in *The Prince,* and noble, as in republics described in the *Discourses.* Leaders, then, are those who either must struggle under degenerate conditions or create and manage 'good' laws, aiming preferably to channel people's motivations from self-interest into the service of the state. It is in Machiavelli that a model for university leadership exists that can move universities away from the corporate form they have taken under the New Public Management, subject to market forces, towards a cooperative and scholarly form.

In the third chapter I present the two most important modern idealist figures in political philosophy, Kant and Hegel, both of whom occupied a variety of educational roles, including administrative ones, and strove to articulate a vision of largely liberal democracy built upon moral foundations and aimed at producing peace and individual independence. They discussed in some detail the proper nature and role of the state, including the bureaucracy or civil service, and identified the ethical and professional principles upon which leaders should act, the constraints that should exist, and the desired effects on society, which should be oriented towards the common weal and individual freedom. Their arguments, in somewhat different ways, both require educational institutions to prepare everyone for the reflective and critical abilities necessary to fulfil civil service roles in a modern society, and require the state including its civil service to provide for educational freedom. The main educational concept guiding Kant and Hegel was *Bildung,* which found perhaps its highest form at the university level in the Humboldt model of the University of Berlin, the model that has found most successful expression internationally.

Peter Milley explores the contributions Jürgen Habermas has made to political analysis relevant to education goals and 'how educational processes and institutions should work.' Higher education, for Habermas, should serve to develop capacities to shape cultural life and provide sites for 'unfettered debate,' grounded in ideals of equality, justice, and freedom. Milley examines three sets of key concepts: first, how human interests are related to the politics of knowledge; second, communicative and strategic action as modes of power; and finally, how the model of lifeworld and system contributes to an understanding of how the politics and exercise of power are expressed among the domains of private lives, civil society, the economy, and the state.

Peter Gronn discusses the importance of one of the most influential of conservative theorists, Friedrich Hayek. While Hayek is best known for his work on economics, he had equally, if not more, important things to say about learning, knowledge, knowledge distribution, and the evolution of 'order.' He distinguished and contrasted two ontological orders of being: spontaneous and organised. While he had little to say directly about organised order, he emphasised the autonomous forces in spontaneous order associated with hidden hand explanations of the mechanisms through which social institutions evolve. Hayek had exceedingly strong views about ways in which state activity might pervert 'natural' processes of social and civic ordering, championing nineteenth-century Gladstonian liberty and liberalism. What is not clear here is the role, if any, played by leadership and ideas of authority and influence: on one hand, spontaneous order seems to imply 'self-organising,' obviating the need for leadership altogether, while on the other, organised order, which gives expression to intention and 'design,' suggests there may be a need for it.

Bourdieu's political theory is presented by Carol Harris, who discusses his relevance to current economic and cultural inequalities that in the educational field reflect a conflation of talent or natural giftedness with opportunity. These practices, for Bourdieu, produce inequality that leads to confusion between *social* and *natural* gifts, often accepted uncritically by governments promoting such levelling concepts as 'school ranking' by 'standardised examinations,' student 'achievement' and parental 'choice.' Political implications of Bourdieu's work are compared with Critical Theory and the ideas of Foucault for conceptions of social structures marked by distinctions of discourse, taste, skills, and other forms of capital. She also examines his turn to a social phenomenology and a pedagogy of possibility (i.e., *habitus*), as well as to the shifting locations of power and knowledge. Illustrated, through arts education, the naturalisation of power differentials in schools in Bourdieu's account of inequitable social and economic resources, particularly cultural capital embodied by all social groups as 'distinctions of taste' is presented. She further addresses political implications of Bourdieu's theory, arguing first for a heightened awareness of the political process of education, and examining the nature of a Western pedagogy that might incorporate local traditions with empowering skills and literacy.

Stephanie Mackler discusses, a little-examined or understood figure in educational administration and leadership, apart from frequent short references to the 'banality of evil': Hannah Arendt. This chapter examines the underlying hermeneutic approach to thinking, intelligence, and meaning, and the critique of the 'thoughtlessness' of the bureaucratic and its implications for morality. From this Mackler constructs a model of the three modalities of action, thinking, and judgment upon which responsible, and hermeneutic, educational administration and leadership are built. She argues for changes in graduate professional programmes from a 'problem solving' mode to one that has more to do with cognition and the construction of meaning, and for more opportunities for students to cultivate private reflection of the kind Arendt promotes, and which are more directly supported by arts and humanities disciplines.

Chuck Fazzaro's chapter is a critical enquiry into the effects of structuralist hegemony in American public education, particularly the concept of freedom embedded in the US Constitution, which uses as a framework Foucault's notions of ethics and analysis of societal structural arrangements. Foucault regarded the latter as being constructed through three modes of objectification: systems of inquiry (e.g., biology, economics, linguistics) that try to give themselves the status of sciences while turning the subject into an object of manipulation; institutional practices that divide the subject from others or inside himself; and ways in which individuals turns themselves into subjects. Although some contemporary critics labelled him a 'structuralist,' Foucault never accepted the project of structuralism, which assumes universals and 'just-and-true-for-all' explanations of reality and the locus of 'truth.' For Foucault, 'truth' was more internal to one's conscience and thoughts, an approach consistent with the US Supreme Court's interpretation of the free speech clause of the First Amendment as 'freedom of thought,' not merely freedom of expression. Fazzaro explores the implications of Foucault's work for current schooling structures and technologies in American public education conditioned by structuralism.

The second part of this collection, 'Political Analysis: The Critique,' examines various types of political analyses, such as the politics of the policy process, minority politics, civil society, micropolitics, and community politics. Chapter 9, by Michèle Schmidt, explores the impact of high-stakes accountability on school leaders by problematising the theoretical and practical spaces within school leadership. Using a post-modern policy analysis framework, and drawing from theorists such as Ball and Scheurich, she presents a more current explanation of policy analysis that examines the local experience of those implementing policy and ultimately contributing to the democratic project in education. Schmidt examines the conflicting cultures of learning and environments of regulation that are shaped and defined by prevailing testing policies and, in so doing, illuminates how principles of exclusion found in the politics of accountability are embodied in the inclusive projects of school leadership. A multidimensional analysis provides a discursive platform on which to illuminate politically driven state policy implications as they collide with local policy interpretations as well as commenting on the viability of a postmodern analysis of education policy as a complex and contested process.

The chapter by Michelle Young and Gerardo López argues that studies of educational politics and policies, limited by traditional theoretical and methodological tools, fail to provide a comprehensive understanding of the phenomena being researched and, thus, should not be used as sole sources of information on which educational policy and programme development are based. The many perspectives from which educational researchers could expand the theoretical frameworks for political analysis include the cultural perspective, critical race theory, first nations/indigenous, feminist, critical feminist, black feminist, Chicana, feminist post-structural, spirituality, post-structural policy archaeology, policy reconstruction, and queer theory. They make a case for three such alternatives: critical race theory, feminist post-structural theory, and queer theory. Doing so, they argue, will not only create an opportunity to expose the field to different understandings of educational politics and policy, but it should also disrupt taken-for-granted assumptions of what these phenomena are, what they can be, and what purposes they ultimately serve.

Richard Bates examines the concept of civil society, currently seen as a possible solution to social, economic and political dilemmas and advocated as a way forward by ideologues of right and left. The Right sees civil society as a mechanism for reducing politics and expanding the free market, the Left, as a mechanism for radical social change in the pursuit of social justice. This chapter reviews the contemporary discussion on the idea of civil society as a 'public sphere' of voluntary associations somewhat separate from both state and market, and as a possible global achievement that might both inform and support ideas of the public good in ways that counter the effects of economic globalisation and local politics. The implications of these developments for the administration of education and the potential role of educational leaders in the development of civil society are also explored.

Read Diket examines museums as adult education sites, as they reflect nationalistic agendas and institutional tactics in the politics of art. The early twentieth century mission of the venerable old-line museum was an education of the mind through awe-inspiring interiors and grand narratives in which the museum audience was removed from active participation in the social structure of an art world by being 'given' something, reserving edification for museum directors, collectors, and esteemed art historians. Later in the twentieth century, museums promoted a modernist style of reconstructionist or critical philosophies, expecting an educated museum audience to interpret art, extract underlying tensions in culture, and consider the structure and congruency of beliefs. With postmodernism and a proliferation of cultural opportunities for a paying public, museums need larger audiences to keep the doors open, actively seeking the uneducated and the educated. Drawing on theories of Husserl about how we structure views of the world, and Heidegger, who maintains that we are '"fellow players" in the game of life,' along with the political implications of neurological theories posed by Damasio on emotion, Diket examines the impact of the constructivist museum.

Community politics in education is examined by Lawrence Angus in reporting on the early stages of a research project mapping and interpreting what occurs when a disadvantaged community embarks on a neighbourhood and community renewal programme to rejuvenate its schools. The project challenges the way 'underachievement' continues to be sheeted home to the individual and to the 'backgrounds' of individuals by schools and educators, rather than to social structures, the cultural preferencing of schools, and social and cultural processes of advantaging and disadvantaging. Angus contends that schools and educators are too often complicit in interventionist processes of 'leading' and 'doing' so-called community renewal in ways that employ subtle manipulation of students and community members through forms of 'managed participation.' He argues that schools and government officials, to more fairly and successfully support, encourage, and assist renewal, must realise that community members are capable of challenging mandated 'solutions' derived in remote policy contexts since they are in the best position to recognise that well-intentioned 'solutions' may not be in their interests. This approach requires schools and educators to respect the knowledge, language, class location, culture, and experiences of communities of disadvantage and to recognise that conditions of educational disadvantage need to be confronted and explored from within the communities in which they are experienced.

The last part, 'Current Political Controversies: The Practice,' addresses current topical issues of a political nature. Chapter 14, by Janice Wallace, offers a critique of neoliberalism as it is played out in the particular context of educational governance in three provinces in Canada. In the wake of economic restructuring and the neoliberal politics of the 'New Right,' the work of educational leaders in British Columbia, Ontario, and Alberta is differentially positioned in relation to the provincial governments' economic and political agendas. Using data gathered in informal interviews, document searches, and media accounts, Wallace explores how school administrators are positioned between the market-driven ends and fiscally deprived means of provincial education policies informed by the demands of the new managerialism.

John Smyth's chapter sketches out the nature and scope of student disengagement with education, pursuing a counter-hegemonic 'student voice' perspective that accords young people a more active and democratic part in the construction of their educational futures. Increasingly large numbers of young people are becoming disengaged and 'dropping out' of school. The evidence for this is widespread, incontrovertible, and largely unheeded, with no creative policy thinking addressing the situation. In his examination of the indifference of many young people to the social institution of schooling, Smyth implicates the 'new pedagogy' based on the neoliberal agenda of competition, marketisation, privatisation, international benchmarking, standards, high stakes testing regimes, and the ethos of economic globalisation. The consequence, he maintains, is that we have a contradiction: at precisely the time we need flexible, creative, and humanising schools capable of energising young people for new horizons and productive futures, what we have instead are preferred educational policy trajectories aimed at controlling and warehousing prospective generic workers through compliant and coercive forms learning. The 'pedagogies of indifference,' or 'defensive pedagogies,' and the general 'dumbing down' of education are flowing directly from the neoliberal policy agenda. He proposes as an alternative policies that are committed to building the kind of trust and respect in schools between teachers, students, and communities necessary for creative, flexible, and productive learning in smart knowledge economies.

The neoconservative attack on academia, the 'new McCarthyism,' is the topic of Fenwick English's chapter. He reviews the concerted, focused, and well-funded political assault underway on academic thought in American colleges and universities by a broad front of right-wing authors from neoconservative think tanks and agencies. He contends that while there has always been an undercurrent of unrest among conservatives about ideas, issues, and programmes they deem politically threatening, dangerous, frivolous or absurd, the current assault represents a far more serious and far-ranging attack to silence prominent academics who are in the forefront of reactions to cherished neoconservative policies and initiatives, such as the war in Iraq, the long-standing boycott of relationships with Cuba, or support for such neoconservative biases as same-sex marriage, affirmative action, and the continuing prevalence of racism and sexism in American life. This chapter presents a typology of right-wing perspectives, showing how the current assault may be classified appropriately employing the critical element of conspiracy theory and crude interpretations of more well-established conservative political theory.

The final chapter is Michael Bottery's examination of the impact of 'supranational organisations' on nation state education systems. These include organisations of a variety of types: economic, like the World Bank and World Trade Organisation; political, such as the European Union; and educational, particularly the Organization for Economic Co-operation and Development (OECD). Reviewing their origins, missions, and influence, Bottery provides perspectives on how such influence is transmitted to, and mediated by, a variety of nation states. Such influences include increased emphases upon the economic mission of the nation state, greater circumscription of professional roles, and the increased influence of managerialist influences. At the same time, he argues, there are not only movements to centralisation but to decentralisation, which in some cases threaten the legitimacy of nation states and their ability to protect their educational systems.

## REFERENCES

Althusser, L. (1971) 'Ideology and ideological state apparatuses: notes toward an investigation,' in *Lenin and Philosophy and Other Essays*, New York: Monthly Review Press.

Apple, M. (ed.) (1982a) *Cultural and Economic Reproduction in Education: Essays on Class, Ideology, and the State*, London: Routledge and Kegan Paul.

———, (1982b) *Education and Power*, London: Routledge and Kegan Paul.

Bacharach, S. and Lawler, F. (1980) *Power and Politics in Organizations*, San Francisco: Jossey-Bass.

Bachrach, P. and Baratz, M. (1962) 'The two faces of power,' *American Political Science Review*, 56: 947–52.

Baldridge, V. (1971) *Power and Conflict in the University*, New York: John Wiley.

Ball, S. (1987) *The Micro-Politics of the School: Towards a Theory of School Organization*, London: Methuen.

Baum, H. (1983) 'Autonomy, shame and doubt: power in the bureaucratic lives of planners,' *Administration and Society*, 15, 2: 147–84.

Bennet, S. and Wilkie, R. (1973) 'Structural conflict in school organization,' in G. Fowler, et al. (eds) *Decision-Making in British Education*, London: Heinemann.

Bennis, W. (1989) *On Becoming a Leader*, Addison-Wesley.

Blau, P. (1964) *Exchange and Power in Social Life*, New York: Wiley.

Bottomore, T. (1964) *Elites and Society*, New York: Basic Books.

Bowles, S. and Gintis, H. (1976) *Schooling in Capitalist America:Educational Reform and the Contradictions of Economic Life*, New York: Basic Books.

Brinton, C. (1965) *The Anatomy of Revolution*, New York: Vintage.

Brown, G. (1977) *Sabotage: A Study of Industrial Conflict*, Nottingham: Spokesman Books.

Brown, R. (1978) 'Bureaucracy as praxis: toward a political phenomenology of formal organizations,' *Administrative Science Quarterly*, 23, 3: 365–82.

Bukharin, N. (1968 [1914]) *The Economic Theory of the Leisure Class*, London: M. Lawrence.

Child, J. (1972) 'Organizational structure and strategies of control,' *Administrative Science Quarterly* 17: 163–77.

Clegg, S. (1975) *Power, Rule and Domination: A Critical and Empirical Understanding of Power in Sociological Theory and Organizational Life*, London: Routledge.

———, (1989) 'Radical revisions: power, discipline and organizations,' *Organization Studies*, 10, 1: 97–115.

Deal, T. and Kennedy, A. (1982) *Corporate Cultures: The Rites and Rituals of Corporate Life*, Reading: Addison-Wesley.

Della Fave, L. R. (1986) 'Toward an explication of the legitimation process,' *Social Forces*, 65: 476–500.

DiMaggio, P. and Powell, W. (1983) 'The iron cage revisited: institutional isomorphism and collective rationality in organizational fields,' *American Sociological Review*, 48: 147–60.

Domhoff, G. (1967) *Who Rules America?* Englewood Cliffs: Prentice-Hall.

———, and Dye, T. (eds) (1987) *Power Elites and Organizations*, Newbury Park: Sage.

Eagleton, T. (1991) *Ideology: An Introduction,* London: Verso.

Edelman, M. (1971) *Politics as Symbolic Action: Mass Arousal and Quiescence,* Chicago: Markham.

Edwards, J. D. (1998) 'Managerial influences in public administration,' *International Journal of Organizational Theory and Behavior,* 1, 4: 553–83.

Fairholm, G. (1993) *Organizational Power Politics: Tactics in Organizational Leadership,* Westport: Praeger.

Fisher, R. (1983) 'Negotiating power-getting and using influence,' *American Behavioral Scientist,* 27, 2: 149–67.

Foucault, M. (1980) *Power/Knowledge,* New York: Pantheon.

Freire, P. (1973) *Education for Critical Consciousness,* New York: Seabury Press.

French, J. and Raven, B. (1959) 'The Bases of Social Power,' in D. Cartwright (ed.) *Studies in Social Power,* Ann Arbor: Institute for Social Research.

Frost, P. and Egri, C. (1991) 'The political process of innovation,' in L. Cummings and B. Shaw (eds) *Research in Organizational Behavior,* Greenwich: JAI Press.

Gadamer, H.-G. (1998) *The Beginning of Philosophy,* New York: Continuum.

Galtung, J. (1981) 'Structure, culture, and intellectual style: an essay comparing Saxonic, Teutonic, Gallic and Nipponic approaches,' *Social Science Information,* 20: 817–56.

Garfinkel, H. (1956) 'Conditions of successful degradation ceremonies,' *American Journal of Sociology,* 61: 420–4.

Giroux, H. (1981) *Ideology, Culture & the Process of Schooling,* Philadelphia: Temple University Press.

Grace, G. (1978) *Teachers, Ideology and Control,* London: Routledge and Kegan Paul.

Gramsci, A. (1992 [1949–1953]) *Prison Notebooks,* New York: Columbia University Press.

Gray, B. and Ariss, S. (1985) 'Political and strategic change across organizational life cycles,' *Academy of Management Review,* 10: 707–23.

Gronn, P. (1999) *The Making of Educational Leaders,* London: Cassell.

Habermas, J. (1970) *Toward a Rational Society: Student Protest, Science, and Politics,* Boston: Beacon Press.

——, (1975) *Legitimation Crisis,* Boston: Beacon Press.

Hancock, N. and Hellawell, D. (2003) 'Academic middle management in higher education: a game of hide and seek,' *Journal of Higher Education Policy and Management,* 25, 1: 5–12.

Hayek, F. (1994 [1944]) *The Road to Serfdom,* Chicago: University of Chicago Press.

Helmke, G. and Levitsky, S. (2004) 'Informal institutions and comparative politics: A research agenda,' *Perspectives on Politics,* 2, 4: 725–40.

Holden, M. (1966) '"Imperialism" in bureaucracy,' *American Political Science Review,* 60: 943–51.

Hoyle, E. (1982) 'Micropolitics of educational organizations,' *Educational Management and Administration,* 10: 87–98.

Iannaccone, L. (1975) *Educational Policy Systems,* Fort Lauderdale: Nova University Press.

Jermier, J., Knights, D. and Nord, W. (eds) (1994) *Resistance and Power in Organizations,* London: Routledge.

Kaiser, R. (1992) *Why Gorbachev Happened: His Triumphs, His Failure, and His Fall,* New York: Simon and Schuster.

Kavanagh, D. (1987) 'Margaret Thatcher: the mobilizing style of prime minister,' in H. Clarke and M. Czudnowski (eds) *Political Elites in Anglo-American Democracies: Changes in Stable Regimes,* Northern Illinois Press.

Kets de Vries, M. (2006) *The Leadership Mystique: Leading Behavior in the Human Enterprise,* London: Prentice Hall.

——, and Miller, D. (1984) *The Neurotic Organization*, San Francisco: Jossey-Bass.

Kipnis, D. et al. (1980) 'Intraorganizational influence tactics: explorations in getting one's way,' *Journal of Applied Psychology*, 65, 4: 440–52.

Knights, D. and Morgan, G. (1991) 'Strategic discourse and subjectivity: towards a critical analysis of corporate strategy in organizations,' *Organization Studies*, 12, 2: 251–73.

Kolb, D. and Bartunek, J. (eds) (1992) *Hidden Conflict in Organizations: Uncovering Behind-the-Scenes Disputes*, Newbury Park: Sage.

Lasswell, H. (1962) *Power and Personality*, New York: Viking.

Ledeneva, A. (2006) *How Russia Really Works: The Informal Practices that Shaped Post-Soviet Politics and Business*, Ithaca: Cornell University Press.

Lerner, G. (1986) *The Creation of Patriarchy*, New York: Oxford University Press.

Lucas, R. (1987) 'Politico-cultural analyses of organizations,' *Academy of Management Review*, 12: 144–56.

Luke, C. and Gore, J. (eds) (1992) *Feminisms and Critical Pedagogy*, New York: Routledge.

Lukes, S. (1985) 'Introduction,' in V. Havel et al., *Power of the Powerless: Citizens Against the State in Central-Eastern Europe*, Armonk: Sharpe.

Macfarland, J. (1999) 'Machiavelli's imagination of excellent men: an appraisal of the lives of Cosimo de' Medici and Castruccio Castracani,' *The American Political Science Review*, 93, 1: 133–46.

Mastenbroek, W. (1980) 'Negotiating: a conceptual model,' *Group & Organizational Studies*, 5, 3: 324–39.

Mawhinney, H. (1999) 'Reappraisal: the problems and prospects of studying the micropolitics of leadership in reforming schools,' *School Leadership & Management*, 19, 2: 159–70.

McClelland, D. (1975) *Power: The Inner Experience*, New York: Irvington.

McConnell, G. (1966) *Private Power and American Democracy*, New York: Knopf.

Meier, K. (1989) 'Bureaucratic leadership in public organizations,' in B. Jones (ed.) *Leadership and Politics: New Perspectives in Political Science*, University Press of Kansas.

Meyer, J. (1984) 'Organizations as ideological systems,' in T. Sergiovanni and J. Corbally (eds) *Leadership and Organizational Culture: New Perspectives on Administrative Theory and Practice*, University of Illinois Press: Urbana.

Meyer, J., Scott, W. and Deal, T. (1981) 'Institutional and technical sources of organizational structure: explaining the structure of educational organizations,' in H. Stein (ed.) *Organization and the Human Services: Cross-Disciplinary Reflections*, Philadelphia: Temple University Press.

Meyer, J. and Rowan, B. (1992) 'Institutionalized organizations: formal structure as myth and ceremony,' in J. Meyer and W. Scott (eds) *Organizational Environments: Ritual and Rationality*, Sage: Newbury Park.

Meyerson, D. and Scully, M. (1995) 'Tempered radicalism and the politics of ambivalence and change,' *Organizational Science*, 6: 585–600.

Michels, R. (1958 [1911]) *Political Parties: A Sociological Study of the Oligarchical Tendencies of Modern Democracy*, Glencoe: Free Press.

Miliband, R. (1969) *The State in Capitalist Society: The Analysis of the Western System of Power*, London: Quartet Books.

Mills, C. W. (1956) *The Power Elite*, New York: Oxford University Press.

Mintzberg, H. (1978) 'Patterns in strategy formation,' *Management Science*, 24, 9: 934–48.

——, (1983) *Power in and around Organizations*, Englewood Cliffs: Prentice-Hall.

Moe, T. (1989) 'The politics of bureaucratic structure,' in J. Chubb and P. Peterson (eds) *Can the Government Govern?* Washington DC: Brookings Institute.

Morley, D. and Shockley-Zalabak, P. (1986) 'Conflict avoiders and compromisers: toward an understanding of their organizational communication style,' *Group and Organization Studies*, 11, 4: 387–401.

Mosca, G. (1939[1896]) *The Ruling Class*, New York: McGraw-Hill.

Mumby, D. (1988) *Communication and Power in Organizations: Discourse, Ideology and Domination*, Norwood: Ablex.

Nyberg, D. (1981) *Power over Power: What Power Means in Ordinary Life, How It is Related to Acting Freely, and What It can Contribute to a Renovated Ethics of Education*, Ithaca: Cornell University Press.

O'Day, R. (1974) 'Intimidation rituals: reactions to reform,' *Journal of Applied Behavioral Science*, 10, 3: 373–86.

Ouchi, W. and Johnson, J. (1978) 'Types of organizational control and their relationship to emotional well-being,' *Administrative Science Quarterly*, 23: 293–317.

Pareto, V. (1968 [1901]) *The Rise and Fall of the Elites: An Application of Theoretical Sociology*, Totowa: Bedminster Press.

Peters, B. G. (1978) *The Politics of Bureaucracy*, New York: Longman.

Peters, G. (1998) *The New Institutionalism*, London: Cassells.

Pettigrew, A. (1973) *The Politics of Organizational Decision-Making*, London: Tavistock.

Pfeffer, J. (1978) 'The micropolitics of organizations,' in M. Meyer et al. (eds) *Environments and Organizations*, San Francisco: Jossey-Bass.

——, (1981) *Power in Organizations*, Marshfield: Pittman.

——, (1992) *Managing with Power: Politics and Influence in Organizations*, Boston: Harvard Business School Press.

Pollitt, C. and Bouckaert, G. (2004) *Public Management Reform: A Comparative Analysis*, 2nd edn, Oxford: Oxford University Press.

Porter, L. et al. (1983) 'The politics of upward influence in organizations,' in R. Allen and L. Porter (eds) *Organizational Influence Processes*, Glenview: Scott, Foresman.

Poulantzas, N. (1973 [1968]) *Political Power and Social Classes*, London: NLB.

Raven, B. and Knuglenski, A. (1970) 'Conflict and power,' in P. Swingle (ed.) *The Structure of Conflict*, New York: Academic Press.

Richardson, E. (1973) *The Environment of Learning: Conflict and Understanding in the Secondary School*, London: Heinemann.

Rubin, J. (1983) 'Negotiation: an introduction to some issues and themes,' *American Behavioral Scientist*, 27, 2: 135–47.

Said, E. (1978) *Orientalism*, New York: Pantheon Books.

Samier, E. (ed.) (2003) *Ethical Foundations for Educational Administration*, London: RoutledgeFalmer.

——, and Bates, R. (eds) (2006) *Aesthetic Dimensions of Educational Administration and Leadership*, London: Routledge.

*School Leadership & Management* (1999), 12, 2.

Skocpol, T. (1979) *States and Revolutions: A Comparative Analysis of France, Russia, & China*, Cambridge: Cambridge University Press.

Slaughter, S. and Leslie, L. (1997) *Academic Capitalism: Politics, Policies, and the Entrepreneurial University*, Baltimore: Johns Hopkins University Press.

Smyth, J. (ed.) (1989) *Critical Perspectives on Educational Leadership*, London: Falmer Press.

Storey, J. (1985) 'The means of management control,' *Sociology*, 19, 2: 193–211.

Tullock, G. (1965) *The Politics of Bureaucracy*, Washington DC: Public Affairs Press.

Turner, R. (1981) *Politics as Leadership*, Columbia: University of Missouri Press.

Van Maanen, J. and Barley, S. (1984) 'Occupational communities: culture and control in organizations,' in B. Staw and L. Cummings (eds) *Research in Organizational Behavior*, Greenwich: JAI Press.

Weiler, H. (1985) 'Politics of educational reform,' in R. Merritt and A. Merritt (eds) *Innovation in the Public Sector,* Beverly Hills: Sage.

West, W. (1985) *Administrative Rulemaking: Politics and Processes,* Westport: Greenwood Press.

Zaleznik, A. (1970) 'Power and politics in organizational life,' *Harvard Business Review,* 48: 47–60.

# Part I

# Political Philosophy

## The Foundations

# 2 Beyond Foxes and Lions

## Machiavelli's Discourse on Power and Leadership

*Andrea Migone*

## UNDERSTANDING MACHIAVELLI

This chapter deals with Niccolò Machiavelli's notion of leadership, and advances some thoughts about its relation to educational leadership for universities. Writing about Machiavelli is like reconstructing a mosaic: the tiles are all there, but it is easy to argue about their individual placement. One needs a guiding principle, and in Machiavelli the *fil rouge* is the analysis of leadership. The right leaders, who operate according to Machiavellian *virtù,* understand what surrounds them, are realistic about it, prepare for the twists and turns of *Fortuna,* are not afraid to act as both the fox and the lion, can adapt actions to changing conditions, and can elevate the city from a state of corruption to a state of 'good laws.' Today, to apply his precepts we must extrapolate the normative rules from the implementation processes. Mass executions have no place in democracies, but the concept of getting rid of those administrators who may hinder the smooth running of the political process is surely reflected in the spoils' system.

There is little work done in the area of educational leadership directly connected with Machiavelli, one excellent exception being English's (1992) article on school principals. He looks at decision-making as a central notion in Machiavelli's work, and notes how a strong school executive will be instrumental in forwarding the interests of the school. In this context much the same is true for universities; educational leadership must focus on the improvement of the educational structure itself. Weak or distracted leadership is dangerous for the university, just as it is dangerous in a prince.

There is an imbalance in the biographical information available for Machiavelli: most of it refers to the latter part of his life (Viroli 2000). Born in Florence on 3 May 1469, he spent his early life calmly and with the privilege of a good humanistic education. After working for a Florentine bank in Rome, he returned to his hometown in 1494, just as the Medici were overthrown and Girolamo Savonarola rose to power in Tuscany. In 1498, after the brief Savonarola interlude, Machiavelli entered into the service of the Florentine Republic as second chancellor, and secretary to the Council of Ten for War. For the following fourteen years, he had various important diplomatic postings, including in France and Rome. In 1512, the Medici regained power in Florence and Machiavelli was dismissed. The following year he was accused of plotting to bring back the Republic. Arrested, he was held for three weeks and tortured before being released. Now forced outside of the political sphere of the Florentine state, he still tried to regain a political posting. After the death of Lorenzo di Piero de Medici, grandson of Lorenzo the Magnificent, in 1519, thanks to Cardinal Giulio de Medici, he partially returned within the good graces of the rulers of Florence. The Medici's policies, though, had antagonised the emperor, Charles V, who moved against them. Machiavelli undertook the organisation of Florence's defence, but imperial forces overran the city and the Republic was restored. Because of his involvement with the Medici, republican leaders now marginalised Machiavelli. He died soon after, on 21 June 1527.

Machiavelli was a prolific and multifaceted author. Besides *The Prince* (1513) and the *Discourses on the First Ten Books of Titus Livy* (1512–1517), his most renowned efforts, which will be the main focus of this analysis, he also penned a variety of other works. Some tackled the political arena, such as the *Discorso sopra il Riformare lo Stato di Firenze* (1520) and the *Art of War* (1520), and his production as a Florentine diplomat, such as the *Discorso Sopra le Cose di Pisa* (1499), and historical narratives like his essays on the lives of Cesare Borgia (1502) and Castruccio Castracani (1520) and the *Florentine Histories* (1520–1525). Finally, Machiavelli produced a set of respectable literary works, including the novel *Belfagor Arcidiavolo* (1515) and the prose comedy *The Mandrake* (1518).

He also is one of the most controversial and debated figures in political philosophy. In 1990, Silvia Ruffo-Fiore (1990) had accumulated 600 pages of bibliographical references on the Florentine writer. Theologians and philosophers like George Bull and Friedrich Hegel prefaced *The Prince;* political philosophers like Isaiah Berlin and Benedetto Croce discussed his work, figures like the Archbishop of Canterbury, Reginald Pole, the French jurist Jean Bodin, the encyclopaedist Denis Diderot and Frederick the Great of Prussia all variably commented on the nature and effects of his writings. Yet, for all of the enormous mass of debates, commentaries, attacks, praises, and rejoinders that emerged, little common ground can be found on the intent and nature of Machiavelli's production.[1]

His work has been rated as amoral, immoral, and belonging to a 'new' morality. He has been labelled a man gazing forward upon the dawn of a 'modern revolution' and one looking backwards, drawing inspiration from the lingering sunset of Italy's Roman past. Described by some as the first true technical political scientist (Olschki 1945), applying a Galilean method to the historical-political analysis he carried out (Burnham 1943), and by others as using a deeply flawed, selective methodology that amounted to nothing more than 'an elaborate and irrelevant superstructure' (Anglo 1969: 243).

Finally, how do we reconcile the two apparently strident voices found in *The Prince* and the *Discourses?* Was Machiavelli the apologist of wily, cruel princes or the hopeful herald of republican virtue? Could we, with Meinecke (1957), consider the Florentine secretary a republican, who had enough of a realist attitude to know when to bow to *realpolitik?* Or was *The Prince* the result of his political employment and the *Discourses* of the freer reflections of the years after his dismissal (Baron 1961)? Perhaps his accounts were meant for different realities: *The Prince* for the difficult political times of his life and the *Discourses* for the hopeful republican future (Skinner 1981). If the two works are related, is it because they belong to an interconnected project (Chabod 1958) or because the creation of the republic depended on the previous emergence of a leader who could lead the polity out of corruption (Viroli 1990)?

Machiavelli remains a very complex subject and some of the questions asked about him and his work are not likely to receive a final answer. Bearing this in mind, we still can put forward some thoughts and attempt to reconnect three main themes of his production: his method, his political analysis, and the figure of the leader. After describing his reception in the next section, I deal, in order, with these topics.

## MACHIAVELLI'S RECEPTION

Machiavelli was immediately received, as Strauss (1958) would put it four centuries later, as a 'teacher of evil.' The so-called 'Machiavel stereotype' (Anglo 1969) spread quickly and thoroughly: from John Leslie, Bishop of Ross (1569), to Gentillet (1576), to Bodin (1576), the ideas of Machiavelli generated widespread and lasting opposition if not revulsion. Consider Frederick the Great's comment:

> Machiavelli's *The Prince* is for Morals what the Work of Spinoza is for matters of Faith. Spinoza weakened the basis of Faith, and tried nothing less than to overthrow the edifice of Religion; Machiavelli corrupts Politics, and undertakes to destroy the precepts of healthy Morals. (Frederick II von Hohenzollern 1742: xxx)

Machiavelli's bad reputation endured from the sixteenth to the middle of the nineteenth centuries when it was finally reviewed and his writings on democracy properly contextualised (Skinner 1981). Still, most Straussians believe that his abandoning the notion of traditional morality makes him a relativist. Harvey Mansfield (1979; 1996) came some way from this reading by arguing that this separation of moral and political principles is 'liberating' the latter from the former and is not just a modernist mistake.

Today Machiavelli is often seen as proposing a strand of moral voluntarism (Kocis 1998), or an interesting mix of 'act' and 'rule' utilitarianism

(Femia 2004). However, his approach remains 'disturbing' (Berlin 1971), especially because of his contrapositioning of two different moral systems, the emerging one and the old one that was dying in Renaissance Italy, none of which he believed held any assurance of 'truth' for human choice. His appeal to nationalism and his belief that agents embracing freedom must be moral cynics (even going as far as using the same methods of those who are against freedom), remain problematic and have given pause to many of his readers. Yet, Machiavelli was no moral relativist: moral judgment is present in his works, especially the *Discourses*.

> The disturbance in Machiavelli's writings is that we are forced to choose among competing moralities, one comfortable if demanding, supported by church and tradition, and the other disquietingly new and uncertain, but promising new freedoms and new well-being. (Kocis 1998: 19)

It is arguable that most of the issues with Machiavelli's advice stemmed from the fact that it broke with an established tradition that bound the ruler's actions to strict moral principles. The idea that human beings could behave in an evil manner was certainly not new (Chabod 1958); what must have been shocking was the statement that the good ruler may and should do so. The whole edifice of the right of resistance, after all, depended on the king's compliance with Christian morality. If we disassociate the one from the other how can we judge properly? Machiavelli introduced the problem of 'dirty hands' in politics to the modern period (Calhoun 2004; Walzer 1973). His ultimate statement is that the political ruler faces an inescapable dilemma: creating and maintaining a just state may require less than savoury methods. According to Femia (2004: 85), Machiavelli has a dual approach to morality: one for private morality that can be understood as 'rule' utilitarian, and one for public morality that is 'act' utilitarian.[2] 'Both "rule" and "act" utilitarianism . . . have the effect of bringing morality down to earth. What counts is not adherence to transcendent norms or divinely ordained purposes, but the maximization of empirically ascertainable well-being' (Femia 2004: 85). Finally liberated from the burden of the charge of immorality, Machiavelli's writings yield a different image of the Florentine secretary's vision, both methodologically and substantively.

## MACHIAVELLI'S METHOD

Machiavelli's methodology is integral to his work. He used an empirical method, borrowing freely from the historical record to support his own argumentation, and discarded the teleological tools that had previously been commonplace (Femia 2004). He never superimposed the medieval approach, so reliant on the connection between polity and religion, upon Renaissance society, wholeheartedly discarding the theological lining of the thinkers who preceded him in favour of pragmatic and empirical (but not immoral or amoral) concerns. His works, within the context of this approach, are closely interrelated. There, we find an important vein of republicanism, but not an Aristotelian one, most likely because the Greek *polis* strengths and needs are not those of sixteenth-century Italy, and Machiavelli better related to the *Res Publica*, the Roman commonwealth.[3] Just as he seemed to have a closer kinship with Roman stoicism, with its pragmatism and ultimately with the sense of purpose that it gave mankind, than he had with the abstract universal concepts of Plato or Aristotle, and the theological straightjacket they had fitted over medieval societies.

In Derrida's (1980) sense, Machiavelli shakes the teleological and other-worldly 'centre' of medieval philosophy and lays the foundations of modern political thought. His approach, grounded in the notion of empowered, independent human beings, whose passions, both base and high, are starkly and unadulteratedly depicted, replaces the transcendent, universalised truths and moulds of the Middle Ages. It represents a critical break with tradition (Femia 2004). Mansfield (1983; 1996) is correct in noting that the Florentine secretary did not single-handedly pull political thought out of its premodern mould and Femia (2004) is also right in stating that Machiavelli, *pace* Berlin (1971), did not create this shift to modernity on his own. Yet, there is no denying that his precepts were crucial in recasting the way in which we understood and thought about the political system and the notion of leadership that he always closely associated with it.

Still, how good was Machiavelli's method and what consequences did it engender? The Florentine author often used historical examples and statements to underscore his points.[4] Yet, there is little doubt that this was not done in proper 'academic' fashion, following what we would call historical method, nor could we altogether call him a neutral observer of the history he used (Anglo 1969; Gilbert 1965). Even if Butterfield (1940: 57) was too harsh when he noted that the Florentine secretary could 'see the shape of things only in the mould that his own mind had made for them,' sample selection definitely is a problem in Machiavelli's work. Nor did he achieve great success in delivering strict laws of political behaviour. Surely, though, we should both contextualise Machiavelli's work and perhaps look a bit deeper into his intentions. Not much of what we call scientific method was in place at the time he wrote and his understanding of Roman history was more limited than our own. Yet, much that is positive can be found if we look at his work more closely (Femia 2004: Ch 4). First, Machiavelli geared his method towards the deduction of trends in the actions of political leaders, not in discovering immutable principles. In fact, he speaks of rules rather than social laws.[5] Furthermore, he was purposively selective in choosing his examples. Like other writers in the Renaissance (Pitkin 1984: 11), he made a crucial contribution to a tradition that was to use the historical record to criticise extant political systems: 'the Enlightenment did not invent criticism; it emancipated and published the old royal tradition of politics, which grew from the winding roots of the Machiavellian method' (Soll 2005: 126–7). Very few writers before or since him painted a more vivid image of the reasons and methods of politics.

## MACHIAVELLI'S POLITICAL THEORY

The true linchpin of Machiavelli's work is the analysis of the nature of political systems and the advice to those seeking change. His approach is based on four main elements. Machiavelli is a realist, with little interest in teleology or metaphysics. He also is an ontological pessimist, but without assuming that people cannot act positively. Third, sociopolitical change is rooted in human nature and it is cyclical. Finally, commitment to seek glory rather than naked power, and a keen understanding of the role that *Fortuna* can play in human activities are the grounding for the proper political leader. Machiavelli is eminently interested in the reality of politics, in what actually happens and how princes can modify their behaviour to match the evolving conditions and maintain their polity.

The Florentine secretary has little use for teleology or metaphysics because he describes the polity as revolving around power struggles and has no qualms in shedding the utopian imagery previously used for both states and people (*The Prince* XV). This meant breaking the medieval bond between religion and politics for a new, lay morality. Machiavelli's realism is grounded in his understanding of the political system as based on power (*The Prince*) and self-interest. Actions are motivated by the nature of human beings who 'can desire everything but are unable to obtain everything, so that their desire is always greater than their power or acquisition, and discontent with what they posses and lack of satisfaction are the result' (*Discourses* I: 37).

Power is the most important resource in maintaining the state, but naked force will not go very far in supporting a ruler: laws and customs are ignored at one's peril (*The Prince* III–V). Yet, because of human nature, coercion is important: 'For one can say this generally of men: that they are ungrateful, fickle, hypocrites and dissemblers, evaders of dangers, lovers of gain' (*The Prince* XVII).

If they do not fear the prince, they can be trusted to be loyal only as long as things go well, 'but fear is maintained by a dread of punishment which never abandons you' (*The Prince* XVII). Yet, there are bounds.

> A prince, nevertheless, ought to make himself feared in such a mode that if he does not acquire love, he then avoids hatred; for being feared and not hated can go very well together; and he will always bring this about if he abstains from the goods of his citizens and subjects, and from their women. (*The Prince* XVII)

While he notes that 'it is necessary for anyone who organizes a republic and establishes laws in it to take for granted that all men are evil' (*Discourses* I: 3), Machiavelli believes in the potential of human beings to choose to do good and be noble. It may pay to think the worst, so as not to be blind-sided, but we may get the best out of them yet (Kocis 1998: 28–29). The ability to do good or evil depends on the existence of laws and a certain equality of wealth distribution (*Discourses* I: 3 & I: 37). Societies are functional structures aimed at satisfying the needs of human beings, as are laws. While there is no superior moral imperative to respect good laws, if no such laws exist we should strive to create them, because they will influence the nature of societies.

Deeply steeped in the humanist notion that 'social laws' ruling over the changes in social structures are immutable (*Discourses* I: 2), Machiavelli's analysis is aimed at discovering the bases for a free society (*Discourses* I: 1–3). This exercise is operationalised differently in his two best-known works. In *The Prince,* the goal is perhaps narrower, as it 'was written as advice to a potential ruler in corrupt, degenerate conditions' (Kocis 1998: 93). In the *Discourses,* the focus is, rather, on the management of a republic governed by good laws. The creation of laws was to be praised above all because it drew human beings out of the 'state of nature,' out of the corruption that stops them from exercising their good side (Kocis 1998: 98). This is a systematic process, not applicable everywhere. A republican structure will not do if the people are not ready to embrace the legal structures that are at the bases of the republican order (*Discourses* I: 5). Still, if the background is right, a ruler who forces good laws upon the people in time will see a self-sustaining republican system emerge (*Discourses* I: 55; I: 9–11; I: 28, III: 1; III: 3, 8).

Machiavelli's work is about sociopolitical change, about the transition between a corrupt polity and one based on good laws. He was convinced that societies went through cycles: climbing to a zenith and then plunging to a nadir (*Florentine Histories*). This was not a determinist vision; rather, he believed that recurrent paths of human actions could be delineated (Femia 2004: 66–7). Particularly interested in the upswing phase of societies, Machiavelli argued that to move out of unlawfulness the action of a leader was required:

> Also, this must be taken as a general rule: that it never or rarely does it happen that a republic or a kingdom is organized well from the beginning or is completely reformed apart from its old institutions, unless it is organized by one man alone. (*Discourses* I: 9)

However, the prince cannot act simply because of a power-lust, but must be driven by glory, which contains a moral element (Price 1977). Glory also gives the prince a clear goal: leading the people out of corruption (Kocis 1998).[6] Along with being motivated by glory, the prince needs to have *virtù*.

But this is not a simple, intuitive concept. De Alvarez (1980), in his intro-duction to *The Prince*, notes how carefully Machiavelli shapes the multiple hues of the term, but ultimately we can argue that *virtù* is closely correlated to action. A mix of realist analysis, ability to adapt to change, and deter-mination, *virtù* allows rulers to act as needed to create the republic. Yet, Machiavelli's princes cannot be immoral, they cannot be Agathocles: 'one cannot call it virtue to kill his fellow citizens, to betray his friends, to be without faith, without pity, without religion; which modes enabled him to acquire imperium but not glory' (*The Prince* VIII).

In the *Discourses* (I: 10), Machiavelli reiterates the point by saying that, after the founders of religions, the people who show the most glory are the founders of republics and kingdoms. At the same time, princes may find themselves in dire straits. According to Machiavelli, initial conditions determine what limits the ruler faces when acting; Kocis (1998) summarises them below.

In *The Prince,* Machiavelli argues that, while a certain 'bestial' action may be warranted by having to deal with enemies in a state of corruption, this cannot be the ultimate or only manner of action.

> You ought to know, then, that there are two kinds of fighting: one with the laws, the other with force. The first one is proper to man, the second

| HUMAN CONDITIONS | MORAL ASSUMPTIONS | TYPE OF MORAL REASONING |
|---|---|---|
| Nobility or *Gloria* → | Duty | → Deontology |
| ◯ - - - - - System of Laws | | |
| Corruption → | Decency and Civilization | → Consequentialism |

*Figure 2.1* Drawing moral assumptions from human potentials.

*Source: Kocis 1998: 118.*

to the beasts; but because the first proves many times to be insufficient, one needs must resort to the second. Therefore it is necessary for a prince to know well how to use the beast and the man . . . he ought of the beasts to pick the fox and the lion; for the lion cannot defend himself from snares, and the fox cannot defend himself from wolves. One needs, then, to be fox to know snares, and lion to terrify wolves. Those who rely simply on the lion do not understand this. (*The Prince*, XVIII)

The imagery of the fox and the lion has been one of the most quoted, and, perhaps, most misunderstood points in *The Prince*. Timothy Lukes' (2001) excellent review of the topic fills a great gap in the area and reestablishes the relevance of the lion in the book, because it represents the necessary physical, communitarian, and charismatic counterpoint to the fox. Just as Machiavelli noted that princes cannot simply rely on the lion, Lukes (2001) reminds us that no successful polity can dispense with it.

The ultimate goal of the prince will be a political order based on good laws. Machiavelli argues in the *Discourses* that the best model for this polity is the republic. This was not the democratic, universal franchise model of today. His vision was rather for restricted political participation within the Roman republican form of government. Ever the pragmatist, he argued that republican institutions are superior to kingship because, to ensure a consistent flow of capable leaders, they are allowed to recruit from a broader pool of talent (*Discourses* I: 20; III: 9). Traditionally more cautious and open to innovation, republics tend to benefit all citizens instead of being mired in private goals as kingdoms often are. Republics naturally fight against the tendency towards degeneration that is engendered by the dominance of private interests in the polity, because they rely on mixed constitutions that, by balancing power, allow us to channel the inherent selfishness of human beings and put it to the service of the state (*Discourses* I: 2).

One final tile in the Machiavellian mosaic is the notion of *Fortuna*. Machiavelli held a humanist view, asking that people refer to their human side, rather than to God, to understand their world (*The Prince* VI; *Discourses* I: 2), and was interested in dealing with those facets of human life that are accessible to human control. 'And only those defenses are good, are certain, are durable, which depend on you yourself and on your virtue' (*The Prince* XXIV). However, there are no guarantees in our universe, which is, rather, a continuous negotiation of various states of existence in which Prudence, the intellectual ability to recognise the need for compromise in human action, has a key role in navigating difficulties. Rulers must be ready to adapt to the conditions of their times (*Discourses* III: 9). This may not be enough however, because *Fortuna*[7] plays an important and sometimes unpredictable role in human life. The effect it may have upon even the most resilient of rulers is shown clearly in the *Life of Castruccio Castracani of Lucca* (1520). Born in humble conditions, he rises through his own efforts and good luck to a position of dominance in Lucca and in Tuscany itself. However, after inflicting a crushing defeat on the Florentines he falls ill and dies soon after. *Fortuna* became envious of Castruccio, Machiavelli writes, and even this successful prince is brought low.


## WHAT LEADERSHIP?

Machiavelli's complexities can appear as daunting as rebuilding a mosaic, but if we step back frequently and try to place his work and life in proper context there is much we can learn. The Florentine writer is attempting to advise a potential ruler on how to build and maintain a republican political order, but his realism and his experience dictate his abandonment of utopian or metaphysical approaches. The highest duty of the prince is to the polity, the most important goal is the safety of the state, the protection of an order of good laws from which the *vivere libero,* the living free, may emerge. Depending on the situation, determined action and violence may be necessary as well as cunning, because the bigger crime would be to allow a just polity to crumble. Princes exist in a difficult, hostile, and changing world, therefore they must be gifted with *virtù,* the ability to always keep theirs eyes on the ultimate goal of creating a republic, they must be ready to struggle against the mutable *Fortuna,* to adapt their strategy to her changing, and must be motivated by *Gloria,* not lust for power. When all the tiles are finally back in place the image in the mosaic is about outstanding leadership.

Leadership is obviously central in Machiavelli's work, both because of the historical context in which he operated and the role that he assigns to it in his writing. Historically, Renaissance Italy depended heavily on the presence of powerful leaders in both the economic and political spheres: the Medici in Florence, the Sforza and Visconti in Milan, the Doria in Genoa, and the host of petty lords and soldiers of fortune like Castruccio Castracani who peppered the whole peninsula. Therefore, it is not surprising that this figure would emerge in Machiavelli's accounts. However, leaders at the time of Machiavelli enjoyed considerably more latitude than they do today (Calhoon 1969), and so we should refrain from assimilating them. We can draw similarities and seek lessons from a comparison, but must always being mindful of the differences that abide between the two periods. Management literature has, at times, insisted very heavily on an out-of-context perception of Machiavelli as an hyperrealist who inherently suggested immoral action (Bing 2000; Borger 2002; Buskirk 1974). Recently, this has thankfully been noted in the better literature (Galie and Bopst 2006; Swain 2002).

What is the leader to Machiavelli? The Florentine secretary was definitely against the corruption that gripped Italy at the time (*Discourses* I: 54) and argued that the greatest goal of any ruler would be to eliminate this corruption and turn a city into a haven of good laws (*Discourses* I: 10). Only a prince blessed by *virtù* can do so but only by seeking glory rather than by pursuing power alone. To affect such an important transition, the prince may need to use all means at his disposal, including those that would appear to be morally repugnant. Failure to do so may spell the end of the process and force the polity into the state of corruption. However, once a government of good laws is achieved, everyone and especially the leaders are bound by those rules themselves (*Discourses* I: 45).

Perhaps we can borrow from Viroli (1990) and see the role of leadership in Machiavelli as part of a general feel for the emergence of the modern state. While Machiavelli is neither Bodin nor Suarez, and while Harvey Mansfield (1983) did make an interesting case for the difference between the modern, impersonal concept of the state and the rather more patrimonial and personal version the Florentine writer presented, his criticism may be too strong. Machiavelli is the first modern writer to use 'state' in the meaning of the sovereign political community, even if he was acutely aware of the relevance of individual rulers. However, it is true that his was a 'long view' perspective and that he may more properly be seen as one of the originators of a modern vision. In this sense, Machiavelli's project is, according to Mansfield (1996), neither a purely Renaissance/humanist one, nor is it a classically republican one. The Florentine secretary went beyond the immediate historical contexts of both his time and the past from which he drew inspiration, and understood the differences between the 'old' political model he mistrusted and the 'new' one he hoped for. It is unlikely he imagined a modern impersonal state. Rather, he was interested in a post-Renaissance state, led by rulers who submitted to its 'good laws,' and were tempered by the participation of part of the people in the process of government.

How do we reconnect the discourse on Machiavelli to the issue of educational leadership in universities? Machiavelli's rulers are decisive and realistic, they can adapt to the changing conditions of their environment but, most of all, they seek to better the society in which they operate. They would create, under a system of good laws, the conditions for the *vivere libero* of the people (*Discourses* II: 2). If this is the goal of the political ruler, what should leadership aim to do in the university system? I argue that it should focus on educational matters and accessibility. In an era of New Public Management, the university has often been turned into a quasi-corporate model, more interested in budgeting and administration than in education. Two main problems have resulted from this: first, there has been a mushrooming of the bureaucratic personnel in the universities; second, scholars have been turned into employees upon whom a model of competition has been thrust.[8] A Machiavellian model of university leadership would move away from this competitive model and towards a cooperative and noncorporate one, where scholarship and collegiality can blossom.

## NOTES

1. Part of the confusion stems from the great disparity in Machiavelli translations, especially *The Prince*. In this chapter, quotes are drawn from Leo de Alvarez's 1980 translation, which remains the best and closest to the Italian text.
2. A rule utilitarian, when facing a choice, apprises what would happen if a rule were to be followed constantly. If this produces more happiness than pain, the rule is morally binding. An act utilitarian, instead, would try to evaluate the possible results of individual actions and choose the one that maximises utility.
3. On a different tack, Docherty (2006: 130) argues that Machiavelli was 'interested in establishing a major distance between his own contemporary state and that of the Roman Republic . . . this is an integral part of establishing a version of Italy as a foundational instance of that great modern and modernising political entity, the nation state.' Machiavelli did not want to replicate Rome, but certainly preferred Roman civic engagement to the Christian contemplative outlook, because it helped to ground republican political participation (Femia 2004: 81).
4. However, in the introduction to the second book of the *Discourses*, Machiavelli notes that one should not blindly follow history.
5. When Machiavelli speaks of laws he refers to legal statutes, not social laws; the latter are always cast in terms of general rules or trends.
6. Machiavelli was not the first to write about glory. Bartolomeo Sacchi, known also as Platina (1421–1481), did so in his *De Optimo Cive*. He looked at the true goal of politics, which he equated not with the quest for and maintenance of power, but with the search for glory. The glory of the prince was, for Platina, the recognition of the general superiority of one's virtue by all issuing from the prince's approach to power: always directed to the service of the community and of the *res publica*.
7. Much has been written regarding the notion of *Fortuna* in Machiavelli. A straightforward translation would render luck; but it is unsatisfactory. Arguably, *Fortuna* refers to the Roman goddess Fortuna. In the Roman pantheon, she represented Fate, Luck, and Fortune. She had a variety of aspects, not all of them positive. At times she could be *Fortuna Bona* (Good Luck), but she could also be *Fortuna Brevis* ('Brief'—Fickle Luck), *Fortuna Mala* (Bad Luck), *Fortuna Dubia* (Dubious Luck), *Fortuna Mobilis* (Shifting Luck), and so forth. Fortuna's representations are also multiple: sometimes she is depicted as blindfolded, distributing her gifts (or sorrows) randomly; in other cases she has a rudder, symbolising her capacity to steer the lives of people; and at times she has a cornucopia, symbol of prosperity. Romans prayed to her different aspects according to their needs. In Machiavelli, *Fortuna* should probably be understood in the Roman sense, as a powerful, shifting force, that cannot be controlled, but that can certainly be influenced and struggled against.
8. Consider, for example, how rare it is for publishable academic ideas to be freely discussed among colleagues in North American universities.

## REFERENCES

Anglo, S. (1969) *Machiavelli: A Dissection*, London: Victor Gollancz.

Baron, H. (1961) 'Machiavelli: the republican citizen and the author of "The Prince"', *English Historical Review*, 76: 217–53.

Berlin, I. (1971) 'The originality of Machiavelli,' *New York Review of Books*, 4: 20–32.

Bing, S. (2000) *What Would Machiavelli Do? The Ends Justify the Meanness*, New York: Harper Business.

Bodin, J. (1576) *Les Six Livres de la République*, Paris.

Borger, H. (2002) *The Corporate Prince: Machiavelli's Timeless Wisdom Adapted for the Modern CEO*, Bloomington: First Books Library.

Burnham, J. (1943) *The Machiavellians*, New York: The John Day Co.

Buskirk, R. H. (1974) *Modern Management and Machiavelli*, Boston: Cahners Books.

Butterfield, H. (1940) *The Statecraft of Machiavelli*, London: Bell and Sons.

Calhoon, R. P. (1969) 'Niccolo Machiavelli and the twentieth century administrator,' *The Academy of Management Journal*, 12, 2: 205–12.

Calhoun, L. (2004) 'The problem of "dirty hands" and corrupt leadership,' *The Independent Review*, 8, 3:363–85.

Chabod, F. (1958) *Machiavelli and the Renaissance*, Cambridge: Harvard University Press.

De Alvarez, L. P. S. (1980) 'Introduction,' in *The Prince*, Irving: University of Dallas Press.

Derrida, J. (1980) 'Structure, sign, and play in the discourse of the human sciences,' in J. Derrida (ed.) *Writing and Difference*, London: Routledge.

Docherty, T. (2006). *Aesthetic Democracy*, Stanford: Stanford University Press.

English, F. W. (1992) 'The principal and the prince: Machiavelli and school leadership,' *NASSP Bulletin*, 76, 540: 10–15.

Femia, J. V. (2004) *Machiavelli Revisited*, Cardiff: University of Wales Press.

Frederick II von Hohenzollern. (1742) *Anti-Machiavel, ou Essai de critique sur le Prince de Machiavel*, Amsterdam.

Galie, P. J. and Bopst, C. (2006) 'Machiavelli & modern business: realist thought in contemporary corporate leadership manuals,' *Journal of Business Ethics*, 65, 3: 235–50.

Gentillet, I. (1576) *Discourse contre Machiavel, Florentin*, Geneva.

Gilbert, F. (1965) *Machiavelli and Guicciardini*, Princeton: Princeton University Press.

Kocis, R. A. (1998) *Machiavelli Redeemed: Retrieving his Humanist Perspective on Equality, Power, and Glory*, Bethlehem: Lehigh University Press.

Leslie, J. (1569) *Ane Brieff Declaratioun of the Wikit and Ungodlie Proceedings of Certane Inveterat Conspiratoris Agains the Quenis Majestie*.

Lukes, T. J. (2001) 'Lionizing Machiavelli,' *American Political Science Review*, 95, 3: 561–75.

Machiavelli, N. (1980 [1513]) *The Prince*, trans. L. de Alvarez, Irving: University of Dallas Press.

——, (1996) *Discourses on Livy*, trans. H. C. Mansfield and N. Tarcov, Chicago: University of Chicago Press.

Mansfield, H. C. (1979) *Machiavelli's New Modes and Orders*, Ithaca: Cornell University Press.

——, (1983) 'On the impersonality of the modern state: A comment on Machiavelli's use of Stato,' *American Political Science Review*, 77, 4: 849–57.

——, (1996) *Machiavelli's Virtue*, Chicago: University of Chicago Press.

Meinecke, F. (1957) *Machiavellianism: The Doctrine of Raison d'état and its Place in Modern History*, London: Routledge.

Olschki, L. (1945) *Machiavelli the Scientist*, Berkeley: University of California Press.

Pitkin, H. F. (1984) *Fortune is a Woman: Gender and Politics in the Thought of Niccolò Machiavelli*, Berkeley: University of California Press.

Price, R. (1977) 'The theme of gloria in Machiavelli,' *Renaissance Quarterly*, 30, 4: 588–631.

Ruffo-Fiore, S. (1990) *Niccolò Machiavelli: An Annotated Bibliography of Modern Criticism and Scholarship*, New York: Greenwood Press.

Skinner, Q. (1981) *Machiavelli*, Oxford: Oxford University Press.

Soll, J. (2005) *Publishing The Prince: History, Reading, and the Birth of Political Criticism*, Ann Arbor: University of Michigan Press.

Strauss, L. (1958) *Thoughts on Machiavelli*, Seattle: University Of Washington Press.

Swain, J. W. (2002) 'Machiavelli and modern management,' *Management Decision*, 40, 3: 281–7.

Viroli, M. (1990) 'Machiavelli and the republican idea of politics,' in B. Block, Q. Skinner, and M. Viroli (eds) *Machiavelli and Republicanism*, Cambridge: Cambridge University Press.

———, (2000) *Niccolò's Smile: A Biography of Machiavelli*, New York: Hill and Wang.

Walzer, M. (1973) 'Political action: The problem of dirty hands,' *Philosophy and Public Affairs*, 2, 2: 160–80.

# 3 Administration as a Humanistic Pursuit

## Kant and Hegel on the Political Critique of Educational Administration

*Eugénie A. Samier*

At first glance, two of the most influential philosophers in the modern period, Kant and Hegel, seem to have little relationship to educational administration. In the case of Kant (1724–1804), there are a number of misleading references to his ethics (Samier 2003). There is some reason for his under-representation—it is difficult to appreciate his political theory without first tackling the underlying critical groundwork in his three critiques of reason. The *Critique of Pure Reason* and *Critique of Practical Reason* are relevant to administrative decision-making, and recent cultural studies and organisational aesthetics have provided purchase for relating Kant's discussion in the *Critique of Judgment* (Samier 2006). The recent fad for leadership also opens the door to Kant's analysis of genius in the *Critique of Judgment,* his analysis of teleological reasoning—the judgments of things in terms of final causes, ends, or purposes—would be useful in discussions of the disciplinary integrity of administration (see e.g., Hood 1990; Ostrom 1973) and critiques of its ideological character.

Hegel (1770–1831) has played an even lesser role, reduced to occasional references to his dialectic influencing Marxism and Critical Theory. This is surprising considering Hegel's influence in educational philosophy, championed in the US by William Torrey Harris as a model for individual rational development and involvement in social institutions leading to freedom, adopted by Susan Blow, a major force in the Kindergarten movement based in part on Hegel's dialectic and concept of mind, and borrowed by John Dewey, who incorporated Hegel's notions of the virtuous individual and concerns for a strong republic (see Chambliss 1960). More recently, Hegel's continuing relevance for education has been developed in the UK by Tubbs (1996; 2005) and Tubbs and Grimes (2001).

It is the main aim of this chapter to demonstrate the relevance of these thinkers to educational administration against the problem of *epigonentum* affecting Freud, Marx, and other major intellectuals, in which selected fundamental principles are transformed into an often misrepresentational orthodoxy (Collins 1998). Their work has also influenced many of the schools of thought shaping the field. This includes the critical method, ethics, politics and government, and Prussian educational reform leading to the modern research university and principles of academic freedom. First, a number of biographical features are discussed, demonstrating that Kant and Hegel were involved in very practical and political matters in education, contradicting the usual 'ivory tower' conceptions of them. In fact, both were acutely aware of and involved in Realpolitik. Kant was a tutor, lecturer, university professor, dean, rector, collegial opponent, champion of intellectual freedom, educational reformer, and opponent of absolute monarchs and state education authorities. Hegel was a tutor, lecturer, Gymnasium rector, and university professor inspired by the French Revolution and the Enlightenment to work towards individual liberty and social institutions operating as ethical communities.

Secondly, Kant and Hegel's conceptions of individual freedom and the ethical character of the state and its administrative apparatus are discussed. Of particular importance are their arguments for the right to resist government, which are compatible with a practical concept of personal freedom, legislative development, and the establishment of civil rights and international peace. Requisite for these ideas are their conceptions of the goals and values of academic freedom, a suitable role for the state in education, and enlightened professional development.

## BIOGRAPHICAL AND HISTORICAL CONSIDERATIONS

Usually the biographies of philosophers are not important, however, knowledge of Kant and Hegel's experience lends legitimacy to their discussions of education and administration. Their stories are problematic, particularly in English, due to unfortunate stereotypes influencing not only interpretations of their basic principles, but their relevance to a field of action. Kant is popularly regarded as obsessively driven to organising his life by an unchangeable and precise schedule and teaching in a German backwater town and university, reinforcing an image of him as a puritanical pedant. This truncated portrait befits one who is supposed to have created a categorical imperative devoid of feeling and discretion, and removed from ordinary political experience, however, it bears little relationship to his actual life and work, as recent Kantian scholarship has demonstrated. Hegel is also distorted in both biography and popular perception, relatively little studied in Anglophone philosophy, and misrepresented by Marxists, Bertrand Russell, and Karl Popper. It is only since the 1970s that a flowering of Hegelian studies in English has more comprehensively and accurately represented his work.

Kant and Hegel came to their intellectual powers at a time of social, political, and intellectual ferment caused in part by industrialisation and the transition from absolute monarchies to constitutional democracies, punctuated by the French Revolution. They were key figures in the German Enlightenment, whose major tenets, shared with other northern European enlightenment movements (see Dupré 2004), were revolutionary at the time—emancipation from state and religious authority promoted through the humanitarian reaction to the intolerance and persecution of religious wars in France and Germany and the revolution in England in the seventeenth century (see Greene 1960). A central tenet was the examination of authorities, and the 'courage to use your *own* understanding' (Kant 1991a: 54). Given the violence of the previous century, it is understandable that Kant and Hegel placed reliance on rationality. Hegel was heavily influenced by Kant, but, as with all 'disciples' who come into their own, departed from Kant in some significant respects discussed later in this chapter, and in turn had a significant influence on existentialism, British idealism, Marxism, Deweyan pragmatism, phenomenology, hermeneutics, and analytic philosophy. What distinguishes Hegel from Kant is the former's synthesis of Enlightenment rationalism with selected elements of romanticism, 'his absolute idealism, his organic conception of nature, his critique of liberalism, his communitarian ideals, his vitalized Spinozism [pantheism], his concept of dialectic' (Beiser 2005: 35). Both also played a significant role in educational reform emerging from the German Enlightenment as *Bildung.* Scholars saw themselves as *Volkslehreren,* 'teachers of the people,' politicised with an intent to 'fight superstition, oppression and despotism' in preparing people for the ideals of a republic (Beiser 2005: 10–11).

Throughout Kant's years at the university, a very different portrait from the caricature invoked most often in the academic world emerges from his contemporaries' accounts of his social and professorial demeanour (see Kuehn 2001: 126–35). Herder has provided us with a 'less pedantic, Prussian, and Puritanical' individual, in a truer portrait:

> In his prime he had the happy sprightliness of a youth; he continued to have it, I believe, even as a very old man. His broad forehead, built for thinking, was the seat of an imperturbable cheerfulness and joy. Speech, the richest in thought, flowed from his lips. Playfulness, wit, and humor were at his command. His lectures were the most entertaining talks. . . . No cabal, no sect, no prejudice, no desire for fame could ever tempt him in the slightest away from broadening and illuminating the truth. He incited and gently forced others to think for themselves; despotism was foreign to his mind. (in Beck 1956: xxii)

Kant was born into a poor artisan family (Kuehn 2001; Pluhar 1987). While neither parent received a school-based education, they were adherents of Pietism and in this way brought intellectual matters into the household. He attended the Collegium Fridericianum and the University of Königsberg. Königsberg and its university are popularly, and anachronistically, regarded as a backwater, a myth exposed in Manfred Kuehn's 2001 biography of

Kant, where its centrality to trade routes, cosmopolitan character, history as the political capital of Prussia, occupation by Russian forces for a period, and relatively large university size at the time are discussed.

While serving for nine years as a tutor for a number of aristocratic households (a position typical for young intellectuals at the time), he continued his studies, enabling him to qualify for an appointment as an instructor at the University of Königsberg, where he remained for fifteen years, lecturing in natural sciences, mathematics, and philosophy until he received his professorship appointment in logic and metaphysics in 1770, later serving as dean and rector a number of times. It is only in 1770 that Kant published his first 'critical' text; previously, he had published a number of 'precritical' works in science and religion that had already garnered him a reputation in German academia. Kant's career fell into what Kuehn calls the 'silent years' from 1770 to 1781, during which time he worked on the *Critique of Pure Reason,* followed by an intense period of publication lasting until 1798.[1]

Kant was widely discussed in the 1780s as a key figure in the intellectual revival of Prussia, with the number of publications on his work reaching 2,832 (Guyer 1992: 449). This was driven in part by a bifurcation in his academic reception: on one hand, those who enthusiastically embraced the new critical philosophy, and on the other, those who broke friendships or attacked him for his emphasis on rationality, accusing him of 'old, cold prejudice in favour of mathematics,' of a '*Gnostic* hatred of matter' and a '*mystical* love of form' (in Berlin 2000: 308).

Probably the most serious politics Kant engaged in during his academic career involved his dispute with the theological faculty and Frederick William II's censors over the independence of the philosophy faculty, which finally occasioned his last published work, *The Conflict of the Faculties* (1979). Intent on 'stamp[ing] out the Enlightenment,' the king's censors silenced criticism of religious matters, eventually issuing an order to the Königsberg University senate forbidding anyone to lecture on Kant's philosophy of religion (Gregor 1979: xi). The importance of this text is its declaration of academic freedom in relation to both the state's legitimate role in seeking obedience from its citizens and the boundaries of a theological faculty's rightful power. It also establishes grounds for civil disobedience where the state has overstepped its province and the individual is pursuing rightful practice of profession.

Hegel had a long and varied history of educational positions, as private tutor, university lecturer in Jena, head teacher of the Nuremberg Gymnasium, professor at the University of Heidelberg, and, finally, professor at the University of Berlin. In all respects, he was successful in tackling the poor financial, administrative, and pedagogical circumstances of a gymnasium and creating enthusiasm for higher standards of learning (Tubbs 1996; Pinkard 2001).

Pinkard's extensive intellectual biography provides a portrait of Hegel as reform-minded, influenced by the French Revolution and the Enlightenment.

He was born into a family of third-generation civil servants. His maternal grandfather was a lawyer at the High Court of Justice in Württemberg, and his father, paternal grandfather and great grandfather served as secretary to the revenue office, ducal commissioner or high bailiff for the town of Altensteig, and another type of ducal commissioner for the town of Rosenfeld, respectively. His family moved in the social circles of the Privy Council in Stuttgart, by then evolved into a professional class of bureaucrats. Influenced by his education and experience of Württemberg's political development through constitutionalism and political rights aimed at an enlightened and cosmopolitan polity, he was shaped by, and later became a proponent of, the German *Bildung* ideal, 'that included the ideals of education, art, culture, and the formation of cultivated taste' (2001: 16), later translated into the internationally influential Humboldt University model.

Hegel, too, experienced a bifurcation in regard for his work: 'he was either highly admired and even idolized, or he was disparaged' (Pinkard 2001: 115). This is no surprise, as Hegel took a vigorous part in contentious issues of the time, including the nature and role of religion and constitutionalism, seeking a legitimate 'basis for moral, spiritual, and social reform in modern times' (Pinkard 2001: 148). He derived inspiration from the French Revolution, Rousseau, and involvement in the Prussian liberal reform movement of Hardenberg and von Stein, two 'mandarins' of this administrative transformation (Pinkard 2001: 418–25; Westphal 1993: 238). His understanding of Realpolitik came through personal experience, the aftermath of the Battle of Jena that resulted in hardship for the university community through Napoleon's rationalisation of the German universities, conflict with political authorities over academic freedom at the University of Heidelberg, and the authorities' investigations of Jacobinism at the University of Berlin (Pinkard 2001: 366–9, 436–45).

## SUBSTANTIVE CONTRIBUTIONS

Kant and Hegel as idealists adopted a number of the same principles and concepts, including the active role of the mind, the normative character of concepts (Brandom 1999), and their practical value in making judgements—in other words, the practical value of philosophy in personally committed political action and the construction of community. However, where Kant's critique was a subjective idealism based on a psychological overcoming of impulses, Hegel's was objective, grounded in historical process and the overcoming of impulse through social and political response (Westphal 1993: 245). Kant's conception of reason is a '*formal* or *abstract*' conception of the self as rational and individual, self-determination as the 'power of reason over sensibility,' and freedom as 'independence from the causality of nature.' Hegel's conception of reason is a '*material* or *concrete*' conception of self as realised 'through internalizing the other' in community, self-determination as an integration of reason and sensibility; and freedom as realised 'within the realm of nature . . . according to the necessity of one's own nature and the universe as a whole' (Beiser 2005: 201; Hegel 2003: 225–39).

## Kant

Along with Rousseau in the eighteenth century, Kant strongly influenced the development of moral and political liberal humanism, arguing that the individual is transcendent of natural causality, and, by rising above irrationality (passions and physiological needs) through reason, should be socially autonomous from the will of others. This applies not only to the irrationality of others expressed as abuse or exploitation in organisations, but also to the rational dictates of others in organisational imperatives. Revoking Machiavelli's separation of morals and politics, Kant integrated them into a 'revolutionary new conceptual framework' (Kersting 1992: 343), embedding politics in higher order moral precepts and judgement intended on an international level to produce a confederacy of free nations (see Kant 1991b). Most importantly for administrative studies, Kant's rationality is wholly different from the technical or scientific rationality driving bureaucratic-style decision-making and the organisational design in which the intrinsic moral worth and autonomy of individuals is sacrificed to political and bureaucratic authority's use of them as instruments of policy. Berlin criticises those who transformed 'Kant's severe individualism into something close to a pure totalitarian doctrine on the part of thinkers, some of whom claimed to be his disciples' (1969: 152–3), in other words, extending his principle of rationality to a rule of experts who believe that they can impose their 'rationality' on others.

Kant's political theory rests upon the principles of his practical philosophy, discussed in a number of writings, primarily, the *Metaphysics of Morals* and the *Critique of Practical Reason*. The latter develops the role of an autonomous and self-ruling reason in ethics and in a public and private philosophy of right, as well as in the rationally determined ends of human activity. These writings are accompanied by his political essays, 'Perpetual Peace: A Philosophical Sketch' and 'Idea for a Universal History from a Cosmopolitan Point of View,' in which he attempted to discover the preconditions for freedom as a peaceful world order, including the role of the state and its administration. His rights-oriented liberalism has provided a strong alternative to two other major perspectives: utilitarianism shaping Anglo-Saxon political theory and administration derived from Bentham and Mill, and libertarian liberals like Hayek (1960). Important features of rights-oriented liberalism derived from Kant and represented through Rawls (1971) are that: 1) rights are not dependent upon utilitarian or consequentialist concerns; 2) individuals' civil and political liberties are dependent upon the provision of basic social and economic needs met through redistributive policies; and 3) government should be neutral about competing conceptions of the good, meaning that our rights are prior to any particular conception of the good (Sandel 1998: 184–6).

Kant's political philosophy consists in a number of principles grounding his understanding of the role and responsibilities of the state, and therefore its civil service (including public education staff). First, we require government because people are inclined to act egoistically through self-interest by treating others as a means or 'things' (Sullivan 1994: 9–10). It is necessary, therefore, for government to provide a social contract that protects lives and property and a peaceful tribunal to resolve disputes. Its fundamental task is negative, imposing those constraints necessary to protect and promote each individual's freedom. The legal system establishes conditions under which peaceful community is created by constraining both sovereign and citizens (Sullivan: 1994: 10), setting out obligations or duties that prohibit both from interfering with the freedom of others, rather than granting entitlements. Therefore, citizenship is a responsibility to contribute to those moral conditions, and rights are derivative, arising only from corresponding duties that the state enforces (Sullivan 1994: 11). Kant's three principles for judging 'good citizenry' consist of: '1) The *freedom* of every member of society as a *human being;* 2) The *equality* of each with all others as a *subject;* 3) The *interdependence* of each member of a commonwealth as a *citizen*' (1991c: 74). Kant assumes here the rational ability of each individual to be self-governing. Freedom for Kant means using an intellectual compulsion rather than self-interest (1933: 465), producing the moral community.

Secondly, his universal prepolitical principle of justice is based on the authority of reason alone, rather than the church, rulers, or citizen's self interest—the only formal and moral legal structure is that which promotes as an imperative those civil arrangements allowing the most freedom for everyone alike (Kant 1969: 22–4; Sullivan 1994: 11–12). Kant defined the power and responsibility to act on the Universal Principle of Justice as 'autonomy,' granting each person moral authority and status against the might of the state (1969: 67–8). Kant's 'laws of natural justice' are also based on autonomy; these laws forbid any behaviour infringing on the person of others, their status, their ability to be self-determining and to function responsibly and with dignity, or on anything to which they have title (property and caring for children) (Sullivan 1994: 14). Complementing these general principles would be more definitive legislation, or positive laws, governing matters that are otherwise arbitrary, such as rules of the road, which may vary from place to place, and culture to culture. The only proviso is that they do not conflict with the Universal Principle of Justice (Sullivan 1994: 14).

While the state has the right and duty to enact laws, and obedience to them is a civic duty and moral obligation, reciprocal respect underlies two other coordinate principles of liberalism: equality as equal respect before the law, since everyone has the same innate moral status; and universality, in that the administration of justice should be impersonal with only secondary importance applied to specific historical associations and cultural forms

(Sullivan 1994: 16). For laws to hold universally they must bind absolutely; otherwise they become generalities to which a number of exceptions can be made for particular individuals and groups. This also means that the executive and judicial branches must be constitutionally insulated from direct popular pressure that could reintroduce arbitrary privileges for the majority or for minorities over the majority (Sullivan 1994: 17–18).

It is clear from these principles that Kant was acutely aware of political excess at the state, organisational, and interpersonal levels. And it is his moral principle of treating people as ends in themselves that establishes administrative and organisational principles as well as a critique of bureaucracy. The role of public administration is to serve the citizenry collectively and individually. The worst sin is to use others, whether clients or colleagues, for one's own or organisational ends, and to degrade or humiliate them in the process. In other words, administrative imperatives reflecting bureaucratised hierarchy and senior-level privilege are at odds with Kant's ethical imperatives. Worse, from Kant's view, than the use or abuse of people by each other are determinism and an empirical law of causality (Berlin 1999: 73), typical of mechanistic or structural-functional approaches to administration. Freedom runs contrary to the 'principle of benevolence' in administrative paternalism, which infantilises the adult citizens for whom it makes judgements; it is the 'greatest conceivable despotism' and 'destroys all freedom' (Kant 1991c: 74). As Berlin argues, for Kant 'any kind of use of other people for purposes which are not these other people's, but one's own, seems to him to be a form of degradation' and 'dehumanisation' (1999: 71).

A Kantian critique of bureaucratic reason can be found in the *Critique of Judgement,* the relevant part of which involves distinguishing between determinant judgement practiced in the world of objects (mechanistic or instrumental models), and reflective judgement for establishing principles of ethics and politics (1951: 232–3). Beiner emphasises this latter type of judgement for political purposes: rather than a doctrine of ends, it is a way of thinking of the particular in relation to universal categories as an inherently social activity. Persuading others of the validity of a judgement is the *raison d'être* of judging, a necessary quality, for example, in administrators and leaders in the policy process and organisational change and reform (1982: 119–20).

The state is not a moral institution per se, but it can create a favourable climate for moral action, eliminate impediments to moral growth, and establish humanistic educational values. In 'Perpetual Peace: A Philosophical Sketch,' Kant appeals to politicians to pay tribute to a morality whose maxims of action derive from obligations whose principles are given a priori by reason rather than empirical principles of political wisdom (1991b: 129–30). This morality also has an inescapable responsibility and right to be concerned about citizens' welfare or 'happiness,' which includes satisfaction of needs and desires, the enjoyment and contentment of a fulfilled life, and reasonable confidence in its continuance (Kant 1969: 38-41).

What duties, then, from a Kantian perspective, are administrators, including those in educational organisations, charged with? As instruments of the state, they are constrained by a concept of right by which actions must allow for everyone's freedom of will and for the holding of unpopular political and ethical convictions (Kersting 1992: 344–5). The essence of administration is not contained in bureaucratic policies and procedures, rather, it is a critical judgment in accord with moral and political principles constituting individual responsibility. Their obligation is to ensure the conditions for others' legitimate freedoms and rights, obligations that cannot be delegated away or transferred to higher positional authority. Even though they are the means through which the state expresses its will, they cannot shirk higher order individual responsibilities. And, if educational administrators, they have the added responsibility of ensuring others' rights to a critical and enlightened development.

## Hegel

Hegel is highly problematic in the Anglophone world. Pinkard sums up the misrepresentation of his work in the following:

> Hegel is one of those philosophers just about all educated people think they know something about. His philosophy was the forerunner to Karl Marx's theory of history, but unlike Marx, who was a materialist, Hegel was an idealist in the sense that he thought that reality was ultimately spiritual, and that it developed according to the process of thesis/antithesis/ synthesis. Hegel also glorified the Prussian state, claiming that it was God's work, was perfect, and was the culmination of all human history. All citizens of Prussia owed unconditional allegiance to that state, and it could do with them as it pleased. Hegel played a large role in the growth of German nationalism, authoritarianism, and militarism with his quasi-mystical celebrations of what he pretentiously called the Absolute. (2001: ix)

Following this opening paragraph, Pinkard then writes: 'Just about everything in the first paragraph is false except for the first sentence' (2001: ix). Stewart (1996), also, tackled what he called the 'myths and legends' of Hegel, that he: was an apologist for authoritarianism, totalitarianism, the Prussian state, and German nationalism; glorified war and promoted imperialism through a militaristic political philosophy; had announced the end of history; advanced a thesis/antithesis/synthesis formula of dialectic (one that Hegel never used); and was an arch-rationalist, ignoring existential and irrational factors.

Despite relatively poor commentary in English prior to Pinkard (2000), an adequate secondary literature has existed since the mid-1960s from which administrative studies could have drawn. These writings explore

Hegel's theory of history, the state, government, work, bureaucracy, plural-ism, ethics, and critique of instrumentalism (see Avineri 1972; Kaufmann 1965; Löwith 1964). Inwood's comprehensive *Hegel* (1983) and Rauch's discussion of the *Phenomenology of Spirit*[2] (1999) examine a number of topics more recently accepted as important foundational principles for edu-cational administration and leadership: perception, subjectivity, objectivity, language, conceptualisation, reflexivity, freedom of thought, identity forma-tion, authority and power relations, contextualisation of thought and ideals relevant to policy studies, the formation of community, and a critique of positivism. Beiser (2005), Cristi (2005), and Neuhouser (2000) have subse-quently discussed a number of political principles such as civil society, liber-alism, and the constitutional state that have implications for administrative responsibility in advancing social freedom and institutional ethics.

Hegel radicalised Kant's theory of the mind, extending knowledge to the noumenal as part of an evolving historical process based on the principle of action and negation, or dialectical process, producing higher levels of consciousness. His dialectic is an interplay of the particular and universal in which 'man seeks recognition of his own particular self from all men; he seeks universal recognition of his particularity' (Mills 1998: 243). This is a truer conception of the Hegelian dialectic than the triadic thesis-antithesis-synthesis, an 'overcoming or resolution of opposing dualisms': it is instead a formation and reformation of consciousness in which differences are seen to be irresolvable, however understood in greater depth (Tubbs 2005: 330–1). One social formulation of dialectic serving as a caution to authorities is the 'ironical reversal of the roles of master and servant' discussed by Hegel, in which the 'servant becomes self-reliant because he depends on his own work, while the master comes to depend on the servant' (Kaufmann 1965: 169; Hegel 2003: 104–12).

He saw being as a process of self-creation and re-creation through self-annulment and self-transcendence, issuing from a complex organic inter-relation of individuals and their social context (Westphal 1993: 236). It is upon this conception of consciousness that his theory of knowledge rests: knowledge itself is not passively acquired but demands action, confron-tation, and immersion. Referred to by Hegel as 'conceptual thought,' the world is a construction of the mind through the mediating role of conscious-ness between the individual and the 'spirit' of the times, or *Geist,* enabling normative judgement to free one from habituation (Hegel 1956: 19; 2003: 252; Pinkard 2001: 173). One's consciousness of the world and self-con-sciousness of what one does in using judgement to create goals achieved through a 'negative' relation to natural states of desire and sensation, is the main theme of the *Phenomenology.* It is through this historical process that Hegel evaluated the normative failures in society producing a cultural crisis as a long development of 'negativity' in the self-undermining scepticism that ultimately produces freedom and a just state (Pinkard 2001: 207–8; Hegel 1956: 63–5).

Underlying social institutions he examined—the family, civil society, and the liberal constitutional state—is a set of normative standards used to judge them. In the *Philosophy of Right* he proposed three conceptions of freedom in an increasing hierarchical order: personal freedom, being able to do as one pleases as an individual; the freedom of moral subjectivity, which consists in determining the normative principles governing one's actions; and social freedom, or 'substantial freedom,' realised only through social institutions as both objective laws and subjective social conditions required for others to realise freedom while avoiding the alienation and anomie of modern society (Hegel 1956: 43; Neuhouser 2000: 5–6, 14, 27). For Hegel, there are three principles upon which people could be united and identify with the state yet achieve individual freedom: have 'the immutable maintenance of rights as its objective; bind people to the state through law; and citizen representation in the making of laws and the management of the state' (Pinkard 2001: 151). For Hegel, 'morality is a political affair' (1956: 71) for which leaders (politicians) and administrators have primary responsibility.

Hegel championed republicanism as the appropriate form of government in which all citizens take a part in community as a normative paradigm for politics (Habermas 1973), rejecting the contract tradition because of its omission of necessary membership in society and its inevitable effect on individual development (Westphal 1993: 242, 244). Hegel argued that the state is first and foremost an ethical community with dignity and sacred absoluteness, similar to Aristotle's *koinonia politike* (Hegel 1956: 43–50), a view in part occasioned by his critique of modern industrialised society's increasing atomisation, centralisation, and bureaucratisation (Beiser 2005: 48). In this respect he departed from Kant by distinguishing between *Sittlichkeit,* as the virtue of membership in community involving social and political activities encompassing both rights and duties that produce political obligations and its highest expression, the state (Cristi 1989: 732; Hegel 2003: 253), and Kantian *Moralität,* as virtue conceived in isolation as an individual. An important feature of *Sittlichkeit* is the right to civil disobedience, reflected in Hegel's treatment of Sophocles' *Antigone* in *The Philosophy of History* and the *Phenomenology,* where Antigone has a moral obligation to oppose a tyrant and an authoritarian state.

Hegel has been read as a liberal for whom individual rights have priority over duties to higher political authority and obligations need to be grounded in consent, as well as a conservative for whom duty has priority over individual rights and subservience to the state is owed by the individual. Cristi proposes a more balanced view that takes into account the full text of *Philosophy of Right*:

The authority of his conservative State, which maintains a monopoly on politics bolstered by a hereditary monarch, preserves the freedom of individuals, in a liberal civil society. At the same time, the rights of these individuals, exercised in the context of an unalloyed market economy, demand a strong, autonomous State. ... A dialectical argument allows Hegel systematically to derive a conservative State from the liberal principles embodied in civil society. ... The key to Hegel's dialectical derivation lies in the spontaneous order that springs naturally from the self-seeking behaviour of individuals. This order safeguards the freedom of individuals and at the same time disciplines and reconciles their divergent aims. (1989: 718–9)

Social institutions arise from the expression of individual freedom as civil society, modulated by the more conservative, and stable, character of the state. In *Natural Law,* Hegel regards leadership as individuals who, through praxis and spontaneity, are able to intuitively apprehend the whole of subjective idealism and empiricism, and, through their genius, are able to concentrate all the empirical particularities into a unitary whole (Cristi 1989: 726–7). Leaders can evoke and carry the spirit of the times as it evolves through the historical process. And it is administrators who are responsible for ensuring that laws and favourable conditions are met for individual and collective freedom, including taming the 'natural selfishness of the business classes (Cristi 2005: 73), that is, a market-oriented impulse. They also have a formative or educational responsibility in producing individuals capable of bearing free will. Educational administrators carry a special burden in this respect (Hegel 1996: 205–25; Neuhouser 2000: 148–65). Hegel regarded three conditions to be necessary for freedom, all deliberations that administrators are obliged to exercise: universality, in which one acquires self-awareness by abstracting oneself from specific situations; particularity, in which one chooses particular options among those possible; and individuality, the synthesis of the other two and commitment to a course of action (Beiser 2005: 199). In other words, one should not succumb to ideologies, including those of management and leadership such as the New Public Management and charisma.

Hegel's conception of bureaucracy differs significantly from the Weberian view in some respects. While they both see bureaucracy historically as part of modernity, where Weber regards it as technical, Hegel views it as a practical wisdom demanding a higher standard of knowledge—broader, contextualised, and requiring judgement (Shaw 1992: 4). The institutions providing for needs—the public administration of justice, education and social services, and central government—are intended to transform natural impulses into the higher order ends of civil and political rights through citizen participation, codified into legitimate law and political education (Westphal 1993: 257–62). The role of authority is to maintain an order that provides the conditions for freedom, the two reconciled through the dialectic (Cristi 2005: 55, 67). The ideal civil service Hegel describes as a 'universal class' since its interest is the 'universal interests of society' (1996: 202), dispassionate, tenured, motivated by an ethos of service to the commonwealth, and insulated from the pressures of civil society, in other words, selected on the basis of merit (1996: 284) and salaried rather than appointed through patronage and operating through venality, as was commonplace when he wrote (Avineri 1974: 155–61). Above all, those in public service, including education, must not yield to 'subjective dependence and influences' (Hegel 1996: 302), a feature undermined by the entrepreneurial nature of the New Public Management. Consultancy and other private sector management and provision practices would necessarily be excluded.

## KANT AND HEGEL ON EDUCATION

Kant and Hegel's writings on education are part of the idealist tradition carried through Schiller, Shelley, and Northrop Frye. They were participants of the *Bildung* tradition, an educational concept originating in classical Greece, later adopted by neohumanists in the seventeenth century, who distinguished it from upbringing (*Erziehung*), based in the Medieval educational tradition, and teaching (*Unterricht*) in the modern era. Its distinguishing characteristic is 'an individual process of *self*-formation' (Nordenbo 2002: 345), in contrast to a religious or state control of education, in which the individual must actively take part in his or her own formation or development. *Bildung,* as an education predicated upon an individual's nature rather than social demands, placing it against governance for social order, was harmonised by a curriculum encompassing the seven liberal arts, leading toward maximum individual freedom as a cultivated person, and in harmony with 'universal principles of the world and society' (Nordenbo 2002: 346). Kant's method provided the foundation for a critical epistemology, examining the conceptual presuppositions of all fields, including theology, medicine, and law, and contributing to the university reform instituted by Wilhelm von Humboldt in creating the 'Humboldt' model for the University of Berlin in the early 1800s. As a synthesis of research and teaching it produced the modern research university internationally, 'the key organizational base for intellectuals ever since, we are all post-Kantians, ever since anchored around the centrality of critical epistemology' (Collins 1998: 852).

The responsibility of teachers and administrators in this kind of university is to provide an educational experience that aims at an investigation of the nature and limits of reason and knowledge, conducted in a manner that avoids dogma and scepticism. Kant argues in 'What Is Orientation in Thinking?' for the need to make public use of one's reason, to make it 'suitable for *use in the experiential world*' (1991d: 237). These practices are to be protected by professional autonomy and academic freedom, and it is administrators' responsibilities to create the policies and environment in which they can flourish.

Educational history, philosophy, and curricular studies have taken notice of Hegel in discussion of educational ideal, the role of the teacher, and professionalism, all of which are also relevant to administrative and leadership activities. Tubbs, in particular, has advocated Hegel's discourse as an important foundation in these areas. He was progressive in establishing necessary discipline to support a rich teaching and learning environment and a more interactive and independent style of teaching and curriculum (Tubbs 1996; Pinkard, 2001). Hegel's advocacy of *Bildung,* implemented in his successful rectorship of and teaching at the Nuremburg Gymnasium and reorganisation of the Nuremburg school system, is primarily discussed in *Philosophy of Mind,* in which 'the public or objective sphere (that is, the world in its historical development) . . . [is] internalised by the individual, who is thus (in virtue of the dialectical method) led from subjective belief to objective knowledge or wisdom' (Nordenbo 2002: 350). For Hegel it promised a necessary preparation for citizens to take up political authority in an independent manner (Pinkard 2001: 270).

Tubbs (1996) has identified four Hegelian principles of continuing relevance: 1) the establishment of self-discipline in behaviour and learning based on respect for teachers and fellow students and obedience to legitimate teaching authority regarding curricular requirements; 2) a humanistic approach to curriculum that supports an integration of substance and higher order 'speculative thinking'; 3) an integrative approach to teaching that combines curricular content with student experience to develop interpretive and critical skills and knowledge based on dialectical reasoning; and 4) a teacher role conceptualised as a reflective practitioner based upon self-critique, dialectical activity, and praxis oriented toward emancipation and empowerment. As an educational goal, teachers, administrators, and policy-actors at the government level should be striving in curriculum for the abstract, the dialectical, and the speculative. Extrapolating from Tubbs' characterisation of the teacher's role as presented in *Philosophy of Mind,* they should be both master, establishing moral codes grounded in respect, and slave, taking a personal interest in students' individual development to an extent that rejects rote teaching (2005: 336–7).

## CONCLUSION

Not only can we draw implications for educational administration from Kant and Hegel's political theory, but the philosophers explicitly dealt with the role of the state via its administrative cadres in enforcing individual liberty and in fashioning education as a pursuit ensuring freedom and civic responsibility. They cast a long shadow over bureaucratised, rationalised administration and teaching, which to Kant constituted '*civil coercion*' (1991d: 247), and to Hegel was 'capricious' (1996: 302). Above all, administration and leadership are moral and civic roles, developed first in the individual and then through social institutions, including the laws and educational system that ground the state and its administration (see Kant 1991e). As a critique of administrative and educational reason, both set a higher professional bar than obedience for political authority and socioeconomic pressures. Duties and obligations are characterised by higher order values, not only for their own sake, but to ensure that the social institutions necessary in state-building meet the requirements of universal rights for citizens.

Tubbs and Grimes describe the teacher training programme at King Alfred's College, Winchester, which is based on the idealism of Kant and Hegel, as one that could be applied to the professional preparation of educational administrators. The conception derived from the cultural education of the *paideia* and Romantic and idealist *Bildung* traditions is 'at its heart the aesthetic, religious, historical, philosophical and spiritual significance of education when it intervenes in and seeks to reform modern social relations' (2001: 5), and it produces 'critical and reflective human beings' (2001: 13). The structure of the programme reflects Kant and Hegel's principles of pedagogy, the relationship between theory and practice and thought and being, 'in such a way that *the difficulty of their relationship was not itself suppressed*' (Tubbs and Grimes 2001: 5). Designed around the key themes of gender, race, and power, it is a programme of 'the philosophy of cultural critique' (6) and an overt critique of political relations, consisting of a three-fold model integrating experience, theory, and critique in an interdisciplinary manner over a three-year period. The first two years concentrate on a critical and interpretive approach to theory, and the final year focusses on theory in practice.

## NOTES

1. His most influential works include the three *Critiques* (*of Pure Reason* in 1781, *of Practical Reason* in 1788, and *of Judgment* in 1790), *Foundations of the Metaphysics of Morals* (1785), *On Using Teleological Principles in Philosophy* (1788), *Perpetual Peace* (1795), *Metaphysics of Morals* (1797), and *Anthropology from a Pragmatic Point of View* (1798).
2. Also translated as *Philosophy of Mind*.

## REFERENCES

Avineri, S. (1974 [1972]) *Hegel's Theory of the Modern State*, Cambridge: Cambridge University Press.

Beck, L. W. (1956) 'Sketch of Kant's life and work,' in I. Kant, *Critique of Practical Reason*, New York: Macmillan.

Beiner, R. (1982) 'Hannah Arendt on judging,' in H. Arendt, *Lectures on Kant's Political Philosophy*, Chicago: University of Chicago Press.

Beiser, F. (2005) *Hegel*, New York: Routledge.

Berlin, I. (1969) *Four Essays on Liberty*, Oxford: Oxford University Press.

———, (1999) *The Roots of Romanticism*, Princeton: Princeton University Press.

———, (2000) *Three Critics of the Enlightenment: Vico, Hamann, Herder*, Princeton: Princeton University Press.

Brandom, R. (1999) 'Some pragmatist themes in Hegel's idealism: Negotiation and administration in Hegel's account of the structure and content of conceptual norms,' *European Journal of Philosophy*, 7, 2: 164–89.

Chambliss, J. J. (1960) *The Origins of American Philosophy of Education,* The Hague: Martinus Nijhoff.

Collins, R. (1998) 'The skeleton of theory,' in *A Global Theory of Intellectual Change,* Cambridge: Harvard University Press.

Cristi, F. R. (1989) 'Hegel's conservative liberalism,' *Canadian Journal of Political Science,* 22, 4: 717–38.

——, (2005) *Hegel on Freedom and Authority,* Cardiff: University of Wales Press.

Dupré, L. (2004) *The Enlightenment and the Intellectual Foundations of Modern Culture,* New Haven: Yale University Press.

Greene, T. (1960) 'Introduction' in I. Kant, *Religion within the Limits of Reason Alone,* New York: Harper & Row.

Gregor, M. (1979) 'Translator's introduction,' in I. Kant, *Conflict of the Faculties,* Lincoln: University of Nebraska Press.

Guyer, P. (1992) 'Bibliography,' in P. Guyer (ed.) *The Cambridge Companion to Kant,* Cambridge: Cambridge University Press.

Habermas, J. (1973) 'On Hegel's Political Writings,' in *Theory and Practice,* Boston: Beacon Press.

Hayek, F. (1960) *The Constitution of Liberty,* Chicago: University of Chicago Press.

Hegel, G. W. F. (1956) *The Philosophy of History,* New York: Dover.

——, (1996) *Philosophy of Right,* Amherst: Prometheus Books.

——, (2003) *The Phenomenology of Mind,* New York: Dover.

Hood, C. (1990) 'Public administration: Lost an empire, not yet found a role?' in A. Leftwick (ed.) *New Developments in Political Science,* Aldershot: Gower.

Inwood, M. J. (2002 [1983]) *Hegel,* 2nd ed. London: Routledge.

Kant, I. (1933) *Critique of Pure Reason,* London: Macmillan.

——, (1951) *Critique of Judgement,* New York: Macmillan.

——, (1969) *Foundations of the Metaphysics of Morals and Critical Essays,* New York: Macmillan.

——, (1979) *The Conflict of the Faculties,* Lincoln: University of Nebraska Press.

——, (1991a) 'An answer to the question "what is enlightenment?"' in *Kant: Political Writings,* Cambridge: Cambridge University Press.

——, (1991b) 'Perpetual peace: a philosophical sketch,' in *Kant: Political Writings,* Cambridge: Cambridge University Press.

——, (1991c) 'On the common saying: "this may be true in theory, but it does not apply in practice,' in *Kant: Political Writings,* Cambridge: Cambridge University Press.

——, (1991d) 'What is orientation in thinking?,' in *Kant: Political Writings,* Cambridge: Cambridge University Press.

——, (1991e) 'Idea for a universal history,' in *Kant: Political Writings,* Cambridge: Cambridge University Press.

Kaufmann, W. (1965) *Hegel: Reinterpretation, Texts, and Commentary,* Garden City: Doubleday & Co.

Kersting, W. (1992) 'Politics, freedom, and order: Kant's political philosophy,' in P. Guyer (ed.) *The Cambridge Companion to Kant,* Cambridge: Cambridge University Press.

Kuehn, M. (2001) *Kant: A Biography,* Cambridge: Cambridge University Press.

Löwith, K. (1964) *From Hegel to Nietzsche: The Revolution in Nineteenth-Century Thought,* New York: Columbia University Press.

Mills, P. J. (1998) 'Hegel's *Antigone*,' in J. Stewart (ed.) *The Phenomenology of Spirit Reader: Critical and Interpretive Essays,* Albany: SUNY Press.

Neuhouser, F. (2000) *Foundations of Hegel's Social Theory: Actualizing Freedom,* Cambridge: Harvard University Press.

Nordenbo, S. E. (2002) '*Bildung* and the thinking of *Bildung*,' *Journal of Philosophy of Education,* 36, 3: 341–52.

Ostrom, V. (1973) *The Intellectual Crisis in American Public Administration,* Tusca-loosa: University of Alabama Press.

Pinkard, T. (2001[2000]) *Hegel: A Biography,* Cambridge: Cambridge University Press.

Pluhar, W. (1987) 'Translator's Introduction' to the *Critique of Judgment* . . .

Rauch, L. (1999) 'A discussion of the text,' in L. Rauch and D. Sherman, *Hegel's Phenomenology of Self-Consciousness: Text and Commentary,* Albany: SUNY Press.

Rawls, J. (1971) *A Theory of Justice,* Cambridge: Harvard University Press.

Samier, E. A. (2003) 'A Kantian critique for administrative ethics: an alternative to the "morally mute" manager?' in E. A. Samier (ed.) *Ethical Foundations for Educational Administration,* London: Routledge.

———, (2006) 'Imagination, taste, the sublime, and genius in administration: a Kantian critique of organisational aesthetics,' in E. A. Samier and R. Bates (eds) *Aesthetic Dimensions of Educational Administration and Leadership,* London: Routledge.

Sandel, M. (1998) *Liberalism and the Limits of Justice,* 2nd ed., Cambridge: Cambridge University Press.

Shaw, C. (1992) 'Hegel's theory of modern bureaucracy,' *American Political Science Review,* 86, 2: 1–12.

Stewart, J. (ed.) (1996) *The Hegel Myths and Legends,* Evanston: Northwestern University Press.

Sullivan, R. (1994) *An Introduction to Kant's Ethics,* Cambridge: Cambridge University Press.

Tubbs, N. (1996) 'Hegel's educational theory and practice,' *British Journal of Educational Studies,* 44, 2: 181–99.

———, (2005) 'Chapter 6: Hegel,' *Journal of Philosophy of Education,* 39, 2: 329–55.

———, and Grimes, J. (2001) 'What is Education Studies?' *Educational Studies,* 27, 1: 3–15.

Westphal, K. (1993) 'The basic context and structure of Hegel's *Philosophy of Right,'* in F. Beiser (ed.) *The Cambridge Companion to Hegel,* Cambridge: Cambridge University Press.

# 4 On Jürgen Habermas' Critical Theory and the Political Dimensions of Educational Administration

*Peter Milley*

Politics exist when competing human interests collide, producing conflicts resolved through the use of power (Morgan 2006). Wherever people interact—whether in families, communities, workplaces, or formal political venues—their different needs, interests, and expectations will produce some level of conflict and result in some type of power dynamic. Following this definition, it is not hard to imagine that politics form an inherent aspect of social processes, including education and its administration.

In western nations, the state tends to play a major role in policy direction and oversight for all levels of formal education. And schools and universities bring a range of participants and stakeholders together who often have different needs, interests, and values. So education and its administration have both big and small 'p' political aspects to them. These politics pertain to questions about both educational goals and how educational processes and institutions should work. Yet, popular ways of thinking about educational organisations and their administration often mask these political dimensions. Effectiveness perspectives that emphasise administrative roles and behaviours and organisational structures and functions do not capture well the political aspects of policy and decision-making processes (Hodgkinson 1996), interpersonal and group dynamics (Morgan 2006), bureaucratic pathologies (Perrow 1986), and individual wilfulness (Greenfield 1993: 53–73). Cultural perspectives, especially those relying on a consensus rather than conflict view, often present too homogeneous and harmonious an image of the idiosyncratic, conflict-ridden nature of organisations and their administration (Greenfield 1993: 75–91). Most importantly, these popular views sidestep the significance of power, the lifeblood of politics.

There are many theories of politics and power that can provide lenses for guiding research and practice in educational administration. All of them have philosophical underpinnings, and it is important to make them explicit since politics and power are not just instrumental to administration—they have profound social, moral, and educational implications. Politics can be practiced in democratic or autocratic ways (Morgan 2006). The former builds capacity in people and organisations for informed, reflective thought and action, while the latter does not. Power can be enacted through inspiring ideas and exemplary actions that nourish the human spirit or it can be exercised inhumanely through the use of threats and physical force.

This chapter explores the contribution that Jürgen Habermas' well-regarded version of critical theory can make to an understanding of the political dimension of educational administration. Habermas has spent four decades integrating a complex set of concepts from a range of disciplines to develop a theory that addresses social, cultural, economic, political, psychological, aesthetic, and historical dynamics of western society and its institutions. His work has been subject to critiques from a range of perspectives, including postmodernism (e.g., Lyotard 1984; Seidman 1998), feminism (e.g., Cohen 1995; Fraser 1995), and postcolonialism (e.g., Yeatman 1994), and has responded to these criticisms over time.

Habermas (1970) has not written directly on the topic of educational administration, but he has argued that higher education should be focused on developing the capacity of people to shape the cultural life of their families, communities, and societies. Its economic contributions are important but secondary. He also claims that universities should primarily serve as sites of unfettered debate, where cultural, political, and economic practices can be subject to ongoing critique (1987). In the educational literature, researchers such as Barnett (1993), Lakeland (1993), Milley (2005), and Ostovich (1995) have taken up his ideas about higher education. Scholars in other subfields of education have also taken up concepts from his critical theory. Examples include Gibson (1986) and Young (1990) in education, Bates (1989), Foster (1986, 1989), Harris (2002), Milley (2002a), and Sergiovanni (2000) in educational administration, Brookfield (2005), Connelly (1996), Mezirow (1995), and Welton (1995) in adult education, and Hart (1992), Milley (2002b), and Welton (1991) in experiential and workplace learning.

Habermas' work appeals to educational scholars and practitioners in part because it aims to recuperate the power of modern reason and the democratic ideals of equality, justice, and freedom that ground a great deal of educational thinking (if not practice) in the west. These ideals stem from an enlightenment tradition that has been subject to a great deal of criticism for not living up to its promises (Horkheimer and Adorno 1993; Lyotard 1984). Habermas encourages reflection on the troubling contradictions associated with an uncritical acceptance and application of this tradition. He shows where things have gone wrong historically, conceptually, and practically in the process of enlightenment, and offers potential solutions. Finally, he (1979) holds that socially progressive societies are developed through certain kinds of learning processes. His social theory is also a learning theory, facilitating its use in the educational field (Outhwaite 1994; Young 1990).

Three key sets of concepts from across Habermas' oeuvre are explored here for educational administration. The first is a typology of human interests and corresponding forms of knowledge offering a fruitful way of thinking about the politics surrounding the development and application of a knowledge base. The second is Habermas' perspective on communicative and strategic action, which offers a helpful way to think about the sources and effects of power in everyday practice. The third is his model of life-world and system, which provides a comprehensive perspective of multiple domains—private lives, civil society, economy, and state—and of how politics play out and power is exercised within, but more particularly, between these domains. In order to understand these concepts a little better, it is important to situate them in the overall context of political interests in the critical theory tradition.

## POLITICAL INTERESTS OF THE CRITICAL THEORY TRADITION

The critical theory movement began in the 1920s with scholars from the Institute for Social Research at the University of Frankfurt (Agger 1992). Attempting to remedy Marx and Engel's (1972) theory of historical materialism and Weber's (1968) rationalisation thesis, the 'first generation' sought in different ways to analyse the theoretical and empirical prospects for achieving socially just, nonviolent, and nontotalitarian societies so that the universal ideals of freedom, truth, and justice could be reconciled with the individual desire for happiness (Wellmer 1994: 45–6). Their findings were not flattering: despite the enormous increase in knowledge, productive forces, and wealth, enlightenment and modernisation had also resulted in social, cultural, and political regression, evidenced by profound social divides and inequalities, abject forms of culture, and relentless violence (Horkheimer and Adorno 1993).

Subsequent researchers have taken the tradition of the Frankfurt School in new directions (Seidman 1998), but at the heart of most critical theories lie the normative concerns of freedom, equality, and social justice (Cannon 2001). Critical theories are thus always political at some level. The interests of marginalised, subordinated people and groups are key concerns. Most critical theorists see ideology as an important source of power that dominant social groups draw upon to keep other groups subordinated. Dominant ideas become ideology proper when subordinated groups come to identify with them as truly representing their interests when, in objective terms, they do not (Althusser 1984). Ideology masks conflicting interests that exist between social groups and conceals the social, cultural, economic, and political arrangements that sustain existing patterns of domination and subordination (Bottomore et al. 1988).

With this central concept of ideology, it is not surprising that many critical theorists view ideology critique to be one of their key tasks. Some identify specific ideologies, determine their sources, describe their effects, and work both theoretically and practically to dissolve their efficacy (e.g., Apple 2000; Bourdieu 1977; Giroux 2004). Others begin their research from the standpoint of subordinated people to investigate the ways in which ideologies and social structures and practices delimit how marginalised people are able to interpret their needs, voice their interests, and engage in political action (e.g., Freire 1970; Smith 1996).

Habermas is considered to be second generation from the Frankfurt School (Duvenage 2003). He supports its core values, but his conceptual approach is different. Instead of criticising particular ideologies that enable the subordination of groups, he is more interested in defining the conditions under which people *in general* are able to identify and criticise ideologies, authentically express their interests, and resolve conflicts rationally and nonviolently. He takes this position out of a concern that people in advanced industrial societies continually run the risk of losing their capacity for critical reflection and authentic self-expression. Without this capacity, they and their societies can readily succumb to various forms of domination. For Habermas (1984, 1989), the most legitimate power that can be used to resolve conflicting interests is that of reason, derived from and through genuine, inclusive dialogue. This requires a robust public sphere, enabled by key institutions in civil society such as universities, in which genuine public dialogue can take place about needs, interests, issues, and goals.

## HUMAN INTERESTS AND CORRESPONDING FORMS OF KNOWLEDGE

Early in his career, Habermas (1971) promulgated a typology of fundamental human interests and corresponding forms of knowledge that had emerged in western societies as they modernised and purportedly became enlightened, aiming to debunk the ideological stranglehold that 'positivism' had on the human sciences. He believed the ubiquitous and unreflective application within the human sciences of the interests, epistemologies, and methods from the physical sciences was a significant intellectual and moral failing. It allowed researchers to focus on causal explanations and predictions of human behaviour with a view to enabling greater control over people and their social environments. This facilitated the use of the human sciences in psychological and social domination. His solution was to show how the human sciences address moral, aesthetic, and scientific interests, a broader range than those addressed by the physical sciences. The human sciences, therefore, ought to rely on a wider range of epistemologies and validity claims. Table 4.1 presents an interpretation of Habermas' typology, including concepts he later introduced (1984).

Scientific and instrumental knowledge support the interests people have in explaining, predicting, and, ultimately, controlling their natural, social (including educational) environments. Scientific knowledge is deemed to be valid if it reliably represents a state of affairs, fact, or truth; instrumental knowledge, if it is effective in meeting the objectives to which it is put to use. In educational administration, polling to predict employee, student,

*Table 4.1*   Human Interests and Corresponding Forms of Knowledge

| Human interest | Form of knowledge | Validity claim | Cultural sphere |
| --- | --- | --- | --- |
| description, explanation, prediction, control | scientific-instrumental | truth, effectiveness | science and technology |
| mutual understanding, action coordination, justice | moral-practical | rightness | morality |
| self-expression, emancipation | aesthetic -expressive | truthfulness, authenticity | arts |

or stakeholder responses to a proposed educational initiative would be an example of a scientific approach. The use of software to standardise the implementation of an initiative would be an instrumental approach. Instrumental knowledge also informs political thinking and action in terms of strategy formulation.

Moral-practical knowledge informs all interests people have in establishing legitimate interpersonal relations to coordinate their actions with others in mutually agreeable and just ways. It can be deemed valid based on how right or just it is. In the context of educational administration, it can be viewed as framing moral reasoning, ethical judgments, and policy-making, shaping political thinking and action, at least in the case of reflective and morally well-developed administrators.

Aesthetic-expressive knowledge informs the interests people have in conveying their needs, interests, and identities and in freeing themselves from domination and repression, whether psychological, social, cultural, economic, or political. It is deemed valid based on its truthfulness and authenticity. As the source of self-awareness, virtue, and charisma, this knowledge can be seen to be foundational to educational leadership (Samier 2006). It would also shape political thinking and action, particularly with respect to challenging barriers to truthful interpretations of need and authentic self-expression.

Habermas (1971; 1997) suggests that these sets of human interests and forms of knowledge are not mutually exclusive. In advanced industrial societies, however, communities of interest have arisen around them, forming distinct cultural spheres, and groups have developed specialties within these communities, forming distinct subcultures. They have the tendency to become insular, in part because of the increasing specialisation of interests and knowledge into subfields. To be sure, complex, knowledge-intensive societies require specialists in each of the spheres in order to function properly. But he also argues that an appropriate balance needs to be struck between specialised learning in each and integrative learning that bridges them. Integrative learning offers a system of checks and balances within and between the spheres, and provides for innovations to occur. Socially progressive societies are constituted and sustained by these kinds of learning.

Habermas (1971; 1997) observes that people in advanced industrial societies emphasise the development of technologies to ensure their economic competitiveness and survival. As a result, they privilege instrumental interests and knowledge. When instrumental rationality takes precedence over scientific, moral, or aesthetic reasoning, people become less able to express themselves authentically and begin to lose their capacity for making sound moral choices and setting appropriate directions. Totalitarianism is one possible, if extreme, consequence of an imbalance in learning. He further notes that a paradox exists in the specialised claims used to justify and evaluate knowledge and action in each of the three cultural spheres, observing how, on one hand, the use of specialised validity claims makes it difficult for people to communicate and build understanding between communities of interest. This can increase misunderstanding, conflict, and politics within and between cultural spheres. On the other, the use of specialised knowledge and validity claims helps deepen understanding within communities of interest, protecting them from inappropriate 'outside' influences. Following Habermas (1979), the inappropriate application of interests, knowledge, and evaluative standards from one sphere to another can distort communication, learning, and action within and between them, producing negative social and cultural effects. But it can also lead to socially progressive learning processes, if approached with a view to increasing mutual understanding between the social actors. For their survival, complex, modern societies require art that has moral content and technical sophistication, moral reasoning that is authentic and supported by effective procedures for developing and adjudicating social norms, and science that has a strong ethical base and is imbued with a sense of virtue.

An example from the educational administration context that helps to elaborate Habermas' analysis is Hodgkinson's (1996) observation that all administrative decisions are, in the final instance, value judgments. Decision-making engages moral-practical interests and knowledge. The validity of decisions should thus generally be assessed on the grounds of how 'right' they are. But Hodgkinson observes that effectiveness is a metavalue in educational administration. As a result, instead of deciding to do what is right, administrators often follow the path of least resistance and do what is efficacious. This tendency in administrative thinking and action impoverishes educational institutions because it fails to infuse them with intellectual rigour, moral character, and wilfulness.

In Habermas' view, many conflicts can only be legitimately resolved through the power of a philosophical discourse that recognises and considers interests as well as knowledge claims. Hodgkinson (1996), who is by no means enamoured of critical theory, supports this perspective with his well-known claim that educational administration ought to be viewed, taught, and practiced as philosophy-in-action. For Habermas (1979; 1984), philosophy provides a metalanguage that can (and should) serve to connect actors across cultural spheres. The kind of philosophical discourse he has in mind requires people to decentre themselves *vis à vis* how they conceive social reality. Scientific-instrumental interests and knowledge involve an objective worldview; moral-practical interests and knowledge rely on an intersubjective worldview; aesthetic-expressive knowledge draws on a subjective worldview. The ability to assume multiple subject positions, to reflect on and discuss the implications of different standpoints in terms of their interests, knowledge, and relationships with self, others, and their natural environments, are central to progressive forms of social evolution.

Habermas' typology and related analysis offer political insights for educational administration because he demonstrates how particular forms of knowledge have been promulgated to further certain types of interests. To be sure, intellectual debates can be solely about contesting knowledge claims. This is often the case when specialists within particular cultural spheres have disagreements. An example is researchers who, drawing on systems theory from biology, argue about whether educational organisations should be treated as open or closed systems (Evers and Lakomski 2001). But debates are not always just about contesting knowledge claims. They can often represent underlying political struggles around conflicting interests. An example is the influential debate that occurred in the 1970s between Daniel Griffiths and Thom Greenfield as to whether educational administration was best understood and practiced as a scientific or moral and aesthetic endeavour (Dolmage 1992). Their communication was often strained (see Griffiths 1975; Greenfield 1993) because they appeared to be arguing about knowledge claims but were also battling fundamental interests—explanation and prediction versus understanding and subjective expression. This debate may have been even more enriching if its political dimensions were explicitly teased out and addressed in a less partisan manner (Donmoyer 2001).

Following Habermas, there are also times when people may openly engage in political struggles around particular interests, but may not be drawing on appropriate knowledge and validity claims. For example, researchers from the scientific-instrumental community of educational administration sometimes experience critical researchers as doing this (Hoy and Miskel 1996). The moral claims critical researchers make about how certain administrative practices are harmful for some groups may not register with scientific-instrumental researchers unless they are, at minimum, backed up with factual evidence. Even then there can be arguments about facts, including how they were derived and interpreted. This process can also work in reverse, with critical researchers claiming, for example, that research informed by an interest in exercising control over people is unethical. In such cases, scientific-instrumental researchers may need to approach critical researchers on the basis of moral-practical knowledge claims in order to enter a productive dialogue.

## COMMUNICATIVE AND STRATEGIC ACTION

The twin concepts of communicative and strategic action are central to Habermas' critical theory. He introduced them in the context of the linguistic turn that occurred in the social sciences and philosophy in the 1970s and 1980s (Lafont 2002). He was aiming, in part, to find a way around the impasse that the first generation of the Frankfurt School had reached about the fate of the ideals of the Enlightenment and modern reason (Horkheimer and Adorno 1993). For Habermas, the 'philosophy of consciousness' at the centre of the Enlightenment project needed to be replaced with a philosophy of communication (1989: 1). This would rid philosophy—in particular, its political variant—of the unified conception of subjectivity that provides grounds upon which people can justify their domination over others. In the place of a unified subject, he offers the concept of intersubjectivity, in which human reason, identity, will, and action are seen as properties of their communication and interaction. This dialogical perspective recasts the spirit of the Enlightenment by placing collective will formation front and centre. And it provides a theoretical and practical framework within which people can challenge and alter the courses of action of those who would commit political excess.

Communicative action exists when people interact in consensual ways to coordinate their activities; strategic action, when people use communication that aims to achieve individual, organisational, political, or social objectives. The primary role of communicative action is to foster mutual understanding, whereas that of strategic activity is to pursue and attain goals. Both are required to maintain individual lives, families, communities, organisations, and societies, and are dialogically related. But Habermas makes it clear that communication exists to support communicative action, an ideal case of 'normal' human communication creating understanding: 'What raises us out of nature is the only thing whose nature we can know: language. Through its structure autonomy and responsibility are posited for us. Our first sentence expresses unequivocally the intention of universal and unconstrained consensus' (1984: 396). In contrast, strategic forms of communication are derived from this fundamental type. Lying is a concrete example of how strategic action is derived from the communicative foundation of human communication—it would not be possible for one person to lie if the other did not presuppose the interaction was an attempt to establish a genuine mutual understanding (i.e., a truth). Figure 4.1 presents the different modes of each type of social action, adapted from Habermas (1984: 333).

Where a genuine mutual understanding exists, people have implicitly reached a consensus with respect to at least four types of validity claims, comprehensibility, truth, rightness, and truthfulness. These claims form the backdrop for all communication in that people could justify them if requested (Habermas 1984). For example, in conversation people can seek

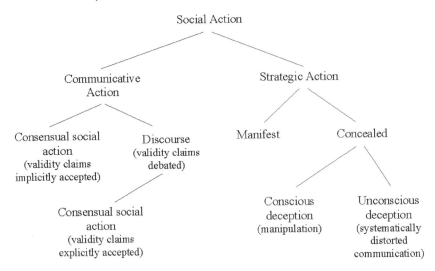

*Figure 4.1*   Modes of communicative and strategic action.

to clarify terminology, question the veracity of certain facts, or assess how sincere their interlocutor is. In cases where speech is oriented to mutual understanding, but an agreement cannot be reached, a variety of approaches is possible. They can adopt explicit forms of strategic communication to influence each other, for example, invoking a formal role of authority to control the discussion. Alternatively, people can use deceptive or manipulative communication. This takes place, for example, when someone acts disingenuously and harbours relevant information or lies. As a last resort, people can break off communication altogether, but it is important to note that unresolved disputes are sometimes resolved through psychological or physical force.

Habermas (1984) describes an additional form of concealed strategic action he calls systematically distorted communication. This unconscious form of deception occurs when people falsely believe they are interacting to reach a mutual understanding. False beliefs come from distorted self-understanding, which stems, in turn, from an unconscious repression of conflict. Stable totalitarian regimes are a good example of this: authoritarian leaders often come to truly believe their abusive actions are in the best interests of those they rule, while the people come to accept these actions as legitimate. Situations of systematically distorted communication are difficult to recognise because they appear in the guise of communicative action, and are also difficult to rectify. Doing so involves addressing both internal psychological and interpersonal communication issues (Habermas 1984). Analyses of systematically distorted communication offer potentially rich sources of insight into the deep conflicts inherent within the cultural, political, and economic contexts and institutions in advanced industrial societies. Once a light is shone on these hidden conflicts, people, groups, or societies can envision how they are engaged in practices that are not in their best interests (Braaten 1991).

For Habermas (1990), strategic actions, apart from abuse and violence, of course, are necessary parts of human interaction. They help to make economic, political, and administrative systems, institutions, and processes work. But strategic communication is a key contributor to the repression of conflicts in and between people, communities, organisations, and societies. Habermas (2001) worries that people in advanced industrial societies rely too heavily on it. This reliance contributes to unstable and hostile sociopolitical arrangements.

As an alternative to strategic action, Habermas suggests that people more regularly attempt to enter into a special mode of communicative action whereby they make explicit and debate the problematic validity claims that form the implicit or repressed backdrop to their interactions. He calls this mode of interaction 'discourse' (1984: 117). Historically, discourse has required some very special conditions to work. Habermas frames these conditions in his concept of the ideal speech situation:

1.  All those potentially affected by the discussion have an equal opportunity to speak;
2.  Each person involved is motivated to reach consensus and can overcome their inhibitions and strategic motivations;
3.  Each participant in the dialogue observes the norms of honesty and sincerity;
4.  No participant in the dialogue exercises or invokes privileges based on their formal role or authority. (Bernstein 1995)

While these conditions are nearly impossible to achieve, they nonetheless provide a conceptual means by which people can identify the undue influence of power—other than the power of ideas and their rational justification—in their discursive contexts. This can help them gauge the degree to which particular sources and forms of power negatively affect both the process and outcomes. It can also help them name problematic forms and sources of power and find ways to hold them at bay.

Habermas' concepts of communicative and strategic action offer political insights for educational administration because they show how there are two different, but related, ways of addressing and resolving conflicting interests in social systems. There is the collective power of ideas developed through broad participation, authentic communication, and consensus-building. And there are the more customary ways of exercising administrative power, that is, through explicit and concealed strategies such as the invocation of formal role authority, subtle or overt coercion, concealment of information, and so forth. His analysis presents some of the potentially troubling consequences related to customary ways of thinking about and practicing administrative politics. His description of ideal speech conditions provides a useful diagnostic tool for identifying customary forms and techniques of power and how they may negatively affect administrative process and outcomes. The point here is not that using strategic action to resolve conflicts is necessarily bad; however, if administrators rely on strategic communication as their main approach to furthering interests and resolving conflicts, they can do significant psychological and organisational damage. The regular application of strategic sources of power can produce a highly political organisational culture fraught with infighting and misunderstanding (Morgan 2006). The exercise of power as means can become an end in itself, creating systematically distorted communication where everyone, including the administrator, is self-deceived and no one's authentic interests are being furthered. Habermas' ideas also highlight that certain administrative contexts more properly require communicative action than do others. Where the agenda is (or ought to be) about reaching an authentic understanding about what to do and how to coordinate action towards that end, then administrators need a communicative political solution to resolve the conflicting interests that will arise among all those potentially affected by the decision. In such cases, Habermas' ideas encourage administrators to pursue the power of ideas through authentic and inclusive dialogue.

## LIFEWORLD AND SYSTEM

As a core part of his theory, Habermas (1979; 1997) describes how progressive social evolution in advanced industrial societies occurs (or can take place) through a dialogical learning process involving two developmental trajectories. On one developmental path, people can learn to coordinate their lives in increasingly reasonable and nonviolent ways, despite their different values, interpretations of need, interests, and goals. On the other, people can establish and learn to participate productively in economic and administrative systems and institutions that provide the material infrastructure sustaining diverse, large scale populations. Habermas (1984; 1989) refers to the former developmental path as cultural rationalisation and the latter as social modernisation.

His aim in introducing these concepts was, in part, to address problems he perceived in Weber's (1968) rationalisation thesis. Weber saw western societies becoming 'iron cages' of psychological and social domination as a result of their modernisation processes. In Habermas' view, Weber wrongly came to this conclusion because he was only looking at one side of the development puzzle: the growth of economic and administrative systems and institutions and the instrumental form or rationality associated with them. Habermas argues that one should also look at developmental processes in private life and civil society, where a more hopeful picture emerges regarding the overall trajectory of modernisation since the Enlightenment.

Cultural rationalisation relies on the capacity for people to think and interact communicatively. Processes of cultural rationalisation, based on genuine forms of communicative action, create cohesive societies with psychologically healthy populations and vibrant, dynamic cultural institutions. In contrast, social modernisation relies on the capacity for people to organise themselves to achieve goals, solve problems, and materially reproduce their lives. Processes of social modernisation, based on successful forms of strategic action, create well-off societies characterised by efficient organisations and systems of administration.

Both cultural rationalisation and social modernisation are required to maintain and reproduce advanced industrial societies (Habermas 1984; 1989). And these processes need to be dialogically connected in order that healthy, socially progressive ways develop. Habermas' (1989) influential model of advanced industrial societies consisting of lifeworld and system establishes the importance of the dialogical relationships between processes of cultural rationalisation and social modernisation and the communicative and strategic action that facilitate them. It is useful to think of the lifeworld and system in a multifaceted way: in addition to representing sites of social learning and development processes, they designate physical domains of advanced industrial societies that have institutional infrastructures. They also represent particular standpoints (or orientations) to perception, analysis, and action. Figure 4.2 provides an interpretation of this model. The italicised portions of this figure suggest how the model can be adapted, at least indicatively, to the context of educational administration.

In the lifeworld, people coordinate their private and public activities with others in reciprocal ways through communicative action. In the system, people engage in actions that implement decisions to which they consent in the lifeworld. Communicative action in the lifeworld gives rise to personal and civic ends (e.g., personal and cultural values, normative expectations), while the system exists to provide effective means for achieving those ends. The outcomes from communicative action and the trajectory of cultural rationalisation should thus steer the strategies and processes of social modernisation, even as the latter influence the capacity for, and direction of, cultural rationalisation. The media of power and money facilitate the dialogical relationship between the lifeworld and system, steering both forms of social action and the two developmental processes.

A healthy lifeworld is central to the establishment and maintenance of a functional system, while a functional system offers some of the key infrastructures that support a healthy lifeworld. Habermas (1989: 153) observes a tendency in advanced industrial societies for cultural rationalisation and social modernisation to 'uncouple,' improving economic and administrative efficiencies in the short term. It can also free people up from instrumental concerns related to their economic lives, allowing

| Lifeworld<br><br>(site of cultural rationalization through communicative action) | Steering Mechanisms<br><br>P = Power<br>M = Money | System<br><br>(site of social modernization through strategic action) |
|---|---|---|
| Private life<br><br>*Sociocultural development (incl. identity politics) through formal and non-formal education and life course*<br><br>*Administration of individual learning in educational institutions* | (P) Labour power →<br>← (M) Income from labour<br>(M) Consumer demand →<br>←(P) Goods/services<br><br>*(P) Financial means →*<br>*(P) cultural capital →*<br>*← (P) definition of employability*<br>*← (P) Tuition fee policy*<br>*(M) Tuition →* | Economic system<br><br>*Human capital development through formal education and workplace learning*<br><br>*Administration of economic and financial aspects of educational institutions* |
| Civil society<br>(public sphere)<br><br>*Sociocultural development (incl. cultural critique and politics) through formal and non-formal education, and participation in public discourse*<br><br>*Administration of collective learning in educational institutions* | (M) Taxes →<br>← (P) Political decisions<br>← (M) Infrastructure<br>(P) Mass loyalty →<br><br>*← (P) Administrative acts*<br>*(P) Critique →*<br>*(P) Political activism →* | Governance and administrative system<br><br>*Educational policy development through political machinery and policy implementation through educational bureaucracies*<br><br>*Formal governance and management of educational institutions* |

*Figure 4.2*   The lifeworld and system.

them to concentrate on personal, cultural, and social development. But Habermas sees crucial problems arising in the long term from such situations. He worries about the propensity of social modernisation processes to 'colonise' (1989: 186) cultural rationalisation. This occurs when system goals take priority over lifeworld goals, where the accomplishments of the latter goals are essential to the maintenance of the lifeworld and to the maintenance of the system itself (Braaten 1991). In such situations, social cohesion may begin to unravel as agreed upon norms and values are disturbed. Cultural institutions may suffer a crisis of legitimacy as people cease to find them relevant. And individuals may suffer identity crises or other psychosocial problems as a result of disrupted processes of socialisation (Habermas 1989).

As an example of colonisation, Habermas cites the contemporary pressure on educational institutions to 'close circuit [themselves] with the employment system' (1989: 371). This administrative process narrows the scope of discussion among educational participants and stakeholders about the purposes of education. Instead, employers, state policy makers, and educational administrators determine educational purpose based on labour market conditions. But labour markets are prone to structural and cyclical crises in under- and unemployment, so they may not serve as a reliable beacon of educational purpose (Livingstone 1998), rendering educational institutions, labour markets, employers, educational policy makers, and administrators faulty. Some may pursue political action against different authorities and institutions in the system. Others may internalise their situations as personal failure, leading to crises of motivation whereby they detach themselves from their academic identities, educational endeavours, or the labour market. Either way, the economic and administrative actors and their institutions face threats, particularly during downturns in the labour market. At this point, both the infrastructure that supports the lifeworld and the functional capacity of the system are drained.

The parallel processes of cultural development and social modernisation require a means for reintegration. Following Habermas (1989), decisions about whether to uncouple or (re)integrate processes of cultural rationalisation and social modernisation properly rest under the purview of the lifeworld. But the relationship between processes of social modernisation and cultural rationalisation are ultimately altered through media of money and power. Criticism can be launched, for instance, with a view to undermining the legitimacy of particular administrative authorities. Or political activism can be undertaken against aspects of the system. A significant amount of political acumen and competence is required to keep the development of societies and their institutions on a socially progressive trajectory.

Political action also takes place within the lifeworld and system. Identity and cultural politics occur, for example, in the lifeworld. These can contribute to processes of cultural rationalisation, particularly if they are practiced communicatively and take the shape of philosophical discourse discussed above in the section on human interests and knowledge. Some of these political struggles generate full-fledged social movements, which express their power through the steering mechanisms, transforming aspects of the system and processes of social modernisation (Welton 1993). The effect that environmental movements have on legal regimes and consumption patterns offers an example of this. Politics in the system take the shape of the customary political behaviours associated with formal roles in the machinery of governance or bureaucracies.

Habermas' model of the lifeworld and system offers a comprehensive framework for thinking about where and how politics play a role in educational administration. It explains how different political dynamics feature in administrative action. These venues include private and public spheres and economic, governance, and bureaucratic systems, at the level of the state and educational organisations. Equally important, the model provides a lens for researchers and practitioners to identify different forms and sources of power in administration. And it encourages them to think about which of these are the most valid, particularly in terms of fostering socially progressive educational processes, institutions, and, ultimately, societies.

In private and public spheres of administration, legitimate power tends to stem from a communicative approach. For example, elementary school principals likely will not be able to find durable solutions to the competing interests that spark conflict in their schools around the inclusion in the curriculum of a book about a family with same-sex parents by using manifest strategies (e.g., excluding certain people from the debate, making unilateral decisions) or concealed strategies (e.g., hiding behind the 'bureaucracy,' pointing fingers elsewhere, feigning to be working on the issue). Following Habermas, the power to truly resolve an issue such as this would likely come from bringing the interested parties together into an 'ideal speech situation.' And this might not be a one-time event, consisting instead of an ongoing dialogical process that leads to a decision about the issue. Equally important is that in taking a communicative approach, an administrator would build capacity within the school community to tackle other, equally difficult issues in the future.

In getting goals approved and supported through governance and bureaucratic venues, administrators may sometimes have to rely heavily on a strategic approach that draws on more customary forms of power (e.g., targeting information in ways that appeal directly to specific interests, taking advantage of absences of people who disagree with the initiative, calling in past debts from people who have influence). And in the interrelationships between the sociocultural (or lifeworld) and the economic, governance, and bureaucratic (or system) venues of action, administrators may find they need to confront other forms of power, such as open letters in newspapers criticising state policies or loss of tuition revenue when students choose to go elsewhere due to administrative policies.

The model of lifeworld and system also directs attention to where and how education and its administration play an important role in the political processes of society. Habermas is clear that education is (or ought to be) first and foremost a contributor to sociocultural development of individuals and civil society more generally. As a site for communicative action and public discourse it is (or can be) an important enabler of socially progressive forms of cultural rationalisation. Core functions of education are to build and sustain capacity in individuals and society more generally for rigorous critique, contributing to a robust, highly reflexive civil society, and to provide a source of power for steering the economy, governance, and public administration. The capacity for and outcomes from critique also support political activism within the lifeworld and against the system. The model implies that an important task of researchers, educators, and practitioners of administration is to view their work as contributing to sociocultural capacity, including political competence in its communicative form.

## CONCLUDING THOUGHTS

Those who research and teach educational administration may provide incomplete perspectives in their publications and classrooms if they do not incorporate considerations of politics and power. Without political lenses through which to view their work, administrators may misapprehend situations and issues, potentially making them less effective in their work. They may also not be as fully aware as they could be of the moral aspects of their work related to the power they exercise over others by virtue of their formal authority, the power that others exercise against them, and, importantly, the power others exercise through them and their organisations (Apple 1995). Whichever political concepts researchers draw upon to better understand administration, their work should not act as a blinder. The overuse of a political lens can make organisational realities appear more political than they are. Administrative practices that rely too heavily on the use of political strategies and tactics can antagonise people, exacerbate conflicts, and unnecessarily increase the level of political behaviour in organisations (Morgan 2006).

The dialogical nature of Habermas' theory is one of its key strengths in this regard. It shows that politics in administration are not just about 'working the system' to achieve individual, organisational, or large 'P' policy objectives. Power in administration should not stem only from the customary strategic sources and behaviours. Politics of a different kind can inform the creation of vision and ideals that give rise to worthy educational and administrative objectives. In this realm of administrative action, power stems from authentic, collective dialogue. When pathologies emerge, such as organisational culture rife with patterns of domination and subordination, too much strategic or instrumental action may be a root cause. A shift to communicative action should improve the situation.

Finally, Habermas' work serves as an important reminder that, while politics play a role in educational administration, educational administration also plays a role in politics. Schools and universities exist, in good measure, to develop the capacity of people to participate productively in their societies, including in politics. Administrative research and practice set the conditions for this. Researchers and practitioners need to be vigilant that their often necessary interests in explanation, prediction, control, and effectiveness in educational administration do not override the other fundamental educational interests in understanding, justice, and emancipation that form the basis for an increasingly rational, inclusive, and social body politic.

## REFERENCES

Agger, B. (1992) *The Discourse of Domination: From the Frankfurt School to Post-modernism*, Evanston: Northwestern University Press.

Althusser, L. (1984) *Essays on Ideology*, London: Verso.

Apple, M. W. (1995) *Education and Power*, New York: Routledge.

——, (2000) *Official Knowledge: Democratic Knowledge in a Conservative Age*, New York: Routledge.

Barnett, R. (1993) 'Knowledge, higher education and society,' *Oxford Review of Education*, 19, 1: 33–47.

Bates, R. (1989) 'Leadership and the rationalization of society,' in J. Smyth (ed.) *Critical Perspectives on Educational Leadership*, London: Falmer.

Bernstein, J. M. (1995) *Recovering Ethical Life: Jürgen Habermas and the Future of Critical Theory*, London: Routledge.

Bottomore, T. et al. (eds) (1988) *A Dictionary of Marxist Thought*, Oxford: Basil Blackwell.

Bourdieu, P. (1977) 'Cultural reproduction and social reproduction,' in J. Karabel and A. Halsey (eds) *Power and Ideology in Education*, New York: Oxford University Press.

Braaten, J. (1991) *Habermas's Critical Theory of Society*, Albany: SUNY.

Brookfield, S. (2005) 'Learning democratic reason: the adult education project of Jürgen Habermas,' *Teachers College Record*, 107, 6: 1127–68.

Cannon, B. (2001) *Rethinking the Normative Content of Critical Theory: Marx, Habermas and Beyond*, New York: Palgrave.

Cohen, J. L. (1995) 'Critical social theory and feminist critiques: the debate with Jürgen Habermas,' in J. Meehan (ed.) *Feminists Read Habermas: Gendering the Subject of Discourse*, New York: Routledge.

Connelly, B. (1996) 'Interpretations of Jürgen Habermas in adult education writings,' *Studies in the Education of Adults*, 28, 2: 241–52.

Dolmage, R. (1992) 'The quest for understanding in educational administration: a Habermasian perspective on the 'Griffiths–Greenfield Debate,' *Journal of Educational Thought*, 26, 2: 89–113.

Donmoyer, R. (2001) 'Evers and Lakomski's search for leadership's holy grail (and the intriguing ideas they encountered along the way),' *Journal of Educational Administration*, 39, 6: 554–72.

Duvenage, P. (2003) *Habermas and Aesthetics: The Limits of Communicative Reason*, Cambridge: Polity Press.

Evers, C. and Lakomski, G. (2001) 'Theory in educational administration: naturalistic directions,' *Journal of Educational Administration*, 39, 6: 499–520.

Foster, W. (1986) *Paradigms and Promises: New Approaches to Educational Administration*, Buffalo: Prometheus.

——, (1989) 'Toward a critical practice of leadership,' in J. Smyth (ed.) *Critical Perspectives on Educational Leadership*, London: Falmer.

Fraser, N. (1995) 'What's critical about critical theory?' in J. Meehan (ed.) *Feminists Read Habermas: Gendering the Subject of Discourse*, New York: Routledge.

Freire, P. (1970) *Pedagogy of the Oppressed*, New York: Seabury Books.

Gibson, R. (1986) *Critical Theory and Education*, Toronto: Hodder and Stoughton.

Giroux, H. (2004) *The Terror of Neoliberalism: Authoritarianism and the Eclipse of Democracy*, Toronto: Garamond Press.

Greenfield, T. B. and Ribbins, P. (eds) (1993) *Greenfield on Educational Administration: Towards a Humane Science,* London: Routledge.

Griffiths, D. E. (1975) Some thoughts about theory in educational administration. *UCEA Review,* 17, 1: 12–18.

Habermas, J. (1970) *Toward a rational society: Student protest, science and politics,* Boston: Beacon Press.

——, (1971) *Knowledge and Human Interests,* Boston: Beacon Press.

——, (1979) *Communication and the Evolution of Society,* Boston: Beacon Press.

——, (1984) *The Theory of Communicative Action: Reason and the Rationalization of Society,* Boston: Beacon Press.

——, (1987) 'The idea of the university-learning processes,' *New German Critique,* 41: 3–22.

——, (1989) *The Theory of Communicative Action: The Lifeworld and the System,* Boston: Beacon Press.

——, (1990) *Moral Consciousness and Communicative Action,* Cambridge: MIT Press.

——, (1997) 'Modernity: an unfinished project,' in M. Passerin d'Entrèves and S. Benhabib (eds) *Habermas and the Unfinished Project of Modernity: Critical Essays on The Philosophical Discourse of Modernity,* Cambridge: MIT Press.

——, (2001) *The Postnational Constellation: Political Essays,* Cambridge: Polity Press.

Harris, C. E. (2002) 'Expanding dimensions of the "knowledge society": technology, discourse ethics and agency in coastal communities,' *The Journal of Educational Administration and Foundations,* 16, 2: 37–65.

Hart, M. U. (1992) *Working and Educating for Life: Feminist and International Perspectives on Adult Education,* London: Routledge.

Hodgkinson, C. (1996) *Administrative Philosophy: Values and Motivations in Administrative Life,* Tarrytown: Elsevier Science.

Horkheimer, M. and Adorno, T. W. (1993) *Dialectic of Enlightenment,* New York: Continuum.

Hoy, W. K. and Miskel, C. G. (1996) *Educational Administration: Theory, Research, and Practice,* New York: McGraw-Hill.

Lafont, C. (2002) *The Linguistic Turn in Hermeneutic Philosophy,* Cambridge: MIT Press.

Lakeland, P. (1993) 'Preserving the lifeworld, restoring the public sphere, renewing higher education,' *Cross Currents,* 43, 4: 488–503.

Livingstone, D. W. (1998) *The Education–Jobs Gap: Underemployment or Economic Democracy,* Toronto: Garamond Press.

Lyotard, F. (1984) *The Postmodern Condition: A Report on Knowledge,* Minneapolis: University of Minnesota Press.

Marx, K. and Engels, F. (1972) *The German Ideology,* New York: International Publishers.

Mezirow, J. (1995) 'Transformation theory of adult learning,' in M. Welton (ed.), *In Defense of the Lifeworld,* New York: SUNY Press.

Milley, P. (2002a) 'Imagining good organizations: moral orders or moral communities,' *Educational Management and Administration,* 30, 1: 47–61.

——, (2002b) 'Human capital 101: querying one-dimensionality in university cooperative education,' *Critical Pedagogy Networker,* 14, 3–4: 1–16.

——, (2005) 'The social and educational implications of university cooperative education: a Habermasian perspective,' unpublished dissertation, University of Victoria.

Morgan, G. (2006) *Images of Organization,* Thousand Oaks: Sage Publications.

Ostovich, S. T. (1995) 'Dewey, Habermas, and the university in society,' *Educational Theory,* 45, 4: 465–77.

Outhwaite, W. (1994) *Habermas: A Critical Introduction*, Stanford: Stanford University Press.

Perrow, C. (1986) *Complex Organizations: A Critical Essay*, New York: Random House.

Samier, E. (2006) 'The aesthetics of charisma: architectural, theatrical, and literary dimensions,' in E. A. Samier and R. Bates (eds) *Aesthetic Dimensions of Educational Administration and Leadership*, New York: Routledge.

Seidman, S. (1998) *Contested Knowledge: Social Theory in the Postmodern Era*, Oxford: Blackwell.

Sergiovanni, T. J. (2000) *The Lifeworld of Leadership: Creating Culture, Community and Personal Meaning in our Schools*, San Francisco: Jossey-Bass.

Smith, D. E. (1996) 'The relations of ruling: a feminist inquiry,' *Studies in Cultures, Organizations and Societies*, 2: 171–90.

Weber, M. (1968) *Economy and Society: An Outline of Interpretive Sociology*, New York: Bedminster Press.

Wellmer, A. (1994) 'Reason, utopia and the dialectic of enlightenment,' in R. J. Bernstein (ed.) *Habermas and Modernity*, Cambridge: MIT Press.

Welton, M., (1991) *Toward Development Work: The Workplace as a Learning Environment*, Melbourne: Deakin University Press.

——, (1993) 'Social revolutionary learning: the new social movements as learning sites,' *Adult Educational Quarterly*, 43, 3: 152–64.

——, (1995) 'In defense of the lifeworld: a Habermasian approach to adult learning,' in M. Welton (ed.) *In Defense of the Lifeworld: Critical Perspectives on Adult Learning*, Albany: SUNY Press.

Yeatman, A. (1994) *Postmodern Revisionings of the Political*, New York: Routledge.

Young, R. (1990) *A Critical Theory of Education: Habermas and Our Children's Future*, New York: Teachers College Press.

# 5 Hayek, Leadership, and Learning

*Peter Gronn*

The anti-historicists [Popper, Berlin, Hayek, and Von Mises] made a deliberate attempt to associate historicism and its inductive methods with totalitarianism of both the fascist and communist kind. Its success owed much to its coincidence with the half century that saw the costly defeat of fascism in Europe and the global cold-war struggle between democracy and communism. Exciting support against one's methodological enemies by charging them with complicity in the rise of totalitarianism and the suppression of liberty and democracy was an easy matter in this environment. (Graeme Snook, *Longrun Dynamics*)

This chapter reviews the work of the Viennese-born thinker, Friedrich August von Hayek (1899–1992), perhaps one of the twentieth century's most influential economic theorists and social philosophers. Hayek was a prolific scholar who, in the words of one of his biographers, 'wrote so much and in so many different areas' (Caldwell 2004: 13). Indeed, a hallmark of Hayek's erudite style was to ground the lengthy argumentation in these extensive writings in a huge corpus of scholarship, encompassing a vast sweep of (mostly) European thinking, from mediaeval times right through to the modern period, the details of which were often crammed into numerous and copious footnotes. An assessment of Hayek's contribution and legacy that does full justice to this extraordinary capaciousness, therefore, is a far from easy task. For the purposes of this brief discussion, I have necessarily had to be selective in my appraisal of Hayek and have restricted myself to the significance of his work for readers with an interest in organisational leadership and, to a lesser extent, learning. My nomination of this particular focus, however, has created an additional difficulty. Hayek's writings include numerous passing usages of terms commonly associated with leadership, such as control, hierarchy, managers, entrepreneurs, rulers, elites, great men, oligarchies, and dictatorships, and even 'Caesaristic paternalism' (1960: 406). Despite this practice, Hayek never really dwelt to any great extent on leadership itself and, apart from the few specific sections of his writings, which I discuss shortly, his mentions of leaders were mostly intensely negative and concerned movements and parties of Nazis, fascists, communists,

and socialists (e.g., 1979: 180)—with the latter typically being characterised dismissively by him as scientistically-minded intellectual authoritarians
(1997: 190)—movements that were the precursors of socialism, such as the
Saint-Simonians, headed (he claimed) by 'new popes with a college of apos-
tles and various other grades of members below them' (1979: 284) or occasional examples of such European dictators as Hitler, Mussolini, Stalin and
Lenin (1978: 134). On the other hand, the major preoccupations of much of
his writing for the last half century or so of his life were concepts and themes
that are closely associated with leadership and sometimes figure prominently
in discussions of it, such as coercion, power, and planning.

From the point of view of scholars with an interest in leadership, then,
much of Hayek's thinking in this area has to be inferred. An example of
what I mean is his reference to such vague conceptual entities as 'central
organisers' (1978: 75). With this limitation in mind about the reliance on
inferences, I address two key strands of Hayek's thought and their implications: first, his view of the inevitability of the social distribution of knowledge and the related idea of the fallacy of omniscient minds; second, his
idea of spontaneous order, its differentiation from, and relationship to, the
parallel realm of organised order. Each of these aspects is discussed sequen-
tially, preceded by a brief overview of Hayek's *oeuvre*, the influence of some
leading Scottish Enlightenment thinkers on his work, and his engagement as
a public intellectual, in particular, his involvement in the Mont Pèlerin Society. In the concluding section I consider the implications and significance of
Hayek's ideas for the contemporary study of organisations.

## WHO WAS HAYEK?

Although he attained preeminent status in economic circles, unlike his fellow
twentieth-century economist John Maynard Keynes (and possibly even J. K.
Galbraith), Hayek's name has not achieved as widespread popular recognition. The explanation for this is probably that, for much of the twentieth
century, the particular brand of economics with which he was associated—
orthodox free market liberalism—became marginal to the mainstream policy
thinking of most national governments. Since the late nineteenth century in
British politics, the tenets and shibboleths of liberal theory had been yield-
ing ground to a rising tide of collectivist thinking. No political party was
immune to its influence. By the time of the New York stock market crash
in late 1929, liberalism was at its nadir and 'the ideological course towards
collectivism was firmly set' (Cockett 1995: 17). On the other hand, Hayek
and his fellow liberals were eventually to come into their own, so much so
that the scale of the revival of interest in, and uptake by, governments of
classical liberal economic reasoning from the mid 1970s to the present day
has been truly astonishing. Apologists for this intellectual *risorgimento* have
become labelled as neoliberals—as, indeed, Hayek referred to them himself

(1981: 83). Emblematic, perhaps, of the beginnings of a shift from the old welfare state order to the new was Hayek's 1974 Nobel Prize for economics. The succeeding three decades or so were to bear witness to the realisation and triumph of a set of ideas whose time, its apologists believed, had well and truly come.

In light of the current popularity of neoliberal and neoconservative labels, and the occasional confounding of these terms in discussions about ideologically inspired right-wing governments that have recently successfully forged electoral coalitions of constituencies of both neo- persuasions (e.g., USA, Australia), it is important to clarify Hayek's status as a liberal. On the matters of his intellectual roots and temperament, he was both emphatic and unequivocal: he positioned himself squarely in the nineteenth century old Whig, Gladstonian version of liberalism (1960: 407). As he explained in his essay 'Why I am not a Conservative,' the distinction for him between a liberal and a conservative turned on the overriding concern of the latter with 'the action of established authority' and that: 'This authority be not weakened rather than that its power be kept within bounds. This is difficult to reconcile with the preservation of liberty' (1960: 401). Moreover, the traditional commitments of conservatives to the importance of persons of superior status, and the idea that their inherited standards and values entitled them to a prominent (even exclusive) role in public affairs, were anathema to a liberal because such claims entailed the defence of privilege and monopoly 'in order to shelter such people against the forces of economic change.' Instead, as far as Hayek was concerned, all elites, including conservative elites, no matter what their intellectual and cultural contributions were to the evolution of civilisation, had to 'prove themselves by their capacity to maintain their position under the same rules that apply to all others' (1960: 403).

Not only did Hayek eschew conservatism, but he was also keen to distance himself from a popular understanding of liberalism. Above all else, Hayek was committed to the supremacy of the value of freedom and its realisation in economic and social arrangements. For this reason, he championed what he referred (interchangeably) to as the Great or Open Society, although he did not have in mind a specifically liberal democratic society, since many of the institutions typically associated with this particular social formation were deliberately designed to fulfil a range of desired ends or purposes. Such design thinking was a manifestation of constructivism, whereas he, by contrast, was an antirationalist and anticonstructivist. The philosophical standpoint from which he dissociated himself was what he regarded as an apostate and ersatz version of liberal theory that he dubbed 'rationalistic liberalism' (1960: 398). This was a doctrine that was heavily influenced by continental, in particular French, radical social thinking, which legitimated state-sponsored intervention policies and forms of planning aimed at meliorating social conditions or improving living standards. In the constant tension that exists between the pressures on governments to intervene and reshape economic and social processes or to let events take their own course, then—briefly, the tension between rational design and spontaneous emergence—Hayek positioned himself as a trenchant opponent of rationality and a forceful advocate of freedom. He contrasted his own 'true' Whig liberalism with the corrupted version that he asserted had taken root in late nineteenth century England, exemplified by thinkers such as J. S. Mill and public figures such as the Welsh politician and prime minister, David Lloyd George, and whose adherents were impelled more by 'a desire to impose upon the world a preconceived rational pattern than to provide opportunity for free growth' (1960: 408; 1948: 26–8).

## A LOVE AFFAIR WITH SCOTLAND

There were numerous intellectual influences on Hayek's thinking. One in particular is worth singling out for special mention because it proved decisive in shaping the view of human institutions and their evolution that was implicit in his antirationalism. This influence was the intellectual tradition that formed part of the Scottish Enlightenment, in particular, the views of the two Adams—the philosopher Adam Ferguson and the political economist Adam Smith—on the evolved and self-ordering nature of much human interaction (1948: 4; 1991: 146). The contrast between Hayek's celebration of Scottish Enlightenment thinking and the scorn he poured on that associated with the other, French, Enlightenment, especially as it developed in the *École Polytechnique* in postrevolutionary France, could not have been starker (1979: 185–211). While the output of the former school of thought symbolised how the institutions of society had 'just grown,' the latter sought to express how, thanks to revolutionary ardour, those institutions had been 'consciously constructed' (1979: 202). *École* thinkers, however, prospered, partly as a result of their admiration for the despot Napoleon, whereas the fortunes of a rival group at the *Collège de France,* the ideologues, devoted to the cause of individual freedom, languished because they were snubbed by their emperor (1979: 204–11).

Two key features of Scottish thinking had a profound impact on Hayek. The first (and the least well known of the two), which he was particularly fond of citing (e.g., 1948: 7n8; 1973: 150n19), was concerned with the origins of society and its institutions. This point was evident in passages early in the section devoted to subordination in Ferguson's history of civil society. The more notable of these include claims that society emerges from, and is shaped by, human activity, although social formations do not represent the realisation of any preconceived plan: 'the forms of society are derived from an obscure and distant origin; they arise, long before the date of philosophy, from the instincts, not from the speculations, of men . . . nations stumble upon establishments, which are indeed the role of human action, but not the execution of any human design' (2003: 119–20). Moreover, although features of society that might subsequently become known solely as a result of experience may be retrospectively ascribed to a 'previous design,' 'no human wisdom could foresee' and 'no authority could enable an individual to execute' any such design (2003: 119–20). Given Ferguson's claim that the attribute which sets mankind apart as a species is an altruistic disposition that accords priority to acting benevolently towards one's fellow humans, rather than the pursuit of one's naked self-interest, and that such action is conducive to the public good of society (2003: 55–9), Hayek's enthusiasm for Ferguson's *An Essay on the History of Civil Society* may be considered somewhat surprising. Such surprise is compounded by the significance Hayek accorded the other feature of Scottish thinking that influenced him so profoundly, the presumed social benefits that accrued as human agents pursued their self-interests in exchange relations with their fellows. This was the virtue that Hayek inferred from Adam Smith's idea of the invisible hand.

There are two well-known passages in Smith's work that express this idea. The first is from *The Theory of Moral Sentiments,* where it is claimed that:

> The rich only select from the heap what is most precious and agreeable. They consume little more than the poor, and in spite of their natural selfishness and rapacity, though they mean only their own conveniency, though the sole end which they propose from the labours of all the thousands whom they employ, be the gratification of their own vain and insatiable desires, they divide with the poor the produce of all their improvements. They are led by an invisible hand to make nearly the same distribution of the necessaries of life, which would have been made had the earth been divided into equal portions among all its inhabitants, and thus without intending it, without knowing it, advance the interest of society, and afford means to the multiplication of the species. (2002: 215)

Later, in the *Wealth of Nations,* Smith showed how by preferring to support domestic rather than foreign industry an individual was seeking to safeguard his own security, and that:

> . . . by directing that industry in such a manner as its produce may be of the greatest value, he intends only his own gain, and he is in this, as in many other cases, led by an invisible hand to promote an end which was no part of his intention. Nor is it always the worse for society that it was no part of it. By pursuing his own interest he frequently promotes that of the society more effectually than when he really intends to promote it. (1976: 477–8)

The significance of both passages is twofold. First, from the substantive viewpoint of economics, each illustrates quite rightly how an agent's pursuit of self-interest need not necessarily generate socially detrimental outcomes. As is indicated by Smith's two caveats, however ('nor is it always' and

'frequently'), he was careful not to accord unqualified or blanket endorsement to self-interested action. Second, these passages also show clearly how
human actions may produce unintended consequences. Hayek drew succour
from both these implications of Smith's work: the first helped bolster his
subsequent arguments for the superiority of the market as an efficient device
for allocating resources, while the second assisted in subverting the foundations of rational constructivist approaches to engineering socially preferred
desirable ends. To secure widespread endorsement for each of these claims,
Hayek and his fellow liberals first had to set about winning the battle of
ideas. To this end, he needed a band of followers to help build an intellectual
movement.

## SCALING MONT PÈLERIN

While it may be arbitrary to single out one event as triggering the revi-
talisation of classic liberalism, Cockett nominates a conference convened
in Paris in mid 1938, known as 'Le colloque Walter Lippman,' as crys-
tallising the commencement of its long march to scholarly and political
redemption (1995: 57). Hayek, then a professor at the London School
of Economics, was one of twenty-six attendees, all of whom (except for
Lippman himself) were academics united in their antipathy to Keynesian
thinking and desirous of arresting liberalism's decline. The outbreak of
war in 1939 delayed the convening of subsequent conferences, but this
Paris meeting provided the model for a subsequent gathering and a society
founded by Hayek in 1947.

Hayek's 'liberal crusade' (Cockett 1995: 105) formally began in April
of that year in a hotel on the slopes of Mont Pèlerin in Switzerland. Some
of the better known luminaries among the thirty-eight intellectuals present
were, in addition to Hayek, Karl Popper, Milton Friedman, Ludwig von
Mises, Michael Polanyi, Bertrand de Jouvenal, Lionel Robbins, and G. M.
Young. An important outcome of this gathering was the creation of the
Mont Pèlerin Society (MPS), with Hayek appointed as its inaugural president. Following two subsequent meetings in 1949 and 1950, the MPS has
continued to convene regularly every couple of years until the present day. By
the 1980s, there were more than 500 delegates in attendance, and the MPS
numbered five Nobel Laureates among its members. While it was largely a
talking shop and published no magazine or propaganda, the MPS did play
a crucial role in reestablishing the long lost legitimacy of liberal ideas and
values, particularly by building bridges with a swag of British Conservative
Party politicians, prominent journalists, and members of free market think
tanks. By these means, it succeeded indirectly for a time in influencing British government policy during the prime ministership of Margaret Thatcher
(Cockett 1995: 118). (In 2008, the MPS is scheduled to convene its sixtieth
anniversary meeting in Tokyo (Mont Pèlerin Society 2007).) This strategy

of influence was perfectly consistent with (and, indeed, may even have been the prototype for) his view of the role of the political philosopher (or, in contemporary parlance, public intellectual) who, while 'he must not arrogate to himself the position of a "leader" who determines what people ought to think,' has a duty to 'show possibilities and consequences of common action, to offer comprehensive aims of policy as a whole which the majority have not yet thought of' (Hayek 1960: 114).

## KNOWLEDGE AND MINDS—OMNISCIENT AND NOT SO OMNISCIENT

Contemporaneously with these developments, Hayek authored two papers on knowledge that, particularly in the case of the first, were to prove pivotal in broadening the range of his subsequent writings (Caldwell 2004: 230–1). These were 'Economics and Knowledge' (1937) and 'The Use of Knowledge in Society' (1945). They were especially significant for the view of mind that they expressed and, arguably, provided the intellectual bedrock for virtually all of Hayek's subsequent thinking. There are two main reasons for this claim. First, these essays demonstrated forcefully the cognitive limitations of human agency. Second, they highlighted the parallel problem for agents of finding means conducive to coordinating human activity in circumstances of dispersed and unequally shared knowledge.

While the shortcomings of equilibrium analysis in economics were the particular target of Hayek's wrath in 'Economics and Knowledge' (i.e., broadly, its presumption of an optimum state in which the plans of competitively interacting agents are compatible), his overriding concern was to demonstrate that its reliance on the ideal of a perfect market was flawed. For there to be a perfect market required of agents that, 'even if they are not supposed to be strictly omniscient,' they are 'at least supposed to know automatically all that is relevant for their decisions' (1937: 45). Further, any claim to a hypothesised state of equilibrium, Hayek reasoned, was founded on a set of subsidiary assumptions about how agents learned from experience and obtained knowledge, all of which was secondary to the problems of the acquisition and communication of knowledge more generally. Taken at face value, these observations display a wholly unremarkable character, except that what Hayek was driving at turns out to be highly significant for the social learning of individual agents. This is because the formulation and subsequent realisation of agents' plans require reference to a framework of expectations and predictions about the likely behaviour of their fellow agents—not to mention those agents' dependence over time on constant and reliable data sources with which to ground those expectations and predictions. If these deficiencies were not enough, then the presumed market behaviour of agents still begged two further questions: viz, what kinds of relevant knowledge (e.g., about current and future commodity prices, where commodities may be acquired, and how they might be utilised) and what amounts of such knowledge were required for their decision-making (1937: 45)?

It was on the basis of this line of attack that Hayek posited the existence of an entirely new and general phenomenon. He called this the division of knowledge, something which he regarded as comparable in status to the division of labour:

> The problem which we [in economics] pretend to solve is how the spontaneous interaction of a number of people, each possessing only bits of knowledge, brings about a state of affairs in which prices correspond to costs, *etc.*, and which could be brought about by deliberate direction only by somebody who possessed the combined knowledge of all those individuals. (1937: 49)

Such a 'somebody' was equivalent to an 'omniscient dictator' or a 'directing mind' (1937: 51, 52), but this was also a somebody, as he suggested in 'The Use of Knowledge in Society,' who not only did not, but could not, exist. For this reason, the real economic problem of a society, as distinct from the false problem posed by equilibrium theorists, was 'the utilization of knowledge not given to anyone in its totality' (1945: 520). Armed with this bottom line reality of dispersed or distributed knowledge, it was in this second paper that Hayek re-directed his guns at central planning—a matter which, in the previous decade in England (from where Hayek was writing at this time), had found increased endorsement across the political divide (Marwick 1964). Hayek had already subjected collectivism and planning to a blistering attack in 1944, in the book which gave him a prominent public profile, *The Road to Serfdom*. The experience of six years of total war, however, appears not to have dented the widespread enthusiasm for planning and there was general agreement that 'if democracy was to work, if it was to recover its appeal, it would have to be *planned*' (Judt 2005: 67, original emphasis). To object to the idea of directed economic planning, as Hayek had just done and would continue to do, was tantamount to tearing up the 'road map of the twentieth century' and inviting marginalization (Judt 2005: 560).

On the cusp of the outbreak of war, in another essay, 'Freedom and the Economic System,' Hayek said that the sole version of planning he was willing to countenance was 'a rational framework of general and permanent rules' (1997: 195), through which production was to be directed—as distinct from planning that substitutes for competition, as he referred to it at one point (1994: 48)—and which entailed no decisions about the particular ends to be furthered by that production. In other words, the only rules that were necessary were those intended to facilitate individually determined initiatives and plans (or ends), and then only in the interests of eliminating uncertainty, and always subject to revision consistent with the growth of knowledge. Later, Hayek was to claim that the object of such rules was to inhibit coercion and encroachments on freedom (e.g., including the protection of property ownership and property rights), that rules were sufficient to unite a social order, and that they were learned by absorption of the cultural traditions of which they formed part (1991: 19–23). While he may have been infuriatingly short on specific details and examples, Hayek's (extremely minimalist) sense of planning amounted to endorsing the most effective means of coordinating individual efforts. By contrast, the prevailing view of planning at this time (i.e., late 1930s) was vitiated, he asserted, by the absence of a 'single mind [that was] comprehensive enough to form even an individual conception of such a comprehensive scale of human aims and desires' that might be the proposed object of planning (1997: 202). Rather than the superior knowledge of a single expert mind, Hayek championed the practical, decentralised, local knowledge of numerous people embedded in 'the particular circumstances of time and place' who were 'performing eminently useful functions based on special knowledge of circumstances of the fleeting moment not known to others' (1945: 521, 522).

Such knowledge dispersal, however, was both a strength and a weakness for, while it validated the worth of the 'man on the spot' (1945: 524) ahead of the planner, it left unresolved the question of how the totality of a society's division of knowledge, which was always incomplete and imperfectly held and understood, might be utilised. Hayek's answer was that, in economics, the price system had evolved precisely as a solution to this problem. Prices, he claimed, 'can act to coördinate the separate actions of different people in the same way as subjective values help the individual to coördinate the parts of his plan' (1945: 526). In short, awareness of supply and demand was conveyed by the information reductively distilled in those commodity prices that diffuse rapidly throughout a market. In effect, the current pricing of a particular commodity records the effects of numerous prior decisions made about that commodity and becomes a guide for subsequent decisions about its future. Compared with cumbersome central planning, then, the price mechanism managed to combine both decentralisation and automatic coordination (1994: 55–6). Just as price systems had evolved without any need for human design, so it was with social institutions more generally, he maintained, such as languages, customs, laws formed through precedent, moral codes, and overall cultural inheritance. To see why Hayek believed that societies had emerged in this way requires an analysis of his idea of orders.

## ORDERS AND ORDERING, LEADERSHIP AND LEADING

An order was defined as 'a state of affairs in which a multiplicity of elements of various kinds are so related to each other that we may learn from our acquaintance with some spatial or temporal part of the whole to form correct expectations concerning the rest . . . ' (Hayek 1973: 36, original italicised). The need for order in social relations arose because the actions of individuals are neither isolated nor self-contained, as all actions are 'directed toward other people and guided by their expected behaviour' (Hayek 1973: 36). There were two broad forms of order, according to Hayek, first, a made, created, or designed exogenous order to which he gave the name 'taxis,' meaning a concrete organised order open to intuitive perception; second (drawing from economic, biological, and cybernetic theories), a self-generating, self-organising endogamous order of abstract relations between elements that have achieved regularised conduct, and that can only be mentally reconstructed, which he labelled 'cosmos' or spontaneous order (1973: 38–9). [Strictly speaking, if account is also taken of Hayek's (1952) examination of the mental, or sensory, order then there are three orders].

The significance for Hayek of this idea of bifurcated ordering was that it offered him a means of better accommodating the parallel and simultaneous existence of patterns of human collaboration which operated on the basis of inducement and/or coercion. Hayek considered that inducement prevailed principally in spontaneously ordered systems in which the elements comprised accrued sets of practices that had adapted to changing circumstances. This meant that there was likely to be an incentive for individuals to align their actions with various ordering forces (e.g., presumably, as when one acts in conformity with the customs or traditions of a community, or in accordance with ecological principles). The quintessential exemplar of a spontaneous order was the market (or catallaxy), because it served competing, rather than a single set of, human ends (1978: 107–8). Made orders, by contrast, existed to serve particular human designs or purposes, and characteristically they included examples of voluntary interest groups, and organisations which mostly arranged their authority relations hierarchically as part of a command structure, as in the cases of firms and public service bureaucracies. The reason Hayek restricted coercion to the made order was because, unlike spontaneously ordering systems, which were not governed by a single superior will (individual or collective), a condition of membership of most organisations and groups for the individuals concerned was their submission to the will of a superior authority figure, such as a founder or an owner: 'While within an organization the several members will assist each other to the extent that they are made to aim at the same purposes, in a catallaxy they are induced to contribute to the needs of others without caring or even knowing about them' (1978: 109). Thus, a spontaneous order such as a market is always superior to an organised order, because an effect of its exchange relations is that everyone derives benefits from them and because only a market is able to reconcile conflicting knowledge and conflicting purposes, by means of noncoercive mutual adjustment (1978: 110).

Despite the apparent clarity of the distinction between Hayek's two orders, there are some potential sources of confusion. These emanate from his attempt to account for relations between sets of real world phenomena by spontaneous or directive ordering principles, except that his switch in usage to the noun 'order' bestows a quasi-entitive status on the process that is implied by the participle 'ordering.' This difficulty is complicated by his additional claims that, while both orders coexist (1973: 48), thereby implying their equivalence in status, every society 'must' possess an order (which is usually spontaneous in nature) (1973: 36) and society is itself a kind of spontaneous order, in addition to being a superordinate one because it both subsumes the made order of organisations (i.e., as these exist within society) and may itself also be disaggregated into 'numerous other spontaneous sub-orders or partial societies' of which individuals may be members (1973: 47). As if to compound these problems, in *The Fatal Conceit,* his final book before his death—in which he was wrestling with issues of cultural evolution, adaptation, variation and selection rules, and their relationship to evolutionary epistemology—Hayek substituted for spontaneous the words 'the extended order of human co-operation' which he identified as capitalism (1991: 6). To what extent is there scope for leadership in these sets of ordering relations and, if there is, what role do leaders play?

Taken at face value, the totality of Hayek's assumptions about cognitively limited minds, the inadvertent forms of social causality arising from the unintended outcomes of actions, the socially dispersed and unequal nature of knowledge, the evolved origins of much of the fabric of social formations, along with the salience of coordinating mechanisms, does not auger well as a justification for leadership, at least of a direct or supervisory type. Moreover, the view of learning inherent in these assumptions suggests that much of it occurs on the basis of personal experience, and in keeping with processes of trial and error, emulation and, in particular, imitation (1991: 20–1). That is, while individuals' views and desires may be acquired by acting in accordance with their own designs and plans, they also 'profit from what others have learned in their individual experience.' At one point in *The Constitution of Liberty,* in which Hayek is discussing democracy and its relationship to the growth of civilization, these two themes of leadership and learning come together in a rather curious way. Whereas the principle of democratic majority rule presupposes that the efforts of everyone are directed by the opinions and standards of the majority, historically, in fact, according to Hayek, the principle of civilised advance was a 'reversal' of this, for it 'consists in the few convincing the many.' In short, 'there is no experience of society which is not first the experience of a few individuals,' and without those who know 'best' and 'more than the rest' being in a position to convince the rest, 'there would be little progress in opinion' (all citations from 1960: 110). In short, social and cultural progress equates to a form of elite-mass diffusion.

The reasoning with which Hayek sought to justify this elite leadership was, to say the least, somewhat eccentric and incomplete. As part of the generation that was deeply scarred by the trauma undergone by European democracies in the 1930s, as noted in the Snooks quote that heads this chapter, Hayek's thinking about leadership was deeply coloured by that experience. It led him to be wary of democratic sovereignty, because on the one hand he feared that elected governments could easily become the playthings of such fickle and potentially coercive majorities, while on the other the potential paralysis of democratic processes sowed the seeds of totalitarian rule. In *The Road to Serfdom,* he suggested three reasons why 'the worst,' rather than the best, rise to the top whenever there is a mass yearning 'to get things done' (1994: 150). First, agreement on values and strength in numbers and the will to impose these values generally arises from a group within the majority of the population that is the repository of lowest common denominator standards, rather than from elites with refined and differentiated tastes. Second, the ill-formed ideas, prejudices, and emotions of this same majority sector prove to be highly susceptible to demagogic appeal and manipulation. Third, the demagogue and his support group prove highly adept at cementing mass support for their totalitarian leadership by fostering both a hatred of out groups and an envy of the better-off classes. Antipathetic to dictatorship and suspicious of democracy, then, there were very few other options than elite rule open to Hayek, particularly given his overriding commitment to minimise encroachments on liberty and his priority to safeguard what he regarded as the self-correcting forces on which civilisation rested.

In Hayek's elite-mass worldview, it is the educated few who provide the source of new ideas, which diffuse gradually 'until they become the possession of a majority who know little of their origin' (1960: 112). The basis of this division of function between elite and mass was between general, abstract ideas, on the one hand, and a preoccupation with mundane particular issues, on the other. Crucially, however, if civilised thinking were to advance, 'the theorist who offers guidance must not regard himself as bound by majority opinion,' and democracy might sometimes be best served by theorists in 'opposing the will of the majority' (1960: 114, 115). Because, as Hayek noted, it was the lot of most people in modern societies to be employed in large organisations, and therefore to be tied into hierarchies of employment in the made or designed order, such possibilities of ideas generation were only likely to be realised by a free-floating group of men of independent means. Not only this, but in an astonishing acknowledgement of the limitations of the extended order of the market, Hayek conceded that there were services to a society that were beyond the capacity of markets to price and to provide, and it was here that leaders fulfilled an important need:

> The leadership of individuals and groups who can back their beliefs financially is particularly essential in the field of cultural amenities, in the fine arts, in education and research, in the preservation of natural beauty and historic treasures, and, above all, in the propagation of new ideas in politics, morals and religion. (1960: 125)

In short, this frank admission amounted to leadership of an entire cultural heritage, albeit provided through philanthropy, wealthy patronage, and the idealism of a class of reformers who, motivated by public conscience, had supported numerous humane causes, such as abolition of the slave trade. Moreover, the existence of this kind of leadership class implied the need for tolerance of the 'idle rich' (1960: 127)—not idle in the sense of indolence, but of disinterestedness. Finally, it was not without a small dose of irony, given the MPS's battle to discredit Keynesian economics and Hayek's own brief exchanges with Keynes—in which he apparently sensed that he got the better of him (Caldwell 2004: 176–81)—that Hayek cited Keynes himself as the twentieth-century embodiment of the public service leadership provided by a man of independent means (while at the same time conveying his envy of him for this very reason), as had once been provided by leisured Victorian scholar-gentlemen (1960: 447n7).

## DISCUSSION

While there is a quaintness about Hayek's nostalgic attachment to a rather Olympian English version of nineteenth-century gentlemanly amateur leadership, the more important point is that it leaves entirely up in the air the question of what influence, if any, such leadership may have on the evolution of spontaneous order. After all, unlike organised order, this was an order without commands, yet it was coterminous with civilisation for Hayek, and such civilised men were meant to contribute to its advance. The mechanism by which this alleged diffusion from the few to the many was to occur, however, remains rather murky. On the other hand, some of Hayek's other claims about orders do raise a few intriguing implications for recent developments in leadership, particularly distributed leadership. Having due regard to space limitations, these points are discussed briefly.

In his elaboration of orders, Hayek allows for the means that sustain a spontaneous order to also operate in organised orders. Thus, the actions of individuals in organisations may be guided as much by rules as by commands, because:

> Every organization in which the members are not mere tools of the organizer will determine by commands only the function to be performed by each member, the purposes to be achieved, and certain general aspects of the methods to be employed, and will leave the detail to be decided by individuals on the basis of their respective knowledge and skills. (1973: 49)

In other words, the same cognitive limitations that operate in the wider society to subvert the whole idea of an omniscient mind apply with equal force in organised orders. Here, 'the organizer,' so-called, is entirely dependent on individuals for knowledge that he does not possess, but that he needs, and with whom he has to cooperate to realise his (or their joint) ends. At the same time, while it is the complexities unleashed by the changing division of labour that, for Hayek, make competition, as a general rule, the superior means for securing coordination, the consequences of these same complexities of the division of labour apply with equal vigour within organisations. Thus, while there might be 'no difficulty about efficient control or planning were conditions so simple that a single board or person could effectively survey all the facts' (1994: 55), the completion of tasks in large organisations, as pointed out by Hayek's fellow MPS member, Polanyi (1951: 115), relied to a significant extent on the mutual adjustment of colleagues, thereby exposing the limitations inherent in the idea of the span of executive organisational control.

There is a clear point of connection between these arguments and recent attempts at revising conventional understandings of leadership (e.g., Gronn 2002; Spillane 2006). While the notion of 'distributed leadership' may be open to the allegation that it represents a somewhat promiscuous approach to leadership—because, instead of offering a normative model of distributed leadership or (which would make no sense) of a distributed leader, it merely describes a situation in which organizational influence is shared—it derives at least some of its legitimacy and scholarly uptake by focusing on the dynamics of coordination and the reality (in effect) of Polanyi's idea of mutual adjustment. Thus, apologists for distributed leadership have criticised the inadequacy in prevailing leadership approaches of assumptions about the division of leadership labour between 'leaders' and 'followers' for grappling with growing environmental complexity and, as alternatives, have sought to bring to light such phenomena as synergies, interdependencies, knowledge-sharing attendant upon an escalating growth of knowledge, and the way in which chains of authority function to institutionalise senior level ignorance and dependence, in much the same way that Hayek (1960: 427n10) did when he cited Kline and Martin's (1958) views about the inherent shortcomings of hierarchies.

Indeed, in allowing for the possibility of spontaneous collaboration between colleagues, I have adopted remarkably similar language to that of Hayek, although I have done so by describing how emergent relations accommodate complexity in a way that tends towards holistic structuring (Gronn 2002), a direction in which Hayek's methodological individualist view of parts–wholes relations would not permit him to go. Taken together, these trends, along with the increased references one finds to networked and cellular modes of organising, point increasingly (adapting Baumann 2007) in the direction of 'liquid organizations.' They provide persuasive evidence of the increased incursion into the made or designed order of forces that Hayek associated with spontaneous ordering more generally. Needless to say, the paradox of this development is that it is exactly the opposite of the one that was of most concern to Hayek and that he devoted so much of his intellectual energies to resisting.

## CONCLUSION

As was suggested in the early sections of this chapter, Hayek was a prolific scholar who devoted the bulk of the second half of his long career to expatiating on developments that, to his way of thinking, were proving prejudicial to the cause of individual freedom. The identification of such threats and the crafting of an intellectually compelling defence of freedom were, from his perspective, the overriding intellectual priorities of his era. These challenges, in turn, stimulated a range of diverse interests that led him increasingly in the direction of a concern with grand questions to do with civilisation and its perpetuation and the evolutionary factors that helped sustain or prejudiced the future of civilised societies. By any standards this was a vast mental landscape.

As a theorist, rather than as an empiricist, Hayek's writing is populated with abstractions, most of which, in the case of leadership, merely hint at or imply a role for leaders of one variety or another. When examined closely, however, the small number of passages in which he addresses leadership directly reveal, as I have endeavoured to show, an odd empathy for the leadership of a bygone era. On reflection, perhaps this strength of attachment is not surprising, because that leadership was associated so closely with the era in which the version of liberty that he defended with such conviction was in the ascendency; viz, the highly engaged public leadership provided by a number of leisured scholars who committed themselves heroically to a range of causes for social and cultural betterment. Ironically, the lives of such men were mostly free of the clutches of the market order that Hayek esteemed so highly. Considered from the perspective of the contemporary organisational and social complexity, such an understanding of leadership is long since defunct. On the other hand, as I hope I have shown, at least some of what Hayek had to say about social orders resonates closely with current discussions of the future of leadership and coordination in organisations. For that reason alone, quite apart from what he had to say about the value of freedom, his work continues to be important.

## REFERENCES

Baumann, Z. (2007) *Liquid Times: Living in an Age of Uncertainty,* Cambridge: Polity.

Caldwell, B. (2004) *Hayek's Challenge: An Intellectual Biography of F. A. Hayek,* Chicago: University of Chicago Press.

Cockett, R. (1995) *Thinking the Unthinkable: Think-Tanks and the Economic Counter-Revolution, 1931–1983,* London: Fontana.

Ferguson, A. (2003 [1767]) *An Essay On the History of Civil Society,* Cambridge: Cambridge University Press.

Gronn, P. (2002) 'Distributed leadership as a unit of analysis,' *Leadership Quarterly,* 13, 4: 423–51.

Hayek, F. A. (1937) 'Economics and knowledge,' *Economica,* 13, 4: 33–54.

———, (1945) 'The use of knowledge in society,' *American Economic Review,* 35, 4: 519–30.

———, (1948) *Individualism and Economic Order,* Chicago: University of Chicago Press.

———, (1952) *The Sensory Order: An Inquiry into the Foundations of Theoretical Psychology,* Chicago: University of Chicago Press.

———, (1960) *The Constitution of Liberty,* Chicago: University of Chicago Press.

——, (1973) *Rules and Order*, Chicago: University of Chicago Press.

——, (1978) *The Mirage of Social Justice*, Chicago: University of Chicago Press.

——, (1979 [1952]) *The Counter-Revolution of Science: Studies on the Abuse of Reason*, 2nd edn, Indianapolis: Liberty Fund.

——, (1981) *The Political Order of a Free People*, Chicago: University of Chicago Press.

——, (1991) *The Fatal Conceit: The Errors of Socialism*, Chicago: University of Chicago Press.

——, (1994 [1944]) *The Road to Serfdom*, 5th edn, Chicago: University of Chicago Press.

——, (1997 [1939]) 'Freedom and the economic system,' in B. Caldwell (ed.) *Socialism and War: Essays, Documents, Reviews, Collected Works of F. A. Hayek*, vol. 10, London: Routledge.

Judt, T. (2005) *Postwar: A History of Europe Since 1945*, New York: Penguin Press.

Kline, B. E. and Martin, N. H. (1958) 'Freedom, authority, and decentralization,' *Harvard Business Review*, 36, 3: 69–75.

Marwick, A. (1964) 'Middle opinion in the thirties: planning, progress, and political "agreement"', *English Historical Review*, 79, 311: 285–98.

Mont Pèlerin Society. Online. Available HTTP: http://www.montpelerin.org/home.cfm (accessed 23 August 2007).

Polanyi, M. (1951) *The Logic of Liberty: Reflections and Rejoinders*, London: Routledge and Kegan Paul.

Smith, A. (1976 [1776]) *An Inquiry into the Nature and Causes of the Wealth of Nations*, Chicago: University of Chicago Press.

——, (2002 [1759]) *The Theory of Moral Sentiments*, Cambridge: Cambridge University Press.

Snooks, G. D. (2000) *Longrun Dynamics: A General Economic and Political Theory*, London: Routledge.

Spillane, J. (2006) *Distributed Leadership*, San Francisco: Jossey–Bass.

# 6 Bourdieu's Distinctions of Taste, Talent, and Power

## Bridging Political Fields and Administrative Practice

*Carol E. Harris*

> Educational administration . . . involves not simply the formulation and implementation of reliable and neutral *techniques* of management but rather the active embracing of a political role involving analysis, judgment, and advocacy and the adoption of an active stance toward issues of social justice and democracy. (Bates 1987: 110)

Although today many North American educational administrators, or more inclusively, educational leaders, take Bates' words of two decades ago seriously (e.g., *Educational Administration Quarterly* 2004; MacKinnon, in press; Maynes 2001), a large segment of the school system still sees its goal as putting into practice the latest theories to emerge from that dominant duo of government and markets. Marshall, in an introduction to a special edition of *Educational Administration Quarterly* (EAQ), points out the relatively short history of equity concerns within the administrative side of education. Rather than focusing on inclusion (or exclusion) of people by gender, sexual orientation, class and race, she notes that administrators' concerns, as reflected in scholarly writing, have tended traditionally to center on such generalisations as 'bureaucracy, hierarchy, [and] efficiency' (2004: 3). Thus, Marshall argues, the field is overdue, especially in light of reactionary reforms in the United States, for a more openly ideological perspective.

The 2004 issue of *EAQ,* with the exception of Shields (2004), addresses an American readership; its message, however, speaks to Canadians who also have been subjected to waves of restructuring and reform. Given the force of globalisation, the challenge to equity is truly international. Canadian educational administration has been, apart from a commendable coverage of gender (e.g., Coulter 1998; Reynolds and Young 1995; Wallace 2003), relatively silent for years on the explicit topic of social justice (Ryan 1991), but it has seen a virtual explosion recently around issues of domination and exclusion. In this, educational leaders (MacKinnon in press; Samier 2003; Shields 2004) have joined forces with the broader field of Canadian education, with sociologists (e.g., Taylor 2001; Corbett 2007), philosophers (e.g., Portelli and Solomon 2001), curriculum theorists (Bickmore 2006;

Cook and Westheimer 2006; Darts 2004[1]; Portelli and Vibert 2001) and adult educators (e.g., Fenwick, Nesbit, and Spencer 2006; Welton 2005).

Yet the tension noted above positions educational administrators and other school leaders 'between a rock and a hard place' (Milley 2006: 80; Shields 2004: 109–10):

> On the one hand, they must concentrate on wresting resources from the larger political and economic systems of administration, while working within a formal structure of roles and accountabilities to meet performance targets. On the other hand, they have a duty to respond to and negotiate the diverse, contradictory and sometimes incommensurable interests and needs of members of their institutions and communities, while faithfully helping these members strive towards wisdom, social justice, autonomy and solidarity, values that . . . comprise the bedrock of public education. (Milley 2006: 80)

In bringing about the social changes advocated theoretically (e.g., Blackmore 1999; Smyth 1989; Stromquist 2005; Wallace 2004)—and that is the perspective I am addressing here—educational leaders must engage in the politics and policy-making of education. It follows that this objective also demands an understanding of the complex connections involved in injustice.

This chapter explores one such connection, that between power (symbolic and real) and cultural capital at work in the field of education. To do so following Bourdieu, however, this one connection points to many more, including his eventual transformation from scholarly intellectual to public persona, a transformation brought about by the threats of neoliberalism and the dominance of globalisation (Swartz 2003). Bourdieu's sociopolitical writings offer an expanded venue for examining social justice, a field he explored frequently in his micropolitical studies of French schools and one that invites analysis in diverse contexts. This I explore in the first section of the paper. In the second, I take the example of Bourdieu's analysis of cultural capital to analyse 'distinctions of taste and talent' as they play out within the mythology of Canadian public school music. I demonstrate that symbolic violence, as played out in arts education, offers a particularly effective illustration of the politics of privilege. In reference to this example of symbolic violence, I return to the tenor of our times, neoliberalism, and the importance of political awareness and resistance to this in our schools. To begin this appropriation[2] of Bourdieu to the administrative realm, I visit several of his concepts and apply them to the field of education, and to the subfield of musical culture within that. I begin with a brief overview of his central observations regarding education.

## BOURDIEU ON EDUCATION

Education and the reproductive forces at work in schooling, from the beginning of his theorising to his most recent activism, remained Bourdieu's central concerns (1973; 1998a; Bourdieu and Passeron 1977). Some thirty years ago, Bourdieu recorded with empirical precision extreme inequalities of economic and cultural conditions among and within societies, reminding readers that the surest route to inequality of outcome in schools is to treat all students similarly (1974: 37–8). As children enter school with far different backgrounds, similar treatment will only exacerbate the differences. In a tightly structured exposé of reproduction, he documented the positive correlation between students who hold (or do not hold) socioeconomic resources and their academic results (Bourdieu and de Saint-Martin 1974). He demonstrated, moreover, the two-way relationship—a 'dialectic of approval' (1973: 111)—whereby the school recognises certain of its members who, in turn, recognise the legitimacy of school.

Of central importance to this chapter on distinctions of taste is Bourdieu's observation that attitudes and assessments of school actors and members of the general public alike lead to a conflation of talent (or natural giftedness) with opportunity. In education, for example, 'judgements that teachers make with regard to students . . . take into account not only knowledge and know-how, but also the intangible nuances of *manners* and *style*' (Bourdieu and de Saint-Martin 1974: 338). These practices of judgement, he maintains, justify the kinds of inequality that, in turn, lead to confusion between *social* and *natural* gifts (1974: 32).

The practices take root, moreover, in a rich soil of scholastic denial and cultural inertia. The denial lies in the myth that schools provide their students equal opportunities to succeed. An appearance of meritocracy is made possible by the presence of power in multiple forms. Not always does the distribution of rewards fall to those with economic power, for cultural capital and social networks occasionally trump economics (Bourdieu 1973); these atypical situations, where cultural strengths are ignored, allow for a failure to recognise genuine opportunity. In cultural terms, the manners of students become the 'half-uttered, unuttered or unutterable' (Bourdieu and Saint-Martin 1974: 339) marks of distinction that place some students on the cutting edge of success and marginalise others.

Although other theorists[3] have applied these and similar pedagogical and administrative theories of inequality in their writing, an examination of the interwoven texture of Bourdieu's work stands to inform administrators today of additional subtleties implicated in the challenge to achieve equity in schools. His later work, especially, offers hope of emancipatory change. The context of his theory includes fields of action, capital in its many forms, *habitus*—that network of presuppositions that propel one to accept gifts of heritage as natural endowments—and finally, the state of illusion (*illusio*) that allows people to proceed unaware of their habitus. The theories, embedded one within another, point to the themes of this chapter: first, that culture plays a significant role in the reproduction of societal, economic, and political power; second, that a peeling away of illusions provides an important space in which school actors can assert individual and collective agency;

and third, that the challenge to effect greater equity in schools is particularly urgent in the face of the destructive effects of contemporary neoliberalism. The challenge, contends Bourdieu, calls not only for the scholarly dissemination of ideas in writing, but also for political action.

## BUILDING A VOCABULARY

### Fields of Action

Bourdieu identifies many fields of action—economic, political, religious, cultural, educational—each demarcated by its peculiar discourse, habits, attitudes, rules, regulations, and guiding assumptions. He holds that we act within each field, more or less understanding the 'game' played by others in the same field. In Western societies as well as in Marxist theories of materialism, for instance, the commonly accepted field is that of economics. In this field, debates may rage about Keynesian and classical theories of wealth and its control and distribution. But the terminology and the references, if not the overriding assumptions, will be understood by each of the combatants.

Public education forms another field of understanding and action. Here we have a common language—often mysterious to those on the outside—that cloaks debate about class size, pedagogy, standards of success, accountability, and other such in-house issues. More or less, within the system of schools, colleges, and universities we understand one another, even when we do not agree.

Within the larger educational field are subfields inhabited by less commonly known areas of the curriculum, such as physical education, visual arts, and music. Again, the discourse of each area and the accepted hierarchies of power and attainment are only vaguely understood by those outside the field. The same holds true for extracurricular activities involving team sports or for 'smart sports' such as chess and bridge (Bourdieu 1973: 111).[4]

In the political field, several games are played (Lukoševiciute-Vidziuniene 1998). The obvious one involves party politics where, in representative politics, we state platforms, positions, and programmes and strive to work and speak on behalf of others. To accomplish this, citizens must pass over or delegate their power and authority to a representative. Then there are the politics of symbolic power, where the social world is created and expressed with words and gestures. This gives one an opportunity to confirm or express what already exists, or to suggest a vision of the world which would have the potential to attract citizens and effect change. Then, too, the political field answers to the symbolism of cultural power, whereby status and prestige work together with, or independently of, economic power. As Bourdieu points out, the ability to know *how* to act and *what* to say in social gatherings brings rewards beyond the social realm itself (1973: 99). Positions of status are related, not only through connections within the field but in regard to exterior relations of difference. These relations of difference, these distinctions, become evident in an examination of capital.

## Capital

Something counts as capital only to the extent that possessing it gives one an ability to gain profits specific to a field (Bourdieu and Wacquant 1992: 97). All forms of power are defined by Bourdieu as capital, and capital exists always in relation to a field. Linguistic capital, for instance, concerns competence in speech and comprehension measured in relation to a specific market where often unrecognised power relations are at stake (Johnson 1993: 7). The way one speaks, in revealing class, ethnicity, gender and other social markers, places one immediately in relation to the exterior world. Thus, rich linguistic capital proclaims cultural positioning and helps the possessor access high positions within social and economic fields.

Academic or educational capital derives from formal education and is measured by schools, diplomas and degrees. It also comes from informal sources of knowledge and information gained through one's family and social milieu—what Bourdieu calls one's educational inheritance. Bourdieu points, for instance, to a 'very high rate of professional heredity' particularly noticeable in the medical profession where one sees a 'veritable dynasty of doctors' (1973: 112). Clearly, in this sense of accumulation, education merges with social capital.

Social capital, marked by the connections formed with family, friendship groups, and school ties, permeates all other forms of capital. Bourdieu explains it as constituted within 'contacts and group memberships which, through the accumulation of exchanges, obligations and shared identities, provide actual or potential support and access to valued resources' (1993: 143). Social capital depends upon the people one knows and the connections one has made, or that have been made by one's parents.

In this paper, primary importance is given to cultural capital. As Reay points out, this is 'primarily a relational concept that exists in conjunction with other forms of capital' (2004: 57), that is, economic, social, and symbolic. By cultural capital and its corresponding field, I mean, therefore, much more than what has often been claimed to be the two central pillars of culture: '"highbrow" aesthetic culture, and analytically and causally acquired skills distinct from other important forms of knowledge or competence' (Lareau and Weininger 2003: 567). How one presents oneself, observes the physical environment, stands, moves, and speaks all illustrate one's cultural placement and symbolic power. Refusing to accept a dichotomy between high and significant matters and low or insignificant matters, Bourdieu consigns a wide range of behaviours to his analysis of culture, including 'various ways of chewing one's food, different forms of dressing, musical tastes ranging from a predilection for "Home on the Range" to a liking for John Cage, home decoration, the kind of friends one has and the films one likes to see' (Moi 1991: 1020). As I define culture, and as I believe Bourdieu intends it to be understood, people also share (or debate) common experiences and perceptions of meaning, employing a vocabulary rich in emotional and aesthetic content.

Within the arts, as we will see, power accessed through culture is not always totally dependent on one's native skill and talent. While talent provides one source of power, as suggested above, it is often supplemented by (and inextricably intertwined with) economic and political capital.

Legitimisation plays an important role in each form of capital. Certain practices within each field—and as contrasted with the outside world— become accepted as naturally superior to others, although such recognition tends to be implicit rather than overt. The hegemonic condition in this occurs as these practices seem superior even to those who do not participate or share the dominant knowledge and skills (Johnson 1993: 24).

## Habitus

Legitimisation takes place according to 'systems of durable, transposable dispositions,' termed *habitus* by Bourdieu (1990). Habitus is that product of history that informs individual and collective practices by guaranteeing 'their "correctness" . . . and their constancy over time, more reliably than all formal rules and explicit norms. Habitus sets the boundaries within which agents are "free" to adopt strategic practices that orient, rather than strictly determine, action' (Harker and May 1993: 174). According to Moi, who has used Bourdieu for feminist analysis, classifications of habitus owe their specific efficacy to their ability to function below the level of consciousness and language, beyond the reach of introspective scrutiny or control by the will. Nevertheless, classifications present 'the totality of general dispositions acquired through practical experience in the field' (1991: 1021); they are the 'objective cognitive structures that organise [people's] resolutions, outlooks and activities' (Lukoševiciute-Vidziuniene 1998). In political terms, the habitus produces a society 'in which the established cosmological and political order is perceived not as arbitrary (i.e., as one possible order among others) but as a self-evident and natural order which goes without saying and therefore goes unquestioned' (Bourdieu 1977: 166).

Intellectual and educational fields, like any other, have their own specific habitus, their specific mechanisms of selection and consecration. The danger lies in verdicts that 'in the name of taste, condemn to ridicule, indignity, shame, silence . . . [people] who simply fall short, in the eyes of their judges, of the right way of being and doing' (Harris 1991: 511). Much like the hidden curriculum in schools, such classifications of habitus constitute norms and values that are inculcated through forms of classroom interaction, rather than through any explicit teaching project.

Within the educational field is a cultural field, where schools work to establish in children habits, dispositions and attitudes of taste. Unfortunately, school actors sometimes fail to recognise their own efforts, thus mistaking already present 'tastes' as signs of skill and talent. 'Taste is an acquired disposition to "differentiate" and "appreciate"' (Bourdieu 1984: 466), that is, to establish and mark differences by a process of distinction that 'ensures recognition of the object . . . without implying knowledge of the distinctive features which define it' (466). We prize certain objects and sounds, for instance, simply because of familiarity. If the familiar is also part of the dominant culture, we inherit a distinct advantage over those for whom the dominant habitus is unfamiliar. Taste, therefore, amounts to 'a practical mastery of distributions which make it possible to sense or intuit what is likely (or unlikely) to befall—and therefore to befit—an individual occupying a given position in social space. It functions as a sort of social orientation, a "sense of one's place"' (Bourdieu 1984: 466). In this sense, taste operates as a highly determined structure of power.

Habitus, as an unconsciously accepted framework of power, also provides the space in education for positive change. Bourdieu identifies *strategies*—directed towards certain ends without being consciously so directed or determined by them—as 'an infinite number of moves to be made, adapted to the infinite number of possible situations which no rule, however complex, can foresee' (1990: 9–10). Subconscious strategies provide opportunities for agentic actions that challenge and sometimes overcome structural barriers of economic, social, and cultural power. Moi (1991) provides an example of such agency in her description of a young woman 'at risk' of failure who obtains, through her seemingly obstructive behaviour, the attention of school counsellors and peers, who manage to assist and keep her from self-defeat.

These spaces in which actors strategise, claims Bourdieu, can appear to our consciousness only when we break with deterministic views of the world. He points to three problematic views in particular. The first occurs when constructions of substance (group numbers, limits, members) become confused with complex relationships within and across groups. For example, the 'working class' as defined by the sociologist is more theoretical than real:

> It is not really a class, an *actual* class, in the sense of a group, a group mobilized for struggle; at most, it might be called a *probable class,* inasmuch as it is a set of agents that will present fewer hindrances to efforts at mobilization than any other set of agents. (1985: 725)

The second troublesome view considers economics as the sole contributor to social status. This chapter has presented several examples of alternative capital such as social, linguistic, cultural, and the all-embracing symbolic capital 'commonly called prestige, reputation, renown, etc., . . . in which the different forms of capital are perceived and recognized as legitimate' (Bourdieu 1985: 724). The third problem area surrounds an excess of objectivism (or rationalism) that, Bourdieu maintains, goes 'hand-in-hand with intellectualism, and that leads one to ignore the symbolic struggles of which the different fields are the site' (723). Each of these three may pose a threat to an adequate understanding of successful strategic action.

In the Canadian study below, I outline aspects of Bourdieu's theory, ending with an example of the kind of individual and collective agency that appeared within the fortifications of accepted—yet inequitable—school practice. I offer, as well, an example of equitable practice that potentially reaches well beyond the cultural field.

## APPROPRIATING BOURDIEU: MYTHS OF DISTINCTION AND TASTE

My own study of the administration of school music programs in Canada, conducted in the early 1990s, unearthed several myths surrounding people's perceptions of talent, taste and intellectual endowment (Harris 1991; 1996). These myths, which appeared in the social milieu (or habitus) of three school boards, one located in British Columbia and two in Ontario, surrounded six perceptions of reality, each perception (or disposition) accompanied by firmly held beliefs and attitudes among teachers and administrators about the nature of music and arts education.

The first myth was of the correspondence and positive equation between student achievement and musical talent. In this, talent was seen as quite distinct from the generalised educational opportunities experienced by children in their formative years. The second myth was that only children from certain homes favour classical music; that is, classical and popular music were enjoyed naturally by different segments of the socioeconomic population. Third, a teacher is a teacher; s/he is a specialist in the art of teaching and can, therefore, teach any subject, especially at primary/elementary levels of schooling. Fourth, an emotional distance sets music teachers, who tend to be 'prima donnas,' apart from other members of staff; the belief here is that music teachers shape their programmes according to their own desires and quite independently of the required curriculum. Fifth, the myth of 'music as fun' is that the important contribution of school music inheres in its potential for entertainment; the role of music in schools is simply to provide joyful experiences for children. In this view, learning takes a secondary place. Sixth, music is equally accessible to all students and the choice not to participate emanates from students' (and parents') lack of interest in the subject. This final myth indicates that children enjoy equal access to musical opportunities in public schools.

In approaching these myths, my task was to demonstrate that each was at the same time based in everyday realities of schooling and deeply rooted in a collective reluctance to appreciate cultural and other forms of capital. From my interviews, I presented the words of school actors to establish each myth and, with the help of Bourdieu and other theorists, was able to question its validity and to offer an alternative reading. The *field* of operation was education and, in this field, I found a language common to all actors. Music educators, however, inhabited a *subfield* in which the discourse was not always understandable to administrators and other teachers. Music teachers (and administrators who had been music teachers) spoke, for instance, of aesthetic appreciation, of music's form and elements (distinct from other subjects and, thus, leading to uncommon learning objectives), of connections between rhythm, melody, and children's emotional responses, the embodiment in children of rhythm and melody through songs and games, and so on.

The cultural complexities involved were, at the same time, social and economic. Simply put, some children enjoyed far more opportunity than others. Although this is widely acknowledged in literature, my surprising finding was that it found little recognition among educators as it might affect their everyday practice. Yet administrators and teachers told me of students who, coming to school with the benefit of private lessons, enhanced school programmes. These students knew the language game of music and were able to apply reading skills, learned at the piano or violin, to school instruments. In these school boards, as Bourdieu points out in his studies, distinctions of student talent and taste as perceived by school educators could be seen clearly.

One board, however, stressed the kinds of learning that no students had enjoyed previously. These included skills of vocal sight reading, listening and writing, composing, games that called for a wide variety of physical dexterity and, as students progressed in their musical learning, the playing of classroom instruments (e.g., recorders, as contrasted with instruments encountered in private lessons) and a common programme of listening that introduced all children to hitherto unfamiliar music. With these children, the achievement gap between socioeconomically privileged and underprivileged children was slight or imperceptible. As Bourdieu maintains, achievement gaps tend to narrow as students move farther from knowledge and skills accumulated in the home (1974: 36, 37). In this instance of music programming, music skills and appreciations were consciously planned by teachers and administrators to do just this—introduce new learning and lessen the achievement gap. The politics of this board were those of equity and the policies of programming followed suit. I found, however, that such beliefs and actions were rarely acknowledged overtly as political. Policies that led to equitable conditions were consciously based, rather, on a particular method of pedagogy (here the Hungarian Kodaly Music Education approach), one proven successful—in terms of learning goals—in other geographical contexts.

Looking back on this study from the vantage point of some thirteen years, and with a deeper reading of Bourdieu, I have a richer understanding of the illusion (or cultural amnesia) that tended to hide from administrators and teachers the extremes of inequality of educational opportunity experienced by students in one school board and, to a lesser degree, in a second board. Educators, while admitting the inadequacies of school programmes, declared that their own children benefited greatly from private lessons, board-sponsored honour choirs, and special schools chosen for their exceptional music programmes. The point I drew from this, although implied rather than stated directly by educators in the study, was that music (and possibly other arts obtained through private lessons) was valued highly. It placed the children of educators at the cutting edge of job preferment and subsequent socioeconomic success. These children, as youth and adults, were able to entertain, perform with others, and appreciate high culture (as well as their own youth culture), thus enhancing their social networks; and they learned, as the result of performing solo and in ensemble, how to project their voices clearly and move with grace and purpose. Such performativity develops from educational fields and, in turn, sustains these fields.

Thus, through the lens of Bourdieu, we have the myths of *habitus,* the capital of socioeconomics, and the overriding cultural capital of arts education. We also see a blindness, or cultural illusion, that obstructs from participants the full impact on students of school processes, administrative choices, and steps that might have been taken towards a pedagogy of possibility (Simon 1992). With the notable exception of one school board, legitimacy surrounds the *status quo* whereby the dominant institution of education, usage, and action was accepted but not recognised as such (Moi 1991: 1021).

One school board, however, presented a more emancipatory pedagogy and administration. At this site, educators tended to include all students, thereby creating space for students from all backgrounds to participate. In so doing, they broke with dominant perceptions of talent and taste, that is, with any assumption that 'high' music belongs to only one class. The dominant discourse at this site differed, as well, with the recognition that teaching an art—music, in this case—requires lengthy training both in the skills of performance and those of pedagogy.

This study of school music education revealed educators engaged in both enabling and disabling strategies of pedagogy. That was the historical context of the early 1990s. I doubt, however, that the interested theorist or practitioner would find an improved situation today.

## WHY BOURDIEU, WHY NOW?

In his later years, Bourdieu moved from political scholar to political activist (Swartz 2003). Having spurned public pronouncements (such as those made by fellow-countryman Jean Paul Sartre) in favour of scholarly writing and teaching, what Bourdieu saw as the threat of neoliberalism propelled him finally into the spotlight of public discourse. Following a prolonged study of dismantled workplaces and suffering workers (Bourdieu 1999), he presented an analysis of neoliberalism that informs all other socioeconomic and cultural fields. A brief overview of this critique is important for two reasons: it tells of our present times, our *Weltanschauung,* and it directs educators today to carve out and occupy a public space where social change may be democratically debated and acted upon.

Bourdieu's critique focuses on the overweening rationality of neoliberalism. The discourse, based on an economic theory of abstraction and individualism, promotes competition and efficiency while avoiding any social logic subject to the rule of fairness. Bourdieu identifies this theory as 'an immense political project underway (although its status is denied) [that] aims to create the conditions under which the "theory" can be realized and can function: *a programme of the methodological destruction of collectives'* (1998a: 95–6). The project is accomplished by various means, some of which are consciously perceived by its victims while many others are merely accepted as 'the way things are.' Bourdieu notes these means, all of which are progressively taking place in the global context, as the 'suppression of market regulation, beginning with the labour market, the prohibition of deficits and inflation, the general privatisation of public services, and the reduction of public and social expenses' (1998a). Moreover, he decries the politics of financial deregulation in which transformative and destructive measures, such as the Multilateral Agreement on Investment (MAI),[5] are designed to call into question any and all collective structures:

> The nation, whose space to manoeuvre continually decreases; work groups, for example through the individualisation of salaries and of careers as a function of individual competences, with the consequent atomisation of workers; collectives for the defence of the rights of workers, unions, associations, cooperatives; even the family, which loses part of its control over consumption through the constitution of markets by age groups. (1998a)

Bourdieu, in discussing individualism as it appears in the language of participative management, throws new light on the presently popular concept of distributed leadership within schools (Gronn 2002). He notes that the pressure toward self-control extends workers' (or teachers') involvement into new realms of rationalized domination. These workers become overinvolved in work that is conducted in stressful conditions. Most destructively, these conditions 'converge to weaken or abolish collective standards or solidarities' (Bourdieu 1998a; for teachers' work internationally see Gunter 2007; Robertson 2000; Smyth 2001). In addition, the security of workers, including teachers, is weakened and their stress and suffering increased through 'precarious arrangements' whereby a reserve army of employees is ready to take their place.

Bourdieu terms these conditions of underemployment, job insecurity, layoffs, and labour intensification the 'structural violence' (Bordieu 1998b) of neoliberal work. Meanwhile, he notes,

Organisational discourse has never talked as much of trust, co-opera-tion, loyalty, and organizational culture as in an era when adherence to the organization is obtained at each moment by eliminating all tempo-ral guarantees of employment. (1998b)

In schools and in the preparation of teachers, I have seen this insecurity fac-ing young teachers who, without permanent jobs, often exist for years on contract work. If new teachers are free of family responsibilities they may find jobs in northern or inner city locations, but for those who must remain where they are contract work, with its insecurity and stress, remains the norm. To counteract such insecurity, teachers with cultural capital in music and the other arts and in language proficiencies tend to enjoy preferment in the hiring game. Others with less cultural capital improve their proficiencies in special education. But above all lurks the spectre of insecurity, strain, and stress.

Bourdieu holds out hope that this 'race into the abyss,' (Bordieu 1998b:102) so disastrous in its effect on individual well-being and social solidarity, will eventually be stemmed. He looks to two sources as the ini-tiators of change: first, the 'very institutions and representatives of the old order that is now in the process of being dismantled,' and second, the 'col-lective work of socially committed workers—familial or otherwise.' (Bor-dieu 1998a)

He warns that the conservation efforts of the first group will be labelled conservative or simply defensive of privilege. Both groups, he maintains, will try to make room for social actors oriented toward the '*rational pursuit of ends collectively arrived at and collectively ratified*' (1998a). In other words, he believes that liberating change will take place only through a socially democratic process.

## TOWARDS ACTION

For the democratic process to take effect, however, educators need a new vocabulary, a way of understanding and expressing resistance to unequal power arrangements (Brown 2004; Shields, Larocque and Oberg 2002). We require, as well, more inclusive forums for discussion, in both our postsec-ondary institutions and public schools. Several examples of university-com-munity collaboration signal resistance to the status quo and an expanded public space. In Canada, Community-University Research Alliances (CURA 2003–04) are encouraged and funded through the federally administrated Social Sciences and Research Council of Canada. At the University of Vic-toria, British Columbia, for instance, several CURA projects have focused on the uses of verbal and artistic forms of communication to broaden understanding between native and nonnative groups (Bannister 2003; Pence 2007). One project was the Cultural Property Community Research Collab-orative, established in 1999 for a five-year period, with these objectives:

- to utilize the research and teaching resources of the University . . . and its CURA partners to benefit regional arts and heritage organizations;
- to encourage innovative research projects of mutual interest to the collaborating partners;
- to provide opportunities for professional training and upgrading in cultural resource management and heritage preservation; and
- to involve student collaboration at the university and community levels. (CURA 2003–04)

Other community development researchers (Bannister 2003; Clover and Harris 2005), through participatory approaches to research in the form of community dialogue, residential workshops, and continuous outreach to the public, have stated more forcefully their intention to bring about greater equality of opportunity and condition. Bannister, for instance, followed a 'science shop' concept of university-community liaison borrowed from the Netherlands to identify 'ethical and other policy issues in research collaboration' that support mutually beneficial partnerships with First Nations communities (2003: 6, 7). The objective is to blend 'expert' knowledge with local and traditional ecological knowledge (LEK and TEK) in the identification of problems to be studied and protocols of action to be followed. Much of the participatory research literature, like that of Bannister, acknowledges that researchers 'strive to equalize uneven or unbalanced social relations, challenge inequities, and help people to develop skills and abilities to exercise greater self-determination and control over their futures' (Clover and Harris 2005: 23).

In the American university context, Brown presents a multilayered model of teaching intended to awaken in aspiring administrators an awareness of equity imbalances and the means whereby they can be challenged and corrected. Brown integrates an unusual multidisciplinary approach to pedagogy, policy and action through an interweaving of three theoretical fields— adult learning, transformative learning and critical social theory—with three pedagogical strategies of critical reflection, rational discourse analysis and policy praxis. Her intention, in the transformative tradition of Freire and other critical adult educators, is to 'stretch [students] beyond [their] comfort zones' (2004: 78) and lead them to 'perceive social, political, and economic contradictions, and to take action against the oppressive elements of reality' (2004: 77). Brown's guidelines for reflection, borrowed from adult learning strategies as outlined by the National Coalition Building Institute, are:

- to celebrate similarities and differences;
- to recognize the misinformation that people have learned about various groups;
- to identify and heal from internalized oppression—the discrimination members of an oppressed group target at themselves and each other;

- to claim pride in group identity;
- to understand the personal effect of discrimination through the telling of stories; and
- to learn hands-on tools for dealing effectively with bigoted comments and behaviors. (Brown 2004: 92)

Although such theory and practice serve a heuristic purpose in alerting administrators to many problems and possible solutions, modelling is not embraced by all professors and political activists.

In my own graduate teaching (Harris in press), and in the spirit of Bourdieu, I turn to an aesthetically nuanced approach to the policies and politics of administration. In all my teaching areas—philosophy, organisation theory and policy—and at the beginning of each class, I ask one student to make a ten-minute presentation of a song, a poem or artwork and, then, lead the class in discussing the implications of the work. Although my experiments in blending the arts with theory were extremely tentative at first, from reading and reflecting on a series of student evaluations I have been able to focus my strategies and purposes more firmly. I have discovered that, as students engage in new sentient experiences (e.g., sound, sight, touch), they come to grips more thoroughly with concepts of difference, taste and distinction than they might otherwise do. Students are introduced, in these few minutes at the beginning of a class, to a wide range of beliefs, experiences, values and assumptions. I see in their written reflections on these aesthetic presentations first steps towards an intellectual awareness that, in turn, holds promise for political discourse and action. As well, student reflections about hitherto unexamined values and assumptions (their and others) indicate aesthetic growth and increased critical awareness. I also see, through follow-up observations and discussions with students, signs in some of an enriched sociopolitical imagination and a growing will to create a world that is not yet apparent. Of course, my findings remain highly qualitative and it is impossible to uncouple aesthetic and theoretical influences. Nor do I wish to do so; my objective is to inspire action in the difficult terrain of school and community relations.

But none of these moves within the university directly involves school-based action and addresses the tension identified by Milley (2006; Foster 2004), whereby school administrators are called upon, at the same time, to serve the equity needs of students and parents and the demands of the larger political and economic system. MacKinnon (in press), in discussing the effect of this ongoing tension, notes that schools, particularly in Western societies, continue to suffer from 'blind spots' concerning the life experiences of others:

In school settings, this lack of awareness results in a plethora of silences and negative (sometimes savage) actions that reinforce inequity and perpetuate social injustice. If unchallenged, as is all too often the case, silence and aggression become normalized and even seen as unremarkable, if not acceptable, by those they marginalize. (MacKinnon in press)

The problem becomes self-perpetuating through inequitable hiring practices that see 'those privileged by injustice as most likely to be hired back into the system as teachers and administrators' (in press). MacKinnon, a university professor, works directly with teachers, administrators and school district personnel to interrupt this cycle

> in a number of ways, such as challenging hiring practices, instituting employment equity policies that slowly change the face of teaching and administration, supporting instances of community resistance, and/or educating current administrators in ways that help them unmask and confront their own assumptions and privileges. (in press)

To effect political, as well as school-based, action, MacKinnon collaborates with other educators in an Educational Leadership Consortium (ELC), and in partnership with the teachers' union, the Department of Education, associations of school boards, aboriginal peoples, and women, and with all universities involved in teacher training, to deliver three- and four-day modules on justice issues in the province of Nova Scotia. Modules are facilitated by practising or retired school administrators, and occasionally by university-based academics, knowledgeable and dedicated to the consortium's purposes. One module, designed specifically for aspiring school administrators, centres on ideologies of privilege (i.e., the administrative habitus) and focuses on 'common understandings of school, notably that they are meritocracies that provide equal chances for all students to be successful' (MacKinnon in press).

Although I have witnessed, during twenty years in the administrative field, several instances of awareness and action (at times radical) among practising administrators, discussion about equity issues and radical action have been relatively rare in my university experience. The work of MacKinnon and his colleagues redirects attention to the importance of teacher and administrative preparation while going well beyond it, as Brown advocates, to the 'necessary complement' of 'professional learning' (2004: 78).

Yet all three examples of active outreach—postsecondary training of school leaders in a critical vein, the application of aesthetics to stimulate other ways of seeing, and training sessions directed specifically towards practising administrators—I believe, would benefit from a closer reading of Bourdieu. As each of the theorist-practitioners discussed above seeks to awaken critique of existing conditions, this critique would be enhanced by an even closer examination of the fields in which we and our students or participants labour, the ethos (or habitus) of different societal environments, the illusions under which we live and work and, most significantly, the intersections of these features with various forms of capital. Cultural capital, in particular, deserves special attention, as it seems to be a largely unacknowledged source of power. Such a reading might move cultural studies (both of the arts and lived cultures) from the periphery of school and postgraduate university curricula to a central position in political decision-making.

## SUMMARY CONCLUSION

This paper outlines a primer for the application of Bourdieu to educational administration and leadership and offers a few examples of political action in the field. All too often in administrative literature, pieces of Bourdieu are abstracted from his theory, leaving an impression that such concepts as *habitus,* field, capital and *illusio* carry stand-alone explanatory power. He insists, however, on the embeddedness of these concepts and an acknowledgement that complexity is essential to successful understanding and action. Although I cannot claim to have covered the essence of any one concept, I have provided an introduction that may engage the politically motivated reader in further study. In the discussion, I introduced a few examples of where the field of educational administration intersects with assumptions—founded or unfounded—of taste, talent and power and how some educators are attempting to bridge the politics of privilege.

Bourdieu, although writing for and about the highly structured society of France, can be appropriated for many purposes, including a micropolitical examination of reproduction in the Canadian school context. In particular, I have detailed tendencies in schools to reproduce cultural inequities. Cultural capital, however, as a relational concept, cannot stand alone but, as noted above, exists 'in conjunction with other forms of capital . . . that together constitute advantage and disadvantage in society' (Reay 2004: 57). In addition to the insights provided by a richly complex reading of society, I chose Bourdieu to illustrate social problems of equity for several reasons. The first is my own interest in the political aesthetics of administration (Harris 2006), which leads me to appreciate the space he relegates to language and aesthetics; another is Bourdieu's highly specific analyses of cultural and social determinants of reproduction of class, status and power that take place in schools; and, finally, that Bourdieu moves beyond structural determinism to uncover spaces available for emancipatory action.

Bourdieu's insistence that the present period of neoliberalism demands political action, as well as a theory of politics, finds wide resonance among educators today. His message is timely, not only because the topic of social justice is fashionable but because it is essential in an out-of-control world.

## NOTES

1. Although Darts' work is not yet in publication, the dissertation exemplifies an innovative arts methodology (a/r/t/ography) for engaging students, through the production of art/visual culture, in an investigation of social issues.
2. Because Bourdieu insisted, from the early 1970s until his death in 2002, that education plays a substantial role in social reproduction, the appropriation of his theories to educational administration involves only a short conceptual leap.
3. Habermas (1971), for instance, talks of the lifeworld wherein habits, attitudes, and commonly held beliefs are second nature to people, and thus beyond con-

scious recognition. Collingwood speaks of presuppositions, by which he refers to 'underlying belief structures that are so much a part of us that they are hidden from our awareness' (Harris 2006: 55, re Collingwood's *New Leviathan* 1942: 17–48).

4. Bourdieu traces reproduction (of power) at work in smart sports; the numbers of students engaged in bridge, for instance, increases the nearer one approaches the pole of economic power. That is, wealthy children are more apt than their less well-off peers to play the game.

5. The MAI was a treaty negotiated among members of the Organization for Economy Cooperation and Development (OECD) between 1995–98 to standardise rules and regulations on financial transactions and investments.

## REFERENCES

*Alberta Journal of Educational Research: Theme Issue, Exemplars of Arts-Based Research Methodologies* (2002) 58, 3.

Bannister, K. (2003) 'Community-University Connections: Building a Foundation for Research Collaboration in British Columbia,' Working Paper Series, Clayoquot Alliance for Research, Education and Training, University of Victoria (www.clayoquotalliance.uvic.ca).

Bates, R. (1987) 'Corporate culture, schooling, and educational administration,' *Educational Administration Quarterly*, 23: 79–115.

Bickmore, K. (2006) 'Democratic social cohesion (assimilation?): representations of social conflict in Canadian public school curriculum,' *Canadian Journal of Education*, 29: 359–86.

Blackmore, J. (1999) *Troubling Women: Feminism, Leadership and Educational Change*, Buckingham: Open University Press.

Bourdieu, P. (1973) 'Cultural reproduction and social reproduction,' in R. Brown (ed.) *Knowledge, Education and Cultural Change*, London: Tavistock.

———, (1974) 'The school as a conservative force: scholastic and cultural inequalities,' in J. Eggleston (ed.) *Contemporary Research in the Sociology of Education*, London: Methuen.

———, (1977) *Outline of a Theory of Practice*, Cambridge: Cambridge University Press.

———, (1984) *Distinction: A Social Critique of the Judgement of Taste*, Cambridge: Harvard University Press.

———, (1985) 'The social space and the genesis of groups,' *Theory and Society*, 14: 723–44.

———, (1990) *In Other Words*, Cambridge: Polity Press.

———, (1993) *Sociology in Question*, London: Sage.

———, (1998a) *Acts of Resistance: Against the Tyranny of the Market*, New York: New Press.

———, (1998b) 'The essence of neoliberalism,' in *The monde diplomatique*. Online. Available HTTP: <http://mondediplo.com/1998/12/08bourdieu> (accessed 14 August 2007).

———, (ed.) (1999) *The Weight of the World: Social Suffering in Contemporary Society*, Cambridge: Polity Press.

———, and Passeron, J.-C. (1977) *Reproduction in Education, Society and Culture*, London: Sage.

———, and de Saint-Martin, M. (1974) 'Scholastic excellence and the values of the educational system,' in J. Eggleston (ed.) *Contemporary Research in the Sociology of Education*, London: Methuen.

——, and Wacquant, L. J. (1992) *An Invitation to Reflexive Sociology,* Chicago: University of Chicago Press.

Brown, K. M. (2004) 'Leadership for social justice and equity: Weaving a transformative framework and pedagogy,' *Educational Administrative Quarterly,* 40: 77–108.

Butterwick, S. (2002) 'Your story/my story/our story: Performing interpretation in participatory theatre,' *Alberta Journal of Educational Research,* 58: 240–53.

Clover, D. E. and Harris, C. E. (2005) 'Agency, isolation and the coming of new technologies: exploring "dependency" in coastal communities of Newfoundland through participatory research,' *Alberta Journal of Education Research,* 51, 1: 18–33.

Collingwood, R. G. (1942) *The New Leviathan,* Oxford: Clarendon Press.

Cook, S. and Westheimer, J. (eds) (2006) *Canadian Journal of Education,* 29, 2.

Corbett, M. (2007) *Learning to Leave: The Irony of Schooling in a Coastal Community,* Halifax: Fernwood.

Coulter, R. (1998) '"Us guys in suits are back": women, educational work and the market economy in Canada,' in A. Mackinnon, I. Elgqvist-Saltzman, and A. Prentice (eds) *Education into the 21st Century: Dangerous Terrain for Women?* London: Falmer.

CURA (2003–04) Cultural Property Community Research Collaborative Program, Community-University Research Alliance Objectives at the University of Victoria. Online. Available HTTP: <http://www.maltwood.uvic.ca/cura/old/contact_objectives.html> (accessed 14 August 2007).

Darts, D. G. (2004) 'Visual culture jam: art, pedagogy and creative resistance, unpublished dissertation, University of British Columbia.

*Educational Administration Quarterly* (2004) 40, 1.

Etmanski, C. (2007) UNSETTLED: An intersectional performance of transformative learning in higher education, unpublished dissertation, University of Victoria.

Fenwick, T., Nesbit, T. and Spencer, B. (eds) (2006) *Contexts of Adult Education: Canadian Perspectives,* Toronto: Thompson.

Foster, W. P. (2004) 'The decline of the local: a challenge to educational leadership,' *Educational Administrative Quarterly,* 40: 176–91.

Gronn, P. (2002) 'Distributed leadership as a unit of analysis,' *The Leadership Quarterly,* 13: 423–51.

Gunter, H. (2007) 'Remodelling the school workforce in England: a study in tyranny,' *Journal for Critical Education Policy Studies,* 5, 1. Online. Available HTTP: <http://www.jceps.com/> (accessed 8 January 2007).

Habermas, J. (1971) *Knowledge and Human Interests,* Boston: Beacon Press.

Hall, B. (1996) 'Participatory research,' in A. Tujnman (ed.), *International Encyclopedia of Adult Education and Training,* Oxford: Elsevier.

Harker, R. and May, S. A. (1993) 'Code and habitus: comparing the accounts of Bernstein and Bourdieu,' *British Journal of Sociology,* 14, 2: 169–78.

Harris, C. E. (1991) Administering school music in three Canadian settings: philosophy, action, and educational policy, unpublished dissertation, University of Toronto.

——, (1996) 'Technology, rationalities, and experience in school music policy: underlying myths,' *Arts Education Policy Review,* 97, 6: 23–32.

——, (2006) 'Collingwood on imagination, expression and action: advancing an aesthetically critical study of educational administration,' in E. A. Samier and R. Bates (eds) *Aesthetic Dimensions and Educational Administration and Leadership,* London: Routledge.

——. (in press) 'Exploring critical awareness through aesthetic experience: Implications for the preparation of educational leaders,' *Educational Administration and Foundations.*

Johnson, R. (1993) 'Editor's introduction,' in P. Bourdieu (ed.) *The Field of Cultural Production: Essays on Art and Literature,* Oxford: Polity Press.

Lareau, A. and Weininger, E. B. (2003) 'Cultural capital in educational research: a critical assessment,' *Theory and Society,* 32: 567–606.

Lukoševiciute-Vidziuniene, A. (1998) 'P. Bourdieu's concept of a political field,' *Sociumas,* 8. Online. Available HTTP: <http://www.sociumas.lt/Eng/Nr8/bourdieu.asp> (accessed 14 August 2007).

MacKinnon, D. (in press) 'Social justice professional development for school leaders: a modular approach,' *Journal of Educational Administration and Foundations,* 18, 1 & 2.

Marshall, C. (2004) 'Social justice challenges to educational administration: introduction to a special issue,' *Educational Administration Quarterly,* 40: 3–13.

Maynes, B. (2001) 'Educational programming for children living in poverty: possibilities and challenges,' in J. P. Portelli and P. Solomon (eds) *The Erosion of Democracy in Education: From Critique to Possibilities,* Calgary: Detslig.

Milley, P. (2006) 'Aesthetic experience as resistance to the "iron cage" of dominative administrative rationality,' in E. A. Samier and R. Bates (eds) *Aesthetic Dimensions and Educational Administration and Leadership,* London: Routledge.

Moi, T. (1991) 'Appropriating Bourdieu: feminist theory and Pierre Bourdieu's sociology of culture,' *New Literary History,* 22, 4: 1017–49.

Pence, L. (2002) 'Drawing on identity: CURA project documents, Okanagan native children's art.' Online. Available HTTP: <http://ring.uvic.ca/02feb21/cura.html> (accessed 14 August 2007).

Portelli, J. P. and Solomon, R. P. (eds) (2001) *The Erosion of Democracy in Education: From Critique to Possibilities,* Calgary: Detselig.

——, and Vibert, A .B. (2001) 'Beyond common educational standards: towards a curriculum of life,' in J. P. Portelli and R. P. Solomon (eds) *The Erosion of Democracy in Education,* Calgary: Detselig.

Reay, D. (2004) 'Gendering Bourdieu's concepts of capitals?: Emotional capital, women and social capital,' in L. Adkins and B. Skeggs (eds) *Feminism after Bourdieu,* Oxford: Blackwell.

Reynolds, C. and Young, B. (1995) *Women and Leadership in Canadian Education,* Calgary: Detselig.

Robertson, S. (2000) *A Class Act: Changing Teachers' Work, the State, and Globalisation,* New York: Falmer.

Ryan, J. (1991) 'Observing and normalizing: Foucault, discipline, and inequality in schooling,' *Journal of Educational Thought,* 25, 2: 104–19.

Samier, E. A. (ed.) (2003) *Ethical Foundations for Educational Administration: Essays in Honour of Christopher Hodgkinson,* London: Routledge-Falmer.

Shields, C. (2004) 'Dialogic leadership for social justice: overcoming pathologies of silence,' *Educational Administration Quarterly,* 40: 109–32.

Shields, C., Larocque, L. and Oberg, S. (2002) 'A dialogue about race and ethnicity in education: Struggling to understand issues in cross-cultural leadership,' *Journal of School Leadership,* 12: 116–37.

Simon, R. (1992) *Teaching Against the Grain: Texts for a Pedagogy of Possibility,* Toronto: OISE Press.

Smyth, J. (ed.) (1989) *Critical Perspectives on Educational Leadership,* New York: Falmer Press.

Smyth, J. (2001) *Critical Politics of Teachers' Work: An Australian Perspective,* New York: Peter Lang.

Stromquist, N. P. (2005) 'Comparative and international education: a journey toward equality and equity,' *Harvard Educational Review,* 75: 89–111.

Swartz, D. L. (2003) 'From critical sociology to public intellectual: Pierre Bourdieu and politics,' *Theory and Society,* 32: 791–823.

Taylor, A. (2001) *The Politics of Educational Reform in Alberta,* Toronto: University of Toronto Press.

Wallace, J. (2004) 'Educational *purposes economicus:* globalization and the reshaping of educational purpose in Canadian provinces,' *Canadian and International Education,* 33: 99–117.

––––––, (2003) 'Encountering resistance to gender equity policy in educational organization,' *Canadian Journal of Educational Administration and Policy.* Online. Available HTTP: <http://www.umanitoba.ca.ezproxy.library.uvic.ca/publications/cjeap/articles/wallace.html> (accessed 14 August 2007).

Welton, M. (2005) *Designing the Just Learning Society: A Critical Inquiry,* Leicester: NIACE.

# 7   Hermeneutic Leadership

## Hannah Arendt and the Importance of Thinking What We are Doing[1]

*Stephanie Mackler*

> Thoughtlessness—the heedless recklessness or hopeless confusion or complacent repetition of 'truths' which have become trivial and empty— seems to me among the outstanding characteristics of our time. What I propose, therefore, is very simple: it is nothing more than to think what we are doing. (Arendt 1958: 5)

More than anything else, Hannah Arendt wanted us to think. [2] However, this was not often her explicit concern: Arendt insisted that she was a political theorist, with an emphasis on the *political*. As a German Jewish refugee who experienced up close the political disasters of the twentieth century, Arendt was concerned with real people and political events. Indeed, *The Human Condition,* one of her most lauded works, is devoted to a careful discussion of the *vita activa,* which Arendt laments has lived for too long in the shadow of the *vita contemplativa.*

Given Arendt's explicitly political interests, it makes sense to turn to her political philosophy to shed light on educational leadership. For instance, we might look at her ideas related to authority, the public versus the private, or her controversial claims in 'The Crisis in Education' (1993) and 'Reflections on Little Rock' (2003) (for essays on Arendt and education, see Gordon 2001). But I believe her most important contribution to educational administration is her more purely philosophical work on thinking, namely her plea that we *stop and think.* Although many scholars deny the relationship between Arendt's more philosophical writings and her political theory, an argument can be made that her philosophy of the mind is directly related to her political aims. For instance, Steinberger writes, 'Indeed, current scholarship perhaps overestimates the sense in which *The Life of the Mind* was for Arendt a departure, a return to "philosophy," and thus underestimates the sense in which it continues and supports her central project in "political theory"' (1990: 804). Though thinking would seem to be *apolitical,* if not *anti*political (in fact, Arendt herself argues that it is), I hope to show how Arendt's notion of thinking is implicated in politics and, by extension, must therefore be implicated in educational leadership.

Before we explore Arendt's understanding of politics and thinking, I want to be clear about my Arendtian diagnosis of the problems in educational administration today. To say that thinking is good is something we can most likely agree does not, in itself, make an interesting argument. But the kind of thinking Arendt describes, and the force behind her argument, are unique.

Arendt's journalistic coverage of the trials of Nazi leader Adolf Eichmann resulted in her controversial claim that there is a 'strange interdependence of thoughtlessness and evil' (1994: 288). Thoughtlessness, she avers, is characteristic of modern bureaucracy in which 'officialese,' a language of clichés and prepackaged answers, dominates speech.[3] One need only listen to the clichéd language of contemporary news media, politics, popular culture, and, indeed, education discourse to conclude that officialese is today's predominant idiom.

Although I am not specifically concerned that educational leaders will commit evil acts of the magnitude of Eichmann's, I am concerned that they are likely to fall prey to banality of thought and speech. Banality in the sphere of educational leadership is particularly dangerous considering that educational administrators determine policy for institutions whose purpose is to teach others to think—a function arguably unique to schools. Educational leaders must be able to think deeply about the principles that underlie their actions and they must be able to think about the meaning of what they do. I realise this is a contentious claim, both because educational institutions have many other aims (citizenship, socialisation, job training) and because they so often fall short of teaching anything that looks like thinking. Nonetheless, I think it is uncontroversial to assert that educational institutions are, *or should be,* in their essence at least partly devoted to the development of the mind.

Moreover, according to Arendt, the distinctly human world (as opposed to the natural environment) can exist only when we come together to talk about it, and such talk must be as diverse as the individuals who utter it. To succumb to officialese, and the thoughtlessness that accompanies it, is to sacrifice having a world; it is to sacrifice our humanity. Herein lies the particularly ethical force of our concerns in this chapter. As Suzanne Duvall Jacobitti suggests,

> In a world in which the greatest dangers may be mindless bureaucrats, obeying orders and thoughtless conformism in society (which Arendt implied in writing of the 'banality of evil'), [thinking about the reasons or justifications for what one is being asked to do] is not an insignificant moral function. (1991: 285)

The suggestion that educational administrators are thoughtless might seem condescending or, at least, inaccurate. But Arendt distinguishes thinking from intelligence and, furthermore, she depicts a type of thinking—what I call *hermeneutic thinking*—that is concerned with *meaning,* as opposed to knowledge. (Arendt does not use the term 'hermeneutic,' though her work clearly falls within the category of hermeneutic philosophy insofar as she is concerned with interpretation, meaning, and understanding.) To understand hermeneutic, or interpretive, thinking requires also understanding Arendt's concepts of action and judgment, for Arendt's interest in thinking is tied to these two more political activities. Collectively, these three activities—*action, thinking,* and *judgment*—can be considered three modalities of what I call here *hermeneutic leadership.* It is important to note that this is my term, not Arendt's. But a concern that we make meaning and act meaningfully runs throughout Arendt's work, making the introduction of this term helpful for identifying the common thread of her ideas and positing an ideal toward which educational administrators might strive.

The remainder of this chapter offers an account of each of these three modalities and of their interrelationship. My account follows Arendt in being phenomenological—that is, I explain what it is like, existentially speaking, to do any of these things. However, I conclude with practical suggestions for the graduate education of educational leaders.

## ACTION

Arendt's conception of action is grounded in the ancient Greek idea that to be human is to be engaged in a life of civic action and that we humans actualise our freedom in the *polis*—that is, among other free human beings with whom we exchange ideas and begin projects. Arendt distinguishes action from the other two activities of the *vita activa,* labour and work, because action alone is free from necessity and utility; action, the highest of these three activities, is good in itself. We realise our humanity in action by displaying those parts of us that are most human—that is, the *who* I am that is not anything biological (we are the same at the species level), but rather, is known through the unique things I say and do among others.

This notion of action becomes more interesting when we consider the way Arendt juxtaposes action with behaviour: To behave is to adhere to the norms established by society, while to act is to do something that could not have been predicted or foreseen by society—that is, to do something that only you could have done.

The distinction between behaviour and action rests on the relationship of each to what Arendt calls 'plurality' and regards as an unquestionable good. Plurality refers to the fact that 'men, not Man, live on the earth and inhabit the world' (1958: 7). What seems like a relatively obvious phenomenon—that humans are many and live among one another—is significant for Arendt.[4] Arendt grounds our commonality in our difference: what we have in common is that we are all different. That humans live together and that no two humans can ever be the same is the condition of plurality.

Plurality is both the condition of human life and the condition through which humans achieve meaning because humans 'can experience meaningfulness only because they can talk with and make sense to each other and themselves' (Arendt 1958: 4). Without a common space in which to reveal our differing viewpoints in relation to a common object, the world (reality) cannot appear: 'Only where things can be seen in a variety of aspects without changing their identity, so that those who are gathered around them know they see sameness in utter diversity, can worldly reality truly and reliably appear' (Arendt 1958: 57). In this way, plurality is a condition that unites individuals in what Arendt calls a 'world' by emphasising what distinguishes them from one another in terms of their perspectives on that world.

Arendt argues that plurality is currently eclipsed by a ubiquitous society (see Pitkin 1998 on Arendt's concept of the social realm). Although Arendt's work was inspired by the rise of twentieth-century antiplural totalitarian regimes that produced such 'well-behaved' characters as Eichmann, Arendt argues that antiplural behaviour is not unique to totalitarian regimes. Rather, it has become a part of everyday life, with the rise of the 'mass society or mass hysteria, where we see all people suddenly behave as though they were members of one family, each multiplying and prolonging the perspective of his neighbor' (1958: 58). The social realm is not grounded in difference; rather, it requires sameness from its members, negating plurality.

Behaviour is the *sine qua non* of society, for it is the common standard to which we refer in order to guarantee likeness. Behaviour is what we today more frequently call conformity. It is ironic that our individualist Western culture distinguishes between behaviour and conformity: we want our children to behave, while we frown upon conformity. But the behaviour we love is actually just a normalised version of the conformity we disdain. Behaviour violates plurality.

Action, on the other hand, is inextricably tied to plurality: 'While all aspects of the human condition are somehow related to politics, this plurality is specifically *the* condition—not only the *conditio sine qua non,* but the *conditio per quam*—of all political life' (Arendt 1958: 7). There can be no action without plurality, and likewise, plurality is revealed through action. Arendt explains that 'action would be an unnecessary luxury, a capricious interference with the laws of behavior, if men were endlessly reproducible repetitions of the same model' (1958: 8). Action is the way in which individuals paradoxically come together to attain their common humanity through the revelation of their distinctness as individuals.

This emphasis on the uniqueness of our actions points to another quality of action: it *must* disrupt our expectations—it must be 'infinitely improbable' (Arendt 1958: 178). We notice something *as* action only if it is unexpected; anything that could have been predicted falls within the realm of behaviour. This is not to say that to act we must set out to do something radically new. In fact, Arendt claims that we cannot know in advance how our deeds will be received by others. Rather, newness, according to Arendt, is inherent in the human condition. The fact that we were born once, against all odds, and that we entered the world as a distinct somebody who was never here before, lays the groundwork for other such improbable beginnings we will initiate throughout our lives. Simply being who we are, which is to say doing and saying what occurs to us, can itself be a form of action.

Arendtian action could appear to be self-aggrandising and self-centred, but Arendt insists that it is not (see Arendt 1958: 195). But action inevitably inspires a chain of reactions, creating a 'web of relationships' among people. We humans can only have a world—can only experience reality—if we come together to talk about it. We are more isolated, Arendt argues, when we lack a public space in which to reveal our differences.

Thus far, I have discussed action in broad strokes and implied that speech is a form of action. But it is important to point out that, for Arendt, speech is an essential form—if not the fullest form—of action. Arendt insists that speech is not merely useful. If speech were intended only to communicate basic needs, grunting would suffice. Rather, 'finding the right words at the right moment, quite apart from the information or communication they may convey, is action' (1983: 26). Speech is significant in a few ways: First, speech makes actions (the things that happen in our lives) intelligible, thereby creating a shared conceptual world that links people together. Brute action would not *mean* anything to us if we could not explain it verbally. Second, speech itself is a form of action insofar as what is said can be as disruptive and unique as any physical action. In fact, given Arendt's emphasis on public discourse, it seems that she is most interested in the way our explanations act in the world. As George Kateb explains,

> [The content of political action] is talk about public matters, the public thing; it is talk about what to do (rather than . . . actual doing or executing or administering of it). But this is not to suggest that political speech is idle, academic, or gratuitous. It grows out of the need to respond to events . . . The result of talk is often to start something new, to begin a process. (1977: 156)

This latter point should make it clear why I have offered such a lengthy discussion of action. Arendt's notion of action provides an alternative, more robust notion of what political work should look like than the usual image of the boardroom meeting. If a discussion of action were enough, then we could conclude here. However, as concerned as she was with action, it can be argued that Arendt was even more concerned that we *stop and think* about what we are doing. Without thinking, action lacks meaning. As we explore the connections between thinking and action, a picture of hermeneutic leadership emerges.

## THINKING

It is important to note that Arendt is not yet another voice in the chorus of academics calling for a union of theory and practice. In fact, Arendt sharply distinguishes thinking from action, suggesting that they have nothing to do with each other. We will have to explore first what she means by thinking before we can see how, ultimately, thinking can relate to action.

To understand thinking requires that we set aside two dominant notions: first, the notion offered by cognitive science that thinking is merely a set of neural processes; second, a notion especially common in education discourse, that thinking is a problem-solving activity. While these are potential ways to define thinking, Arendt offers another.

According to Arendt, our mental faculties consist of two distinct parts. She draws upon Kant's distinction between *Verstand* and *Vernunft,* which she translates as 'intellect' and 'reason,' respectively (1978: 13).[5] The former corresponds to the activity of knowing, or cognition, and deals with what can be verified with certainty; it searches for truth. The latter, reason, corresponds with the activity of thinking and deals with what cannot be known; it searches for meaning. Arendt explains:

> Kant drew this distinction between the two mental faculties after he had discovered the 'scandal of reason,' that is, the fact that our mind is not capable of certain and verifiable knowledge regarding matters and questions that it nevertheless cannot help thinking about. (1978: 14)

While cognition (or intellect) wants to know about something, reason wants to understand what it means for that something to be at all. The aim of cognition is not to begin, but rather, to end: to know. If complete knowledge were possible, then cognition ultimately would extinguish itself. Reason, on the other hand, does not seek answers. Arendt posits that people have 'an inclination, perhaps a need' (1978: 11–12) to search for meaning that is apart from their need for knowledge. To ask about the meaning of something is not to ask what or whether something is (these are questions for cognition), but rather, '*what it means for it to be*' (1978: 57–8).[6] It is erroneous, Arendt insists, to try to conceive of meaning and knowledge in the same way because they have different aims (1978: 62). The fact that we can ask questions for which there are no definite answers is predicated on the fact that there are answerable questions. Arendt suggests that behind every question that has an answer that can appear 'there lurks the unanswerable one' that thinking pursues (1978: 62).

We search for explanations of meaning in response to things that occur in the sensory world but, factually speaking, lack meaning. Suzanne Duvall Jacobitti explains:

> To think, as Arendt defined it, involves stopping from one's activities in the world and asking 'Why am I doing this?' or 'What is the meaning of what we are doing?' . . . [Thinking] arises out of the most mundane everyday occurrences, especially things one has done oneself. (1991: 285)

To relate to our earlier discussion, we can say that the quest for meaning responds to action because action is unexpected and thus cannot already have been understood. To make meaning requires abstraction, which uses concepts and ideas, ordered into a story, to explain the significance of things apart from the factual details. The fact that we can imagine in our minds things that actually did appear means we can also imagine general concepts, which cannot appear: 'Thinking always "generalizes," squeezes out of many particulars—which, thanks to the de-sensing process, it can pack together for swift manipulation—whatever meaning may inhere' (Arendt 1978: 199).

Because concepts cannot appear (in the same way that a tree can), thinking 'never produces unequivocal results' (Arendt 1954: 308). As such, thinking is justified on its own terms: we think about meaning for its own sake. The mind creates an interpretation, but that interpretation cannot be certain, and thus it thinks of yet another: 'The quest for meaning, which relentlessly dissolves and examines anew all accepted doctrines and rules, can at every moment turn against itself, as it were, produce a reversal of the old values, and declare these as "new values"', (Arendt 2003: 177). In this way, thinking, like action, is an initiating activity.

However, unlike action, thinking is *apolitical,* which is to say that it is private and detached from the world we share with others. When we think, Arendt says, we may look paralysed to the outside world, though there is no scarcity of movement in the mind (1978: 173). Of course, she does not mean that we literally stop moving our bodies while we think. Rather, the idea of paralysis is a metaphor for the way our public selves are frozen while our private minds are activated. It is important to note, particularly for our purposes, that for Arendt, 'private' thinking remains connected to the world because what we think about comes *from* the world.[7] Still, if there are degrees of publicity and privacy, then thinking can be said to be a particularly private event.

The opposite is also true: just as the body appears inactive while the mind is active, the mind is inactive while the body is active. Arendt argues that we have a 'sixth sense,' common sense (*sensus communis*), that provides answers, quick rules and principles for our everyday lives. Thinking does not belong among our quotidian activities: 'Absence of thought is indeed a powerful factor in human affairs . . . [T]he very urgency . . . of human affairs demands provisional judgments, the reliance on custom and habit' (1978: 71).

Furthermore, thinking challenges common sense because it examines what in 'the daily business of living' must remain unexamined (Arendt 1978: 176). The questions raised by thinking cannot be answered, nor are they immediately 'useful' to common sense; likewise, thinking is uninterested in common sense except insofar as it can dismantle it and thereby rob it of its social function: '[Thinking] does not confirm but rather dissolves accepted rules of conduct' (Arendt 1978: 192). This is why, as I said above, Arendt separates politics from thinking. It is important to understand this antagonism between thinking and politics so that we do not erroneously assume that there is a cause-effect relationship between the two or that one can think while one acts. Thinking is not political, according to Arendt. Just as we had to *stop and think* about meaning, we must also *stop thinking* to take a stand on the meaning of that about which we think.

But to say that thinking and action are separate is not to say that they are unrelated. Rather, there is a dialectic between the everyday world (the polis) and thinking. An event—*action*—that takes place in our shared world but is noticeable for its nonaccordance with ordinary understanding requires us to think. And, yet, what we think will disrupt the ordinary understanding of the world in which the action took place. Educational leaders move within this dialectic: they must be able to engage in action *and* reflect on the meaning of action (their own and that of others—in the school, boardroom, in domestic or international affairs). Thinking is 'political by implication' (Arendt 2003: 188). It is judgment that facilitates the dialectic, making thinking political and thus completing the picture of hermeneutic leadership.

## JUDGMENT

Although thinking is private, the products of thinking—what Arendt calls 'thought-things'—can be shared. In fact, Arendt suggests that we have an urge to translate our private thoughts into the public world (1978: 98). Through speech and writing, thinking's products (thoughts), which are temporary answers to the question, "Why?," can become part of the realm of action. Judging enables thinking to become public and therefore political. As George Kateb writes, '[Arendt] says the thinker . . . may trigger in others this politically usable version of thinking, the faculty of judging . . . Judging is [a] mode by which automatism is broken; it is "the most political of man's abilities"' (1977: 172).

As Arendt scholars are quick to point out, she never fully developed her work on judgment. The first two sections of her work on the mind (published posthumously as *Life of the Mind*) had been written, but the final section on judgment had only its section heading in place at the time of her death. Thus, one must cobble together lectures and written works to understand her concept of judgment. Arendt scholars will note that there is some debate about the extent to which judgment can be considered political (see Beiner 1982; Bernstein 1986; Biskowski 1993). Moreover, Benhabib (1988) points out that Arendt uses judgment in three different ways, making it difficult to determine one definition of Arendtian judgment.

According to Arendt, a judge is a storyteller who reflects upon past events and explains their meaning in terms beyond a literal factual description. The judge tells why things happened as they did, suggesting the implications of events in the larger human drama of which they are a part. Like thinking, judgment is concerned with meaning. But whereas thinking can continuously ask questions about meaning, judging is responsible to the events that, first, inspired thinking but, second, require a response.

This notion of judgment is fairly uninteresting until we contrast it with our ordinary notion of judgment as the application of general rules to particular cases. For instance, I might judge a particular case of murder in self-defense to be morally acceptable based upon my belief in a preformed, universal maxim that murder in the case of self-defense, though it ideally should be avoided, is acceptable. However, Arendt, drawing upon Kant's notion of aesthetic judgment, offers a unique view of judging. Judging, she argues, does not apply general rules to particulars, but rather, derives rules from particulars.

When we endeavor to make sense of something we ask, 'What is the meaning of X happening?' That is, we do not ask about the meaning of any happening, but of a particular happening. If a presupposed rule could suffice, then there would no need to seek an interpretation in the first place. Once the question of meaning has been asked, we search for a conceptual explanation of the event that compelled our search. Or, in other terms, we derive a universal rule from a particular event. Arendt writes,

> The chief difficulty in judgment is that it is 'the faculty of thinking the particular' but to *think* means to generalize, hence it is the faculty of mysteriously combining the particular and the general. This is relatively easy if the general is given—as a rule, a principle, a law—so that the judgment merely subsumes the particular under it. The difficulty becomes great 'if only the particular be given for which the general has to be found.' For the standard cannot be borrowed from experience and cannot be derived from outside. I cannot judge one particular by another particular. (1978: 271)

Although judging includes thinking (thinking and judging can be understood as two points along a spectrum), judgment must tie abstract thinking to worldly life. In judging, the urgency of everyday life demands an interpretation of an event to help those who have been affected by that event

and will need the explanation in order to carry on in light of it. As Peter
Steinberger explains,

> Just as the aim of thought in general is to create structures of meaning,
> so the aim of judgment is to establish for any society a common concep-
> tual apparatus on the basis of which social actors can come to share the
> kinds of understandings and discriminations that allow for intelligent
> collective action. (1990: 813)

Judgment's connection to others makes all the more sense, Arendt explains,
considering that the standards of judging are not abstract ideals, but rather,
common sense (*sensus communis*). Because he bases judgment on taste,
which is a subjective faculty shared among people, Kant requires that the
products of judging be agreeable to others. The perspectives of others matter not only after thinking (when we produce a 'thought-thing'), but also, in
the process of thinking itself. A judgment is made in relation both to already
known, general interpretations *and* to the shocking as yet uninterpreted
incident requiring judgment. In judging, we think with an 'enlarged mentality': we interpret the meaning of *this* event through consideration of others'
perspectives on past events (or current explanations of this event that we
have not yet accepted) (Arendt 1978: 257–8). The result of 'going visiting'
with others' standpoints is that we become more aware of our own perspectives. We test commonly accepted understandings against actual experience
in search of an adequate interpretation (Arendt 1978: 257–8).

With an understanding of judgment on its own, we can now consider how
it relates to action: it is a means of response to action and can become a form
of action itself. The unexpectedness of a distinct person's action creates a
situation that is not immediately intelligible, thereby demanding judgment
to explain it: 'Thinking [about meaning] then arises out of the disintegration
of reality and the resulting *dis*unity of man and world, from which springs
the need for another world, more harmonious and more meaningful' (Arendt
1978: 153). It is important to emphasise that there would be no need to
come to terms with events of the past if they could have been predicted and
if they had not changed the course of human affairs. In such cases, the interpretations already at our disposal are revealed to be insufficient, requiring
us to create a new interpretation. In this way, the ability to judge provides a
kind of intellectual reconciliation, or safety net, against the unpredictability
of human action so that actors can act and the world can cope.

At the same time, judgment, expressed in speech, can be a form of action:
what is said is as new as the action that inspired it and can thereby help others form judgments. In this way, judgment is a form of political discourse.
Biskowski explains,

> By making judgments, we take a stand with respect to what we have seen,
> heard, and reflected upon. This quality of judgments—the necessity of

taking a stand—seems indispensable not only to historians or storytellers, but also to agents participating in democratic politics. (1993: 873)

My interpretation, which is my judgment, can become others' interpretations, or can help others arrive at an interpretation (see Smith 2001 for a discussion of Arendtian political judgment).

It is helpful, then, to think of the educational leader as a judge, or storyteller—one who makes sense of world events. The impulse for judgment to become action provides the link between continuous thinking and thoughtless action. In facilitating this connection, judgment ensures that action is informed by thinking, not banality. Of course, when judgments result in concrete things, like policy, there is a risk of banality.[8] But, administrators must rely on accepted interpretations if they are to implement policies. Still, policies arrived at through thinking are more likely to be sound than those arrived at through the groupthink that is so prevalent today. Hermeneutic leadership consists of moving among thinking, judgment, and action to ensure that the most meaningful decisions possible are made—to ensure that we think what we are doing.

## IMPLICATIONS FOR THE PREPARATION OF EDUCATIONAL LEADERS

The primary purpose of this discussion is to provide an Arendtian account of the three interrelated modalities of what I am calling hermeneutic leadership. But it is helpful also to consider some 'practical' implications of Arendt's thought.[9] Above all, I propose that future education leaders receive an education in hermeneutic thinking. Although graduate programs teach what we colloquially call thinking, they tend to emphasise problem solving; such assignments have more to do with cognition than reason—with knowledge rather than meaning. Moreover, theories (of management, behaviour, educational policy) are often presented as something to apply, but Arendt's point is that Eichmann succumbed to the impulse to apply pregiven rules without awareness of the particularities of the situation. Thinking is something other than this.

To cultivate the habits of mind for hermeneutic thinking, students must have opportunities for the kind of private reflection on meaning that Arendt describes. As Eduardo Duarte cogently argues, the current trend for group projects and 'teamwork' (a banal term in the management lexicon) threatens the possibility for thinking: 'Because cooperative learning is structurally incompatible with the event of *withdrawal* from the company of others, upon which thinking is based, the result is the eclipse of thinking . . . cooperative learning models may be creating conditions of "nonthinking"' (2001: 202). Rather, assignments that inspire students to *stop and think* about meaning would cultivate the reflective capacities necessary for hermeneutic leadership.

To inspire such thinking requires engaging with exemplary hermeneutic texts that challenge students' interpretive views and develop their sensitivity to meaning. The interpretations others offer can attune students to the importance of meaning, provide models of good meaning-making, and serve as perspectives with which students visit in making judgments (see Smith 2001 for more detail). This activity is impractical insofar as it does not entail simulations of policy situations or direct application of theories, but again I follow Duarte who challenges: 'Should it not be that "practicality" is out of order within that context where "thinking" *must* be taught?' (2001: 219).

This latter point leads to my final suggestion that to teach hermeneutic thinking requires engagement with the arts and humanities, the disciplines most explicitly concerned with meaning (on Arendtian judgement and policy (see Bleiman, Hammer and Park 1999). Too often, graduate education resembles technical instruction. Can there not be a place for the liberal arts in the graduate education of educational leaders?

## CONCLUSION

These suggestions are but a modest attempt to elucidate possible implications of Arendt's ideas for the preparation of a new generation of educational leaders; indeed, they address explicitly only one of our three modalities (thinking)—the one that seems most pressing at this time. Regrettably, I have neither the space nor the expertise to offer more practical advice (on hermeneutic education see Mackler 2004; 2007; forthcoming a; forthcoming b). Nonetheless, I hope it is clear by now that Arendt would not want us to conclude with a 'to do' list, for action cannot be prescribed, and thinking does not leave us with quick and easy answers. If we agree that how we interpret bears upon how we act, then the very act of understanding differently can broaden the possibilities for administration and leadership.

Moreover, as I implied in the introduction, my aim is to offer an ethical picture of leadership. Education leaders possess immense ethical responsibility, because they guide the curriculum, institutions, and people that prepare future citizens, politicians, teachers, business leaders, mothers, and fathers. Our institutions of education do not need technocrats fluent in officialese at the helm. Rather, they need people who can think well and speak well about what has happened and about what will happen—about the meaning of what they have done and aim to do. They need people who are willing to ask unanswerable questions and to come up with the best possible answers for the unpredictable and idiosyncratic people they serve. This alone could make all the difference in the world.

## NOTES

1. I owe many thanks to Kerri Timmerman, my research assistant, and to Anne Peters, for making final formatting edits. Thanks also to Mordechai Gordon for his support of my work, and to Eduardo Duarte for helping me gain clarity

on the ideas developed here. Finally, I am grateful to Eugénie Samier for her patience with my queries and for inviting me—and Arendt—to be a part of this volume.

2. I owe many thanks to Kerri Timmerman, my research assistant, and to Anne Peters, for making final formatting edits. Thanks also to Mordechai Gordon for his support of my work, and to Eduardo Duarte for helping me gain clarity on the ideas developed here. Finally, I am grateful to Eugénie Samier for her patience with my queries and for inviting me—and Arendt—to be a part of this volume.

3. Arendt asserts that she is only drawing a 'lesson' from the events and not positing a thesis. Nonetheless, her work on Eichmann and her subsequent works reflect an interest in thinking and, ultimately, judgment as an attempt to systematically explain this phenomenon. Unfortunately, I do not have the space here to explain further this premise of my argument (see *Eichmann in Jerusalem* 1994).

4. Arendt's use of the word 'plurality' resembles our current use of the buzzword 'diversity.' An important distinction between plurality and diversity, however, is that the latter tends to refer to group identity. We say a classroom has diversity, not because each and every student is inherently distinct (plurality), but because it has *X* number of black students and *X* number of Latinos, and so on. We tend to lack appreciation for plurality, instead categorizing people according to the extent to which they adhere to cultural or biological categories.

5. Arendt acknowledges that *Verstand* is usually translated as 'understanding' but states that she believes this to be a mistranslation.

6. This is not to say that the search for unanswerable questions is disconnected from the search for answerable ones, such as the search for answers in scientific research. Arendt suggests that scientific findings could not result if it were not for this initial search for meaning.

7. Arendt describes the dialogical character of thinking, which she says is in some ways *more plural* than the social world. See especially: 'The two-in-one' in *The Life of the Mind*.

8. The creation of policy probably falls into Arendt's category of 'work' rather than action. For more on these distinctions, see *The Human Condition*.

9. Arendt insists that education and politics should be separate, but her claims are specifically related to K–12 education. It is unclear whether she would have approved of graduate education for political actors.

## REFERENCES

Arendt, H. (1954) 'Understanding and politics (the difficulties of understanding),' in J. Kohn (ed.) *Arendt: Essays in Understanding 1930–1954*, New York: Harcourt Brace & Company.

———, (1958) *The Human Condition*, Chicago: University of Chicago Press.

———, (1978) *The Life of the Mind*, San Diego: Harcourt Brace & Company.

———, (1982) *Lectures on Kant's Political Philosophy*, Chicago: University of Chicago Press.

———, (1983) *Men in Dark Times*, New York: Harcourt Brace & Company.

———, (1993)'The crisis in education,' in *Between Past and Future: Six Exercises in Political Thought*, Harmondsworth: Penguin Classics.

———, (1994) *Eichmann in Jerusalem: A Report on the Banality of Evil*, New York: Penguin Books.

———, (2003) 'Reflections on Little Rock,' in J. Kohn (ed.) *Responsibility and Judgment*, New York: Schocken Books.

——, (2003) 'Thinking and moral considerations,' in J. Kohn (ed.) *Responsibility and Judgment,* New York: Schocken Books.

Beiner, R. (1982) 'Hannah Arendt on judging,' in H. Arendt, *Lectures on Kant's Political Philosophy,* Chicago: University of Chicago Press.

Benhabib, S. (1988) 'Judgment and the moral foundations of politics in Arendt's Thought,' *Political Theory,* 16: 29–51.

Bernstein, R. (1986) 'Judging: the actor and the spectator,' in R. Bernstein (ed.) *Philosophical Profiles,* Philadelphia: University of Pennsylvania Press.

Biskowski, L. J. (1993) 'Practical foundations for political judgment: Arendt on action and world,' *Journal of Politics,* 55: 867–87.

Bleiman, J., Hammer, D. and Park, K. (1999) 'Between positivism and postmodernism: Hannah Arendt on the formation of policy judgments,' *Policy Studies Review,* 16,1: 148–82.

Duarte, E. (2001) 'The eclipse of thinking: an Arendtian critique of cooperative learning,' in M. Gordon (ed.) *Arendt and Education,* Boulder: Westview Press.

Gordon, M. (ed.) (2001) *Arendt and Education.* Boulder: Westview Press.

Jacobitti, S. D. (1991) 'The public, the private, the moral: Hannah Arendt and political morality,' *International Political Science Review,* 12: 281–93.

Kant, I. (1951) *Critique of Judgment,* New York: Hafner Press.

Kateb, G. (1977) 'Freedom and worldliness and the thought of Hannah Arendt,' *Political Theory,* 5: 141–82.

Mackler. S. (2004) 'Natality seduced: Lyotard's differend and the birth of the improbable,' in D. Beckett (ed.) *Philosophy of Education 2003,* Urbana: Philosophy of Education Society.

——, (2007) 'Educating for meaning in an era of banality,' in B. Stengel (ed.) *Philosophy of Education 2007,* Urbana: Philosophy of Education Society.

——, (forthcoming a) 'Reviving the liberal arts: learning for meaning's sake,' *Policy Futures in Education,* 6, 3.

——, (forthcoming b) Toward the Hermeneutic University: Learning for Meaning's Sake, Rottterdam: Sense.

Pitkin, H. F. (1998) *The Attack of the Blob: Hannah Arendt's Concept of the Social,* Chicago: University of Chicago Press.

Smith, S. (2001) 'Education for judgment: an Arendtian oxymoron,' in M. Gordon (ed.) *Arendt and Education,* Boulder: Westview Press.

Steinberger, P. J. (1990) 'Hannah Arendt on judgment,' *American Journal of Political Science,* 34: 803–21.

Villa, D. R. (1992) 'Beyond good and evil: Arendt, Nietzsche, and the aestheticization of political action,' *Political Theory,* 20: 274–308.

Young-Bruehl, E. (1982) 'Reflections on Hannah Arendt's *The Life of the Mind,*' *Political Theory,* 10: 277–305.

# 8 Democratic Ideals, Ethics, Foucault, and the Hegemony of Modern Thought in American Education

## A Critical Enquiry

*Charles J. Fazzaro*

[T]he freedom of the subject and its relationship to others is the very stuff [*matière*] of ethics.

Michel Foucault

The American experiment in government was intended to free individuals from the tyranny of social class structure. The United States was to be a country of opportunity where hard work and talent, not social class, would ultimately determine successes and failures. To the contrary, Scott and Leonhardt report that ' . . . fewer families moved from one quintile, or fifth, of the income ladder to another during the 1980s than the 1970s and still fewer in the 1990s than in the 1980s' (2005: 12). Ironically, after over 216 years since the ratification of the U.S. Constitution with the attached Bill of Rights, which explicitly and implicitly guaranteed equal opportunity, social mobility in the United States is lower now than in Britain, France, Canada, and some Scandinavian countries (Scott and Leonhardt 2005: 14). What went wrong?

To secure the rights guaranteed by the Constitution, some of the Founders, in particular Thomas Jefferson, believed that it would be only through an educated citizenry that fundamental democratic ideals could eventually be realised. In Jefferson's words, 'If a nation expects to be ignorant and free in a state of civilization, it expects what never was and never will be' (1816). In short, the ideal ethical character of each citizen would be to act politically to ensure the fulfilment of the full range of guaranteed fundamental rights to all citizens, not merely for their own self-interest.

Heeding Jefferson's call for an educated citizenry, all states eventually developed a system of state sponsored and locally administered free public schools. The primary purpose of these was to educate children to a level appropriate to assume the fundamental political office of *citizen*. Education legal historian Newton Edwards succinctly summarises why American public education is so important to government: 'Public education is not merely a function of government; it is *of* government [emphasis added]' (1955: 23). This view of American public schools has extended into the twenty-first century. In 2003, Justice Sandra Day O'Connor, delivering the opinion for the

United States Supreme Court upholding the law school admissions standards of the University of Michigan, quoting from the landmark 1954 decision in *Brown v. Board of Education,* stated that, 'This Court has long recognized that "education . . . is the very foundation of good citizenship"' (*Grutter v. Bollinger, et al.* 2003).

So how can the failure to achieve such basic democratic rights as access and equity, guaranteed in the Founding documents, be explained in light of a nearly 150 year history of universal, compulsory education intended to prepare children to fulfil these rights? This critical enquiry provides a possible explanation.[1] The enquiry unfolds from: (1) a consideration of how Michel Foucault's views of ethics are essential relative to fulfilling the American democratic ideals; (2) an explication of a model for viewing how the knowledge about humans became infected with science; (3) a brief overview of Foucault's work relative to subjectification and its implications for ethics and governing; and (4) a discussion of how subjectification became hegemonic in the American society.

## FOUCAULT AND ETHICS

Ethics and morals are often interchanged in discussions of human beings' behaviour towards one another and one's behaviours relative to some standard of conduct. In this regard, morals are subjective because moral rules have no objective, transcendent grounding. For example, Kant's views of duty and obligation qualify as moral principles. Ethics, on the other hand, can be considered to be objective in that they relate to an assumed transcendent set of rules. For example, Aristotle's approach to practical reasoning was based on virtues. For Foucault, ethics involves 'the freedom of the subject in relation to others' (1984: 300). For Americans, the Constitution serves as a transcendent set of rules. These rules, in particular here, the Bill of Rights, are about what the government *ought not* to do to an individual citizen. But the relationship between the government and the individual is circular, given the opening words of the Constitution, 'We the People of the United States, in order to form a more perfect Union, establish justice . . . and secure the Blessings of Liberty to ourselves and our Posterity.' Significant here for Foucault's views of ethics and the American form of governance is the collective pronoun 'We.' It signifies that as a group the 'We' (the People) would govern itself, leaving no division between a sovereign and the population. In short, the 'We' would be its own sovereign. In terms of Foucault's ethics, this relationship of one-to-the-other as both citizen and sovereign demands that citizens must be responsible for not only themselves as individuals, but all other citizens as well. Consequently, in the ideal philosophical sense Americans ought not to act politically as the People to promulgate, maintain, and enforce policies that would effectively discriminate one citizen from another in the distribution of fundamental rights. Despite the public schools purpose relative to citizenship, the equitable distribution of rights has not been the case for almost the entire history of the United States. The widely recognised and documented long and difficult struggle of women and African Americans is evidence enough. Less well understood is how the institution of public education has functioned not in the service of promoting a democratic ethic of equality of opportunity, but as a mechanism of social stratification through the technologies that divide, categorise, and rank. The contradiction between the Jeffersonian belief that the public schools would educate citizens consistent with a democratic ethic and their eventual transformation into mechanisms of discipline might best be understood within the contexts of Western intellectual history.

## THE ENLIGHTENMENT AND KNOWLEDGE

The American experiment in government was born near the end of the eighteenth century, as the Enlightenment was coming to a close. Beginning in the middle of the seventeenth century, the Enlightenment was characterised by dramatic changes in the two major discourses that have existed from the dawn of recorded human history—the discourse of *humanity* and the discourse of *reality* (the discourse constituting the laws governing the order of the world). The discourse of humanity is manifold. Included among these often intertwined discourses are those that constitute a society's social, economic, political, and legal structures along with cultural aspects such as religion. Like the discourses of humanity, the discourse of reality changed periodically throughout history. Foucault, in his archaeological search for disruptions in the '*episteme*' of Western culture, recognised 'two great discontinuities.' 'The first inaugurates the Classical age (roughly half-way through the seventeenth century) and the second, at the beginning of the nineteenth century, marks the beginning of the modern age (1973: xxii–iii).' The later *episteme* will be referred to here as 'modern thought'[2], or, more specifically, *science,* including the categories of thought passing themselves off as science, such as the 'social sciences.' Modern Thought claims objectivity in that it justifies its conclusions on the existence of a transcendent discourse, a *metadiscourse*. Unlike the discourse of reality, the discourses of humanity might claim either objectivity or subjectivity depending on the issue in question. Many religions, for example, credit a supernatural transcendent being for all occurrences.

During the Enlightenment, the discourse of humanity, nourished by the works of the likes of Jean Jacques Rousseau, Thomas Paine, and John Locke, would serve as a justification to liberate the human from the repressive tyranny of the sovereign legitimated by birthright and/or reference to a divine will. As the Enlightenment was drawing to a close, Immanuel Kant was fashioning from the spoils of more than 150 years of intellectual warfare between rationalism and empiricism the intellectual scaffolding for a new reality discourse (modern thought) that the modern human, only recently liberated from the shackles of conformity imposed by tyrannical sovereigns and religious absolutists, would use to explain the world and all of its complexities—ultimately truth itself. These two discourses, humanity and reality, each with its unique criteria of distinction—just/unjust for humanity and both true/false and efficiency/inefficiency for reality—would each compete for dominance over the other (Lyotard 1984). As we shall see later, early in the nineteenth century the discourse of reality, often disguised in the social sciences as the discourse of humanity, would be used to reconstruct the human into a more docile, governable entity.

## FOUCAULT, ETHICS AND GOVERNMENTALITY

In brief, Foucault was concerned with the ways that humans develop knowledge about themselves. Through his unique analytic approach, he wrote critical histories of the 'sciences' of medicine, psychiatry, penology, economics, language, and biology. The critical aspect of his histories is that he did not accept the 'knowledge' that these new sciences claimed to have uncovered, but analysed these so called 'social sciences' as ' . . . very specific "truth games" related to specific techniques [*technologies*] that human beings use to understand themselves' (1982a: 224–225). Foucault found four major types of these technologies. The first two are those we use in the sciences and linguistics. The third type he refers to as 'technologies of domination,' 'which determine the conduct of individuals and submit them to certain ends or dominations, and [objectivize] the subject' (1982a: 225). The fourth type are the 'technologies of the self,' 'which permit individuals to effect by their own means, or with the help of others, a certain number of operations on their own bodies and souls, thoughts, conduct, and ways of being, so as to transform themselves in order to attain a certain state of happiness, purity, wisdom, perfection, or immortality' (1982a: 225). The encounter between the technologies of domination of others and the technologies of the self Foucault called 'governmentality.' For Foucault, 'governmentality makes it possible to bring out the freedom of the subject and its relationship to others—which constitutes the very stuff [*matière*] of ethics' (1984: 300).

By the end of the sixteenth century the administration of the state through the 'art of governance' associated with the ancient notion of governing the family was being replaced by the 'science of government,' as the notion of *population* replaced that of *family.* This new science of the state was 'statistics.'

> It was through the development of the science of government that the notion of economy came to be recentered on to that different plane of reality which we characterize today as the 'economic,' and it was also through this science that it became possible to identify problems specific to the population; but conversely we can say as well that is was thanks to

the perception of the specific problems of population, and thanks to the isolation of the areas of reality that we call the economy, that the problem of government finally came to be thought, reflected and calculated outside of the judicial framework of sovereignty. And that 'statistics' which, in mercantilist tradition, only ever worked within and for the benefit of a monarchial administration that functioned according to the form of sovereignty, now becomes the major technical factor, or one of the major technical factors, of this new technology. (Foucault 1978: 99)

Foucault argued that because Descartes made possible the belief that direct evidence was enough to establish *truth* he effectively cut scientific rationality loose from ethics. 'Before Descartes, one could not be impure, immoral, and know the truth. . . . After Descartes, we have a nonascetic subject of knowledge. This change makes possible the institutionalization of modern science' (1983: 279). By the beginning of the eighteenth century, the growth of science, with its assumption of objectivity, would have a profound effect on how institutional practices would be developed in the service of governance. For the United States, at least, this would have significant implications for the ethics necessary for its citizen ('We the People') government to fulfil Constitutional guarantees of liberty.

## Establishing and Maintaining Socioeconomic Structures

Through his historical analytics, Foucault (1977) was able to show that in modern Western societies, socioeconomic structures are forged and maintained through a transparent discursive carceral network of disciplinary technologies that transform the body into a productive force. This three-stage transformation began in mediaeval times. The first stage extended into the early seventeenth century and emphasised technologies that exercised control over the body through exclusion, later coupled with confinement. The second stage generally paralleled the Enlightenment. While continuing practices of exclusion through confinement, institutions set about correcting the morals of transgressors through a pastoral power exercised through work, training, and education. Those isolated and confined, including prisoners, the insane, those in the military, and students in schools, would become, from the early nineteenth century until the present, subjects for study and analyses, which would constitute the knowledge of the modern social science.

Significant here is that of the three stages, only the last is not dependent exclusively on the discursive nature of architecture (e.g., prisons, asylums, the factory floor, hospitals, military barracks, and schools). The technologies of control legitimated through the modern social sciences are predominantly linguistically discursive. As such they are constructed and communicated through the exclusive language of social science professionals, including educators, who closely supervise and control what counts as knowledge about humans. These 'professionals' acquired their power during the late nine-teenth century when the notions and assumptions of scientific objectivity were being applied to business, manufacturing, and, in the case at hand, the public schools. This insertion of scientific rationality into the discourse of humanity came about despite the then dim voice of critics such as Friedrich Nietzsche who warned of the subjective nature of the language of science.

> Scientists do no better when they say 'force moves, force causes' and such like—all our science, in spite of its coolness and freedom from emotion, still stands exposed to the seduction of language and has rid itself of the changelings foisted upon it, the 'subjects' (the atom is, for example, just such a changeling, likewise the Kantian 'thing-in-itself'). (Nietzsche 1994: 28)

It is at this stage in modern history that the discourse of reality becomes intertwined with and overpowers that of humanity. Science in all of its forms becomes a technology of domination and the control of the body as a pro-ductive force becomes a political economy. Given that in its most elementary form, *politics* is the allocation of values and resources in a society, then the character of socioeconomic structures is an expression of a dominant socio-economic ideology maintained through the political control of discourse. Political pressure both inside and outside of the institution of public educa-tion came to bear on school administrators to be more 'efficient.' Having suc-cumbed to this pressure, the structures and technologies of schooling would soon resemble those of factories (Callahan 1962). But long before this trans-formation, two assumptions about the nature of things would significantly change the character of institutional practices. Both would ultimately serve to transform the human into a docile subject. The first of these assumptions is that human characteristics, both physical (what can be seen) and mental (what cannot be seen directly but exist only as constructs) are 'normally' dis-tributed within any particular population. The second is that human behav-iours, once made quantifiable, can be subject to the principles of accounting.

## Normality

How the notion of *normal* acquired its transcendent quality in the modern social sciences can be marked by the work of Adolphe Quetelet (1796–1874). His work, when linked to that of Francis Galton, James Clerk Max-well, Charles Sanders Peirce, and Karl Pearson, constitutes a genealogy of discursive elements that presently operate as modern technologies of sub-jectification. When these are exercised through institutional practices they ultimately contribute to human subjugation. The notion of 'normal' as it applies to human populations would not have come about without it's first having been linked to mathematical analysis. Although in 1662 John Graunt was reported to have used descriptive mathematics to analyse data about purely physical human attributes, scientific principles were not yet accepted widely enough to be applied widely to humans. It would take nearly 200 years before such applications would be accepted as 'fact.' In the early part of the nineteenth century, Quetelet would use descriptive mathematics to make judgements about nonphysical (unseen) attributes from purely observable (seen) physical characteristics.

Quetelet was an astronomer by profession, but gained his fame by applying mathematical calculation in the form of the 'astronomical error law' to a wide variety of physical data about humans. The error law was represented in the now familiar bell-shaped curve, which was later standardised by the famous statistician Karl Pearson as the 'Normal curve' (Porter 1986: 311–12). Quetelet used the term 'average man' (*l'homme moyen*), not 'normal,' in his depiction of physical measurements such as chest size, weight, and heights. Quetelet made a significant contribution to the evolving social science by using inference while interpreting statistical data. In the early 1840s he was commissioned to examine data representing the heights of 100,000 conscripts into the French army. When he plotted the data he discovered a bimodal curve instead of the almost perfect bell-shaped curve that the error law demanded. To the left of the larger mode was a smaller mode representing the frequency of those conscripts that would be deemed too short for military service. Quetelet concluded that what caused the smaller mode was not an irregularity in the continuous range of heights, but something that caused the conscripts near enough to the exclusion height to corrupt the measurement. That is, they cheated, thus, he made a judgment about something he could not see directly, *morals*. Later, Quetelet's analysis was shown to be inaccurate because his bimodal curve did not represent a single homogeneous population but, in fact, two somewhat distinct populations, one on average shorter than the other. Quetelet's intellectual leap across the metaphysical abyss separating science and philosophy would prove to be immensely useful to human engineering generally and education in particular (Fazzaro 1998).

The assumption of normality is fundamental to the most powerful statistical techniques. Even though many phenomena in such areas as biology, economics, psychology, and education are not exactly normally distributed they are described by the normal curve of distribution. The notion of normality became essential in the development of technologies of classification in education, in particular, for Alfred Binet and his claim to be able to measure human intelligence. When reported as a numerical quotient the values were used to justify division, separation, and hierarchal stratification of students for educational purposes (Fazzaro 1998: 16).

## Accounting

Besides the institutionalising of the notion of 'normal' within the social sciences, the introduction of accounting principles into educational practices would make it much easier to transform schools to institutions of discipline that would more firmly solidify social order. Principles of accounting were first introduced into American education at West Point in 1817 by Sylvannus Thayer. As superintendent, Thayer began assigning numerical values to various aspects of cadet training and education. He did this in order to correct what he thought were 'serious discrepancies' in the cadet corps (Hoskins and Macve 1988: 46). This form of accounting in education would be common practice before the end of the nineteenth century and fully exploited in the twentieth century. The data necessary for these elaborate accounting systems in education would come from instruments that evaluated just about everything a student did or thought. For example, Oscar Buros' first bibliography of testing, published in 1934, was only forty-four pages. By 1938, the now familiar *Mental Measurement Yearbook* (MMY) had more than 400 pages, listing about 4,000 tests (Haney 1981:1029). The 1995 edition has 1,259 pages, and far too many tests to easily count.

## The Confluence of the Discourses of Normality and Accounting

As the discourse of normality rapidly spread within the social sciences it would find utility in many institutions, in particular, business and manufacturing. The work of Frederic Winslow Taylor and his approach to applying scientific rationality and statistical analyses to maximize efficiency in manufacturing processes would quickly be applied to the public schools (Callahan 1962). In the early twentieth century, school administrators found Taylor's work useful in forging a model for both structuring and managing educational programmes within the ubiquitous factory-like 'Quincy box' schools common in virtually every community. By the middle of the twentieth century school administration would find even greater use for statistical analyses. As achievement testing gained momentum within both state and federal politics, statistical analysis would be used to measure the quality of individual schools. By the 1990s the notion that schools could be understood best by scientific analysis is no more evident than in the official policies of the US Department of Education in its attempts to evaluate the effects of the 2002 No Child Left Behind Act, designed to significantly reduce if not completely eliminate the achievement gaps between schools. According to the NCLB *Research Primer,* 'scientifically-based research is rigorous, systematic, objective, empirical, peer reviewed and relies on multiple measurements and observations, preferably through experimental or quasi-experimental methods' (Lauer 2006).

Regardless of its use, the notion of 'normal' carries the mark of authority both for the speaker and the transcendent quality ascribed to it because of its connection to mathematics and science. Its power to divide one from another is significant for both those characterised as 'normal' on some criterion and those characterised as somewhat 'less than normal.' When the less-than-normal label is applied to children who cannot enter into the discourse of the 'professionals' who use these dividing and labelling technologies, it is little different than branding cattle. The child will forever be publicly known to have a 'deficiency,' often no more than a discursive invention of well-intended but misguided 'professionals' claiming to be acting in the best interest of the child. This is not to say that all differences in human behaviours are mere social constructions. For example, anorexia, schizophrenia, and paranoia have known physical, material causes directly observable through clinical tests. On the other hand, there is little or no such evidence for many of the nearly 400 psychopathologies listed in the fourth edition of the *Diagnostic and Statistical Manual of Mental Disorders* (DSM-IV). The only justification for most is embedded in the notion of 'construct validity.'

Significant for this inquiry is the question, Why are less-than-normal human behaviours (e.g., actions, conduct, demeanour, deportment) and/or attributes (e.g., characteristics, qualities, traits, virtue) subsumed within the notion of a *construct*? In their widely used text in education research, Meredith D. Gall, Walter R. Borg, and Joyce P. Gall define a *theoretical construct* as 'a concept that is *inferred* from observed phenomena [emphasis added]' (Gall et al. 1996: 9).' As examples of constructs, they include '[s]elf-concept, learning style, introversion, and achievement motivation . . . They are constructs because they are *not* directly observable, but rather must be *inferred* from their observable effects on behavior [emphasis added]' (249–250). In short, they are nothing more than linguistic contrivances that help explain why some humans behave differently from others in any particular cultural context, such as the classroom (Fazzaro 1997). The proliferation of instruments that purport to 'scientifically' divide one from another on some notion constructed from mere language serves not the individual being classified but, more important, to expand the language that institutions use to construct humans into an image consistent with the social structure best suited to the interests of the politically powerful. For Foucault, '[The] turning of real lives into writing is no longer a procedure of heroization; it functions as a procedure of objectification and subjection (1979: 192). But what accounts for the distribution of political power?

Why do some have it and others do not?

## HEGEMONY AND SUBJECTIFICATION

Although Foucault would argue that resistance always operates within institutions, the organised resistance necessary to change American public schools from mechanisms of division, classification, and hierarchical classification to schools that promote behaviours consistent with liberating democratic ethics are, at present, nowhere to be found. Antonio Gramsci's notion of hegemony might provide an adequate explanation for this lack. Gramsci believed that the state was the instrument for conforming civil society to the economic structure. To be successful, the state must first be willing to exert its control; and secondly, the state itself must be controlled by representatives of the economic structure (Hoare and Mathews 1977: xii–xiii). But Gramsci did not believe that the state could accomplish its task through propaganda and persuasion alone, at least in advanced capitalist societies. His view was that cultures in advanced capitalist societies were too sophisticated for coercion; thus, the masses must freely give their consent to be governed (Fazzaro 1991). There should be little doubt that in the United States, wealth is a, if not the, major factor regarding access to opportunities and that those in the upper socioeconomic level control most of the wealth, giving them enormous power over state and federal politics. This relation between wealth and power was recognised early in the development of a universal system public education in America. For example, in 1848, Horace Mann warned in his *Twelfth Annual Report* that without an educated electorate the American democratic ideals relative to the influence of wealth could not be fully achieved. Without universal education for all, the majority of the people would be 'the vassals of as severe a tyranny, in the form of capital, as the lower classes of Europe are bound to in the form of brute force' (1848: 17).

Thomas Frank, a columnist for the *New York Times* who writes extensively on economic issues, reports that in 1986, one percent of Americans owned 35.7 percent of the nation's wealth. By 1997 it rose to 40.7 percent. By 1995, the next nine percent of the wealthiest Americans owned 33.3 percent of the wealth. Referring to the Gini Index, a comprehensive standard of inequality, the lowest levels of inequality were in the 1960s and the highest in the late 1920s. By the end of the 1990s 'wealth polarization' was about that of the late 1930s (Frank 2000: 7).

The importance of education to social mobility cannot be understated. David L. Levine, a University of California, Berkeley, economist and mobility researcher, concluded from the current research on social mobility that '[b]eing born in the elite [class] in the United States gives you a constellation of privileges that very few people in the world have ever experienced' (Scott and Leonhardt: 14). Likewise, the very high correlation between family wealth and school achievement as measured by standardised tests is widely recognised. The more wealth a family has, the more opportunities the children have to acquire the language skills necessary for good test performance. Compared to students in European schools, American students often score significantly lower on such areas as mathematics and science. This difference in test scores might be adequately explained in terms of family wealth. The rapid expansion of the American economy compared to that of Europe since World War II masks the forces of inequality at work in the United States. Since the beginning of the 1980s at least, entrance to the middle class has been rapidly closing for Americans, as good paying factory jobs with pension plans and medical benefits have declined sharply. Scott and Leonhardt note that '[b]ecause income inequality is greater here [than in Europe], there is a wider disparity between what the rich and poor parents can invest in their children' (2005: 14). But how does disparity in family wealth operate through schools to solidify class structure? The answer is that government serves as the agent for repression of mobility. It does so through what Foucault calls 'governmentality.'

## CONCLUSIONS

After over two centuries the American experiment of government by and for the people to be achieved through public education has yet to be proven a success. This is not to discount the value that many millions of Americans have gained from their public school experience. Perhaps in a material sense, at least, the schools fulfilled their needs and expectations. What has been argued here is that American public education failed in its responsibility to educate a citizenry that would ultimately act politically to insure that all citizens would be able to freely exercise the rights guaranteed by the Constitution. Because Americans were to be both the governor and the governed the form of education would have to be such that it would foster ethical behaviour consistent with Foucault's belief that '[T]he freedom of the subject and its relationship to others is the very stuff [*matière*] of ethics.' But the schools serve not to free the subject, but to discipline the subject through a plethora of often interacting modes of objectification. In this regard, the schools have succeeded in 'constructing' generations of disciplined, compliant citizens for the demands of the economy. This has led not to a society where constitutionally guaranteed freedoms are nourished and acted upon, but to a very different kind of society—one in which citizens are made to compete with one another for the wealth necessary to fulfil a commercialised notion of their very *being*.

It is all too common in the United States to hear one speak of living, of *being* itself, only in degrees of materiality and sensory pleasures. Unlike Descartes' notion of *being*, 'I think therefore I am,' the American notion of *being* appears to be, 'I shop, therefore I am.' Reproduction and efficiency have displaced uniqueness, originality, and compassion. In all of this present-day, modern sense of *being*, where is the ethics demanded by American democratic ideals? Where is education? Both the explanation and justification for the modern sense of *being* is governed by the disciplines of economics, sociology, and history. Regarding the dominance of history and sociology, the French philosopher Luce Irigaray argues that,

> We should be what apparently we are, what we have already shown of ourselves. As for the rest, our becoming would be prescribed by our genes, or by what has already been deciphered of them. Our growth is to have stopped one day. We are to have become at best objects of study. Like the whole living world, destroyed little by little by exploration—exploration of what it is instead of cultivating what it could become. (2002: vi)

## NOTES

1. The *Critical Enquiry* (CE) referred to in the chapter title signifies an ongoing project I am undertaking with my students. The purpose of the project is to develop approaches to American public education policy enquiry that emphasise the analysis and interpretation of discourses that create, maintain, and justify the structures and technologies of institutions functioning within particular social, political, economic, and legal contexts. The notion of *discourse* relative to the CE project includes meanings consciously expressed through narratives, including not only phonetic and graphic texts, signs, and symbols, but individual and group behaviors and institutional practices. The capital 'C' in *Critical* emphasises social criticism at the most fundamental level of what ought to constitute ideal, just, democratic social structures. The capital 'E' in *Enquiry* recognises that the more traditional spelling is best used when engaged in 'asking about' at a fundamental philosophical level. In this regard, the CE project challenges the assumptions of traditional quantitative and qualitative approaches to policy 'research.'
2. I use the term 'modern thought' interchangeably with 'structuralism.' Both terms explain the phenomena of human life in 'laws' that transcend human consciousness. Of the two terms, modern thought is broader in that it encompasses everything in the physical sciences and anything attempting to pass itself off as 'science.'

## REFERENCES

*Brown v. Board of Education of Topeka,* Supreme Court of the United States, 1954. 347 U. S. 483, 74 S. Ct. 686, 98 L. Ed. 873 (1954).

Callahan, R. E. (1962) *Education and the Cult of Efficiency,* Chicago: University of Chicago Press.

Edwards, N. (1955) *The Courts and the Public Schools,* Chicago: University of Chicago Press.

Fazzaro, C. (1991) 'Antonio Gramsci, hegemony, and education,' *Proceedings of the Southwestern Philosophy of Education Society,* 41: 64–74.

——, (1997) 'From Port Royal to education research: a postmodern inquiry into construct validity,' *The Journal of Philosophy & History of Education,* 47: 73–81.

——, (1998) 'What is normal? a postmodern inquiry into the relations between education and social order,' *The Journal of Philosophy & History of Education,* 48: 11–17.

Foucault, M. (1973) *The Order of Things: An Archeology of the Human Sciences,* New York: Vintage Books.

——. (1978) 'Governmentality,' in G. Burchell, C. Gordon and P. Miller (eds) (1991) *The Foucault Effect,* Chicago: University of Chicago Press.

——. (1979) *Discipline and Punish: The Birth of the Prison,* trans. A. Sheridan, New York: Vintage Press.

——, (1982a) 'Technologies of the self,' in P. Rabinow (ed.) *Michel Foucault: Ethics, Subjectivity and Truth,* vol. 1, *The Essential Works of Foucault 1954–1984,* New York: The New Press.

——, (1982b) 'The subject and power,' in H. L. Dreyfus and P. Rabinow (eds) *Michel Foucault: Beyond Structuralism and Hermeneutics,* 2nd edn, Chicago: University of Chicago Press.

——, (1983) 'On the genealogy of ethics: an overview of work in progress,' in P. Rabinow (ed.) *Michel Foucault: Ethics, Subjectivity and Truth,* vol. 1, *The Essential Works of Foucault 1954–1984,* New York: The New Press.

——, (1984) 'The ethics of the concern of the self as a practice of freedom,' in P. Rabinow (ed.) *Michel Foucault: Ethics, Subjectivity and Truth*, vol. 1, *The Essential Works of Foucault 1954–1984*, New York: The New Press.

Frank, T. (2000) *One Market Under God: Extreme Capitalism, Market Populism, and the End of Economic Democracy*, New York: Doubleday.

Gall, M., Borg, W. and Gall, J. (1996) *Educational Research: An Introduction*, 6th edn, White Plains: Longman.

Gramsci, A. (1977) *Antonio Gramsci: Selections From Political Writings (1910–1920)*, London: Lawrence and Wishart.

*Grutter v. Bollinger, et al.* 02-241 Supreme Court of the United States 539 U.S. 306; 123 S. Ct. 2325; 156 L. Ed. 2d 304; U.S. LEXIS 4800 (2003).

Haney, W. (1981) 'Validity, vaudeville, and values: a short history of social concerns over standardized testing,' *American Psychologist*, 36, 10: 1021–34.

Hoare, Q. and Mathew, J. (1977) *Antonio Gramsci: Selections from Political Writings 1910–1920*, London: Lawrence and Wishart.

Hoskins, K. and Macve, R. (1986) 'Accounting and the examination: a genealogy of disciplinary power,' *Accounting Organizations and Society*, 11, 2: 105–36.

——, (1988) 'The genesis of accountability: the West Point connections,' *Accounting Organizations and Society*, 13, 1: 37–73.

Irigaray, L. (2002) *Between East and West: From Singularity to Community*, trans. S. Pluhácek, New York: Columbia University Press.

Jefferson, T. (1816) *Letter to Charles Yancey*, 1816. ME 14: 384 Online. Available HTTP: <http://etext.virginia.edu/jefferson/quotations/jeff1350.htm> (accessed 12 August 2007).

Lauer, P. A. (2006) *An Education Research Primer: How to Understand, Evaluate, and Use It*, San Francisco: Jossey-Bass.

Lyotard, J-F. (1984) *The Postmodern Condition: A Report on Knowledge*, trans. G. Bennington and B. Massumi, Minneapolis: University of Minnesota Press.

Mann, H. (1848) *The Massachusetts System of Common Schools: Twelfth Annual Report of the Massachusetts Board of Education*, Boston: Massachusetts Board of Education.

Nietzsche, F. (1994) *On the Genealogy of Morality*, Cambridge: Cambridge University Press.

Porter, T. (1986) *The Rise of Statistical Thinking 1820–1900*, Princeton: Princeton University Press.

Scott, J. and Leonhardt, D. (2005) 'Shadowy lines that still divide,' in B. Keller (ed.) *Class Matters*, New York: Times Books.

# Part II
# Political Analysis
## The Critique

# 9 Risky Policy Processes
## Accountability and School Leadership

*Michèle Schmidt*

The Western educational world has recently been powerfully influenced by an inexorable march toward accountability. My intention in this chapter is to explore the way such a phenomenon affects the work of school leaders. I attempt here to promote a theme that advocates a philosophy claiming that leaders must acknowledge the strength of this trend and see the inevitable implications it possesses for shaping choices available for educational policies and practices, while also maintaining the integrity of local cultural contexts. Furthermore, accountability processes seem to have both serious consequences and opportunities for transforming leading, teaching, learning and assessment, particularly in local settings (Burbules and Torres 2000). I employ a postmodern policy analysis approach to examine the nuances of the accountability policy landscape and how such a theory can facilitate leaders to maintain the integrity of their locale. This analysis is grounded primarily in the works of Foucault (1980), Ball (1994), Scheurich (1994), and Rosenau (1992). Finally, in conclusion, I comment on the viability of such an approach for the purposes of policy analysis.

## ACCOUNTABILITY CONTEXT

Accountability demands have now pervaded most educational institutions of the Western world. There exists a myriad of accountability definitions in various professional literatures, in education as well as other fields. However, a persistent definition in education seems to remain restricted by and bound up within large-scale assessment frameworks that focus primarily, if not uniquely, on testing (Earl and Torrance 2000). The most widely promulgated legislation in North America currently is possibly the US Federal Act entitled *No Child Left Behind* (NCLB). The evidential foundation on which NCLB seems to be grounded is an accountability system built on student test results. That is, an accountability system that seems to be premised solely on evaluating the performance of the whole school system in terms of student achievement, with rewards or sanctions reinforcing or deterring those results (Stecher and Kirby 2004).

While it is beyond the scope of this paper to describe the varied account-ability systems universally available beyond the US, generally more emphasis is placed on other forms of assessment. The focus is not only on determining student achievement but also on monitoring learning. These alternative formats include classroom assessments and teachers' input to provide anecdotal details of student achievement and value-added assessments, with emphasis placed on contextualising results and capacity-building strategies that include leadership development, networking, lateral capacity building, teacher education, and school/district reviews (Fullan 2005). Yet, the conditions within which alternatives to standardised testing are implemented are increasingly challenged by a climate of neoliberalism.

## THE POLICY DILEMMA

The current political and economic climate seems to influence policies in a variety of ways. Neoliberal definitions of schooling have pervaded the new accountability agenda, driving forward reforms that include standardisation, competition, and stratification. To varying degrees, schools have become complicit in market solutions in their efforts to remain competitive and achieve outputs unavailable to them otherwise (Berliner and Biddle 1995). Indeed, many of these notions highlight an emerging climate of high stakes testing as a replacement for learning and localised classroom assessment. It is therefore difficult to view accountability without acknowledging the increasing conflict between paradigms of schooling—one of *learning,* and one viewing students as *clients* and learning as a *product.*

Critics claim that neoliberal governments have been able to maintain legitimacy by blaming the education system for not providing industry and the economy with a skilled and well-educated workforce (Hursh 2005). Apple (2001) calls this phenomenon 'exporting the blame.' Others claim government has manufactured the blame (Berliner and Biddle 1995). Within such an ideological context, government also becomes a saviour by appearing to address the problem. In the US, for example, NCLB has become a panacea for improved education and equal opportunity (Giroux and Schmidt 2004). In this context, certain reforms in education have become not only widely acceptable, but also benign (Apple 1996). The present level of government involvement, therefore, is radically detached from an education system that was historically a communal affair. The usual scenario of communities, parents and teachers working together to design curricula and to assess students is gone (Hursh 2005). Some might claim that government has usurped local control by 'steering a system of standards, testing and choice from a distance' (Apple 1996).

More recently, however, what is becoming increasingly evident to not only scholars and educators, but also the general public, is that the NCLB's purported mandate of 'increased opportunity for all' does not necessarily result in equality. Reports of low income, minority students dropping out, or being forced out, of schools are rampant in the US (Haney 2000). Resistance to NCLB is emerging from a number of interest groups—scholars, educators, and parents. Even individual states are resisting NCLB due to their own complaints, which range from a dissatisfaction with the additional costs associated with NCLB requirements to resentment towards federal government interference with their rights (Dillon 2005).

In the US, therefore, despite the mandated implementation of NCLB, localised methods of accountability have begun to proliferate in some states, broadening the criteria of student success to include local initiatives of assessment at the state, school, and classroom levels. Some recent examples of state-level initiatives include Nebraska's state learning-measurement system and its academic standards and assessment system. These institutions do not rely on standardised tests in meeting the accountability requirements of NCLB (Borja 2007). Illinois also has a number of local assessment initiatives that attempt to connect assessment to curriculum, instruction, and school improvement (Vogel, Rau, Baker and Ashby 2006). Recently, the Maine Department of Education developed a local assessment system that provides school systems with criteria necessary to comply with NCLB while also providing flexibility for local decisions (Maine State Department of Education 2004). Similarly, Vermont developed a framework of standards and learning opportunities that provides a structure from which standards-based district, school, and classroom curricula can be developed (Vermont Department of Education 2004). While these examples are not exhaustive, they provide illustrations of the types of state assessment initiatives being developed to work in concert with or outside the realm of federally legislated accountability policies (e.g., NCLB).

In addition to these recent state-level assessment initiatives, school-level assessments are equally important. These approaches are widely used outside of the US (e.g., Wales, the UK, New Zealand, Australia, and Canada). Here, classroom assessment often goes beyond paper and pencil tests to include such alternatives as portfolio and performance-based assessment (Marzano, Pickering and McTighe 1993). Such assessments encourage students to take responsibility for their own learning and place primacy on high-order learning (Earl 1995).

With increasing state-level and a resurgence of classroom-level assessment reform in the US, a backlash has begun to destabilise externally mandated accountability. Connecticut, for example, is suing the federal government for not providing adequate funds to implement testing. Utah is considering measures that will place primacy on state educational goals rather than federal objectives (Dillon 2005). In Ohio, a campaign called, 'Say No,' is comprised of parents who choose to exempt their children from the 4th, 6th, and 12th Grade Ohio Proficiency Tests. In Texas, the Mexican-American Legal Defense Fund turned to the courts to deem test requirements unconstitutional. And in Chicago, the Local School Councils Summit worked with

FairTest to create parent-friendly information outlining the inherent problems with standardised tests (Dotterweich and McNeal 2003). Parents are
also beginning to question the federal rating system. This is especially true
when the schools their children attend are rated as failing by the government, yet deemed successful at the local level as a result of state- or school-
level assessments (Hursh 2005). It is not surprising, then, that these local
accountability systems (that include state- and school-level assessments) and
the external federal accountability systems involving standardised testing
are often at antipodes in their relationship. In fact, they each reflect different
paradigms in thinking about learning, schooling, teaching, and assessment.

For states with an existing accountability system in place at the state or
school level, NCLB is often added on as a separate entity alongside these
other systems. When this happens, as Linn (2005) points out, there is a
danger of mixed messages of differing outcomes from the two systems.
That is, schools may meet the goals of one accountability system but not
the other. Indeed, researchers (e.g., Linn 2005) stress the need for clear
links between federal, state, regional, and school-level accountability systems. For example, Kentucky, Florida, and Colorado have state accountability systems that reveal more positive results than NCLB (Linn 2005).
Consequently, mixed messages sent to students and parents have become
of great concern for schools, educators, and leaders. Leaders at the district and school level in these situations increasingly face external and local
assessment needs that frequently collide in purpose, demonstrating that
educational leadership within an accountability context is risky business.
The policy problem, therefore, evolves into one of compatibility: How do
leaders reconcile federal accountability initiatives that often collide with
state and local policy initiatives?

## POSTMODERN POLICY ANALYSIS

One often hears that we have entered a postmodern era of shifting demo-
graphics, changing economies, technological advancements, a growing
knowledge economy, commodification of education, standardisation,
branding, marketisation, and accountability as surveillance (Berliner and
Biddle 1995). This postmodern condition highlights complexity, diversity,
and uncertainty. Indeed, the confusing influx of knowledge and information
has the capacity to modify and restrict what is deemed essential for teaching, learning, and assessment (Hargreaves, Earl and Schmidt 2002).

Traditionally, modern policy frameworks exist as evaluative processes,
focusing on the extent to which policy succeeds or fails to meet its objectives (Spencer 2001). Critics of traditional policy analysis approaches argue
that power relations are not adequately explored and do little in the way
of illuminating the implications of the problems they attempt to address
(Ball 1994; Scheurich 1994). When viewed from a postmodern perspective,

however, we are able to delve into the problem and ultimately illuminate the underlying values. This enables us to employ a theoretical mechanism for (re)interpreting a given policy landscape and its surrounding contextual influences (Ball 1994; Taylor et al. 1997).

A more contemporary explanation of policy analysis, therefore, is helpful in exploring the local experiences of those implementing policy and in highlighting conflicting cultures and definitions of accountability. Scholars assert that efforts to retain a modern view of policy are difficult within a postmodern society (Taylor et al. 1997). Traditional policy processes are a modern invention—one that privileges process, reason, and expert knowledge, reflects government intentions that are purposeful, and intends to address a problem with actions that are designed to achieve certain goals (Taylor et al. 1997). Policy processes, therefore, tend to be focussed on the benefit of the bureaucracies and those in power, becoming a technology of control with political implications (Ball 1994; Foucault 1980). Policy often becomes a power struggle with cross-purposes and competing understandings and intentions. Furthermore, traditional policy analysis might preclude us from asking social justice questions such as: Who defines the problem? Who allocates resources? Who determines goals?

Observations by postmodern and post-structural scholars (Ball 1994; Foucault 1980) maintain that policy is actually multidimensional in nature, as well as value-laden and contextual. Furthermore, policies interact with each other, are neither straightforward nor rational, and frequently result in unintended and even detrimental consequences. These characteristics challenge conventional policy phenomena that have traditionally striven to be value-neutral and free from contextual issues (Taylor et al. 1997). Ball (1994) and Foucault (1980) stress that policy as discourse becomes a power exercise as to whose meaning is legitimated, whose voices are heard, and whose values are recognised or authoritatively allocated. A more contemporary policy lens, then, acknowledges that policy implementation must consider context, placement, and purpose of implementation and become an approach to solving long-term, value-laden problems.

Despite postmodernism's limitations, this paradigm offers more than just a critique of modernism or even modern policy initiatives. Its strength lies chiefly in the potentialities of human culture, the enactment of democratic government, and a self-conscious public administration that relies more on stewardship than regulation. Postmodern policy analysis offers the latitude to discover appropriate theory rather than applying a particular theory narrowly that inhibits further interpretation (Ball 1994). Furthermore, it enables an examination of the moral order of reform and its relationship to existing patterns of social inequality, bringing to bear those concepts and interpretive devices that offer the best possibility of insight and understanding. All of this can help to legitimise a space for local voices as well as local accountability initiatives and their results, and perhaps show the linkages between external contexts and local practices. By making room for local interpretations, public, parental, and teacher concerns are reflected. In fact, there is increasing evidence that support from the aforementioned interest groups (or lack thereof) can influence the implementation of a policy (DeBray 2005).

## THE IMPORTANCE OF LOCAL PRACTICES

Local practices offer important opportunities for schools to consider their own distinctive organisational characteristics and problems: unique student populations, diverse communities, students' existing skills, teachers' beliefs and personal goals, student behaviour, and a school's institutional history (Abelman et al. 1999). Abelman et al. argue that external accountability measures typically stress that all schools are held accountable to the same expectations, despite local or school differences. This approach does not accurately reflect the various contexts within which administrators and teachers find themselves, and which are typically bounded 'by their own conceptions of who they are, who they serve, what they expect of students, and what they think of as good teaching and learning' (1999: 10).

Arguments presenting notions that schools have conceptions of accountability embedded within their organisational structure, thus shaping school cultures, driving teachers,' administrators,' students,' and parents' beliefs and actions and mediating external mandates, are becoming more prominent (Abelman et al. 1999). In fact, different purposes drive external and internal accountability agendas. External systems often place primacy on improving academic performance while local initiatives focus on contextual issues that affect learning, such as teachers' individual and collective responsibilities to their students for student learning, conduct codes, and students' well-being (Wagner 1989). Researchers often note that despite external mandates, within the walls of their own classrooms, teachers are more likely to focus on their own beliefs for which they feel personally and professionally responsible (Mathers and King 2001). When external policy is not aligned with collective expectations, teachers tend to follow the extant internal accountability system.

Typically, schools with an enhanced organisational capacity are more responsive and able to meet external demands (Acker-Hocevar and Touchton 2001). Indeed, increasingly researchers are able to describe attributes of local assessment programmes that augment statewide testing programmes. These might include: setting priorities and goals, meeting with state officials, developing budgets and funding sources, forming development teams, providing professional development, and piloting and revising assessment tasks (Rabinowitz 2001). This kind of capacity is fostered by educational leaders who encourage collective responsibility and nurture assessment literacy. In these cases, leaders often model instructional leadership in their attempts to build trust among stakeholders (Charles A. Dana Center 1999). More often, however, external reforms do not make it to the classroom; that is, teachers do not connect policy within their professional lives (Datnow, Hubbard and Mehan 2002).

## LINKAGES BETWEEN EXTERNAL AND LOCAL ACCOUNTABILITY SYSTEMS

What, then, can be done to reconcile external and local policy initiatives and practices? Researchers (e.g., Hargreaves and Fullan 1998; Newmann and Wehlage 1995) have written much on the benefits of professional learning communities and assessment literacy. They also note the value of these tools in helping to establish links with external initiatives. For example, individually and collectively, educators can interpret achievement data and develop action plans to change instruction, implement appropriate classroom assessment strategies, and enhance other school- and classroom-level conditions to improve student learning. When teachers and leaders are better-informed and understand the implementation process of external accountability systems and their outcomes, they can make meaningful linkages with internal assessment and accountability systems (Fullan 2000). This approach often relies on reculturing schools so that everyone, including parents and the community, are collaborating. More importantly, schools that are able to link external and internal demands, particularly those policy demands that work at cross-purposes, are often reliant upon leaders who are selective about the policies they implement, with primacy being placed on integrating and connecting external policy with the inner workings of their environment. In such cases, leaders make sure professional development is cohesive and relevant to developing these linkages as they work at 'attacking incoherence' (Fullan 2000: 583).

It seems, then, that a critical component of any accountability system is the shared responsibility for outcomes—the administrator in a school should not alone be liable. For example, key groups such as students, parents, teachers, schools, universities, government, and business all play a role in any given outcome (California Master Plan for Education 2002). Some believe that the best chance for accountability policies to work occur under the following conditions: when sanctions are minimised or eliminated; multiple assessments are used; implementation occurs in stages; there is a focus on capacity building, trust and relationship building; there is an emphasis on assessment literacy; and there is state pressure and support (Mintrop and Trujillo 2005). These approaches provide a deeper definition of accountability that relies on collaboration and results in the positive and constructive involvement of all stakeholders, but most importantly, builds trust among them (California Master Plan for Education 2002). Acker-Hocevar and Touchton (2001) argue that to enhance linkages between internal and external systems leaders must have the authority to make decisions related to financial capital, resources, and curriculum. More importantly, they must have input into defining success. Finally, they must promote assessment literacy and high standards in their schools as well as collaboration and communication with stakeholders. Equally important, leaders must engage in a critical examination of accountability policies by challenging the tensions between education as a public good and education as a commodity (Datnow, Hubbard and Mehan 2002). This is increasingly apparent in schools with an inquiry-minded focus to improve student learning. There, educators are continually asking questions such as the following: How can schools help all students meet high standards? Who sets those standards? How is student progress best assessed? Who should do the assessing—the state, the district, the school? What is the relationship between the external mandates and student achievement? Such schools, according to Rallis and MacMullen (2000), illustrate that what happens inside a school is critical. In other words, an institutionalised process of asking the hard policy questions, followed by implementation (or not) based on reflection and research is key.

Indeed, much evidence shows that it is dangerous for federal policy to rely solely on the results of externally mandated tests to assess educational success or failure without questioning whether the tests represent what society wants schools to pursue and which student populations the tests are intended to serve. It should be noted, however, that by and large when teachers are asked whether they oppose testing or accountability in general, they typically express concerns about the nature of the tests, that is, the high-stakes emphasis on testing, rather than suggesting tests be abandoned entirely (DeBray 2005). Instead, they would prefer a lessening of the high-stakes nature of external accountability and better linkages with classroom assessment. In fact, administrators and teachers typically express support for the goals of external reforms, while remaining concerned about such embedded assumptions being made by policymakers: that the test will motivate students and teachers to work harder; that the state goals are attainable for all students; that the aggregate performance of all students in the system will be raised over time; and that the statewide gap between low and high-performing schools will be diminished (DeBray 2005). Findings such as these suggest that it is incumbent on policymakers to take a broad view of the problem of high-stakes tests and of possible solutions, as well as to consult with the varied locales in which the tests are being administered. '[Externally mandated] testing can be an important ingredient in a reform initiative, but it constitutes only one of a number of necessary policy changes. Testing certainly is not and cannot be the main engine of school reform' (McLaughlin 1991: 251). When they are well-devised and implemented, academic standards, tests, and associated accountability provisions can improve teaching and learning.

This chapter suggests, therefore, that standardised tests are not necessarily the problem; rather, their alignment with local accountability initiatives should be synchronised more closely than they have been in the past. In that vein, Gandal and Vranek (2001) have stated that large numbers of teachers and parents have legitimate concerns about the focus on testing in schools. These concerns may have more to do with specific issues in specific local precincts than with a broad disagreement about using higher standards to drive school improvement.

## VIABILITY OF A POSTMODERN
## POLICY ANALYSIS APPROACH

How viable is a postmodern policy analysis within an accountability context? To begin with, the entire concept of postmodernism remains ambiguous and controversial (Bogason 2001). The term is often plagued by disputes between modernists and postmodernists, as each remains at antipodes, criticising the other's positional ideology. Modernists often view postmodernism negatively, granting it little merit, while postmodernists critique the modernists' need to categorise the theory (Rosenau 1992). Scholars claim there are a number of types of postmodernists (e.g., affirmative and sceptic postmodernists, see Rosenau 1992). Sceptics like Heidegger, Baudrillard, and Nietzsche often see an anomic world replete with fragmentation, instability, disintegration, social malaise, meaninglessness, and societal chaos. Sceptics typically employ deconstructive and linguistic analyses of phenomena, diminishing the value of dialogue with the 'other' or the necessity to remediate problems. Such a viewpoint perceives a neglected environment caused by the domination of exploitive capitalism.

Affirmative postmodernists (e.g., Baumann, Rorty, Burrell) present a more positive worldview, with an interest in understanding the processes that promote change through agency, political action, and social movements. They do not necessarily view postmodern and modern organisations as either independent or inimical towards each other. In this way, contexts, values, and consequences of actions become important to analyse and to understand (Boje 1999; Rosenau 1992). Affirmative postmodernists typically engage in discussions of how to organise, engage in discourse, and understand the world around them from particular perspectives. Therefore, they often include populations who have been oppressed (e.g., by gender, race, class). Nevertheless, it still remains difficult to resolve issues using only one solution or listening to just one voice, since postmodernism is not about a one-voiced world (Rosenau 1992).

Despite claims by postmodernists that essential elements of their discipline attack theory and methodology and relinquish attempts at creating new knowledge in a systematic manner, some scholars disagree (e.g., Rosenau 1992). They argue that there are, in fact, two main methodologies employed by postmodernists that involve deconstruction and interpretive narrative inquiry. Deconstruction seeks to expose hierarchies within texts that disenfranchise certain populations and, in doing so, offer new definitions of text by reversing or undoing presuppositions and exposing silences and gaps within the text (Weiss and Wesley 1999). Secondly, postmodernism leaves room for interpretation through narrative and dialogic communication. Some postmodernists (e.g., Foucault) claim that everything is interpretation and that no one interpretation is superior to another. While postmodernism is fraught with criticisms and contradictions, its strength lies in fostering democratic spaces for interpretation and the unveiling of oppressive practices.

From a postmodern policy perspective, then, we begin to see that policy is messy, unpredictable, and includes a wide range of human elements. While accountability may be viewed from a technical perspective, it is ultimately a human endeavour with human consequences that may be unexpected or unintended. There is a need for cooperation, communication, and transparency between external and local systems. There is a need to ask important questions such as: How do assessment and accountability systems best represent students and schools fairly so that the representation is not really misrepresentation? What are the hegemonic consequences of doing so for leadership practices? (Mabry 2005: 4). We can see that there is a need to broaden the definition of accountability so that it inherently asks the following: Is educational measurement a modernist enterprise irreconcilable in a postmodern world where testing is merely a form of surveillance imposed on the powerless by the powerful, making it possible to qualify, classify, degrade, and ultimately punish? (Dreyfus and Rabinow 1983) Leaders themselves must ask the same questions: What is meant by performance? What is it that makes education so important to individuals, the state, and society at large? What are leaders' own expectations of effectiveness? What about breadth of opportunity and depth of achievement? Postmodernism brings to the forefront the idea that one size does not fit all, that no one method of teaching or assessing is suitable for every student, and that each student is unique with unique learning styles (Jacobs and Kritsonis 2006). In fact, Hargreaves, Earl and Schmidt maintain that 'a postmodern perspective on . . . assessment is based on the view that in today's complex and uncertain world, human beings are not completely knowable. No assessment process or system can therefore be fully comprehensive' (2002: 88).

When taking a postmodern policy analysis approach, we are able to arrive at some very cogent critiques for and against large-scale external accountability initiatives and local, classroom assessments. A postmodern perspective opposes normalisation and exposes the ways in which high-stakes testing solidifies the normalisation of the subject leading to homogeneity or reindividualisation. In other words, individuals are 'remade as sets of comparative reference measures' (Gunzenhauser 2006: 250). Foucault's (1980) notions of power force us to ask questions such as the following: What forms of discipline do high-stakes testing authorise or inculcate in us? In this vein, examinations combine the techniques of an observing hierarchy of surveillance and those of a normalising judgment. It is a normalising gaze, an inspection that makes it possible to qualify, classify, and punish. More importantly, what is lost is the linkage between these measures and the subjects' history—tests conflate values, that is, they confuse the measurement with who is being measured, leaving the dialogue to fixate on the achievement score rather than the individual student. English encourages educators to go beyond data-driven decision-making to 'take the human factor into account' (2003: 208).

Furthermore, such testing policies undermine the importance of the social context by labelling academic progress based upon norm-referenced, hegemonic judgments. High-stakes decisions based on the results of standardised, norm-referenced tests marginalise certain students and are not able to reliably capture other important variables that might contribute to success, such as faculty morale, student morale and motivation, parental apathy and so forth (English 2003). Critics claim that tests can misdirect student motivation, result in teaching to the test, discriminate against minority and socioeconomically disadvantaged youth, and result in higher dropout rates for those who cannot pass (Schmidt et al. forthcoming). There are also the difficulties of incorporating the diversity of instructional programmes and skills taught across districts in one test and of conducting reliability and validity tests on the exams (Stiggins 1991). In fact, the practice of making promotional decisions based on a single test score is inconsistent with professional standards (American Psychological Association and National Council on Measurement in Education 1999). The high-stakes nature of these tests can also lead teachers to cheat on the test to increase students' scores (Roderick, Jacob and Bryk 2002) or to increase retention rates of low-performing first year high school students (Haney 2000).

Despite these negative factors, advocates argue that these tests motivate students, teachers, and school administrators to work harder, serve as a good measure of the validity of the curricula, and identify areas for improvement based on test reports. Additionally, researchers claim that student course-taking patterns contribute to poor performances on standardised tests, in which case a basic curricular focus on the tests may especially benefit low-achieving students. There is evidence to indicate that greater instructional time is associated with greater achievement (Roderick, Jacob and Bryk 2002). In fact, schools with a high concentration of at-risk students may be motivated to mobilise an entire community to institute changes in curriculum, pedagogy or school organisation (Roderick, Jacob and Bryk 2002).

Similarly, when examining localised classroom assessment practices, these approaches are also not exempt from criticism nor are they necessarily a panacea for the accountability problems discussed thus far. Critics argue that the postmodern condition challenges the credibility of many types of classroom assessment. For example, 'authentic assessment' can be far from authentic if 'the meanings and the existential experiences we describe as authentic are fundamentally questionable' (Hargreaves, Earl and Schmidt 2002: 88). By its very nature, the definition 'stresses fidelity to actuality and fact,' and its authenticity runs counter to this, when viewed from a post-modern perspective, in its celebration of diversity and encouragement of a range of perspectives on what might be deemed as facts (Hargreaves, Earl and Schmidt 2002: 89). There is also the contrived nature of assessment in the staging of parent- or student-led conferences, when there is an exaggerated focus on glossy portfolio covers rather than content and self-assessment becomes a narcissistic endeavour (Hargreaves, Earl and Schmidt 2002).

From a more positive perspective, classroom assessment cultivates a forum for diversity and multiple representations of learning styles in a variety of forms. Furthermore, classroom assessment empowers students and diminishes 'hierarchical distinctions of worth' (Hargreaves, Earl and Schmidt 2002: 91). We might conclude, then, that both external and local accountability systems are victim to misuses and both must be designed and implemented purposefully with clear objectives.

## IMPLICATIONS FOR LEADERS

We might ask a final question: What are the implications of a postmodern perspective on both external and local accountability for leaders? Leaders must recognise their own strategic agency and be aware of the norms, values and symbols of society underlying their own cultural and social rules and the potentially limiting informal normative structure in which they find themselves working (Campbell 1998). In this way, they begin to engage in practices that rewrite the cultural landscape and move away from grand narratives (Barnett 1999). Keohane and Martin (1995) claim that leaders too often ground policy decisions within formal normative parameters. This practice is criticised for promoting a narrow understanding of ideas and demarcating theory from practice without fully taking into consideration how the cultural context might shape local practices (Keohane and Martin 1995). The challenge for leaders, then, is to overcome the ways in which policies are 'deliberately packaged and framed to convince . . . the general public that certain policy proposals constitute plausible and acceptable solutions to pressing problems' (Campbell 1998: 381). Through a postmodern lens, decisions made by leaders are grounded in their interpretations of the world around them, interpretations that depict a certain personal and professional narrative of past, present and future experiences and aspirations. By recognising and legitimating their own narratives, leaders can strategically mobilise opportunities to address injustices, inequities, and disenfranchisement within their own cultures, enabling them to 'recast or challenge the prevailing definitions of the situation, thus changing perceptions of costs and benefits of policies and programmes and the perception [and actualities] of injustice of the status quo' (Barnett 1999: 15). Barnett (1999) calls this the 'moment of reframing' where contradictions and tensions are reconciled, where events are situated in ways that align with the extant cultural terrain, and where the costs and benefits of a policy according to context are reconsidered.

Dennard (1997) suggests that leaders distinguish problematic symptoms from the broader set of relationships and processes from which they emerge and move away from decision-making models that obscure the reality of everyday life. They should try to transcend problems rather than simply reformulating them and avoid creating long-term realities by embedding short-term problems through repeated restructuring. Primacy should be placed on nurturing relationships that will sustain democracy and respecting the unique perspectives among staff and faculty. The challenge, however, is that contemporary leaders do not always have the knowledge and strategies to reform current economic and political structures of schools. Consequently, they do not distinguish the inadequacies inherent in standards and tests, nor do they always reflect upon and analyse systemic boundaries that protract educational hierarchies, or even extrapolate beyond their own sociopolitical milieu to determine what can enhance or detract from their local context (English 2003).

In closing, a postmodern policy lens forces us to consider broader definitions of policy. While postmodernism does not necessarily offer a theory to solve problems, it opens our awareness to other approaches and the possibility of accommodating differences: 'In government, we spend an enormous amount of personal energy and public resources trying to make a multidimensional reality fit a one-dimensional model' (Dennard 1997: 157). Embracing diversity and even antagonistic models, Dennard (1997) maintains, requires that we suspend judgment in order to extrapolate the relationship of extremes into terms of moral action, as opposed to merely correcting deviation and marginalising the disadvantaged by maintaining a pseudointellectual status quo.

Docherty (1990) argues that postmodernism accommodates new democratic social relationships that arise from individuals rather than from theory. In this way, postmodernism 'is not simply a method of linguistic and social analysis; it is an articulation of the breakdown of social structures as well as an articulation of the process by which this breakdown generates a new social equilibrium' (Dennard 1999: 151). In summary, postmodernism advocates self-organisation, diversity, and multiplicity of paradigmatic hermeneutics. In this respect, postmodernism becomes a vehicle for change rather than a hostile and oppositional alternative to modernism (Dennard 1997). If viewed as a transitionary approach to governance and administration, the alleged negatives of postmodernism may be mitigated, and postmodernism itself may be viewed merely as a portal or serve as a proxy to heighten our acuity of possible social ills in society and injustices and hierarchal but misdirected hegemony within the bureaucracy. It is counterproductive to view modernism and postmodernism as adversarial and competitive. Rather, what postmodernism emphasises is the collaboration of multiple perspectives (Taylor 1995).

## REFERENCES

Abelman, C. et al. (1999) *When accountability knocks, will anyone answer?* Philadelphia: Consortium for Policy Research in Education (CPRE-RR-42).

Acker-Hocevar, M. and Touchton, D. (2001) 'Principals' struggle to level the accountability playing field of Florida graded 'D' and 'F' schools in high poverty and minority communities,' paper presented at the Annual Meeting of the American Educational Research Association, Seattle.

American Psychological Association and National Council on Measurement in Education (1999) Online. Available HTTP: <http://www.apa.org/science/standards.html> (accessed 23 July 23 2007).

Apple, M. (1996) *Cultural Politics and Education,* Buckingham: Open University Press.

———, (2001) Comparing neo-liberal projects and inequality in education,' *Comparative Education,* 37, 4: 409–23.

Ball, S. J. (1994) *Education Reform: A Critical Post-structural Approach,* Buckingham: Open University Press.

Barnett, M. (1999) 'Culture, strategy and foreign policy change: Israel's road to Oslo,' *European Journal of International Relations,* 5, 1: 5–36.

Berliner, D. C. and Biddle, B. J. (1995) *The Manufactured Crisis: Myths, Fraud and the Attack on America's Public Schools,* Reading: Addison-Wesley.

Bogason, P. (2001) 'Postmodernism and American public administration in the 1990s,' *Administration and Society,* 3, 2: 165–93.

Boje, D. M. (1999) 'Alternative postmodern spectacles: the skeptical and affirmative postmodernist (organization) theory debates,' paper presented at the Business and Economics Society International Conference, Spain. Online. Available HTTP: <http://business.nmsu.edu/~dboje/canary.html> (accessed 20 June 2007).

Borja, R. R. (2007) 'Nebraska swims hard against testing's tides,' *Education Week,* 26, 24: 32–4.

Burbules, N. C. and Torres, C. (2000) 'Globalization and education: an introduction,' in N. Burbules and C. Torres (eds) *Globalization and Education: Critical Perspectives,* New York: Routledge.

California Master Plan for Education (2002) Online. Available HTTP: http://www.network-democracy.org/camp/bb/plan/contents.shtml (accessed 23 July 2007).

Campbell, J. (1998) 'Institutional analysis and the role of ideas in political economy,' *Theory and Society,* 27: 377–409.

Charles A. Dana Center, University of Texas at Austin. (1999) *Hope for Urban Education: A Study of Nine High-performing, High-poverty, Urban Elementary Schools,* Washington DC: US Dept. of Education, Planning and Evaluation Service.

Datnow, A., Hubbard, L. and Mehan, B. (2002) *Extending Educational Reform: From One School to Many,* London: RoutledgeFalmer.

DeBray, E. (2005) *A Comprehensive High School and a Shift in New York State Policy: A Study of Early Implementation,* Chapel Hill: University of North Carolina Press.

Dennard, L. F. (1997) 'The democratic potential in the transition of postmodernism: from critique to social evolution,' *American Behavioral Scientist,* 41, 1: 148–62.

Dillon, S. (2005) 'Connecticut to sue US over cost of testing law,' *New York Times,* 6 April. Online. Available HTTP: <www.nytimes.com/2005/04/06/education/06child.html> (accessed 9 June 2007).

Docherty, T. (1990) *After Theory: Postmodernism/Post-marxism,* London: Routledge.

Dotterweich, L. and McNeal, R. (2003) 'The No Child Left Behind Act and public preferences,' paper presented at the Annual Meeting of the American Political Sciences Association, Philadelphia.

Dreyfus, H. and Rabinow, P. (1983) *Michel Foucault, Beyond Structuralism and Hermeneutics*, Chicago: University of Chicago Press.

Earl, L. (1995) 'Assessment and accountability in education in Ontario,' *Canadian Journal of Education*, 20, 1: 45–55.

———, and Torrance, N. (2000) 'Embedding accountability and improvement into large-scale assessment: what difference does it make?' *Peabody Journal of Education*, 75, 4: 114–41.

English, F. W. (2003) *The Postmodern Challenge to the Theory and Practice of Educational Administration*, Springfield: Charles C. Thomas.

Foucault, M. (1980) *Power/Knowledge: Selected Interviews and Other Writings, 1972–1977*, Brighton: Harvester Press.

Fullan, M. (2000) 'The three stories of education reform,' *Phi Delta Kappan*, 81, 8: 581–84.

———, (2005) 'Turnaround leadership,' *The Educational Forum*, 69: 174–81.

Gandal, M. and Vranek, J. (2001) 'Standards: here today, here tomorrow,' *Educational Leadership*, 59, 1: 6–13.

Giroux, H. and Schmidt, M. (2004) 'Closing the achievement gap: a metaphor for children left behind,' *Journal of Educational Change*, 5: 213–28.

Gunzenhauser, M. (2006) 'Normalizing the educated subject: a Foucaultian analysis of high-stakes accountability,' *Educational Studies Association*, 39, 3: 241–59.

Haney, W. (2000) 'The myth of the Texas miracle in education,' *Education Policy Analysis Archives*, 8, 41. Online. Available HTTP: <http://epaa.asu.edu/epaa/v8n41> (accessed 9 June 2007).

Hargreaves, A., Earl, L. and Schmidt, M. (2002) 'Perspectives on alternative assessment reform,' *American Educational Research Journal*, 39, 1: 69–95.

Hargreaves, A. and Fullan, M. (1998) *What's Worth Fighting for Out There?* New York: Teachers College Press.

Hursh, D. (2005) 'Neo-liberalism, markets and accountability: transforming education and undermining democracy in the United States and England,' *Policy Futures in Education*, 3, 1: 3–15.

Jacobs, K. D. and Kritsonis, W. A. (2006) 'National strategies for implementing postmodern thinking for improving secondary education in public education in the United States of America,' *National Forum of Educational Administration and Supervision Journal*, 23, 4: 1–10.

Keohane, R. and Martin, L. (1995) 'The promise of institutionalist theory,' *International Security*, 20, 1: 39–51.

Linn, R. L. (2005) 'Conflicting demands of No Child Left Behind and state systems: mixed messages about school performance,' *Education Policy Analysis Archives*, 13, 33: 1–17.

Mabry, L. (2005) 'Strategies for high school accountability: a response to Marion,' paper submitted to Reidy Interactive Lecture Series, National Centre for the Improvement of Educational Assessment and West Ed.

Maine State Department of Education (2004) *LAS Guide with Embedded Components for Accommodations and Alternate Assessment: Principles and Criteria for the Adoption of Local Assessment Systems*, Augusta: Maine State Department of Education.

Marzano, R. J., Pickering, D. and McTighe, J. (1993) *Assessing Student Outcomes: Performance Assessment Using the Dimensions of Learning Model*, Alexandria: Association for Supervision and Curriculum Development.

Mathers, J. K. and King, R. A. (2001) 'Teachers' perceptions of accountability,' paper presented at the Annual Meeting of the American Educational Research Association, Seattle.

McLaughlin, M. (1991) 'Test-based accountability as a reform strategy,' *Phi Delta Kappan*, 73, 3: 248–51.

Mintrop, H. and Trujillo, T. (2005) 'Corrective action in low performing schools: lessons for NCLB implementation from first-generation accountability systems,' *Education Policy Analysis Archives*, 13, 48: 1–27.

Newman, F. and Wehlage, G. (1995) *Successful School Restructuring*, Madison: Center on Organization and Restructuring of Schools, University of Wisconsin.

Rabinowitz, S. (2001) 'Balancing state and local assessment,' *School Administrator*, 58, 11: 16–20.

Rallis, S. F. and MacMullen, M. M. (2000) 'Inquiry-minded schools: opening doors for accountability,' *Phi Delta Kappan*, 81, 10: 766–73.

Roderick, M., Jacob, B. A. and Bryk, A. S. (2002) 'The impact of high-stakes testing in Chicago on student achievement in promotional gate grades,' *Educational Evaluation and Policy Analysis*, 24, 4: 333–57.

Rosenau, P. M. (1992) *Post-modernism and the Social Sciences: Insights, Inroads and Intrusions*, Princeton: Princeton University Press.

Scheurich, J. J. (1994) 'Policy archeology: a new policy studies methodology,' *Journal of Education Policy*, 9, 4: 297–316.

Schmidt, M., Tapales, A., Castellano, M., Stringfield, S., and Stone, J. (forthcoming). 'The implications of an exit exam on a vocational high school,' *Review of Research Sociology of Education*.

Spencer, B. L. (2001) 'The seduction of the subject/citizen: governmentality and school governance policy,' paper presented at the Annual Meeting of the American Educational Research Association, Seattle.

Stecher, B. and Kirby, S. N. (eds) (2004) *Organizational Improvement and Accountability: Lessons for Education from Other Sectors*, Santa Monica: RAND.

Stiggins, R. J. (1991) 'Assessment literacy,' *Phi Delta Kappan*, 72, 7: 534–39.

Taylor, C. (1995) *The Politics of Multiculturalism*, New York: Basic Books.

Taylor, S., Rizvi, F., Lingard, B., and Henry, M. (1997) *Educational Policy and the Politics of Change*, New York: RoutledgeFalmer.

Vermont Department of Education (2004) *Grade Expectations for Vermont's Framework of Standards and Learning Opportunities*, Montpelier: Vermont Department of Education.

Vogel, L. R., Rau, W. C., Baker, P. J. and Ashby, D. E. (2006) 'Bringing assessment literacy to the local school: a decade of reform initiatives in Illinois,' *Journal of Education for Students Placed at Risk*, 11, 1: 39–55.

Wagner, R. B. (1989) *Accountability in Education: A Philosophical Inquiry*, New York: Routledge.

Weiss, S. and Wesley, K. (1999) 'Postmodernism and its critics,' in M. D. Murphy (ed.) *Anthropological Theories: A Guide Prepared by Students for Students*. Online. Available HTTP: <http://www.as.ua.edu/ant/Faculty/murphy/pomo.htm> (accessed 20 June 2007).

# 10  Putting Alternative Perspectives to Work in the Politics of Education

*Michelle D. Young and Gerardo R. López*

> The social sciences have sought to transcend history in three ways. They have hidden their Eurocentric origins behind universalistic knowledge claims; they have perpetuated and justified the original division of disciplines by naturalizing and eternalizing their distinctive objects (the capitalist triumvirate of economy, state, and society); and they have secured their scientific truth by defining their methodology (positivism) as context-free. (Burawoy 2005: 508)

'The politics of education can no longer rely solely on conventional perspectives, topics or analyses' (Rorrer and Lugg 2006: 6). Like any other field, the study of the politics of education has traditionally overlooked a constellation of interests, issues, and theoretical frameworks, and, as a result, is subject to what Heck and Hallinger called 'blank spots' and 'blind spots.' Blank spots refers to research areas in need of further investigation, including areas in a field's knowledge base that have been neglected but would enhance understanding if pursued; blind spots, on the other hand, are described as knowledge that is unknown or curtailed because of our limited theoretical lenses. Similar to the arguments made in Kuhn's *The Structure of Scientific Revolutions* (1970), Heck and Hallinger argued that researchers tend to over-rely on a single ontological and epistemological framework that 'impede[s] us from seeing other facets of phenomena under investigation' (1999: 141). It is not until we switch our framework (or our paradigm) that we can shift our vantage point and shed light on our blind spots. Accordingly, our theories function as lenses as well as blinders, providing discursive spaces to explore and come to understand a particular 'truth' as well as blinders to hide competing 'truth regimes' (Foucault 1972).

Having been schooled in educational politics and policy studies, we are familiar with the field's knowledge base and would argue that it suffers from both blank and blind spots. Moreover, we believe that these are due, in large measure, to the narrow methodological and theoretical frameworks underpinning much of the work in the field. In our own research we have found alternative perspectives useful in expanding our understanding of phenomena and helping us to challenge taken-for-granted beliefs and concepts.

Although we understand there are many theoretical frameworks that could provide helpful perspectives and approaches to developing our knowledge of educational politics, we limit our discussion in this chapter to three: critical race theory, feminist post-structural theory, and queer theory.

## REFRAMING INQUIRY IN THE POLITICS OF EDUCATION

The key position of this paper is that scholarship on the politics of education needs to include a broader range of perspectives. Traditionally, research in the politics of education has, like many social science fields, tended to rely on logical positivism as its preferred lens or method of scientific inquiry (Rorrer and Lugg 2006). This mode of inquiry, which relies on a particularly functionalist view, searches for consistent, generalisable, and predictable empirical laws that explain behavioural regularities (Buroway 2005; Steinmetz 2005). This approach, like all approaches, emerges from a specific ontological and epistemological framework, one which is itself the object of intense criticism and debate (e.g., Buroway 2005; Foucault 1972; Kuhn 1970; Steinmetz 2005).

There are many frameworks from which educational researchers may choose, such as the cultural perspective, critical race theory, first nations/indigenous, feminist, black feminist, chicana, feminist critical policy analysis, post-structural policy archaeology, policy reconstruction, and queer theory—just to name a few. Each dictates the way one identifies and describes research problems, the way one researches a problem, the findings that are highlighted, the implications that one considers, and the approach one takes to planning and implementation. As we expand our theoretical understanding of 'what' we know and 'how' we know, so too must we expand our understanding of the relationship between research methods, methodology and epistemology.

In the remainder of this section, we will illustrate our position by overviewing the traditional perspectives used in the field and then highlighting three 'alternative' frameworks for conducting research in our field—critical race theory, feminist post-structural theory, and queer theory. Although we present these three frameworks as unitary and all-encompassing, most researchers who work within these perspectives often borrow heavily from different theoretical strands of research (Rorrer and Lugg 2006; Young 1999). As such, our aim is not to totalise these approaches but, rather, to highlight key aspects and explore how these frameworks illuminate alternate understandings of educational politics and policy.

## TRADITIONAL APPROACHES TO THE STUDY OF EDUCATIONAL POLITICS

Although American public education has involved politics since its inception, the study of the relationships between politics and education, according to Scribner, Aleman and Maxcy (2003), did not develop until 1959 when an article by Eliot called for the 'study of institutions, ideologies, interests, decision making, and voting behavior,' suggesting that 'if all the significant political factors are revealed, the people can more rationally and effectively control the governmental process' (1959: 1036). Since that time, the study of educational politics has largely focused around the questions of 'who gets what, when, and how' (Laswell 1936) or, as restated by López, around 'those mechanisms—formal and informal, visible and unseen—by which individuals, or groups of individuals, influence the decision-making process as well as the resulting policy outcomes' (2003: 72). Such mechanisms, López points out, influence other political behaviours, such as conflict and conflict resolution as studied by Schattschneider (1960), power (Bachrach and Baratz 1962), pressure and influence (Dye and Zeigler 1970), agenda setting (Malen and Ogawa 1988), and voting behaviour (Iannaccone and Lutz 1970; Wirt and Kirst 1982). By the mid-1970s, Scribner and Englert (1977) identified the core concepts of the field as: government, power, conflict and policy—concepts that have served as 'archetypes that structure much of the work we do in the field' (López 2003: 73).

Two developments strongly influenced the culture of research on educational politics. First, within the academy many were enamoured of the promises of a strong predictive science and felt compelled to adopt the methods of positivism in order to develop generalisable theories in the social sciences. This compulsion solidified the centrality of logical positivism in both the academy's aspirations and its procedures (e.g., theory and methods) (Scribner and Englert 1977). A second development was the growth of federal government programmes, which generated both funding for research and a growing interest in the study of educational politics, particularly as a way of assisting educational leaders and policy makers in their work (Scribner, Aleman and Maxcy 2003).

The status of logical positivism in the field has resulted in a marginalisation of alternative theoretical frameworks as well as a narrow and bounded set of research findings on educational politics—a collective 'blind spot' in our field—that is gathered through a confined and circumscribed grouping of theory and method (López 2003; Lugg 2003; Marshall 1997; Young 1999). Because our research methods largely dictate the phenomena we study, another result is the production and reification of 'blank spots.' In effect, the framework through which scholarship on educational politics has been conducted has resulted in time-worn assumptions, norms, and traditions of/about the appropriate way to 'do' research, as well as the appropriate phenomena and/or concepts on which our research should focus, creating a circular relationship between the tools of inquiry we use and our commonly accepted ideas of what we know or need to know.

In making this argument, we are not suggesting that scholars of educational politics cannot, or do not, subscribe to other philosophical and methodological traditions in their work. Indeed recent research, such as that published in Rorrer and Lugg's (2006) PEA yearbook demonstrates that this is not the case. Nor are we suggesting that the methodologies used in our field are entirely unidimensional. Rather, we are arguing that our commonly accepted research and theoretical frameworks provide a partial heuristic for understanding the epistemological and ontological 'baggage' of the field as a whole (Denzin and Lincoln 1994; Steinmetz 2005). As Denzin and Lincoln argue, researchers within a field inquire about their world 'with a set of ideas, a framework (theory, ontology) that specifies a set of questions (epistemology) that are then examined (methodology, analysis) in specific ways' (1994: 11), resulting in a 'gap' that questions the possibility—or impossibility—of truthfully capturing reality.

Over the past decade, an unprecedented number of researchers questioned the beliefs and practices associated with traditional frameworks. For example, Ball (1994), Scheurich (1994), and Young (1999) problematised the rational model in educational policy research as being overly mechanistic and controlling. Marshall (1993; 1997) critiqued research and practices in educational politics as being male centred. Lugg (2006) has questioned the ingrained hetero-normativity in our field. Moreover, the scholarship of Stanfield (1993), López and Parker (2003), and Scheurich and Young (1997) have problematised the traditional approach to educational research, arguing that our epistemologies and ways of knowing are racially biased. In short, there is a wealth of scholarship in our field that consistently documents the failure of traditional educational research to adequately explain, understand, and change educational practice.

Like the scholars described above, we contend that most educational research, and particularly research on the politics of education, takes place within—and is constrained by—traditionally accepted positivist research frameworks. This circumscription results in a number of serious limitations, such as viewing research problems as 'natural' (Scheurich 1994; Young 1999); viewing research as 'value-free' (Marshall 1997); and viewing the information necessary for policy and planning as obtainable, objective, and shared (Adams 1991). Additionally, the mainstream bias resulting from this tradition has 'resulted in a systemic de-emphasis, mischaracterization, or outright avoidance of the concerns and politics of marginalized groups' (Scribner, Aleman and Maxcy 2003: 20).

Because inquiry in educational politics has historically been undertaken within a narrow framework, broader frameworks for understanding the politics of education are needed. By expanding our theoretical and methodological lenses to include perspectives that stand outside traditional discursive configurations, we not only create an opportunity to expose the field to different understandings of educational politics and policies, but we will also disrupt our taken-for-granted assumptions of what educational politics is, what it can be, and what purposes it ultimately serves.

## CRITICAL RACE THEORY APPROACHES TO
## SCHOLARSHIP IN EDUCATIONAL POLITICS

The first of the three alternative perspectives that we will review is critical race theory (CRT). CRT emerged as an outgrowth of the civil rights movement and the critical legal studies movement of the 1970s to analyse the pervasiveness of racism in society and to investigate how the law reproduces, reifies, and normalises racism in society (López 2003). This perspective became widely popular following the success of 'crossover' books such as Derrick Bell's *And We Are Not Saved* (1987), Patricia William's *Alchemy of Race and Rights* (1995), and Richard Delgado's (1995a) *Critical Race Theory: The Cutting Edge*. Since its inception, CRT has developed strong scholarship in both legal (Crenshaw, Gotanda, Peller and Thomas 1995; Delgado 1995a; Delgado and Stefancic 2001; Valdés, Culp and Harris 2002) and educational circles (Ladson-Billings 1999; López and Parker 2003; Solorzano and Yosso 2002; Villalpando and Delgado Bernal 2002). The emerging scholarship in this area has resulted in poignant accounts, analyses, narratives, and 'counterstories' (Delgado 1995a) of the various faces of racism in law, education, and broader society.

CRT maintains that issues of race and racism are not anomalies, but are permanent social conditions that are endemic components of our social fabric. 'CRT scholars suggest that the reason why society fails to see racism is because it is such a common/everyday experience . . . often taken for granted' (López 2003: 83–4). By focusing on the 'permanence' of racism (Bell 1987), CRT contends that beliefs in neutrality, equal opportunity, meritocracy, democracy, objectivity, colour-blindness, and equality 'are not just unattainable ideals, they are harmful fictions that obscure the normative supremacy of whiteness in American law and society' (Valdés, Culp and Harris 2002: 3). CRT scholars argue that claims of social neutrality not only obscure the interests of dominant groups, but they also facilitate the reification of social relations by masking issues of racial power and privilege in society.

Within the CRT perspective, racism is seen as both an individual construct as well as a social and 'civilizational' construct (Scheurich and Young 1997). By placing race at the centre of its discourse, CRT analyses both overt and hidden manifestations of racism in the political, legal, organisational, and social arenas. According to Solorzano and Yosso (2002), CRT centres around five fundamental points: (a) the centrality and intersectionality of race and racism; (b) the challenge to the dominant ideology of racial neutrality; (c) the commitment to social justice; (d) the importance of experiential knowledge; and (e) the reliance on and use of interdisciplinary perspectives. These five tenets are briefly described below.

The first tenet of CRT places issues of race and racism at the centre, but also views its intersections with other forms of oppression, such as gender

(Iglesias 1998), language (Pabón López 2001), and immigration status (Johnson 1998). CRT claims that the struggle against racism is tightly interwoven with the struggle against other forms of oppression and subordination. Thus, an intersectional perspective is necessary because 'race itself is the product of other social forces—for example as the product of heteropatriarchy in a post-industrial, post-colonial, capitalist society' (Valdés, Culp and Harris 2002: 2).

The second tenet of CRT challenges the notion of neutrality—where racism is perceived as an *individual* and *irrational* act in a world that is otherwise neutral, rational and just (Scheurich and Young 1997). In the traditional view, racism is not necessarily connected to the larger 'distribution of jobs, power, prestige, and wealth' (Crenshaw, Gotanda, Peller and Thomas 1995: xiv); rather, it is viewed as an individual construct. Critical race scholars, however, contend that such views serve primarily to preserve and reinforce the notion of a neutral social order, which camouflages power relations and white privilege in the larger social order (López 2003; Scheurich and Young 1997).

The third aspect of CRT is the commitment to social justice, defined as a deep commitment to end racial oppression and eliminate other interlocking systems of subordination such as sexism, language discrimination, and economic exploitation. In this regard, CRT has a critical or transformative purpose, as well as a political and ethical commitment toward antiracist scholarship and political action (Mendez-Morse 2003). This work is done with 'eyes wide open,' so to speak, to what Bell (1995) has called 'Interest Convergence,' or the belief that Whites will tolerate and advance the interests of people of colour only when they promote the self-interests of whites and at a pace that they determine is reasonable and judicious.

The fourth tenet of CRT privileges experiential knowledge—particularly the stories and counter-stories of people of colour (Delgado 1995b). CRT scholars believe there are two differing accounts of reality: the dominant reality that 'looks ordinary and natural' (Delgado 1995a: xiv) to most individuals, and a racial reality that has been filtered-out, suppressed, and censored. The counter-stories of people of colour are those stories that are not told, stories that are consciously and/or unconsciously ignored or downplayed because they do not 'fit' socially acceptable notions of 'truth.' An example would be the counter-story of the Harlem race riots (López 2003).

The final CRT tenet relies on interdisciplinary perspectives to understand the lived reality of people of colour. As such, the use of a single, ahistorical, and 'monocular' lens (Bakhtin 1968) is discarded in favour of multiple lenses that provide a more 'binocular' and historical tapestry to understanding issues of race and racism in society. This includes the use of lenses that are more sociological, psychological, and historical in nature as well as the utilisation of postmodern, post-structural, and postcolonial frameworks.

## FEMINIST POST-STRUCTURAL APPROACHES TO SCHOLARSHIP IN EDUCATIONAL POLITICS

In recent years, feminist researchers in the field of educational politics have found an ally in post-structuralism. Researchers like Catherine Marshall, who made use of feminist perspectives in their early analyses of educational politics, have taken their work to another level by combining the concerns and insights of feminism with those of post-structuralism.

Grounded in such disciplines as philosophy, sociology, psychology, and history, feminism (though certainly not a unitary category) primarily explores the significance of gender relations and other 'distinctively feminist issues [which are] the situation of women and the analysis of male domination' (Flax 1990: 40; see also Britzman 1991; Chodorow 1989; Collins 1991; 1995; Harding 1987; Hartsock 1985; Pillow 2006; St. Pierre 2000). According to Flax feminist theory aims 'to analyze gender relations: how gender relations are constituted and experienced and how we think or, equally important, do not think about them' (1990: 40). Moreover, feminist scholarship has at its core a praxis. It advocates action that results in a more equitable distribution of resources and opportunities for those who have been marginalised.

Like feminism, post-structuralism is comprised of concepts that enable us to understand educational politics in terms different from those that have been used in the past. Post-structuralism—a continuation of the French philosophical movement of the 1960s that fed the intellectual curiosity of such theoretical luminaries as Foucault, Derrida, Baudrillard, and de Beauvoir—has gained increased significance in academic circles as a vehicle to understand such concepts as: discourse, subjectivity, power and knowledge, and resistance. Feminist post-structuralism, as the name suggests, combines feminist and post-structural perspectives. Working from post-structural conceptions of discourse, subjectivity, power and knowledge, and resistance, feminist post-structuralism focuses these concepts on issues of concern to feminists (e.g., power, gender roles, inequity, oppression).

The fundamental aims of feminist post-structural theory are to identify how patriarchy functions in the world, to understand how women and men are impacted—linguistically, socially, materially—within humanism's discourse, to reveal the relationship between power and knowledge, and to open opportunities for resistance. Conceptions of knowledge and power are central to feminist post-structural thought. The notion of universalising truths (i.e., theories that purport to provide comprehensive explanations) is strongly rejected. Rather, this framework suggests that social reality can only be known locally and contemporaneously.

> This approach respects knowledge and understanding that comes from local stories for instance, that comes from a critical awareness of the particular historical situatedness of the set of conditions that contribute

to the local context. Instead of seeing a local context as *merely* representative of wider social, political and economic trends and forces, it allows us to pay attention to the distinctive features of a local context and to hear the local players in their particular places and times. (Grogan 2003: 20)

However, feminist post-structural theory also reminds us that knowledge (even local knowledge) and truth are neither 'fixed' or stagnant—they are slippery, unstable, and open to a multitude of readings/inscriptions. Indeed, all knowledge is contested; what counts as knowledge depends on who creates it, anoints it, and communicates it (Foucault 1972).

Yet, the problem remains that certain 'truths' tend to be circulated over others. Foucault (1972) suggests that the reason this happens is because power, knowledge, and truth are intricately connected: truth does not exist 'out there' but is actively produced and proliferated within discourses of power. The reason why specific truths (e.g., that females are generally not very good at math or that female leaders are more caring than male leaders) are privileged is because other truths are actively constrained, controlled, and afforded a different status. Truth, therefore, is not 'objective,' or 'waiting to be discovered' but is pregnant with the 'values, politics, and desires' (St. Pierre 2000: 484) of society.

The goal of feminist post-structuralism is to critically engage the limits of humanism's subject by examining the structures it creates and normalises as well as the structures created and normalised by humanism's subject). It specifically aims to reinscribe the 'normal' and open up new avenues for understanding and knowing the world, by disrupting and exposing the categories, structures, and processes that give it meaning (Foucault 1972). Key to understanding the concept of subjectivity is that humanism creates and defines through discourse, that is, through the very act of speaking and writing we are subjectified. 'Subjectivity' is a term used to signify the thoughts and emotions of an individual (both conscious and unconscious), how one understands oneself and how one understands her or his relationship with and within larger society (Weedon 1997).

The final feminist post-structural concern is resistance. If, as suggested above, knowledge and truth are to be troubled and/or expanded to include many voices (rather than the voices of the powerful alone), then one can expect that the 'new' knowledge and truths that emerge will include a resistance to the formerly accepted claims to knowledge and truth (Grogan 2003). Moreover, as questions arise and doubt grows, a productive lack of certainty about 'the way things are' as well as a constructive appreciation of multiple perspectives may emerge. Feminist post-structuralism thus encourages a cognitive resistance upon which individuals may (or may not) take action. How and whether cognitive resistance is translated into action depends upon the individual actor and what power is at her or his behest.

## QUEER THEORY APPROACHES TO
## SCHOLARSHIP IN EDUCATIONAL POLITICS

Queer theory—a cultural study, a philosophy, a political analysis and social critique—troubles taken-for-granted assumptions of 'normality' by examining the processes, structures, discourses, and cultural texts that inscribe meaning in a culturally and historically situated subject (Britzman 1995; 1997; Dilley 1999; Sedgwick 1990; Tierney 1997). Mainstream politics of education scholars have paid little attention to the deep structural issues regarding sexual orientation or how they shape interests, the allocation of resources, and other aspects of schooling (Lugg 2003). Yet these same taken-for-granted assumptions and structures disable public education as a public good to be distributed equitably. The lens of queer theory facilitates the identification of how such assumptions and structures, as well as identities, get constructed through language and discourse (Sedgwick 1990).

Queer theory aims to understand why and how specific discourses, structures, behaviours, and actions become inscribed, normalised, and reproduced through linguistically codified and culturally sanctioned rules and norms. It undermines the homo/hetero, masculine/feminine, male/female binaries, while inverting traditional assumptions of what one considers to be 'normal.' As such, queer theory places queerness—both as essence and social construction—at the centre of the discourse, celebrating the normality of queerness while questioning the queerness of normality.

Tierney (1997) identifies five tenets of queer theory: (a) it seeks to understand sexual identity over time; (b) it seeks to uncover norms and deconstruct ideological practices within social institutions; (c) it is confrontational rather than consensual; (d) it seeks to understand sexual identity as being more than sexuality; and (e) it sees society and culture as interpretive and political (see Britzman 1995; Dilley 1999; Sedgwick 1990). The first tenet contends that sexual orientation has not been a stable or stagnant category across time and space, because different social discourses give rise to different understandings of sexual identity. For example, history has documented same-sex relations, as well as stable same-sex relationships, since antiquity. The societal meaning of 'homosexuality,' however, has shifted throughout time (Foucault 1977). Tracing the history of sexuality over time—its archaeology, its embeddedness in popular discourse, its regulation by social institutions—is a critical first step in understanding how society normalises and regulates issues of sexuality.

Closely related, the second tenet of queer theory is to uncover social norms around issues of sexuality and deconstruct heterosexist ideological practices that are often taken for granted on an everyday basis. By uncovering examples of heterosexual privilege in everyday life, queer theory helps us understand that heterosexism is deeply ingrained and rampant in society: it permeates our practices, discourses, and ways of thinking about the world.

The third tenet of queer theory is confrontation rather than consent, meaning that it is not satisfied by status quo or facile understandings of homophobia and heterosexual privilege. Queer theory critically interrogates manifestations of power and normalisations, and how they discipline and control identities and individual behaviour. It provides an important theoretical space that reveals the promise and problematic nature of power, while providing a forum for understanding how a direct confrontation of normality exposes the arbitrariness of the social as well as the systems of power that order our world.

The fourth tenet of queer theory insists that sexual identity is comprised of more than the sexual act, extending to the meaning that people give to their sexuality. In this regard, queer theory seeks to move the discourse away from sexual acts as the basis for sexual identity and highlight the ways in which society proscribes identities onto the individual.

Finally, queer theory views society and culture as interpretive and political, suggesting that while ways of knowing and experiencing the world are socially constructed, certain voices, perspectives, and worldviews are circulated and privileged over others (Honeychurch 1996; Tierney 1997). Queer theory takes an unapologetic stance in identifying and deconstructing the discourses and regimes of truth that normalise certain perspectives and 'realities' while marginalising, silencing, and disparaging others. Queer theory reminds us that there are, indeed, real struggles in the world: over discourse, over political interests and power, over identity, to make visible the politics of the invisible, and to define and defend what we come to see, experience, and believe to be 'normal' and 'natural.'

## PUTTING ALTERNATIVE PERSPECTIVES TO WORK IN EDUCATIONAL POLITICS RESEARCH AND SCHOLARSHIP

Our review of inquiry in educational politics revealed the strong influence of logical positivism on the theories, methods, and findings informing the field. Over time, this knowledge base has been criticised, though the criticisms were rarely related to its paradigmatic narrowness (e.g., Wirt and Kirst 1982). Our critique, however, pushes past the issue of what the knowledge base does or does not contain to a consideration of *why* it has blank and blind spots. We contend that the answer to this question of *why* is, in large measure, the theoretical and methodological tools used in educational politics scholarship.

In the section above, we presented an overview of the traditional perspective used in educational politics research as well as three powerful alternatives. When these less used perspectives—critical race theory, feminist post-structuralism, and queer theory—are put to work in the examination of educational politics, they hold the potential of expanding knowledge, pushing theory, and revealing complexity. In the following three subsections, we demonstrate, through examples, how they have been applied, or put to work, in the politics of education research.

## Putting CRT to Work

While an increasing number of scholars in the field of education have discussed the racism that exists within the theories and methodologies commonly used in education (e.g., Collins 1991), fewer educational politics scholars have addressed race and/or racism in their work (e.g., Anderson and Herr 1993; Larson and Ovando 2001; Marshall 1993; Marshall and Anderson 1995), and even fewer have utilised CRT as a theoretical lens (e.g., Aleman 2006; López 2003; López and Parker 2003; Parker and Lynn 2002; Solorzano and Yosso 2002; Villalpando and Delgado Bernal 2002).

López, for example, uses CRT to critically engage the limits of the discourse surrounding the politics of education by placing race at the centre of his analysis. Through the use of counter-storytelling, he exposes colourblind and racially neutral assumptions within this area of scholarship, while highlighting the notion that the knowledge base largely fails to engage issues of race and racism head-on. López writes:

> If I were to argue that what we study within the politics of education is entirely racist, most scholars in the field—conservative and liberal alike—would be greatly offended, finding such statements preposterous and absurd. Although some would agree there might be certain institutional practices (such as power) that limit the political participation of nonmainstream groups, or perhaps a handful of truly racist individuals whose values and beliefs create policies that negatively affect people of color, most of us would believe that our knowledge base is not largely affected by racism. (2003: 85)

He further suggests that the 'important stuff' in the politics of education is considered apolitical (e.g., governance, organizational theory, and other stable and politically 'safe' topics), and tends to downplay, or altogether ignore, the centrality of race, class, gender, and sexual orientation in the daily life of schools. Such invisibility, López asserts, serves to institutionalise racism by failing to probe and analyse how it permeates the landscape of education, to relegate racism to a 'theoretical footnote' (2003: 70) within the larger discourse of educational politics, and to ignore the importance of equipping educators with the tools to understand how race and racism function in schools and society at large.

CRT can be used to interrogate the counter-narratives of principals, superintendents, teachers, parents, students, and community members of colour—particularly counter-stories that highlight the multiple ways in which racism functions in the politics of daily life (Henry 1998). It can be used as a theoretical lens to understand the apparent racial neutrality of organisational structures (Parker and Lynn 2002; Solorzano and Yosso 2002). It can be used to better understand the limited nature of our knowledge base. In short, placing issues of race and racism at the centre of analysis opens up new possibilities for understanding the politics of education, while disrupting our taken-for-granted assumptions of the apparent apoliticality of the field.

## PUTTING FEMINIST POST-STRUCTURAL THEORY TO WORK

In the time that has passed since Marshall (1993) called for a new politics of race and gender in the Politics of Education Association's yearbook, feminist researchers have begun to develop a significant body of research on gender and educational politics and policy. Within this literature base, several scholars have contributed pieces that made use of feminist post-structural theory (e.g., Ackerman 2006; Grogan 2003; Pillow 2006; Skrla 2003; Young 2003). This research has considered educational politics very differently than either feminist or traditional research in our field.

Ackerman, for example, uses a feminist post-structural perspective to examine the politics of compensation. Specifically, Ackerman explored issues surrounding the low wages provided to child care workers (an overwhelmingly female field) and how wage levels tend to be attributed to market competition. Making use of Bensimon and Marshall's (2003) claim that policies and the analysis of the problems they seek to address are not neutral or apolitical, she shows how conventional explanations are unsatisfactory.

> Given the numbers of children in ECE and the percentage of families who rely on these settings to participate in the workforce, it is puzzling that low wages have both persisted and never been fixed. One also is confronted with the fact, that 97% of the ECE workforce are women. Therefore, given the subtle role that gender can play in creating a marginalized status, its function in the policies and values that support low wages deserves a closer look. (2006: 96)

Ackerman puts feminist post-structural theory to work, questioning the current situation and explanations, uncovering values that lie underneath presumptive explanations, determining what other factors might play a role in low child care wages, and examining how 'child care wages fit into—and are supported by—a broader, interrelated structure of gender-laden policies and values as well as how these values contribute to the persistence of the problem' (2006: 96).

Scholars like Ackerman (2006), Marshall (1993), and Skrla (2003) have used feminist post-structural theory to unpack and trouble taken-for-granted understandings about educational politics. They have demonstrated the political nature of educational policies and policy analysis (Marshall 1997) as well as how the problems that get attention and are ultimately placed on policy agendas reflect the voice and interests of dominant, powerful groups (Marshall 1997; Young 2003). As a result, these scholars have provided helpful standpoints from which educational politics can be reframed (Young and Skrla 2003).

## PUTTING QUEER THEORY TO WORK

'Two of the most prickly political issues involving US public education have been gender and sexual orientation' (Lugg 2003: 96). Since the 1970s a number of laws and school voting initiatives have focused on banning queer people (or those suspected of being queer) from the teaching profession (Lugg 2003). Likewise, prejudicial values and perspectives have shaped many curricular, extracurricular, and student conduct regulations (Blount 1998; Britzman 1995; Clifford 1989; Sears and Williams 1997). Although an increasing number of court decisions have defended queer children (and those suspected of being queer) from physical violence and 'administrative callousness' (Lugg 2003), prejudice and physical violence continue to be tolerated in the US education system.

Using the tenets of queer theory, educational politics scholars have foregrounded blatant homophobia and heteronormativity in educational politics and schools, while describing the structures, processes, and discourses that reify and reproduce sexual hierarchies in society at large. Blount (2003), for example, traced the history of sexuality and gender in educational administration and helped to explain both why men were relegated to the role of administrators and women to the role of teachers, but also how these roles patrolled both gender and sexuality in men and women. In effect, Blount found the education profession 'normalises' gender roles; that is, while both men and women could 'cross' into the other profession, their gender roles could not.

Lugg (2003; 2006) utilises queer legal theory—a fusion of critical legal theory and queer theory—to explore the influence of state sodomy laws on formal and informal school codes regulating behaviour. According to Lugg (2003), the law, as a regulative, disciplinary body, not only reproduces the proverbial closet, but forces gay, lesbian, bisexual, and transgender (GLBT) educators to weigh the costs/benefits of being out against the costs/benefits of being in and encourages straight educators to uphold rigidly normative gender roles in schools.

In short, queer theory can be used in educational politics research to disrupt our taken-for-granted assumptions of how administrators, teachers, students, and community members—of any gender or sexual orientation—'should' behave and act with/in educational organisations and society at large (Tierney 1997). It can be used to analyse how structures—both organisational and ideological—regulate, and are regulated by, a heteronormative social order (Britzman 1995; Butler 1990; Lugg 2003; Tierney 1997). And it can be used to open spaces of possibility in schools—where educators, gay and straight alike, struggle to 'break down the walls of ignorance' (Koschoreck 2003: 46) and create an organisational climate of respect.

Unfortunately, the body of research in educational politics undertaken from a queer theory perspective, like much of the research undertaken from a CRT or feminist post-structural perspective, has remained on the margins of mainstream educational politics literature, limiting its effect on the research practices, theoretical developments, and knowledge production in the field. This is unfortunate. The understandings provided by alternative perspectives offer potentially important contributions. They provide the opportunity to trouble taken-for-granted assumptions about research, to expand knowledge, to push theory, and to reveal the complexity of educational politics.

## CONCLUSION

It has been argued in this chapter that research in the field of educational politics is limited by its overreliance on traditional frameworks. In an effort to push the limits of the field, we reviewed three alternative frameworks. These frameworks,

> [w]hen used heuristically, are lenses or windows that provide a particular view of social phenomena, opening up vistas not to be seen from other windows/theories. In this way, new theoretical perspectives can make visible those aspects of traditional educational phenomena made invisible by previous theoretical frames. (Marshall and Anderson 1995: 169)

For researchers seeking a way to conduct research that is more complex and that breaks from current and more oppressive practices and orientations, critical race theory, feminist post-structural theory, and queer theory offer potentially more meaningful and helpful approaches to studying the politics of education.

While some have argued the incommensurability of research paradigms and theories (see Kuhn 1970), others have recognised that 'incommensurable languages can be compared and rationally evaluated in multiple ways' (Bernstein 1993: 65). Indeed Kuhn argued that the most important advances in the social sciences are likely to occur not within a single paradigm but in efforts to translate across paradigms. Researchers can learn to make use of more than one theory, framework, or paradigm in an effort to understand phenomena. Bernstein (1993), in fact, argues that researchers have an obligation to understand and use more than one framework in their research endeavours. This would of course require that scholars of educational politics become familiar with nontraditional theories and paradigms, that they think carefully about the framework and methodology they choose when conducting research, and that they teach their students to explore alternative theoretical frames. Such efforts, we would argue, would be well worth it. When multiple theoretical frameworks come to bear on educational politics, the usefulness of our knowledge base will be broadened. Researchers will know more about the phenomena they are examining, and they will know more deeply.

## REFERENCES

Ackerman, D. (2006) 'The costs of being a child care teacher: revisiting the problem of low wages,' *Educational Policy,* 20, 1: 85–112.

Adams, D. (1991) 'Planning models and paradigms,' in R.V. Carlson and G. Ackerman (eds) *Educational Planning: Concepts, Strategies, and Practices,* New York: Longman.

Adams, N. (1997) 'Toward a curriculum of resiliency: gender, race, adolescence and schooling,' in C. Marshall (ed.) *Feminist Critical Policy Analysis: A Perspective from Primary and Secondary Schooling,* London: Falmer Press.

Alemán, E. (2006) 'Robin Hood: the "Prince of Thieves" or a pathway to equity?: applying critical race theory to school finance political discourse', *Educational Policy,* 20, 1: 113–42.

Anderson, G. L., and Herr, C. (1993) 'The micropolitics of student voices: moving from diversity of bodies to diversity of voices in schools,' in C. Marshall (ed.) *The New Politics of Race and Gender: The 1992 Yearbook of the Politics of Education Association,* Washington DC: Falmer Press.

Bachrach, P. and Baratz, M. S. (1962) 'The two faces of power,' *American Political Science Review,* 56: 947–52.

Bakhtin, M. M. (1968) *Rabelais and His World,* Cambridge: MIT Press.

Ball, S. (1994) *Education Reform: A Critical and Poststructural Approach,* Buckingham: Open University Press.

Bell, D. A. (1987) *And We Are Not Saved: The Elusive Quest for Racial Justice,* New York: Basic Books.

———. (1995) Brown vs Board of Education and the interest convergence dilemma', in C. Crenshaw, N. Gotanda, G. Peller, and K. Thomas (eds) *Critical Race Theory: The Key Writings that Formed the Movement,* New York: New Press.

Benhabib, S. (1990) 'Epistemologies of postmodernism: a rejoinder to Jean-Francois Lyotard,' in L. Nicholson (ed.) *Feminism/Postmodernism,* New York: Routledge.

Bensimon, E. M. and Marshall, C. (2003) 'Policy analysis for postsecondary education: feminist and critical perspectives,' in C. Marshall (ed.) *Feminist Critical Policy Analysis II: A Perspective from Post-secondary Education,* London: Falmer Press.

Bernstein, R. J. (1993) *The New Constellation: The Ethical-Political Horizons of Modernity/ Postmodernity,* Cambridge: Polity Press.

Blount, J. M. (1998) *Destined to Rule the Schools: Women and the Superintendency, 1873–1995,* Albany: SUNY Press.

———, (2003) 'Homosexuality and school superintendents: a brief history,' *Journal of School Leadership,* 13, 1: 7–26.

Britzman, D. (1991) *Practice Makes Practice: A Critical Study of Learning to Teach,* Albany: SUNY Press.

———, (1995) 'Is there a queer pedagogy? or, stop reading straight,' *Educational Theory,* 45, 2: 151–65.

———. (1997) 'The tangles of implication', *Qualitative Studies in Education*, 10, 1: 31-7.

Burawoy, M. (2005) 'Conclusion: provincializing the social sciences,' in G. Steinmetz (ed.) *The Politics of Method in the Human Sciences,* Durham: Duke University Press.

Butler, J. (1990) *Gender Trouble: Feminism and the Subversion of Identity,* New York: Routledge.

Chodorow, N.J. (1989) *Feminism and Psychoanalytic Theory*, New Haven: Yale University Press.

Clifford, G. (1989) 'Man/woman/teacher: gender, family and career in American educational history,' in D. Warren (ed.) *American Teachers: Histories of a Profession at Work,* Washington DC: American Educational Research Association.

Collins, P. H. (1991) *Black Feminist Thought: Knowledge, Consciousness and the Politics of Empowerment,* New York: Routledge.

———. (1995) 'Reflections on doing difference', Gender and Society, 9, 4: 505-9.

Crenshaw, K., Gotanda, N., Peller, G. and Thomas, K. (eds) (1995) *Critical Race Theory: The Key Writings that Formed the Movement,* New York: New Press.

Delgado R. (ed.) (1995a) *Critical Race Theory: The Cutting Edge,* Philadelphia: Temple University Press.

———, (1995b) 'Legal storytelling: storytelling for oppositionists and others. A plea for narrative,' in R. Delgado (ed.) *Critical Race Theory: The Cutting Edge,* Philadelphia: Temple University Press.

———, (1995c) 'Rodrigo's chronicle,' in R. Delgado (ed.) *Critical Race Theory: The Cutting Edge,* Philadelphia: Temple University Press.

———, and Stefancic, J. (2001) *Critical Race Theory: An Introduction,* New York: New York University Press.

Denzin, N. and Lincoln, Y. (1994) (eds) *Handbook of Qualitative Research,* Newbury Park: Sage.

Dilley, P. (1999) 'Queer theory: under construction,' *Qualitative Studies in Education,* 12, 5: 457–72.

Dye, T. R. and Zeigler, H. L. (1970) *The Irony of Democracy: An Uncommon Introduction to American Politics,* Belmont: Wadsworth.

Eliot, T. H. (1959) 'Toward an understanding of public school politics,' *American Political Science Review,* 53, 4: 1032–51.

Flax, J. (1990) 'Postmodernism and gender relations in feminist theory,' in L. Nicholson (ed.) *Feminism/Postmodernism,* New York: Routledge.

Foucault, M. (1972) *The Archaeology of Knowledge,* New York: Pantheon Books.

———, (1977) *Discipline and Punish: The Birth of the Prison,* New York: Pantheon Books.

Grogan, M. (2003) 'Laying the groundwork for a reconception of the superintendency from feminist postmodern perspectives,' in M. D. Young and L. Skrla (eds) *Reconsidering Feminist Research in Educational Leadership,* Albany: SUNY Press.

Harding, S. (1987) *Feminism and Methodology,* Bloomington: Indiana University Press.

Hartsock, N. (1985) *Money, Sex, and Power,* Boston: Northeastern University Press.

Heck, R. H. and Hallinger, P. (1999) 'Next generation methods for the study of leadership and school improvement,' in J. Murphy and K. Seashore Louis (eds) *Handbook of Research on Educational Administration,* 2nd edn, San Francisco: Jossey-Bass.

Henry, A. (1998) *Taking Back Control: African Canadian Women Teachers' Lives and Practice,* Albany: SUNY Press.

Honeychurch, K. G. (1996) 'Researching dissident subjectivities: queering the grounds of theory and practice,' *Harvard Educational Review,* 66, 2: 339–55.

Iannaccone, L. and Lutz, F. W. (1970) *Politics, Power, and Policy: The Governing of Local School Districts,* Columbus: Merrill.

Iglesias, E. M. (1998) 'Maternal power and the deconstruction of male supremacy,' in R. Delgado and J. Stefancic (eds) *The Latina/o Condition: A Critical Reader,* New York: New York University Press.

Johnson, K. (1998) 'Citizens as foreigners,' in R. Delgado and J. Stefancic (eds) *The Latina/o Condition: A Critical Reader,* New York: New York University Press.

Koschoreck, J. W. (2003) 'Easing the violence: transgressing heteronormativity in educational administration,' *Journal of School Leadership,* 13, 1: 27–50.

Kuhn, T. (1970) *The Structure of Scientific Revolutions,* Chicago: University of Chicago Press.

Ladson-Billings, G. (1999) 'Just what is critical race theory and what's it doing in a nice field like education?' in L. Parker, D. Deyhle, and S. Villenas (eds) *Race is . . . Race isn't: Critical Race Theory and Qualitative Studies in Education,* Boulder: Westview Press.

Larson, C. and Ovando, C. (2001) *The Color of Bureaucracy: The Politics of Equity in Multicultural School Communities,* Belmont: Wadsworth.

Laswell, H. (1936) *Politics: Who gets What, When, How,* New York: McGraw-Hill.

Lincoln, Y. L. and Guba, E. G. (1985) *Naturalistic Inquiry,* Beverly Hills: Sage.

López, G. R. (2003) 'The (racially neutral) politics of education: a critical race theory perspective,' *Educational Administration Quarterly,* 39, 1: 68–94.

———, and Parker, L. (eds) (2003) *Interrogating Racism in Qualitative Research Methodology,* New York: Peter Lang.

Lugg, C. (2003) 'Sissies, faggots, lezzies, and dykes: gender, sexual orientation, and a new politics of education?' *Educational Administration Quarterly,* 39, 1: 95–134.

———, (2006) 'Thinking about sodomy: public schools, legal panopticons, and queers,' *Educational Policy,* 20, 1: 35–59.

Malen, B. and Ogawa, R. T. (1988) 'Professional-patron influence on site-based governance councils: a confounding case study,' *Educational Evaluation and Policy Analysis,* 10, 4: 251–70.

Marshall, C. (1993) *The New Politics of Race and Gender: The 1992 Yearbook of the Politics of Education Association,* Washington DC: Falmer Press.

———, (1997) 'Dismantling and reconstructing policy analysis,' in C. Marshall (ed.) *Feminist Critical Policy Analysis: A Perspective from Primary and Secondary Schooling,* London: Falmer Press.

———, and Anderson, G. (1995) 'Rethinking the public and private spheres: feminist and cultural studies perspectives on the politics of education,' in J. D. Scribner and D. Layton (eds) *The Study of educational politics: The 1994 commemorative yearbook of the Politics of Education Association* (1969–1994), Washington DC: Falmer.

Méndez-Morse, S. (2003) 'Chicana feminism and educational leadership,' in M. D. Young and L. Skrla (eds) *Reconsidering Feminist Research in Educational Leadership,* Albany: SUNY Press.

Nicholson, L. (1990) 'Introduction,' in L. Nicholson (ed.) *Feminism/Postmodernism,* New York: Routledge.

Pabón López, M. (2001) 'The phoenix rises from El Cenizo: a community creates and affirms Latino/a Border cultural citizenship through its language and safe haven ordinances,' *Denver University Law Review,* 78, 4: 1017–48.

Parker, L. and Lynn, M. (2002) 'What's race got to do with it?: critical race theory's conflicts with and connections to qualitative research methodology and epistemology,' *Qualitative Inquiry,* 8, 1: 7–22.

Pillow, W. (2006) 'Teen pregnancy and education: politics of knowledge, research and practice,' *Educational Policy,* 20, 1: 59–84.

Rorrer, A. and Lugg, C. (2006) 'Introduction: education, and the politics of social justice,' *Educational Policy,* 20, 1: 5–7.

Rorrer, A.K. and Lugg, C.A. (2006) 'Power, education and the politics of social justice', Politics of Education Association special issue, Educational Policy, 20, 1: 1-290.

St. Pierre, E. (2000) 'Postructural feminism in education: an overview,' *Qualitative Studies in Education,* 13, 5: 477–515.

Schattschneider, D. (1960) *The Semisovereign People: A Realist View of Democracy in America,* New York: Holt, Rinehart and Winston.

Scheurich, J. J. (1994) 'Policy archeology: a new policy studies methodology,' *Journal of Education Policy,* 9, 4: 297–316.

——, and Young, M. D. (1997) 'Coloring epistemologies: are our research epistemologies racially biased?' *Educational Researcher,* 26, 4: 4–17.

Scribner, J. D., Aleman, E. and Maxcy, B. (2003) 'Emergence of the politics of education field: making sense of a messy center,' *Educational Administrative Quarterly,* 39, 1: 10–40.

Scribner, J. D. and Englert, R. M. (1977) 'The politics of education: an introduction,' in J. P. Scribner (ed.) *Politics of Education: The Seventy-Sixth Yearbook of the National Society for the Study of Education,* Chicago: University of Chicago Press.

Sears, J. and Williams, W. (eds) (1997) *Overcoming Heterosexism and Homophobia: Strategies that Work,* New York: Columbia University Press.

Sedgwick, E. K. (1990) *Epistemology of the Closet,* Berkeley: University of California Press.

Skrla, L. (2003) 'Normalizing femininity: reconsidering research on women in the superintendency,' in M. D. Young and L. Skrla (eds) *Reconsidering Feminist Research in Educational Leadership,* Albany: SUNY Press.

Solorzano, D. G. and Yosso, T. J. (2002) 'Critical race methodology: counter-storytelling as an analytic framework for educational research,' *Qualitative Inquiry,* 8, 1: 23–44.

Stanfield, J. (1993) 'Epistemological considerations,' in J. Stanfield and R. Dennis (eds) *Race and Ethnicity in Research Methods,* Newbury Park: Sage.

Steinmetz, G. (ed.) (2005) *The Politics of Method in the Human Sciences,* Durham: Duke University Press.

Tierney, W. G. (1997) *Academic Outlaws: Queer Theory and Cultural Studies in the Academy,* Thousand Oaks: Sage.

Valdés, F., Culp, J. M. and Harris, A. P. (eds) (2002) *Crossroads, Directions, and a New Critical Race Theory,* Philadelphia: Temple University Press.

Villalpando, O. and Delgado Bernal, D. (2002) 'A critical theory analysis of barriers that impede the success of faculty of color,' in W. Smith, P. Altbach and K. Lomotey (eds) *The Racial Crisis in American Higher Education,* 2nd edn, Albany: SUNY Press.

Weedon, C. (1997) *Feminist Practice and Poststructuralist Theory,* 2nd edn, New York: Basil Blackwell.

Wirt, F. M. and Kirst, M. W. (1982) *Schools in conflict: The politics of education.* Berkeley: McCutchan.

Young, M. D. (1999) 'Multifocal educational policy research: Toward a method for enhancing traditional educational policy studies.' *American Educational Research Journal,* 36 (4), 677–714.

——, (2003) 'The Leadership Crisis: Gender and the Shortage of School Administrators.' In M. D. Young and L. Skrla (eds) *Reconsidering Feminist Research in Educational Leadership.* Albany: SUNY Press.

——, and Skrla, L. (eds) (2003) *Reconsidering Feminist Research in Educational Leadership.* Albany: SUNY Press.

# 11 The Politics of Civil Society and the Possibility of Change

## A Speculation on Leadership in Education

*Richard Bates*

## THE IDEA OF CIVIL SOCIETY

The idea of civil society first emerged during the Enlightenment in the seventeenth and eighteenth centuries. It was an essentially utopian aspiration for a civilisation in which individuals would live together as politically mature, responsible citizens, tolerant of religious, ethnic and cultural diversity, and held together by a social contract based upon natural law and the beneficial, civilising effects of commercial exchange, one of the consequences of which would be a reduction in gross inequality. As such, it rejected the absolutist claims of both traditional religion and the authoritarian state, envisaging an essentially republican politics based on the self-organisation of individuals in the pursuit of common interests under the rule of law. Civil society, in its various versions, was therefore seen as something separate from the state but beyond the domestic sphere of home and family—a society of associations operating in the public sphere in such a way as to articulate various interests into the political process.

During the nineteenth and early twentieth centuries the idea of civil society was discarded in political economy to the point where Hobsbawm (1994: 139) could describe it as 'nostalgic rhetoric' and Margaret Thatcher could famously declare that there was no such thing as society—only individuals and their families. However, during the past two decades the idea has reemerged as a crucial concept in social, political, and economic controversies. The initial impetus for this 'brilliant comeback' (Kocka 2004: 67) was its use in the antidictatorial critique of one-party dictatorships, Soviet hegemony, and Eastern European totalitarianism mounted by Havel, Geremek and Konrad (Kocka 2004). It was also vital to similar critiques developed in Latin America and South Africa (Kaldor 2003; Comaroff and Comaroff 1999). But its use is no longer restricted to such movements and is in wide currency in both left and right political movements as well as by liberals, communitarians, antiglobalisation activists, and social scientists.

Kocka suggests there are three main reasons for the current popularity of the idea of civil society. Firstly, its emphasis on responsibility and self-organisation appeals to those who believe that the interventionist state has reached its limits. Secondly, with its emphasis on discourse, negotiation, and understanding as opposed to competition, exchange, and individualism, the logic of civil society presents an immanent critique of unbridled capitalism. Thirdly, it offers an emphasis on social cohesion as an antidote to the individualism and fragmentation of postindustrial society (2004: 67–8).

In its contemporary form, civil society is argued to be at one and the same time a type of *social action,* a *social sphere,* and a *utopian project.*

As a type of *social action* civil society:

> 1) is oriented towards non-conflict, compromise and understanding in public; (2) stresses individual independence and social self-organization; (3) recognises plurality, difference and tension; (4) proceeds non-violently and peacefully; and (5) is, among other things, oriented towards general things (and) the common good. (Kocka 2004: 69)

As a *social sphere,* civil society is constituted by clubs, associations, social movements, and networks that form 'a complex and dynamic ensemble of legally protected non-government institutions' (Keane 1998: 6).

As a *utopian project,* civil society is currently being advocated in the West as an antidote to both big government and big capital, and in developing countries as a political project of modernisation in the pursuit of democracy and civil rights (Ibrahim 1995; Kaviraj and Khilnani 2001). Here the idea of civil society is defined in contrast to both the constraining authority of the state and the primordial authority of the involuntary bonds of family, village, tribe, and historical cultures (Zubaida 2001).

However, there are significant differences in the politics of civil society. Emerging from the Weberian tradition is a view of a public sphere where various groups consolidate around particular interests and argue out differences in values and priorities that can be subsequently articulated into the formal procedures of politics and legislation. As Kim suggests,

> For Weber . . . the most crucial issue in revitalizing a civil society is to preserve and magnify the elements of contestation under late modern circumstances. Modern individuals need to engage in various associational activities so that they can challenge and compete with each other in a concrete everyday context in which they will be constantly required to define, redefine and choose their ultimate values and to take disciplined moral actions based on their choices. (2004: 188)

Contemporary commentators like Wolin follow this line of argument, suggesting, for instance, that in modern society with its vast concentrations of power in governments and corporations the most desperate problem of democracy is ' to develop a fairer system of contestation over time, especially hard times' (1996: 115).

On the other hand, an alternative view emphasises the associational life it sponsors as a mechanism for establishing social solidarity in the face of anomie and disorder. In this right-Tocquevillian view,

> associational life is frequently imagined in terms of communal conge-
> niality and group solidarity: the civic virtues, in terms of civility, coop-
> eration and trust. In the face of the alleged anomie and disorderliness,
> then, the issue becomes the recovery of this form of solidarity through
> a pluralistic associational life, which, as an unintended consequence is
> expected to engender a more engaged public citizenry and a robust lib-
> eral democracy. (Kim 2004: 189)

These contrasting views of civil society are taken up in two further ideas: contestation in an autonomous *public sphere* and social solidarity through the development of *social capital*.

## CIVIL SOCIETY AND THE AUTONOMOUS PUBLIC SPHERE

The most important contemporary theorist of the public sphere is Jürgen Habermas, who, in *The Structural Transformation of the Public Sphere*, argued the importance of civil society autonomy as

> a domain of our social life where such a thing as public opinion can be
> formed [where] citizens . . . deal with matters of general interest with-
> out being subject to coercion . . . [in order to] express and publicize
> their views. (1989: 105)

Habermas originally conceived of the public sphere as a unitary arena where different voices struggled to articulate a 'public' view free of the constraints of the political power of the state or the economic power of corporations. Public institutions—especially the media—needed to be autonomous and free from political or economic coercion. They were the third pillar of soci-ety, providing the arena within which 'public opinion . . . is worked up via democratic procedures into communicative power [which] cannot "rule" itself but can . . . point the use of administrative power in specific direc-tions' (1994: 9–10). Social movements—such as the feminist, civil rights, and environmental—were argued by Habermas to be the most significant contemporary contributors to the public sphere and the development of communicative power.

His critics, such as Negt and Kluge (1993), however, argued that it was precisely the existence of these multiple social movements that supported the idea that rather than a single, unitary, public sphere, there were in fact many publics and multiple public spheres which constituted (or were consti-tuted by) multiple cultures and forms of communication. In the same vein,

Gitlin (1998) raised the question of whether we should be talking about the 'Public Sphere or public sphericules.'

Moreover, Fraser and Honneth (2003), in part following Felski (1989), argued for the idea of *counter-public* spheres through which marginalised minority groups articulate positions in opposition to those in the broader public sphere, attempting subsequently to move them towards broader acceptance and eventual articulation into state legislation. In many ways, these are arguments about how the public sphere(s) operate rather than about the existence of such an area of discourse, contention, and debate separate from the state and economy within which ideas and interests can be articulated (McKee 2005). But the intersection of public sphere ideas and, by extension, the public interest, with the diversity of contemporary cultures, movements, and associations is an important area of current debate (Bates 2005a; 2005b; Gray 2000; Touraine 2000).

## CIVIL SOCIETY AND SOCIAL CAPITAL

The importance of membership in cultures, movements, and associations is emphasised by the development of the idea of social capital. It is possible to see it developing out of ideas of mutual obligation outlined by such theorists as Adam Ferguson (1966 [1767]) and Adam Smith. Smith's most popular book during his lifetime was *Theory of Moral Sentiments* (1984 [1759]), which took as its starting point the desire of individuals for kindness and esteem. Such desire was seen by Smith as the foundation for associations beyond the family through which networks were established on the basis of trust. Such networks built shared norms and social capital, which in turn facilitated commercial activity and the growth of trade (Bates 1995; 2003a; Muller 1993). These three key ideas—networks, norms, and trust—form the basis for various approaches to social capital in its contemporary forms. Interest in the idea has recently been revitalised by three authors in particular: Bourdieu, Coleman, and Putnam.

Bourdieu (1991; 1997) articulated the idea of social capital as analogous to economic capital which, along with cultural and symbolic capital, combines to determine the social position of individuals. Such capital was argued to derive from networks of relationships in which individuals are embedded and which provide social resources through which they establish an appropriate place in social hierarchies. Although Bourdieu uses the term in a number of different ways, it is essentially presented as a metaphor—one that allows social capital to be seen as capable of being accumulated, invested, and spent in ways analogous to, but somewhat separate from, economic capital.

At the same time that Bourdieu reintroduced the idea of social capital to European social theory through his form of cultural analysis, Coleman developed a similar, but functionalist, analysis in the US. Emerging from his studies of the relationship between educational achievement and social inequality, Coleman suggested that differences in educational achievement could largely be explained by differences in social (somewhat distinct from economic) capital. In this explanation, Coleman defined social capital as 'the set of resources that inhere in family relations and in community social organization and that are useful for the cognitive or social development of a child or young person' (1994: 300). He saw these resources as networks of social relations that were essentially inherited along with economic and political networks, and which consolidated achievement across generations: 'the powerful remained powerful by virtue of their contacts with other powerful people' (Schuller, Baron and Field 2000: 6).

Oddly, despite their mutual interest in social capital and educational achievement, and their collaboration towards the end of Coleman's career, they never acknowledged each other's work in their writings. This was possibly due to Coleman's treatment of social capital and its distribution as relatively unproblematic and 'functional' while, for Bourdieu, the distribution of economic, cultural, and social capital was the result of considerable effort on the part of elites to maintain their ownership of various forms of capital at the expense of the dispossessed.

Perhaps the most popular and influential account of social capital in recent years is Putnam's, whose commentary on the decline of social associations in the US is outlined in his article (later book) *Bowling Alone* (1995; 2000). The three key themes reemerge in his succinct definition of social capital as 'features of social life—networks, norms and social trust—that enable participants to act together more effectively to pursue shared objectives' (1996: 56).

In charting the decline of associational life in the US, Putnam (2000) argues that trust and trustworthiness lubricate social life, and the reciprocity they engender is the touchstone of social solidarity. This does not necessarily mean that all forms of social capital based upon trust and reciprocity are virtuous. Indeed, certain forms of social organisation (organised crime, for instance), may also depend upon quite particular social norms, trust, and networks for their effectiveness. But the interesting thing about Putnam's work is that it is less deterministic than either Coleman's functionalist or Bourdieu's reproductionist accounts of social capital. It suggests, rather, that social capital is variable between communities and over time.

This idea of variability is taken up by Fukuyama (1992; 1995), who associates trust as the dominant feature of social capital, with particular cultural characteristics. For instance, he attempts to explain the relative economic success of various nation states with reference to his assessment of their levels of social capital. Success, he suggests, depends upon communities 'formed not on the basis of explicit rules and regulation but out of a set of ethical habits and reciprocal moral obligations internalised by each of the community's members' (1995: 9). Moreover, 'a nation's well-being, as well as its ability to compete, is conditioned by a single, pervasive, cultural characteristic: the level of trust inherent in the society' (1995: 7).

This being so, Fukuyama argues, 'high-trust' societies, such as Japan, Germany, and the US, will inevitably be more economically successful than 'low-trust' societies, such as China, Italy, and France, as 'high-trust' between managers and workers enables enhanced production. Indeed, the function of social capital in his account now becomes clear: the enhancement of production through the minimisation of dissent. Or, more politely, 'the economic function of social capital is to reduce the transaction costs associated with formal coordination mechanisms like contracts, hierarchies, bureaucratic rules, and the like' (2001: 10). It would seem, therefore, that in order to be economically successful states should sponsor the development of social capital in order to reduce social friction and thus, transaction costs.

There are several major difficulties with this approach, but two are of great importance. First, there are considerable doubts as to its empirical validity, particularly given the rise of China and the very high levels of indebtedness of the US, the failure of firms such as Enron and Arthur Anderson, and the growing disparities between rich and poor, none of which are conducive to the formation of 'high-trust.' Secondly, like most functionalist accounts of social mechanisms, it entirely dismisses the importance of inequality and conflict in the contestation of existing distributions of economic, cultural, and social capital. Despite these criticisms, another attempt to use the notion of social capital in this functionalist manner is articulated through the 'Third Way' movement.

Advocates of the Third Way place considerable importance on the notion of social capital, seeing it first in economic terms and secondly as a mechanism of mobilisation of the disadvantaged through 'social entrepreneurship' (Giddens 1998; 2000). Giddens, for instance, advocates networking among industry as a form of social capital that increases innovation and productivity (2000: 78ff) as well as endorsing the capacity of 'third sector groups' to 'offer choice and responsiveness in the delivery of public services' to the poor (2000: 81). Social capital from this perspective, therefore, seems to involve the sponsorship and/or cooptation of associations and voluntary groups by either the economy or the state. The interests of the economy are served by lowered costs of production combined with higher levels of innovation through networking. The interests of the state are served by more efficient administration of services combined with lowered levels of anomie and resistance (McClenaghan 2000). These are not necessarily unwanted outcomes, but they do indicate the propensity for economy and state to appropriate the supposedly autonomous 'public sphere' for their own ends.

> Indeed, the 'Third Way' project of building social capital among the poor, whether of the First World or the Third, is considered by some as a convenient ideological evasion of the problems of the mal-distribution of wealth and power within and between societies. (Fine 2001)

More broadly, the difficulty with the definition of social capital as primarily concerned with the replacement of the norms, values, and social solidarity threatened by the pressures of globalisation and economic competition is that it obscures the contestation between various groups demanding civil, political, and economic rights and the redress of undeserved inequalities. As McClenaghan observes, in such analyses

> social capital is used in such a way as to place the main emphasis upon social cohesion; an emphasis which gives the analysis a profoundly functionalist and socially conservative bent in that it discounts community organization and mobilisation in defence of citizenship rights and the political articulation of rights-based demands which inevitably generate conflict, in favour of activities designed to enhance social cohesiveness and, by implication, social control. (2000: 580)

## THE DEMOCRACY OF CIVIL SOCIETY

In essence this is, therefore, a battle between the (private) individual and the (public) state, with civil society being the battleground on which individuals, through collective action, attempt to delimit the power of the state and where the state, through collective agencies, attempts to prevent the fragmentation of the nation. Baker, in his discussion of Havel's approach to this problem, makes the point succinctly:

> With Havel, then, the public and the private are intimately related, it is just a matter of how the relationship should be constructed such that the public is not allowed to destroy the private (totalitarianism), nor the private allowed to destroy the public (atomising liberal-individualism). (2002: 149)

The issue for Havel is not that either the public or the private should have primacy over the other, but rather that the private should be a 'holding area' of the self 'from which the self must necessarily emerge to act publicly' (Havel 1988 in Mische 1993: 245). For Havel, it is this emergence of the autonomous human subject into the public sphere that forms the basis of authentic public life—the democracy of civil society (1985, 1988).

In this view, Havel is close to Arendt (1958a; 1963), who argues that 'the political realm rises directly out of acting together, the "sharing of words and deeds"' (1958b: 198). But, interestingly, Arendt defends the idea of civil society against both the incursions of the state and the demands of communities based in national, religious, ethnic, or local traditions:

> Arendt's conception of the public realm is opposed not only to society but also to community: to Gemeinschaft as well as Gesellschaft. While

greatly valuing warmth, intimacy and naturalness in private life, she insisted on the importance of a formal, artificial public realm in which what mattered was the people's actions rather than their sentiments; in which the natural ties of kinship and intimacy were set aside in favour of a deliberate, impartial solidarity with other citizens; in which there was enough space between people for them to stand back and judge one another coolly and objectively. (Canovan 1985: 632)

This is an important issue, for against both collectivist (totalitarian) and liberal (individualist) conceptions of politics, Arendt and Havel argue the importance of civil society as a ground on which both public and private interests can be articulated without the dominance of one over the other; a view similar to Habermas' account of the importance of an autonomous public sphere discussed earlier. As Baker argues, in Arendt and Havel's view,

the individual's private sphere matters, but its preservation is not the sole end of politics, as in liberalism. Yet neither is the collective reified, as in more communitarian visions, since the public sphere is understood not as a thing in itself, but as that artificially constructed (though crucial nonetheless) space in which *individuals* come together. (2002: 154)

But this raises immediately the question of how and under what conditions individuals are to come together in the public sphere. While individuals may make claims as members of particular communities celebrating particular norms, values, and interests, the demand for recognition of the rights accruing to difference may well create friction with those claiming the primacy of alternative norms, values, and interests. As Olssen argues,

pushing the principle of difference too far results in contradiction. While multi-culturalists and those who advocate difference want to celebrate multiplicity and a de-centered polis, the fundamental ambiguity results from the fact that respecting the autonomy of different groups— whether based on religion, race, gender, or ethnicity—is only possible within certain *common bounds*. Central to this perspective is that the notion of difference must pre-suppose a 'minimal universalism' which in turn necessitates a certain conception of community. (2004: 186)

Just what such a minimal universalism would look like is a matter of controversy. It is, perhaps, easier to say what is disallowed than what is allowed. For instance, it seems clear that

cultural minorities whose practices are based on deeply illiberal oppressive relations based on gender, or sex, or any other basis of difference, cannot be tolerated and neither can group practices that fail to respect the fundamentally important principles of democratic politics, such as respect for the other, a willingness to negotiate, tolerance, or the institutional basis of deliberation or the rule of law. (Olssen 2004: 187)

Such a perspective implies a middle ground between *Gemeinschaft* and *Gesellschaft*, where individuals have the right to be respected as members of particular groups, but also the right of independence from the claims of such groups where they so choose: the principle of equal autonomy applies, as Touraine suggests, as the only universal principle that allows reconciliation between the public and the private.

> No multi-cultural society is possible unless we can turn to a universalist principle that allows socially and culturally different individuals and groups to communicate with one another. But neither is a multi-cultural society possible if that universalist principle defines one conception of social organization and personal life that is judged both to be normal and better than others. The call for freedom to build a personal life is the only universalist principle that does not impose one form of social organization and cultural practices. It is not reducible to laissez-faire economics or to pure tolerance, first, because it demands respect for the freedom of all individuals and therefore a rejection of exclusion, and secondly because it demands that any reference to cultural identity be legitimised in terms of the freedom and equality of all, and not by appeal to a social order, a tradition or the requirements of public order. (2000: 167)

Or perhaps, as Taylor puts it more succinctly, 'the struggle for recognition can only find one satisfactory solution, and that is a regime of reciprocal recognition among equals' (1994: 50). But even if this is accepted as the fundamental, democratic principle, the question still arises as to how it is to be articulated in public institutions, and especially, perhaps, educational institutions. How is the democracy of civil society to be constituted in practice?

## THE INSTITUTIONS OF CIVIL SOCIETY

Two approaches to democracy, the classical and the contemporary, compete as an institutional basis of contemporary societies. The classical view was that democracy required participation in the life of the polis by active citizens who collectively defined the norms, values, interests, and institutions through which their collective aspirations might be realised.

> A central feature of this classical conception of democracy, then, is that it is a *moral* concept identifying a form of social and political life which gives expression to the values of self-fulfilment, self-determination and equality—values constitutive of the kind of society in which

all individuals can fulfil themselves by freely and equally determining
the common good of their society. (Carr and Hartnett 1996: 40)

This is not to say that any society has ever realised these principles in
practice, but rather, that as an ideal type, such a conception of democracy allows political and social institutions to be held to account against
such criteria. The implications are that institutions arising from collective
action must be held accountable for their embrace of such principles in
their day-to-day practices.

The alternative, contemporary, account of democracy is based on public
choice theory. In this version of democracy, contemporary life is seen as too
complex and vast for the active participation of all citizens in political processes. Rather than participation, choice is seen as the fundamental principle
between rival political elites through periodic voting for political parties. In
this 'realist' view,

> 'political equality' means an equal opportunity to vote for leaders and
> 'democratic participation' means exercising that vote at periodic elections.
> It thus takes competition between political elites—and not participation
> in decision-making—to be the essence of democracy and the criterion that
> allows the 'democratic method' to be distinguished from other methods
> of political decision-making. (Carr and Hartnett 1996: 42)

Clearly, the 'realist' view of democracy has significant limitations in that
political elites may present alternatives articulating differing versions of the
'public good' between which individuals get to choose, but which may not
articulate their particular interests. Moreover, as footloose capital begins to
operate 'over and above' the institutions of the state, options offered at the
state political level may indeed not bear significantly on crucial issues over
which the state has limited control. As Baumann suggests,

> Having lost much of their past sovereignty and no longer able to bal-
> ance the books on their own or lend authority to the type of social order
> of their choice, contemporary states fail to meet the other necessary
> condition of a viable republic: the ability of the citizens to negotiate and
> jointly decide 'the public good' and so to shape a society which they
> would be prepared to call their own. (1999: 169)

In this view, democracy itself is called into question as decision-making and
alternative futures are removed from the political arena of the state and decisions made by capital are represented as inevitable: 'there is no alternative.'

But, as Dewey (1935) pointed out, such failure is not only of political but
also of educational institutions. While he argued that the interests of individuals, even at the beginning of the twentieth century, had become increasingly
privatised and depoliticised, thereby giving credence to the realist view of

democracy in which participation in the public sphere was regarded as increasingly obsolete, Dewey also argued that the lack of participation in the public sphere was the result of the failure of social intelligence through the failure of educational institutions to provide the opportunity for the development of the knowledge that would allow full participation in the public sphere. Denigrating the intelligence of individuals who were excluded (women, blacks, and those who owned no property) from political participation by lack of knowledge was not the fault of those individuals, but rather of the educational institutions that excluded them from access to crucial knowledge and skills.

> The indictments that are drawn against the intelligence of individuals are in truth indictments of a social order that does not permit the average individual to have access to the rich store of accumulated wealth of mankind in knowledge, ideas and purposes . . . It is useless to talk about the future of democracy until the source of its failure has been grasped and steps are taken to bring about that type of social organization that will encourage the socialised extension of intelligence. (Dewey 1935: 38–9)

For Dewey, prime among these social organisations was education—one that prepared individuals for active participation in the public sphere and the exercise of their democratic rights to participate in the governance of public institutions rather than the 'realist' option of simply choosing periodically between platforms presented by political elites.

## CIVIL SOCIETY AND THE ADMINISTRATION OF EDUCATION

If civil society is both an arena for collective action and a social process, as well as a utopian vision, one, moreover, that has a relative autonomy from the imperatives of the economic state on one hand and the cultural imperatives of traditional communities on the other, a crucial question is what role has education in preparing citizens for active participation in the public sphere? Increasingly, leaders in education are broadening their view of the purposes of schooling to include more than skill formation in the pursuit of efficient economic production, obedience to an all-encompassing state, or subservience to unexamined traditions. As Bottery (2004) suggests, 'big picture' issues are impinging on all of us in ways that cannot be ignored. It is worth quoting him at some length as his presentation of the current dilemmas facing educational leaders encapsulates the issues in a powerful way.

> This is indeed a critical time for education, and for societies in general. It is an age of rapid and far-reaching changes, which no longer occur just at local and national levels, but which have profound effects across the globe. It is a time when we recognize that global warming is no respecter of national borders . . . It is a time then we recognize that humanity continues

to contribute to global pollution, and yet still seems stuck within postures, both political and economic, which prevent this issue from being properly addressed. It is also a time of great paradox, when massive standardizations of global culture contrast with the easy availability of varied cultures and beliefs . . . Perhaps most importantly, with the demise of fascism and communism as state-sponsored ideologies, it is a time when a version of liberal democracy is the only global political ideology, and walks arm-in-arm across a world stage with an economics of free-market capitalism. The results of this twin domination have been remarkable and striking in their extent and intensity. (2004: 3)

Starratt, while taking a somewhat different approach to educational leadership based upon the requirement of schools to develop ways of cultivating meaning, community and responsibility, also does so within the context of the transition of contemporary societies 'between early modernity and the later, more reflexive modernity' in a globalised world (2003: 55).

Although taking a somewhat realist view of democracy and social capital, Rifkin has also argued for the reconceptualisation of both civil society and the form of education appropriate to it:

The new economic and political realities require us to rethink the mission of the civil society in the years ahead. The third sector is likely to play a far more expansive role as an area for job creation and social-service provision in the coming century. The civic sector is also likely to become a more organized force in every community, working with, and on occasion pressuring, the market and government sectors to meet the needs of workers, families and neighborhoods. Thinking of society as creating three kinds of capital—market capital, public capital and social capital—opens up new possibilities for reconceptualizing the social contract and the kind of education we give our young people. (1998: 177)

Similarly, I have argued on previous occasions the need for a global perspective on administration (2002; 2003b) and curriculum (2005b), arguing, in Bottery's summary, for the work of educational leaders to be 'about more than the delivery and implementation of government legislation, curricula and testing, but ultimately to do with learning to live with one another, learning to support one another, learning to listen to one another, and learning to redress issues of equity' (2004:10).

As Starratt suggests, in such processes the idea of community is quite central: not community seen as a restricted form of social solidarity and tradition preventing autonomous individual decision-making and the claustrophobic condition of *Gemeinschaft,* but community seen as an active public association directed towards the solution of public problems articulated in the public sphere. In such an argument the relationship between education and civil society becomes central.

If civil society is that space between the private and the public, between the state and economy on one hand and cultures and traditions on the other, then learning how to use this space becomes a central task of education. But, as argued earlier, civil society is not only a space, but also a social process, a process that is focused on deliberative agreement or mediation:

> Civil society is not only a space but also a process of mediation . . . Understanding civil society as a social process draws attention to how these arenas embody a more constitutive model of communication in which social and political realities, mediated through language, are interpreted and achieve explanatory power in the minds of citizen-actors. As processes of mediation, these networks serve as links between citizens and their understanding of the issues and institutions that confront their respective historical moments. (Murphy 2004: 84)

Within such an understanding of civil society, the role of the school in developing skills of mediation in the formation of communities within the public sphere around issues of public interest is of central importance. Starratt articulates a similar view of the role of educational administrators in 'cultivating community.' Rather than being restricted to the development of commercially relevant skills or the communication of 'virtuous communities' (Sergiovanni 1992) based upon exclusion and the replication of particular cultural traditions, Starratt argues for the development of a public education focussed on areas of public policy, one that encourages the development of community mediation around

> the major issues contested in public debate: ecological preservation; alternative energy sources; full civil rights for various groups disadvantaged by social and political structures; government regulation of global corporations; international agreements on investments in global economic and technological infrastructures; the ownership of the airways, the oceans, the rainforests, the Internet; international responses to terrorist organizations; genetic engineering of food, livestock, medicine, human organs; immigration rights and responsibilities, to name a few. (2003: 90)

Such a view has considerable implications for the administration of curriculum, but also for the administrative and organisational structures of the school for, 'in the formation and building of community within the school, the processes by which a community governs itself, and the corresponding processes whereby individuals govern themselves, are crucial' (Starratt 2003: 91). It also has implications for the administration and management of pedagogical processes, as Murphy suggests in his argument for deliberative education:

> Deliberative education is broadly conceived as instruction that utilizes varying forms of classroom deliberation and deliberative exercises to

enhance the democratic skills of citizenship and to increase understanding of democratic practice. (2004: 74)

Moreover, such an education not only shows students how to 'engage episodes of public controversy' but also how such inquiry 'makes accessible critical learning from the discourses of civil society, performances of public culture, actions of citizen groups, and the struggles of opposition and practices of deliberation' (Goodnight and Hingtsman 1997: 351).

Such an approach to education focuses not only on the importance of preparation and engagement with civil society and the public sphere but also on developing in students the capacity for 'argumentative agency' that encourages in them the 'capacity to contextualize and employ the skills and strategies of argumentative discourse in fields of social action, especially wider spheres of public deliberation' (Mitchell 1998: 45).

This approach, of course, is supported by a long tradition of progressive education going back to Dewey, a tradition that has been somewhat muted during the twentieth century by the ascendancy of a factory model of schooling dominated by vocational skills formation in the service of the economy, and the reproduction of culture and tradition through particular forms of moral education (Bates 2006). However, the limitations and restrictions of these forms of education are increasingly apparent and require a shift of focus in the administration of education towards that area of autonomous activity that is called civil society. Such a shift of focus requires that education become more than an unacceptable administrative activity (Touraine 2000: 287), but one which serves both public and private interests through its engagement with civil society and the public sphere.

## REFERENCES

Arendt, H. (1958a) *The Origins of Totalitarianism,* London: George Allen and Unwin.
———, (1958b) *The Human Condition,* Chicago: University of Chicago Press.
———, (1963) *On Revolution,* London: Faber and Faber.
Baker, G. (2002) *Civil Society and Democratic Theory,* London: Routledge.
Bates, R. (1995) 'Educational research and the economy of happiness and love,' *Australian Educational Researcher,* 22, 1: 1–16.
———, (2002) 'Administering the global trap: the role of educational leaders,' *Educational Management and Administration,* 30, 2: 139–56.
———, (2003a) 'Morals and markets: Adam Smith's moral philosophy as a foundation for administrative ethics,' in E. Samier (ed.) *Ethical Foundations for Educational Administration,* London: Routledge.
———, 'Can we live together? the ethics of leadership and the learning community,' paper presented at British Educational Leadership, Management, and Administration Society Conference, Milton Keynes, October, 2003b.
———, (2005a) 'An anarchy of cultures,' *Asia-Pacific Journal of Teacher Education,* 33, 3: 231–41.
———, (2005b) 'Can we live together? towards a global curriculum,' *Arts and Humanities in Higher Education,* 4, 1: 93–109.

———, (2006) 'Culture and leadership in educational administration: an historical study of what was and what might have been,' *Journal of Educational Administration and History*, 38, 2: 155–68.

Bauman, Z. (1999) *In Search of Politics*, Cambridge: Polity Press.

Bottery, M. (2004) *The Challenges of Educational Leadership*, London: Paul Chapman Publishing.

Bourdieu, P. (1991) *Language and Symbolic Power*, Cambridge: Polity Press.

———, (1997) 'Forms of capital,' in A Halsey, H. Lauder, P. Brown and A. Wells (eds) *Education, Economy and Society*, Oxford: Oxford University Press.

Canovan, M. (1985) 'Politics as culture: Hannah Arendt and the public realm,' *History of Political Thought*, 6, 3: 617–42.

Carr, W. and Hartnett, A. (1996) *Education and the Struggle for Democracy*, Buckingham: Open University Press.

Coleman, J. (1994) *Foundations of Social Theory*, Cambridge: Belknap Press.

Comaroff, J. and Comaroff J. (eds) (1999) *Civil Society and the Political Imagination in Africa*, Chicago: University of Chicago Press.

Dewey, J. (1935) *Liberalism and Social Action*, New York: Capricorn.

Felski, R. (1989) *Beyond Feminist Aesthetics: Feminist Literature and Social Change*, Cambridge: Harvard University Press.

Ferguson, A. (1966 [1767]) *An Essay on Civil Society*, D. Forbes (ed.), Edinburgh: Edinburgh University Press.

Fine, B. (2001) *Social Capital Versus Social Theory*, London: Routledge.

Fraser, N. and Honneth, A. (2003) *Redistribution or Recognition: A Political-Philosophical Exchange*, London: Verso.

Fukuyama, F. (1992) *The End of History and the Last Man*, New York: Free Press.

———, (1995) *Trust: The Social Virtues and Creation of Prosperity*, New York: Free Press.

———, (2001) 'Social capital, civil society and development,' *Third World Quarterly*, 22, 1: 7–20.

Giddens, A. (1998) *The Third Way: the Renewal of Social Democracy*, Cambridge: Polity Press.

———, (2000) *The Third Way and its Critics*, Cambridge: Polity Press.

Gitlin, T. (1998) 'Public sphere or public sphericules?' in T. Liebes and J. Curran (eds) *Media, Ritual and Identity*, London: Routledge.

Goodnight, G. and Hingtsman, D. (1997) 'Studies in the public sphere,' *Quarterly Journal of Speech*, 83: 351–70.

Gray, J. (2000) *Two Faces of Liberalism*, Cambridge: Polity Press.

Habermas, J. (1989) *The Structural Transformation of the Public Sphere: An Inquiry into a Category of Bourgeois Society*, trans. T. Berger and F. Lawrence, Cambridge: MIT Press.

———, (1994) 'Three normative models of democracy,' *Constellations*, 1, 1: 1–10.

Havel, V. (1985) 'The power of the powerless,' in *The Power of the Powerless: Citizens against the State in Central-Eastern Europe*, London: Hutchinson.

———, (1988) 'Anti-political politics,' in J. Keane (ed.) *Civil Society and the State: New European Perspectives*, London: Verso.

Hobsbawm, E. (1994) *The Age of Extremes*, London: Michael Joseph.

Ibrahim, S. (1995) 'Civil society and prospects for democratization in the Arab world,' in A. Norton (ed.) *Civil Society in the Middle East*, vol. I, Leiden: E. J. Brill.

Kaldor, M. (2003) 'Civil Society and Accountability,' *Journal of Human Development*, 4, 1: 5–23.

Kaviraj, S. and Khilnani, S. (eds) (2001) *Civil Society: History and Possibilities*, Cambridge: Cambridge University Press.

Keane, J. (1998) *Civil Society: Old Images, New Visions*, Cambridge: Polity Press.

Kim, S. (2004) *Max Weber's Politics of Civil Society*, Cambridge: Cambridge University Press.

Kocka, J. (2004) 'Civil Society from a Historical Perspective,' *European Review* 12(1) 65–79.

McClenaghan, P. (2000) 'Social capital: exploring the theoretical foundations of community development education,' *British Educational Research Journal*, 26, 5: 556–82.

McKee, A. (2005) *The Public Sphere: An Introduction*, Cambridge: Cambridge University Press.

Mische, A. (1993) 'Post-communism's "lost treasure": subjectivity and gender in a shifting public space,' *Praxis International*, 13, 3: 242–67.

Mitchell, G. (1998) 'Pedagogical possibilities for argumentative agency in academic debate,' *Argumentation and Advocacy*, 35: 41–61.

Muller, J. Z. (1993) *Adam Smith in His Time and Ours*, New York: Free Press.

Murphy, T. (2004) 'Deliberative civic education and civil society: a consideration of ideals and actualities in democracy and communitarian education,' *Communitarian Education*, 53, 1: 74–91.

Negt, O. and Kluge, A. (1993) *The Public Sphere and Experience*, Minneapolis: University of Minnesota Press.

Olssen, M. (2004) 'From the Crick Report to the Parekh Report: multiculturalism, cultural difference, and democracy—the re-visioning of citizenship education,' *British Journal of Sociology of Education*, 25, 2: 179–214.

Putnam, R. (1995) 'Bowling alone: America's declining social capital,' *Journal of Democracy*, 61: 65–78.

——, (1996) 'Who killed civic America?' *Prospect Magazine*, March: 66–72.

——, (2000) *Bowling Alone: The Collapse and Revival of American Community*, New York: Simon and Schuster.

Rifkin, J. (1998) 'A civil education for the Twenty-First Century: preparing students for a three sector society,' *National Civic Review*, 87, 2: 177–81.

Schuller, T., Baron, S. and Field, T. (2000) 'Social capital: a review and critique', in S. Baron, J. Field and T. Schuller (eds) *Social Capital: Critical Perspectives*, Oxford: Oxford University Press.

Sergiovanni, T. (1992) *Moral Leadership*, San Francisco: Jossey-Bass.

Smith, A. (1976 [1759]) *The Theory of Moral Sentiments*, A. Mcfie and D. Raphael (eds), Glasgow: Glasgow University Press.

Starratt, R. (2003) *Centering Educational Administration*, London: Lawrence Erlbaum.

Taylor, C. (1994) *Multiculturalism and the Politics of Recognition*, Princeton: Princeton University Press.

Touraine, A. (2000) *Can We Live Together?* Stanford: Stanford University Press.

Wolin, S. (1996) 'The liberal/democratic divide: on Rawls' *Political Liberalism*,' *Political Theory*, 24, 1: 97–119.

Zubaida, S. (2001) 'Civil society, community and democracy in the Middle East,' in S. Kaviraj and S. Khilnani (eds) *Civil Society: History and Possibilities*, Cambridge: Cambridge University Press.

# 12 The Politics of Education in Museums

*Read M. Diket*

Postmodern theory relies on narrative construction, rather than scientific instrumentation, to grapple with the uncertainty of one's own time. With dialectic modes, modernism stresses innovation and the notion of progress. Art museums and the politics governing institutions of culture and their interaction with the public seem to vacillate between modernist and more recent postmodernist values. Varied ideologies, either drawing on modernist dialogue or postmodernist conversation, seem particularly evident among temporary installations and travelling exhibitions. Extra-school offerings for families and children and adult audiences reflect influences from various education resources, revealed within a landscape of culture. This case study of art museums attempts to map some of the political points around which institutions and the public(s) must work to authenticate institutional missions and charters. The cultural landscape to be charted contains shifting frames of reference:

> [the] postmodern: is to be seen as the production of postmodern people capable of functioning in a very peculiar socioeconomic world indeed, one whose structure and objective features and requirements—if we had a proper account of them—would constitute the situation for which 'postmodernism' is a response and would give us something a little more decisive than postmodernism theory . . . Unfortunately, therefore, the infrastructural description I seem to be calling for here is necessarily itself already cultural and a version of postmodernism theory in advance. (Jameson 1991: xv)

This chapter explores museums as personae caught in the cusp of change. Museum galleries, many lately refurbished as ambiguous spaces with gymnasium floors and cloth-covered walls, arguably signal change (Diket 1997/1998; see discussion of spatial considerations in Hooper-Greenhill 1999). Old style galleries stacked paintings vertically, sometimes overwhelming audiences with the abundance, and loaded glass cases with curiosities mixed freely with furniture pieces and miscellaneous artefacts. Chronology and provenance served as organising themes. The presentation of so much art inspired awe and allowed viewers an opportunity to seek favourite pieces among the multitude of images. The change to fewer works of greater quality, with deemphasised context, caught the public by surprise. Novice museum goers were not sure how to respond when most of the works shown were of high quality. Without wall text and rich image context, understanding an exhibition was intellectually demanding. In 1997 I wrote that many visitors appeared uncomfortable in the refurbished spaces; however, I may have spoken too early in the process of change. It could be argued today that the 'therapeutic positivism and standardization of space' might be a 'telltale sign of the dawning of a new age' (after Jameson 1991: 163). Modernism has as a principal concern for 'coming into being,' while postmodernism seeks breaks, pivotal events that signal new worlds at the moment when things change (Jameson 1991: ix). If a break with modernity had occurred, then standardisation of décor in galleries, along with the installation of meaning-laden sculpture at entry portals can be thought of as signs of change. If modernism continues as the dominant thought in the art museum, what Jameson calls 'late capitalism,' it might be said that culture itself is displayed as commodity.

Arts educators Richard Wink and Richard Phipps (2000) assert that the 'ideal conditions' of modern museums are meant to impact visitors. They discuss the widespread departure from 'collecting' anything and everything to designing exhibitions which convey the uniqueness of holdings. With new acquisitions curtailed by a robust art market, for all but the largest museums institutional focus has shifted to emphasising exhibition goals for holdings, type and number of art works to be viewed, object arrangement, and lighting. Design teams use spatial organisation, with temporary walls, to guide audiences through exhibitions (Hooper-Greenhill 1999). Classical modernism continues as a hyperawareness of pluralism aspects and complexity in late twentieth century thought and practices. Master narratives have all but disappeared in the galleries, replaced by wall texts that reveal social practices and ascribe psychological behaviours to art makers and, by implication, to those same potentials in viewers' lives.

## PERSONAL PERSPECTIVE

From the late eighties through 2007, I visited over seventy-five North American museums and more than fifty European museums (some two or more times during the twenty-year interval). Those visits provided a rich database for semiotic analysis (Diket 1995). One of the early markers of ideological change for me were the exterior signs of an institution's national identity, the late modernist- or postmodernist-themed sculptural objects at entrances and main portals, particularly in front of European and British museums (Diket 1997/1998). Other signs of a cusp appeared in the cohesiveness of permanent collections, room décor and minimal object display. Contrastingly, postmodernist, pluralist sensibilities permeate temporary and travelling exhibitions that counterpoint permanent displays. Together the general presentational features of collections and room décor, selections of travelling shows, placement of objects in permanent installations, along with exterior sculpture and garden areas, revealed much about nationalistic agendas and institutional politics.

I was particularly taken with the presence of a giant sculptural mask installed in a grassy space at the entrance to the British Museum in London. I first wrote about the mask, upon return from extensive travels abroad, 'The gigantic mask, thrown on the ground by the entrance, seemingly exemplifies rejection of truth correspondences between museum held artifacts and a singular historical basis or linage for art' (Diket 1997/1998: 48). Now I might read the mask differently: as evidence of faceless masters constraining existence or, alternatively, as a *pastiche* on the wearing of culture as a mask, similar to using a dead language as one's own lived language. The fact is that I have changed my vantage point; the sculpture having been viewed in person some years ago, now appears an imitation of itself upon reflection. Today I would ask if the mask actually queries if producers of culture have nothing new to say so that they must speak through artefacts and dead languages in the imagined realm or cyberspace of a global museum. The mask begs the question of the public's need to enter, to ponder the collections, and think personally about meaning.

The most recent stage in 'social aesthetics' does not distinguish works of art from practices or organisations, or from everyday events in the lives of participants in a context (Samier, Bates and Stanley 2006). As public spaces, the architectural uniqueness of venerable old world historical museums, the benevolence of early twentieth century American benefactor museums, and the open, light-filled foyers of modernist redesign and newer postmodernist buildings affect viewers psychologically in various ways. Variations among museum institutions enable study of symbolic content, the expression of values and sensibilities, and the quest for meaning within a micro culture. Museums, as public institutions, physically alter the ways in which people interact with each other, with cultural artefacts, and in the outside world (Klein and Diket 2006). These interactions have political implications pertinent to the domain of education.

If the holdings, galleries, and exterior sculptures contain the messages and convey the missions of individual museums, is the public receiving the message? In the later twentieth century, museums with obvious intentionality moved away from awe-inspiring interiors, grand narratives, and didactic presentations of extensive holdings to large spaces and spare displays that relied heavily on viewers' interpretive abilities. There was at least a ten-year delay while new pedagogy caught up with the new style in exhibition.

Neuroscientist Antonio Damasio argues that people need to fit into society; further, they feel embarrassed or lost in what appears to be a social situation with which they are unfamiliar. He says, 'Culture and civilization could not have arisen from single individuals and thus cannot be reduced to biological mechanism . . . [C]omprehension [of culture] demands not just general biology and neurobiology, but the methodologies of the social sciences as well' (1994: 124). Damasio writes about the magnitude of feeling and appreciation of the beauty of feeling, and how the need to survive, and to engage mentally, has a lot to do with education. Educational growth is desirable throughout life.

## POLITICS OF INTENT

John Dewey, in the early twentieth century, criticised museums as cathedrals to high art and as sanctified repositories for the wealth of industrialists. Even so, Dewey maintained a mutually beneficial friendship with wealthy businessman and art collector Albert C. Barnes (the interplay of the friendship is discussed extensively in Constantino 2004). In *Art as Experience,* the role of the collector was tied to capitalist enterprise. Today's museums, particularly American ones still actively building collections, have been criticised for capitalist acquisitions. As a result, codes of ethics have been publicly discussed and new rules defined by museum associations (i.e., American Association of Museums) and international consortia. Museums have dual responsibilities—conservation and education—which now are publicly examined and critiqued by insiders and the press.

The writing of American philosopher John Dewey on the educational role of art museums continues as a major point of reference in museum educational activity in the United States (Berry and Mayer 1989; Csikszentmihalyi and Hermanson 1999). Dewey locates two extremes on a continuum of learning experiences with art: (1) for external agents to impose and dictate, and (2) affording unfettered expression of response to form and content, the locating of personal meaning (Dewey et al. 1929: 175). Dewey's text continues that learning follows from 'two great principles': participation in something with inherent worth, or experience derived from something undertaken as valued human activity; and perception of art as a means to understanding the world. He allows for a third possibility: honing an interest in skill and technique by studying exemplars of art. Dewey's pragmatism posits knowledge as instrumental, with validity claims based in evidence that participants are developing habits of belief, insights, and organising their experiences in a satisfactory manner. Beliefs are conditional and subject to revision.

Barnes' interest was in affording access to great art so that each visitor might say something individual, 'for there is no great merit in repeating what someone else has already said' (Dewey 1929: 185). Thus, the Barnes collection was exhibited without text so that visitors might form their own perceptions directly from the physical properties and forms of the works. He did, however, offer classes to his workers in conjunction with their visits to the collection, and this instruction drew heavily on Dewey's ideas. Participation in the classes was a condition for workers' access to the Barnes collection.

Today the dialectics of authenticity move past Dewey's original ideas about the place for artistic experiences in the self-development of individuals to a consideration of the very space of museums in which many encounter art. As Ameri (2004) observes in 'The Spatial Dialectics of Authenticity,' the problem now centres on the responsibilities of 'our' (Western) civilisation that has allowed artworks to be removed from original provenances and locked away, however safely, in museums (2004).

## POLITICS OF PUBLIC ACCESS

The very earliest museum affording public access to the physical objects of a monarchy was by decree of the newly formed French republic in 1793. Ameri discusses the history of the Louvre museum, starting with the 'Musée Central des Arts,' as the former palace was renamed in 1796. By 1797, the former palace displayed for public view the accumulations of its decimated monarchy. Thus from the first institution, there is a history implicating 'the public and its self-constitution as a sovereign entity' (2004: 62). Implicit in the housing of art is the taking of cult references out of context, giving these instead objectified presence, distanced from 'viewer and the place they happened to occupy' (2004: 63). Ameri continues his thesis by saying that in original contexts cult objects link viewer and referent and collapse space; as art objects, the same forms impose space. He maintains that 'the price of autonomy was the loss of place' and made these 'autoarchic self-referential objects' (63) mere collectibles to be deciphered by the public.

Over a 100 year interval, more national museums were opened in Europe, each seeking wealthy international travellers, scholars of culture, and developing artists to study museum holdings on-site or through photographs (Ameri 2004 argues that these are inverse in importance). In contrast to the benevolent early twentieth century, old-line public and private museums that sought visitors to holdings with the idea of educating their minds (i.e., Dewey et al. 1929), national museums took control over art in the name of their citizens, delegating objects to a special place for safekeeping. As did various industrial benefactors founding private museums, Dewey and Barnes, in their writings, broadened the intended audience. They included working class adults and their families, arguably the least franchised of a possible public.

Edification of the 'sensibilities' was reserved for museum directors, wealthy collectors, and esteemed historians of the art world. Festenstein, in *Pragmatism and Political Theory* (1997), interprets such social arrangements as political acts. The directors made choices about paintings and sculptures selected for purchase; collectors searched out the rare and authentic objects of interest; historians were charged with decisions about provenance and uniqueness. Gradually the roles blurred and merged together. The cabinet collections of collectors and political leaders, formerly viewed in private showings as evidence of the owner's power, moved into the glass cases for public viewing. The museum building thus became a giant cabinet.

The fallacy in Dewey's pragmatism was that museum going was not about obtaining something for the individual, but rather another 'means for creating individuals.' Old-line museums, in effect, removed the museum audience from active participation in the social structure of an art world by 'giving' something to them. When, late in the twentieth century, museums bought into a modernist style that moved away from awe-inspiring interiors and grand narratives, the public was not sure how they were to be involved anymore, turning instead to popular arts and entertainment. Given the popularising effects of reconstructionist and critical philosophies, museums appeared to shift programming toward an educated museum audience. Docent organisations expanded and guides to museum collections were printed. Socially informed viewers were expected to extract underlying tensions in culture from the artefacts and be able to ponder the structure and congruency of beliefs.

Postmodernism brought a proliferation of cultural opportunities; 'high' culture competed with 'popular culture.' With escalating operational costs, museums competed for a paying public, requiring larger audiences to keep the doors open. Museums sought both the uneducated and the educated, and debate arose about how best to approach diversity in the paying public. Hooper-Greenhill's *The Educational Role of the Museum* (1999) expresses a real fear that today's museumgoers are not getting the messages of exhibitions. Late twentieth century structures crowded into the city created a notable absence of paths and signifying portals for entry (also noted by Ameri 2004). Inside, some museums still attempted to portray the endlessness of art on display—one gallery leading to another, then another, then still another. Tucked away in the art maze of today are respites of convenience—restrooms, small art specialty shops, and pleasant places to eat.

If, as Heidegger maintains, we are '"fellow players" in the game of life' then museums might offer the public 'worlds' for viewing that are mediated through aesthetic objects and artefacts. Otherwise, museums become 'the indispensable reserve to the economy that regulates the widespread and free circulation of images outside the museum' (Ameri 2004). Pragmatism's politics flounder by omitting the necessity of practical judgment amongst all viable agents. To be a fellow player implies endeavour on the part of individual and collective agents outside of museum institutional structures, and engagement within with the artefacts of culture. Albert Bandura stresses the necessary bidirectionality of human influence by cautioning: 'The imbalance of social power partly depends on the extent to which people exercise the influence that is theirs to command. The less they bring their influence to bear on conditions that affect their lives the more control they relinquish to others' (1995: 38).

## POLITICS OF CANON

German phenomenologist Edmund Husserl provides insight into the role of the body and human activities through which westerners structure views of the world. As I read Husserl's philosophy (e.g., 1970), visual objects are perceived through cognitive and physical activity: through seeing, focusing, moving, and touching and grasping. All this takes place in living contexts, with material objects and with cultural objects. Intentionality of representation, time and space, and view from one's own body are conditions undergirding understanding. Human beings need to have some grasp of past and future. Husserl posits two domains—a domain of the senses and intuitive propositions and a domain of things, formal states of affairs, and cultural relationships. Importantly, he distinguishes between having something in one's presence and experiencing an empty intention related to a thing and considering what might fill it. Most importantly, Husserl appears to suggest a difference between passive acceptance of value and explicit judging.

Feminist writers became concerned about the male-dominated canon fostered by art museums. Museums are positioned to influence canons relating to art and aesthetics; and museums received heavy criticism for excluding the art of marginalised groups (i.e., Sankowski 1993). Feminist analyses, in contrast to Marxist analyses, indicated that capitalism and patriarchy would 'compromise on the woman question' (Tong 1989: 180), here revealed by the existence of an expanded canon of artworks, including more works of previously marginalised artists, stemming from the past into contemporary times. Feminist theory queried the codes and conditions of selection processes as evidenced in the placement or omission of art in museum settings, selections of contemporary art for exhibition, and paucity of women's contributions extolled in history texts. Wendy Slatkin (1997) discusses a partial reappraisal that came in the form of several 'interventions.' Some careers were reconstituted, gender biases in discourse were identified, the role of women as patrons of the arts was investigated, institutional structures of the art world were deconstructed, and the construction of gender in visual images was celebrated in feminist literature.

In 2007, one of the founding Guerilla Girls, 'Roberta Smith,' spoke at the National Art Education Association annual conference in New York. Wearing her guerilla head, a tailored black suit and heels, 'Roberta' explained to an audience of several thousand educators just how she and her colleagues had used Madison Avenue techniques with a populist twist and 'aestheticized' their anger to force change in museum practices. Though not trained in education, they developed workshops for high school and middle school students. Not trained as social scientists, they used humour to mock the 'oppressors.' They put on masks to be taken seriously as artists. She maintained that they 'claim space, identify an issue, and keep hammering.' The speaker remarked on recent changes in their status—they were 'invited' to speak in Venice and are coming soon on invitation to respond to the collections of the National Gallery in Washington. Philosopher Arthur Danto conditions that the Guerrilla Girls 'envision success in the traditional, let us say, using their concept, white male terms. Its means are radical and deconstructive, but its goals are altogether conservative' (1997: 146).

## Politics of Transparency

A major thrust in museum policy in the twenty-first century argues for transparency in media venues with museum organisation, funding sources, and audience participation; antiquities acquisition; and sales from permanent collections in the public trust. The avowed leader in *transparency* seems to be the venerable Louvre. Transparency can be thought of as a political metaphor for public involvement with the ongoing policies and practices of a cultural institution. The Louvre museum, is advantaged in its stance for transparency because its collections were well-established some 100 years ago, during a period with different playing rules. The Louvre presents its organisational structure on the official website in the most literal way possible. Each staff member has a photo ID and title displayed as part of the organisational structure.

Today's Louvre juxtaposes contemporary work with the art and artefacts of permanent collections predating 1948. The thrust for transparency with museum visitors figures prominently in I. M. Pei's design for the courtyard entrance, which now directs visitors to Louvre wings through the underground labyrinth access. The Louvre's signature glass pyramid immediately became a cultural marker, celebrated in photos and in popular literature (i.e., *The Da Vinci Code*).

## Transparency and the Public 'Eye'

The principle responsibilities of the Louvre are to conserve, protect, restore, and develop France's national art treasures, from the early royal collections to the most recent acquisitions. In carrying out these tasks, the museum's scientific and academic staff display steadfast commitment and universally recognised professionalism:

> The priceless artworks housed in the Louvre are held for the benefit of present and future generations. Hence the vital importance of the museum's mission to make these works available to the greatest number of people possible, from France and all over the world. To do this, it is our job to ensure that every visitor enjoys the best facilities possible. But it is also essential to promote cultural access: to do as much as we can to help each visitor to approach, understand, and enjoy the works they have come to see. With this in mind, we are committed to extend the range of information available at the Louvre in languages other than

French, to further develop the museum's wide range of educational resources and activities, and to make our buildings and collections more easily accessible—in every sense—to people with disabilities and to new audiences. (Louvre 2007a)

The Louvre, with a public history extending back to 1793, is presented on the official website as 'Open to all since 1793.' 'From the outset, the Louvre has *embodied* [my emphasis] the concept of a truly "universal" institution. Universal in the scope of its collections, it is also universal in its appeal to some 6 million visitors every year: a 21st-century museum rooted in 200 years of innovation.' The mission of the museum declares: 'We are also increasingly involved in efforts to encourage access for people who might feel—for whatever reason—that museums are "not for them"' (Louvre 2007a). Finally, the Louvre continues to develop and refurbish new spaces, drawing on the latest concepts in architecture, museum design, and museum-based education (Louvre 2007b).

I visited the greatly expanded and reorganised Louvre in 1996, having viewed construction in the courtyard amidst older presentation aesthetics for the collection during an earlier visit in 1988 (see Klein and Diket 2006). The mid 90s visit began very early in the day, at the museum's opening hour. I spent the day walking through the vast galleries, carefully taking numerous slide photos of the art in context for presentations in college art courses. My visit was in marked contrast to that of travelling companions: my daughter, her friend, and my sister-in-law. They apparently arrived midday. They located the visitor's centre, and set out to view major pieces in the collection using the 'Louvre on the Run' map. They stayed about three hours in the Louvre, revisiting favourite objects and seeking further highlights of the collection. Many of the international visitors appeared to be doing the same thing. Visitors would enter a gallery, scan the room for a particular object, cross quickly to the piece, have their pictures snapped in front of the work, and exit. Few spent any time at all contemplating individual works. What were they getting from their visit—a pictorial artefact of personal proximity with famous work, a facsimile of the art to study later, or simply evidence of a successful scavenger hunt?

Obviously, the Louvre experience required additional educational efforts to be more accessible to a wide range of visitors. The paper guide for visitors, obtained with their ticket, identified the most important pieces in the collection and directed visitors' paths to particular works, but many visitor interactions with the art appeared superficial at best. If, politically, the objects in question were to be truly accessible to 'new' audiences, as the Louvre declares in its mission, the education department needed to address aesthetic, critical, and informational issues in their plans for expanded audiences. As an interim fix, technology moved into the informational void as a personal guide, as was used in 2004 by friends visiting the Louvre.

Visitors are embracing audio tapes as a friendlier way to traverse museum galleries. The disembodied voices gently guide them from one gallery to the next. The conversational tone of the tapes, delivered in a familiar language, do seem to hold visitors for an interim in front of the art under discussion. They listen to the tape and follow its pointers while viewing a piece, or when making their way to the next station. Today's iPod crowd seems particularly comfortable with audio technology as their virtual docent. Their audio guide informs conversation even as they engage in talk with others in their entourage. Guidebooks and wall text do not seem to work as well with postmodern visitors, as it may be more difficult to shift between reading verbal text and image text. The audio guide also helps regulate the zones established between people viewing art in close proximity. Philosopher Marcel Danesi (2004) calls such regulatory zones and body orientation manifestations *metaforms;* polite conventions are understood by participants sharing an environment.

Today, anyone with access to the Internet can preview or experience virtually some works and aspects of the Louvre collections. Virtual visitors can also read about the museum's explicit plans for various audiences (in French only), and view exemplars of materials developed for public use with the collections. The Louvre declares that it regularly shares works with a 'hundred' museums around the world as it implements its mission.

## PUBLIC AS POWER BROKER

How recently do we find such directness of purpose recorded in public domains? Most public and many private museums pose in their mission statements two primary concerns: conserve the collection and serve an audience. For example, the National Archaeological Museum in Athens, founded in the last decade of the nineteenth century, declares its purpose as follows:

> The National Archaeological Museum was founded by presidential decree on August 9, 1893 (Greek Government Journal I, 152, 'On the organization of the National Archaeological Museum'). Its purpose was 'the study and teaching of the science of archaeology, the propagation of archaeological knowledge and the cultivation of a love for the Fine Arts.' Its collections were segregated into: Sculpture, Vases, Clay and Bronze Figurines and other Ancient Figurines made of various materials, Inscriptions, which later went to the Epigraphic Museum, Pre-Hellenic (the Mycenaean collection), and Egyptian. The museum was also equipped with conservation laboratories and a cast workshop. (National Archaeological Museum 2007)

On the roof of the grand building are posed statues celebrating Greece's numerous cultural achievements. Propagation of knowledge and the cultivation of a love for the treasures of the past are hallmarks of this museum.

There is no statuary at the entrance. When I visited the institution in 1999, the museum seemed happily caught between a desire to show everything in rich proximity and new trends toward parsimonious presentation.

There was, in addition, a looming international debate focused on the restitution of the Parthenon marbles, largely held by the British Museum. Transparency politics moved a battle of longstanding directly into the public arena. The British Museum, home to some of the most important of the Parthenon marbles, counters that they have been excellent caretakers of the sculptures, and that display in England ensures continuous access to citizens of the world. Greek officials expect that, through public pressure, the sculptures will be returned to the vicinity of the architectural setting from which they were so crudely wrest, thus sidestepping the issue of 'ownership' with statements of provenance and architectural unity.

The venerable Metropolitan Museum is similarly involved in a dispute with Italy over twenty-two items of uncertain provenance (Riding 2005). American museums appear particularly vulnerable because they acquired collections throughout the twentieth century, many through tax incentives to wealthy private collectors willing to donate desirable objects from their holdings. In contrast to older institutions that maintain that collections built in the late eighteenth and early nineteenth century were 'acquired according to practices of the time' (see Riding 2005: A4), newer museums like the Getty in the US are particularly vulnerable to criticism as they build collections.

In 2002, nineteen 'universal' museums (including the Getty and the Metropolitan) signed a declaration that they would not traffic in illegal cultural artefacts while conditioning that earlier acquisitions would be exempt from the pact. Geoffrey Lewis, Riding reports, as chairman of the Ethics Committee of Council of Museums, was unimpressed and chided the group of museums for evident self-interest in an editorial written for the council's monthly news publication. Riding quotes Lewis as saying, 'The debate today is not about the desirability of "universal museums," but about the ability of a people to present their cultural heritage in their own territory' (Riding 2005: A4).

## PUBLIC 'TRUST'

Egyptian artefacts have benefited from large-scale conservation projects. However, it has only been recently that the public has been given details of the wide-ranging activities of the funds, such as the American Research Center in Egypt's Antiquities Endowment Fund (established 1993), established with funds from the United States Agency for International Development (USAID). In particular, American contributions to Egyptian archaeology and large-scale conservation have been acknowledged as part of a new policy of transparency (USAID 2005).

I have seen several major travelling exhibitions in the United States in the last few years: in Chicago, New Orleans, Memphis (Tennessee), and Mobile

(Alabama). The quality, staging, and texts of these exhibitions seemed to resonate with large audiences in attendance, and to remain viable in memory. Perhaps an outgrowth of transparency can be located in the custom of loaning objects from permanent collections to other museums, even when they must be taken off display in the home institution for an extended exhibition run. In most cases, works receive examination through new scholarly lenses, and many are restored, reframed, or otherwise enhanced by the loan recipients. In return, objects customarily accessible only to citizens and travellers to a specific locale are circulated with related objects through the wider culture. One might ask, is this a feature of what Jameson terms 'multinational capital' (1991: 36)? Are we learning that physical ownership does not preclude intellectual ownership and opportunity to view firsthand cultural objects from distant (physically and temporally) societies as relative to a shared history? Are the artefacts of past and contemporary cultures now considered part and fabric of human experience?

## POLITICS OF VISUAL CULTURE

Arthur Danto discusses the museum and avant-garde theatre as 'outposts of civilization' that upon occasion embrace what he terms 'the art of disturbation.' Disturbation rhymes with masturbation, and like operations of its natural rhyme, 'charged images climax in real orgasms' (1986: 119). I observed an interactive installation built on shadow images accompanied by low angry muttering in Montreal. The experience left me acutely aware of the different actions of men and women in the setting. I acted the role of voyeur with televised segments of Moscow citizens in their homes and public places in San Francisco's Museum of Art—the images were so sad and lonely in their isolation. San Francisco also had human-sized photos of women burned on the breasts by cigarettes that elicited a feeling of pain, even as I wondered if the marks on the breast were wounds or simulations. Even if simulations, such wounds are possible in our society, daily hidden by battered women. Such charged images and thoughts print on the mind; I remember the settings and images vividly, even after years. Danto posits that fear of such power in art, and a belief that artists could possess the power, may have lead to the arts transmutation out of context and history into theory.

Art critic Terry Barrett (2008) describes visual cultural studies as an emerging field that includes fine arts of the type located in museums among 'all humanly made visual items found in daily living' (12). A number of major theories can be applied to all artefacts, thus expanding the usefulness of theory beyond art in museums. Proponents of visual culture seem to insist that the application of theories to the artefacts of daily living must be accomplished through educational venues, and that without such instruction images may be too raw, too deceiving, or too slick to be evaluated. Which task, they appear to ask, is more important? Is it more essential to be able to read and judge the full range of texts, visual and verbal, from a multiplicity of cultures, or should the consideration of culture be confined to what is found in museums? Their answer might be that the artefacts of daily life require more decoding and are more intellectually taxing than those of museums.

Noting a strong draw to popular culture among young people, the Finnish Tennis Palace Art Museum mounted a blockbuster exhibition combining manga art with contemporary Japanese art and Japanese-inspired environments. In museum educator Arja Miller's 2007 presentation during the New York conference of the National Art Education Association, she considered manga as visual culture and discussed the placement of contemporary Japanese comic characters in proximity to a second exhibition of Japanese contemporary artists who grew up reading manga. The manga styles exhibited included examples for boys, girls, and adults. Included with the exhibit were woodblock prints from Hokusai and other old masters of the Japanese print. The exhibition also showed works by Finnish manga artists. The museum involved a group of young people in the planning of the project, who quite successfully reached their peers. Pictures of the opening event showed the array of manga-inspired costumes assembled and worn by young museum attendees. Interest in manga is also strong in the states among older teens and young adults; in college art courses American and international students have shown me with much pride their manga-type images.

For some, manga seems to be a persona or anamie with which adolescents and young adults wish to affiliate themselves. Unlike the constitution of the self as self-sufficient, cut off from the world (what Jameson calls the bourgeois ego, or monad), youth today embrace manga and anamie as alternative selves. The wide-eyed manga belong to some universal culture of youth imbued with power and vision. Manga images have a cult status, and they are 'ironic, defiant and critical' (Tennis Palace Art Museum 2007).

## PERSPECTIVE FROM INSIDE MUSEUM ORGANISATION

In January of this year the Eastman Memorial Foundation invited me to board membership as a trustee for the Lauren Rogers Museum of Art in Laurel, Mississippi. For the previous year I had served on its advisory board, a group drawn from the public supporting museum activities. The new board orientation took place in June of 2007. Some of what I learned there about art museum administration seeped into my writing, particularly on the politics of transparency. With the manuscript all but finished, I used the museum password onto the American Association of Museums website. I have found little hidden from public view. The AAM (2007) espouses voluntary compliance with the benchmarks, standards, and guidelines of the organisation. The organisation worries about protecting collections in emergency conditions, continuing efforts to make collections accessible to all types of visitors, and financial concerns. These concerns are discussed more openly and findings shared at an organisational level; they are not secret from the public.


## HIGH/CLASSICAL MODERNISM

In conclusion, it appears that museums have not transitioned through a cusp, but rather have remained essentially modernist. Art museums serve as economic entities, repositories for culture, and teaching institutions that call to mind a range of cultural products, constrained in the 'space of high modernism.' Recognising where society is, and having stated where society might go, suggests 'an imperative to grow new organs, to expand our sensorium and our body to some new, yet unimaginable, perhaps ultimately impossible, dimensions' (Jameson 1991: 39).

## REFERENCES

Ameri, A. (2004) 'The spatial dialectics of authenticity,' *SubStance*, 33, 2: 61–89.

American Association of Museums. (2007) Online. Available HTTP: <http://www.aam-us.org> (accessed 26 June 2007).

Bandura, A. (1995) *Self-Efficacy in Changing Societies*, Cambridge: Cambridge University Press.

Barrett, T. (2008) *Why is That Art? Aesthetics and Criticism of Contemporary Art*, New York: Oxford University Press.

Berry, N. and Mayer, S. (1989) *Museum Education History, Theory, and Practice*, Reston: National Art Education Association.

Constantino, T. E. (2004) 'Training aesthetic perception: John Dewey on the educational role of art museums,' *Educational Theory*, 54, 4: 399–417.

Csikszentmihalyi, M. and Hermanson, K. (1999) 'Intrinsic motivation in museums: why does one want to learn?' in E. Hooper-Greenhill (ed.) *The Educational Role of the Museum*, London: Routledge.

Damasio, A. R. (1994) *Descartes' Error: Emotion, Reason, and the Human Brain*, New York: HarperCollins.

Danesi, M. (2004) *Poetic Logic: The Role of Metaphor in Thought, Language, and Culture*, Madison: Atwood Publishing.

Danto, A. C. (1986) *The Philosophical Disenfranchisement of Art*, New York: Columbia University Press.

———, (1997) *After the End of Art: Contemporary Art and the Pale of History*, Princeton: Princeton University Press.

Dewey, J. et al. (1929) *Art and Education*, Merion: Barnes Foundation Press.

———, (1934) *Art as Experience*, New York: Minton, Balch & Company.

Diket, R. M. (1995) 'Participating in the performance of semiotics,' *Arts and Learning*, 12, 1: 36–8.

———, (1997/1998) 'Postmodern museum space,' *Arts and Learning Research*, 46–56.

Festenstein, M. (1997) *Pragmatism and Political Theory: From Dewey to Rorty*, Cambridge: Polity Press.

Hooper-Greenhill, E. (1999) *The Educational Role of the Museum*, 2nd edn, London: Routledge.

Husserl, E. (1970) *The Crisis of European Sciences and Transcendental Phenomenology*, Evanston: Northwestern University Press.

Jameson, F. (1991) *Postmodernism, or, The Cultural Logic of Late Capitalism*, Durham: Duke University Press.

Klein, S. and Diket, R. M. (2006) 'Aesthetic leadership: leaders as architects,' in E. A. Samier, R. J. Bates and A. Stanley (eds) *Aesthetic Dimensions of Educational Administration and Leadership*, London: Routledge.

Louvre. (2007a) Online. Available HTTP: <http://www.louvre.fr/llv/musee/institution.jsp?bmLocale=e> (accessed 26 June 2007).

——, (2007b) Online. Available HTTP: <http://www.louvre.fr/llv/musee/mission.jsp> (accessed 26 June 2007).

National Archaeological Museum of Athens. (2007) Online. Available HTTP: <http://odysseus.culture.gr/h/1/eh152.jsp?obj_id=3249> (accessed 26 June 2007).

Riding, A. (2005) 'Why "antiquities trials" focus on America,' *New York Times*, 25 November, A4.

Samier, E., Bates, R. and Stanley, A. ((2006) 'Foundations and history of the social aesthetic,' in E. A. Samier, R. J. Bates and A. Stanley (eds) *Aesthetic Dimensions of Educational Administration and Leadership*, London: Routledge.

Sankowski, E. (1993) 'Art museums, autonomy, and canons,' *Monist*, 76, 4: 535–57.

Slatkin, W. (1997) *Women Artists in History: From Antiquity to the Present*, Upper Saddle River: Prentice Hall.

Tennis Palace Art Museum. (2007) Online. Available HTTP: <www.taidemuseo.fi/english/tenispalatsi/programme/manga.html> (accessed 26 June 2007).

Tong, R. (1989) *Feminist Thought: A Comprehensive Introduction*, Boulder: Westview Press.

United States Agency for International Development. (2005) Online. Available HTTP: <http://www.iht.com/articles/2005/11/25/features/museums.php> (accessed 26 June 2007).

Wink, R. and Phipps, R. (2000) *Museum-Goer's Guide*, Boston: McGraw Hill.

# 13 The Politics of Community Renewal and Educational Reform

## School Improvement in Areas of Social Disadvantage

*Lawrence Angus*

Almost everyone is in favour of solid, decent communities in which people know and support each other; where they trust each other and the service professionals (such as health workers, teachers, and housing officials) who work there, and where the local schools have the confidence of the local community. But not all communities are like that. In Australia, the government of the State of Victoria has introduced neighbourhood renewal programs in fifteen of the state's most disadvantaged localities. One of the most disadvantaged of these is the neighbourhood of Wirra Warra[1], an outer suburb of the regional city of Provincetown.

Informed by a critical social science perspective (Fay 1987), this paper employs critical notions of culture and politics in order to provide an account of the relationships among the micro- and macropolitics of the educational and social community of Wirra Warra. A focus on power relationships and interests, in particular, illuminates the dynamics of social policy in action and is intended to articulate relationships between education and other, larger social contexts. Issues of culture, discourse and the legitimation of meaning are critical in understanding ways in which notions of individualism, standards and school effectiveness have enabled school failure to be represented as the responsibility of particular schools and individuals, and as being related to the adequacy of the educational 'product' rather than to the sociopolitical, cultural and economic factors that contribute to school performance.

## WIRRA WARRA AND THE NEIGHBOURHOOD RENEWAL IDEAL

The policy concept of 'neighbourhood renewal' is applied to neighbourhoods, particularly pubic housing estates, which are characterised by high rates of poverty and unemployment and low rates of school success. These communities are typically ones stigmatised by poor health, particularly mental health, and antisocial activities such as crime and vandalism. Policies of neighbourhood renewal emphasise building 'social capital,' discourses of which typically adopt Putnam's normative ideal that social cohesion is developed through building community trust and social ties. He maintains that in disadvantaged neighbourhoods, 'social networks are not nearly as dense or effective' as they were in the 1960s; they 'have less social capital nowadays than they once did' (2000: 317).

Through building and strengthening trust and social ties, according to this argument, the self-confidence and self-esteem of residents can be enhanced and the consequent community-building capacity, social entrepreneurship, and local leadership will result in shared social vision and improved individual and community livelihoods (McLenaghan 2000). Through a 'whole of community' approach, and by developing partnerships between the community, government departments, and the private and voluntary sectors, neighbourhood renewal can motivate community members and 'empower' them through the development of 'bonding,' bridging,' and 'linking' forms of social capital (Quinn 2005), to take charge of their own social and economic improvement (Millar and Kilpatrick 2005). Such aspirations would seem extremely optimistic for the people of Wirra Warra, a neighbourhood that has been stigmatised and demonised in the city of Provincetown since it was established as a housing estate for recently arrived immigrants from the United Kingdom in the mid 1950s. Any notion that the neighbourhood can be unproblematically turned around through a process of 'community renewal' would seem, on the face of it, rather simplistic.

The notion of community renewal can be criticised for its lack of clarity. Indeed, Lilley associates it with the dreamy, romantic language of 'Wonderland,' in that 'it can mean just what you want' (2005: 63). More importantly, it is not clear how the neighbourhood or community renewal approach can even address, much less resolve, the long-term structural causes of entrenched social and economic disadvantage. The community renewal approach, therefore, is too narrow to respond to the multidimensional nature of macro-factors, such as power and the economy that shape processes of advantaging and disadvantaging. Moreover, the discourse of community typically homogenises, objectifies, and stigmatises the experiences of people in circumstances of poverty. Such people, according to this voluntarist discourse, have the solution to their marginalisation and deprivation in their own hands provided they are willing to take individual and community responsibility for fixing their dysfunctions and becoming more like the middle-class mainstream. The logic of such discourse is clearly one of deficit, which has the effect, as Osei-Kofi puts it, of 'pathologizing the poor' (2005: 267). Such discourse leaves unexamined the entrenched structures of privilege, power, and class. It could be implied from such logic that the best thing teachers can do in disadvantaged neighbourhoods is to be good role models of middle-class norms and, in keeping with current accountability and testing requirements in education, industriously employ in a 'banking'-like fashion (Friere 1970) the supposedly neutral, apolitical techniques of quality instruction as required by currently prevailing notions of 'school effectiveness.'

## SCHOOL REFORM, SCHOOL EFFECTIVENESS AND YOUTH AND RISK

A strong preference for notions of 'school effectiveness' is currently rampant in Australia, as it is England and elsewhere (Angus 1993; Thrupp 1999; 2001). It is important to make this point before discussing schooling in Wirra Warra because it is necessary to understand the dominance of school effectiveness discourse in education policy in order to appreciate the significance in current education debates of concepts like 'standards,' 'accountability,' 'evidence base,' 'high quality instruction,' 'national benchmark data,' 'performance targets,' 'effective schools correlates,' 'effective practice,' 'effectiveness attributes,' 'performance and development culture,' and the like. This terminology is embedded in Victorian Department of Education policy documents such as *School Improvement: A Theory of Action* (Fraser and Petch 2007). This document, and the educational approach it describes, are based largely on 'The Effective Schools Model' (Fraser and Petch 2007: 11), the template for which is adapted from a summary by Sammons, Hillman and Mortimore (1995) of school effectiveness research. This model lists eight of the vague, predictable, 'effectiveness factors' (such as professional leadership, accountability, high expectations) that are said to 'have an evidence-based correlation with improved student outcomes' (Fraser and Petch 2007: 11).

In Australia, Teese (2004) and others argue that school effectiveness factors provide little insight for school reformers who seek to make the educational experience for all young people more democratic and equitable. As Atkinson summarises, school effectiveness 'does not take account of the complexity of the personal, social and cultural world in which teachers and learners move, or of the thinking processes, both conscious and subconscious, that inform their pedagogy' (2000: 323). In other words, the repertoire of teachers' thinking is much more expansive, complex, and deeper than the narrow, utilitarian concern with 'what works' that characterises school effectiveness. Yet the privileging in education policy and accountability requirements of 'school effectiveness' concepts, particularly through the imposition of so-called evidence-based best practice, is likely to have the effect of narrowing the thought and experimentation of teacher-inquirers. The utilitarian evidence-base and theory of action of school effectiveness has little regard for education as 'an ethical activity directed towards morally defensible or socially transformative ends' (Carr in Sikes 2006: 49), such as greater equity, justice, and democracy. As Edwards concludes, school effectiveness thinking 'reinforces contemporary views of pedagogy as knowledge dissemination and consumption, and takes attention away from notions of pedagogy as relational practices of cultural exchange and exercises of power' (2006: 125). The question remains, therefore, whether the school effectiveness mentality can be of any use at all in efforts to make schooling more relevant and appealing.

Neighbourhoods like Wirra Warra, deemed to be in need of 'renewal,' invariably contain substantial numbers of young people who are regarded as 'at risk' of early school leaving and unemployment. The need to manage 'youth at risk' is therefore a major consideration of renewal projects. Deficit thinking is quite explicit in this discourse, as it is in 'neighbourhood renewal' policy, because both assume that disadvantaged or marginalised individuals and communities lack the knowledge, skills, aspiration, and motivation to take advantage of the opportunities for advancement that they have been offered (Bessant 2002; Kelly 2007; Te Riele 2006). Such assumptions betray the tension in 'youth at risk' and 'neighbourhood renewal' policies between their social justice and social control mentalities. This prompts Wishart and her colleagues to speculate whether 'within education, youth at risk discourse may be more about minimizing the risk posed by disadvantaged students to the mainstream than about addressing the risks faced by disadvantaged students' (Wishart, Taylor and Schultz 2006: 294).

The possibility that there are deep structural, economic, and cultural causes of social and educational disadvantage, or even that social institutions like schools might be in part responsible for youth and communities being at risk in the first place, are clearly not on the policy agenda. Therefore, the sad conclusion is that advocates of social justice and equity in schools and society are far from optimistic that government-led efforts will result in much, if any, renewal and empowerment for communities or reform of education in disadvantaged neighbourhoods. Yet, as I illustrate in the remainder of this chapter, there is a strong sense in Wirra Warra, among residents and service professionals, that positive things are happening for the neighbourhood and for young people. I shall then conclude with an analysis of the potential of these 'good things' to contribute to genuine democratic change that may result in improved livelihoods for the people of the community.

## WIRRA WARRA, EDUCATION AND COMMUNITY INCLUSION

The houses in Wirra Warra are typical 'housing commission' dwellings of the 1950s and 1960s. In recent years, about half of them have been sold by government to residents of Wirra Warra or private landlords. The 'best' streets are said to be those in which most houses are occupied by private owners. The 'worst' are those with houses owned by absentee landlords. Many of the renters are reported to be 'ferals'—transient ne'er-do-wells whose reported violent and illegal behaviour is said to give the whole of

Wirra Warra a bad name. One resident jokes, 'Some friends are still too scared to drive through Wirra Warra in case they get carjacked.'

A long-term employee of the Department of Human Services says that Wirra Warra has long been regarded in the department as 'almost like a no-go zone—people said "Don't go there!"' The area's baleful reputation seems to have spread throughout Australia. According to one of the local community spokespeople, Warren Kane, who, after a hard life of crime, jail, alcoholism and drug dependency, requested a priority move from his previous commission home in another state, and says he was told by his caseworker: 'If you are going to Provincetown and you get offered Wirra Warra, you would be better off not taking it.' In the event, it turned out to be a good move for Warren, who says, 'I found that the people here accepted me for what I was not what I looked like and all the drugs I did in the past. I let the caseworker know that he was wrong. It was the best thing that ever happened to us. The stigma came from the outside [of Wirra Warra] not the inside.'

The centrepiece of the neighbourhood renewal program (or simply, 'the renewal') is the 'Community Hub,' construction of which commenced in 2007 on the site of one of the community's two primary schools. During the building of the new school in the Community Hub, staff and students of both schools have amalgamated on the Rose Park Primary School site. That school will be demolished and the grounds used as public space once the new school is completed. The new school, to be called Rose Hill Community School, will be the largest component of the Community Hub. There will also be a kindergarten, community education centre, and new community house. The Hub will house various agencies, facilitate a number of activities, and will signify the worth of the 'renewed' community. It will also play a substantial part in equipping the next generation of Wirra Warra residents with the skills and know-how to pursue better life chances than those of their parents.

The concept 'neighbourhood renewal' includes the idea that a range of government agencies will deliver services in the neighbourhood as an example of 'joined-up' government. The process commenced in 2001 amid plenty of initial suspicions from residents. One resident, who is now secretary of the Community House, recalls: 'At first a lot of people didn't trust the agencies. They had to earn the trust . . . Suddenly they were coming in to help us build or paint and we wondered, "What's the catch?"' An important mediator between residents and officials has been the district's popular member of state parliament, Olive Kennedy, who seems to have won the respect of everyone in Wirra Warra and is a staunch defender and advocate of their rights. Kennedy has been involved in the general development of neighbourhood renewal policy and compares the Wirra Warra experience with other attempts at neighbourhood renewal:

> Neighbourhood Renewals were Labour Party policy as such, but no one knew what shape it would take in places like Marralang, Bonnydale and elsewhere. The difference between those and the Wirra Warra one—there

the bureaucrats went in and decided what the community needed and provided what they thought the community needed with no consultation. When the consultation did happen there was no money left.

Kennedy was determined that such would not be the case in Wirra Warra:

> I was keen on renewal here given the disadvantage . . . I asked to be chair of the committee. The bureaucrats had a blueprint, a committee of thirty with me as chair and not one resident—all thirty were bureaucrats! I said, 'No way. There has to be consultation!'

Kennedy then held a series of public meetings at which, she says, community members were suspicious but, particularly as a few influential residents got involved, started to get interested. As one puts it, 'The renewal got a few residents on side and those residents spread good gossip and they got others on side.' Kennedy targeted individuals and kept pressing participation. She heeded the message that, as one resident puts it, 'There was too much *telling* what we need, instead of *listening* to what we need.' Warren Kane recognises the importance of the groundwork done by Kennedy:

> Olive Kennedy and Molly spent two years setting this up to make sure that residents were involved. They wanted the residents to have input and make the decisions . . . But it's not just about bricks and mortar it's about people . . . When people started to see [things] happening then they started coming on board, and now we are very well supplied with people being part of it—volunteers.

It was not all smooth sailing, however. As department officials put together a renewal plan after consultation with the various stakeholder committees and subcommittees, the residents found they needed to become more assertive. As Warren explains it, 'They [the bureaucrats] brought back the big action plan after listening to us and talking to us—[but] they were purporting to say what we said and we couldn't understand it.' Another resident, Meg Laurens, adds cheerfully:

> We just put [that action plan] in the bin. The one you have is the second one and the residents put that one together. We wrote our vision and interviewed the residents and we decided on the format—not a great big boring document . . . That action plan was very important to us and everything that happens has to come from the residents. If we don't like it it's just not going to happen.

Members of the renewal team accept the view that their role is to facilitate community development in which the local people take leadership. According to the head of the team, Carol Georgiadis:

We said that we're going to call ourselves bureaucrats but we're going to turn it into a nice word . . . We have a clear understanding with this community that we won't stand up and represent them. One of the first things that happened was that all of the eleven Secretaries of all the Departments came here [to Wirra Warra]—a whole-of-government approach. The residents presented them with all the things they wanted, the things that were wrong. They owned it from day one.

Georgiadis's colleague, Harry Truebridge, asserts that the big difference between current reforms and previous attempts at change is the level of trust developed:

The government has been doing things to people here forever. They could never engage with them. So much is about trust. It's a real privilege to work here. It's that level of trust . . . This is different and a lot of people don't get it—it's about putting time into people and not time into project outcomes.

The result has been a healthy level of community involvement, as an activist community volunteer, Janice Morelli, explains: 'The projects—the Community Hub, the education, the BMX track, the men's shed, the tool pool—the residents have driven the changes.' Among the various priorities, education emerged early in the piece as a key theme. Warren Kane left school during his first secondary year, just like many of the current generation of young people in Wirra Warra. Warren now says, 'If I had my life over again I would have education,' and he maintains that 'the first decision we made as a residents group' was about the importance of education—not just school education but also broader community education. He says, 'You are going to see parents and grandparents at the school—school's not the enemy.'

## BUILDING COMMUNITY AND EQUITY THROUGH EDUCATION

Officials of the Midlands Regional Office of the Department of Education are strong supporters of 'the renewal.' Olive Kennedy says they have been 'fantastic.' They agree that the neighbourhood renewal program in Wirra Warra had already become largely resident-led by the time they became involved. The regional director, Norman Jenkins, suggests that the renewal project was characterised by

affirmative action by government to support the people there . . . It was all resident driven—resident empowerment. We see education as being multi-contexted—here was a micro example where we could do something. The university, police, local government were involved and people could see that, 'Hang on. This is ours!' And they drove it.

A renewal subcommittee had by then been set up to consider how educational provision and outcomes could be improved. One of the senior education officials outlines the key issues:

> The educational sub-committee was looking at ways to link people back into education—lack of retention, one of the highest rates of non-continuance of students from junior secondary to senior secondary in the State, one of the lowest adult connectedness, a very low number of students accessing early years [education], very high absenteeism in primary and low transference to secondary school. We felt that we needed a whole of community involvement and a plan.

Norman Jenkins insists that 'it's all about building a community not just a school.' He asserts: 'This is the key factor—if young people are disenfranchised in life, then their opportunities are cut off forever. You start with education [reform].' Jenkins holds that genuine education reform will have a more powerful effect on individual lives and community change than any other initiative. He describes one of the community meetings, at which groups of students, parents, and teachers typed suggestions for discussion at a ring of computers, as 'teary stuff! Grandparents telling us and the eight-year-old kids typing it in; it was heart-wrenching stuff!' He continues:

> Dads and mums had a very negative view of how the schools treated them. Then we tried to turn it around: 'How do you want it to be? Turn it around.' We're talking about great change . . . They were talking about engagement, the need for kids to feel safe came through a lot, and talk about respect—it just kept coming through. It was angry stuff . . . We workshopped all the stuff that had come up and we came up with a vision for education. Then the [Community Hub] building grew out of that. It's built on the concept of a community school. It's about re-engagement of the whole community, not just the kids.

One of the main themes that emerged was that many primary school students were reluctant to proceed to secondary school where, parents say, they 'get lost' and 'can't cope.' This problematic transition was impressed on the regional director by the residents. Jenkins recalls a critical point in the consultations:

> I was talking to the [Hillview Primary] School president, a woman; she said her son loves it here [at the primary school] but he doesn't want to go to [secondary] school next year. I said, 'What if you had something different here? If they want to go to secondary school, OK, but what if they have a different choice?'

The proposed 'different choice' is for students to stay on at primary school, if they want to, for up to two additional years after completing year six. The secondary college has agreed to the arrangement so the new 'super school,' Rose Hill Community School, will cater to children in the first two years of secondary schooling in a primarylike environment. The capacity of young people to move gradually between primary and secondary is expected to make a substantial difference to the sixty percent of students who currently never make it to senior secondary school.

Norman Jenkins, in 2005, referred to 'hundreds' of 'lost kids' in Provincetown, many of whom were from Wirra Warra. They were 'lost to the system.' The LinkUp program, which commenced operating in 2006, has been designed for young people who, for whatever reason, became disconnected from formal education and are seeking to reengage with learning. The success of the program so far has been greater than expected. The LinkUp coordinator, Paul King, explains:

> We were able to enrol twenty students but they never had to attend school. We employed an outreach teacher. We meet the students anywhere except in their homes [and] developed a personalised learning program on what they expressed was important to them.

By the end of 2006, the number of young people participating in the program had grown to 160. By that time the LinkUp team was 'running dozens of programs out of the Wirra Warra community—rusty panels, cooperative learning, playing monopoly, computer programs, learner driving.' King finds this 'exciting' because running programs in places like the Community House is for him 'the way of the future.' He believes young people 'have unique issues that need to be addressed in different ways, and all the players know they have to turn things on their head to make this successful.' Among those engaged in LinkUp are 'kids not connected to any learning [who have been] case managed by various organisations. They had been bullied or been bullies; they were highly motivated to learn but they would not go near a school.' Both King and activist teacher, Ian Patrick, agree that school has been 'toxic' for such students, who are often damaged: 'The ones for us that are difficult are [from] dysfunctional families. We get terrible things to deal with like violence, suicide attempts, a lot of cutters, by and large, young females.' Patrick refers to need for spontaneity and flexibility in the LinkUp program as he follows hunches, pursues contacts through his networks and hunts down favours.

Peter Cambrel, principal of Rose Hill, maintains that the super school will reflect the priorities asserted by the community, including the value of education for all:

> We now have the whiz-bang plans. We had architects from New York—it's very impressive. We are working on the designs to fit the pedagogy. . .

A lot of consultation has been going on . . . it's a unique way of doing things. In communities like these they don't take kindly to big brother imposing things on them. They don't think that they need things handed down to them: 'We're no different than others.' Education was identified as being so important. The design of the building has been driven by the teaching and learning that we want to take place in it.

Numerous teachers at both Hillview and Rose Park schools acknowledge the low proportion of children attending preschool. One stated:

It's a great concern that the children are not coming through kindergarten. Unfortunately, when the fees are due they just drop out. When they come to school they don't know their colours, they don't know numbers and they can't hold scissors. So we are really doing a kinder year in prep (the first year of primary school). We are then so far behind that some kids never catch up.

The low level of preschool attendance is an issue that is being vigorously attacked by the renewal office. But the lack of preschool experience is not the only problem for local young people. Over the past ten years, only two from Wirra Warra have obtained a higher education qualification. Of the families of children who attended Hillview Primary in 2006, only two received income from regular employment, and ninety-four percent of the parents were holders of health cards. As Warren Kane points out, 'Some of our young people have never seen anyone work—mum, dad, or grandma . . . A lot of children never even thought of work.' Kane believes that education and the experience of seeing local parents and peers in jobs will 'enable our kids to dream.' A relatively novice primary teacher in Wirra Warra, Marie Ovens says that the dreaming and thinking about 'alternative futures' has to start early for the pupils because of their narrow horizons:

Our students don't have many of the experiences of everyday life that we take for granted. Lots of them have never been to the beach . . . We get the kids to talk about their futures and their aspirations. We have class goals and personal goals when we encourage them to think ahead about what they would like to achieve. Some talk about what they want to be when they grow up. Some want to be teachers, hairdressers, nurses and so on.

Teachers also speak of children's experiences of having to fend for themselves, take responsibly in various ways for younger siblings, and deal with sometimes violent and chaotic domestic environments. Ovens is aware of several such examples:

They surprise you with what they don't know but sometimes they surprise you with what they do know . . . One little kid has nine brothers and sisters to get organised before he comes to school. A little girl sets her mobile phone so she can get up because the mother is still in bed. These kids really want to be here and they really enjoy it. You tend to think that these kids don't want to learn. I think I had that perception before I came here but it's definitely not the case.

There are also many comments about students at both primary and secondary levels who can unpredictably 'explode.' Another primary teacher, Elizabeth Saunders, provides an example:

> It started to hail. When we looked out the window a kid bumped into another kid and next thing they were throwing punches. Kids bring a certain amount of pent-up anger into the classroom. Monday is usually the worst day because of family issues arising from the weekend.

A high proportion of Wirra Warra children at primary school are classified as eligible for special funding because of their diagnosed 'disability and integration' needs. Teachers at both primary and secondary levels also refer to low levels of nutrition and personal hygiene, absenteeism, and low parental expectations of schooling. Neil Loughran refers to his time at Hillview Primary as 'a baptism of fire.' Turning around some of the problems, he says, is 'slow and challenging,' requiring recognition that student safety and welfare issues have to be dealt with as a 'pre-condition for learning.' Enrolling eighty students in a breakfast program is part of this emphasis, as is a list of initiatives that Loughran reels off.

## CURRICULUM AND CONTROL

Neil Loughran is a strong believer in a 'direct instruction model of learning.' A number of teachers support the literacy program he has introduced, but not everyone. Elizabeth Saunders has found the program too restrictive:

> I found that when I first came here it was so easy to teach. You just went bang, bang, bang, and you didn't even have to think about the lesson. It was easy but I couldn't do it for long. I had to move away from this kind of direct instruction . . . So my program is not so much teacher-directed.

Saunders is particularly concerned that, in the teacher-directed approach, there is 'not enough emphasis on getting kids to think critically.' Others agree with Loughran that providing grounding in literacy and numeracy justifies a structured, even rigid, program. The smaller number of teachers at Rose Park Primary School is critical of the 'direct instruction' that they see as characterising the approach of Hillview staff. This difference has been a major talking point not only of teachers but also parents, officials, and volunteers at the renewal office and Community House. The level of discussion within the community about curriculum and pedagogy is, in itself, indicative of increased interest since the launch of the neighbourhood renewal program. There are other examples of parent interest, as Elizabeth Saunders explains:

> The culture here was that parents wouldn't take part in anything, but recently I had twenty-three out of twenty-four parents come to a parent-teacher interview. It's about how you sell it to the kids. We say to the kids, 'Show Mum and Dad what you've done.'

The parent evening was deliberately set up by school staff as an occasion for 'three-way interviews' involving parent, teacher, and student, and the attendance was remarkable. Saunders plans to strike while the iron is hot and try to attract parents into the school again:

> I'm planning to do a maths day with parents when they can come and play games. The emphasis is on family groups so you can go and be with all of your kids. I think it's a big step to come into a school when you've not had a good experience yourself.

Two single mothers, who are former pupils of Hillview Primary and who, in 2006, were members of the school council, say they do not want their children to leave school early, as they did. They remember an uncomfortable place in which teachers were 'very strict and severe.' They note that there is less bullying now and much greater acceptance of difference among the pupils. Natalie Jovanovich, a local who has been an integration aide at Hillview Primary, defends the community as one that is 'proud and supportive.' She says that many children nonetheless carry enormous 'emotional baggage and pent-up anger,' making them prone to 'hissy fits.' It is at these times, when they are most likely to 'explode,' that the children particularly need understanding rather than punitive behavioural management measures. She concludes: 'Teachers have to earn the trust and respect of kids. This won't happen by asserting their authority.'

## LOOKING TO THE FUTURE

Principal Peter Cambrel says the early days of the 'new' Rose Hill Community School have been very promising. There seems to have been general community acceptance of the merger. Issues of pedagogy and curriculum have not gone away, however, as a former Rose Park teacher demonstrates:

> We are working through the [literacy] program. But I think that we still have some work to do. It's a more literature-based approach—more

prescriptive, directive. We went through the merge process [and] what we were using [at Rose Park] we don't use here anymore. What was at Hillview has just been imposed on us.

According to the regional director of education, Norman Jenkins, this is the time when some 'backward stuff' is likely to happen in teacher and parent morale, so the pressure is on 'to build some stability before the shaky knees happen.' He expects that 'teacher capacity and teacher renewal are going to challenge some staff members; they are all on board but some are going to [have to] rethink the way they will teach and change the way they do things.'

The LinkUp program continues to easily make its target of 160 students and looks likely to keep growing as more of the 'lost kids' find their way to it. LinkUp can no longer be seen as a small, alternative program, and some of its staff are worried that the need to manage the large group might erode some of the program's spontaneity and individuality. Ian Patrick says, 'People say I have to write up the aims and stuff. I can't do that, it's not important.'

The Wirra Warra campus of Provincetown Secondary College has a new principal, Sally Andrews. She is aware that many students from Wirra Warra fail to complete year seven and that few of them make the transition to the Provincetown senior campus. She says, 'we should be doing better for these kids':

> The learning is everything for those kids. That's what it is all about
> . . . It's worth me spending some time down at the community renewal
> talking to parents about their kids down there. In the street smarts they
> are very advanced; we don't acknowledge all the other things that these
> kids know.

Peter Cambrel's ideal of inclusive 'learning communities' that will operate in the super school from 2008 includes open relationships among children, teachers and adults:

> Under one roof you will have three to four staff with helpers but you
> may also have four to five people from the community assisting as
> well. When they work with the students they also learn things from the
> kids—and they are role models for the kids. What we are looking at in
> the learning communities is getting away from the teacher as the focal
> point. The teacher will be the facilitator. Those people will be able to
> work as a team.

There is a strong feeling that making education reform central to the renewal process is the right way to go. Since the plans for the super school have been on display and the two previous primary schools have amalgamated, it appears that community expectations of good things to come have been raised.

## DISCUSSION: THE COMMUNITY IDEAL
## AND THE PROBLEMATIC REALITY

As the above narrative illustrates, there is a great deal of optimism and an emerging community spirit in Wirra Warra. The question is whether the developments provide hope for improved livelihoods and social change. On the evidence to date there is perhaps potential for continuing democratic engagement in shaping the 'renewal' and a commitment to including residents in public forums, local improvements in housing, and considerations of land use and service needs. Many residents say they have influenced decision-making and made a difference.

Although I emphasise that these are the early days, it seems that despite being less advantaged than most citizens of other areas of Provincetown, residents of Wirra Warra are striving to assert their views and exert democratic influence. Government officials, service professionals, and a number of teachers seem to have responded by positioning themselves on the side of local people. The fact is that many residents, who pride themselves on having 'good bullshit detectors' and an ability to 'pick a suit from a hundred paces,' are convinced that this time the bureaucrats are genuine, that they listen, and that it is the residents who are making the decisions. They are rather proud that officials have had to 'earn' their trust, and the officials are proud that they have been able to earn it.

Professional commitment to local people and their livelihoods is particularly strong in the renewal office, where officials regard themselves as turning 'bureaucrat' from a dirty to a positive word. They talk openly about reforming bureaucracy in democratic ways, making it clear that they do not see themselves as simply the recipients of policy directives but as interpreters and reformulators who make policies meaningful and useful in context. Norman Jenkins and a couple of his colleagues are also somewhat radical bureaucrats who are using the 'social justice' background text of Labour Party education policy to create space within the neoliberal, school effectiveness, measurement-oriented policy template to push innovative thinking about promoting equity. Peter Cambrel is also encouraging staff to engage with, understand, and respect pupils, and to work with colleagues and the community.

This last issue touches on debates about curriculum, pedagogy and behaviour management which are rumbling among staff of the new Rose Hill Community School. There has been sufficient consideration of them to anticipate that they are going to be major topics of debate within the community of teachers and among the broader community as well. People have the opportunity to make curriculum relevant to the young people of the community, to use local examples, people, organisations, and stories as curriculum resources. This will require teachers to connect with community colleagues in housing, social work, health work, and other service professionals, volunteers, and community members in exploring local issues and services in educative, inquiring, and engaging ways. Investigations of topics such as civics, poverty, justice, environment, pollution, and health could feasibly be made relevant to the lives of young people by working across agencies with the participation of the students and community.

Active engagement on the side of the residents would now seem to be a feature of the lives of many teachers and service professionals, which in itself is a process of politicisation. Hence there is the potential for residents, young people, teachers, and service professionals to critically question what they previously have taken for granted and to actively take a stance on issues like the purpose of schools in a democracy. The service professionals, through aligning themselves with the interests of the local community, can ultimately make themselves accountable to the community in a reversal of the usual authority positioning. The starting point for such democratic change may be when schools and teachers reach out to young people, move to meet them, welcome them in, and validate their experiences and lives rather than expecting them to adjust to the entrenched school and teacher paradigms (Smyth and Hattam 2004), and when teachers attempt to engage their students in relevant and interesting school experiences in which they can recognise themselves, their parents, their neighbours and their community (Angus 2006). The process of neighbourhood renewal seems, on the evidence so far, to be taking all members of the community seriously, validating their lives and dreams, and to some extent promoting visions of alternative futures.

There are sufficient individual stories of engagement to suggest that many community members have been actively involved, some of whom claim that their lives have changed dramatically for the better. They seem to be becoming active agents of social, educational and institutional reform. Further research will determine whether a sufficient critical mass of social activists can be built such that the interests of disadvantaged people and communities can be asserted.

## NOTES

1. The name 'Wirra Warra' and all other names in this chapter are pseudonyms.

## REFERENCES

Angus, L. (1993) 'The sociology of school effectiveness,' *British Journal of Sociology of Education*, 14, 3: 333–45.
———, (2006) 'Educational leadership and the imperative of including student voices, student interests, and students' lives in the mainstream,' *International Journal of Leadership in Education*, 9, 4: 369–79.

Atkinson, E. (2000) 'In defence of ideas, or why "what works" is not enough,' *British Journal of Sociology of Education,* 21, 3: 317–30.

Bessant, J. (2002) 'Risk and nostalgia: the problem of education and youth unemployment in Australia—a case study,' *Journal of Education and Work,* 15, 1: 31–51.

Edwards, R. (2006) 'A sticky business? exploring the "and" in teaching and learning,' *Discourse: Studies in the Cultural Politics of Education,* 27, 1: 121–33.

Fay, B. (1987) *Critical Social Science,* Ithaca: Cornell University Press.

Fraser, D. and Petch, J. (2007) *School Improvement: A Theory of Action,* Melbourne: Office of School Education, Department of Education.

Friere, P. (1970) *Pedagogy of the Oppressed,* New York: Continuum.

Kelly, P. (2007) 'Governing individualized risk biographies: new class intellectuals and the problem of youth-at-risk,' *British Journal of Sociology of Education,* 28, 1: 39–53.

Lilley, D. (2005) 'Evaluating the "community renewal" response to social exclusion on public housing estates,' *Australian Planner,* 42, 2: 59–65.

McClenaghan, P. (2000) 'Social capital: exploring the theoretical foundations of community development,' *British Educational Research Journal,* 26, 5: 568–83.

Millar, P. and Kilpatrick, S. (2005) 'How community development programmes can foster re-engagement with learning in disadvantaged communities: leadership as process,' *Studies in the Education of Adults,* 37, 1: 18–30.

Osei-Kofi, N. (2005) 'Pathologizing the poor: a framework for understanding Ruby Payne's work,' *Equity and Excellence in Education,* 38: 367–75.

Putnam, R. D. (2000) *Bowling Alone: The Collapse and Revival of American Community,* New York: Simon and Schuster.

Quinn, J. (2005) 'Belonging in a learning community: the re-imagined university and imagined social capital,' *Studies in the Education of Adults,* 37, 1: 4–17.

Sammons, P., Hillman, J. and Mortimore, P. (1995) *Key Characteristics of Effective Schools: A Review of School Effectiveness Research,* London: Education Resources Information Centre.

Sikes, P. (2006) 'Towards useful and dangerous theories,' *Discourse: Studies in the Cultural Politics of Education,* 27, 1: 43–51.

Smyth, J. and Hattam, R. (2004) *'Dropping Out,' Drifting Off, Being Excluded,* New York: Peter Lang.

Teese, R. 'Class war and the war on class: the two faces of neo-conservative research in the Australian media,' Radford Lecture presented at the annual conference of the Australian Association for Research in Education, Melbourne, 2004.

Te Riele, K. (2006) 'Youth "at risk": further marginalizing the marginalized?' *Journal of Education Policy,* 21, 2: 129–45.

Thrupp, M. (1999) *School Making a Difference, Let's be Realistic!* Buckingham: Open University Press.

———, (2001) 'Sociological and political concerns about school effectiveness research: time for a new research agenda,' *School Effectiveness and School Improvement,* 12, 1: 7–40.

Wishart, D., Taylor, A. and Shultz, L. (2006) 'The construction and production of youth "at risk"', *Journal of Education Policy,* 21, 3: 291–304.

# Part III

# Current Political Controversies

The Practice

# 14 At the Service of the (Restructured) State

## Principal's Work and Neoliberal Ideology

*Janice Wallace*

> My focal interest is in human freedom, in the capacity to surpass the given and look at things as if they could be otherwise. (Maxine Greene 1988)

While teaching a summer course on school leadership at a Canadian university, I met a teacher from Switzerland who audited the course at the request of her school in order to learn about North American school leadership practices. As it turned out, we learned a great deal from her about democratic leadership. In her school, 'management' is shared by an elected three-person team of teacher colleagues, while 'leadership' is shared by all school staff on an ongoing basis through consensus-building. Her school mirrors the larger political environment in which all citizens *must* vote and voting is a regular—often monthly—occurrence about all manner of issues of concern to the community and country. My point in introducing this story is not that this is an ideal that should be emulated, but that this model of democratic leadership was so outside our North American experience as to be almost unimaginable. As fascinating as we found this model, we were discouraged to learn that it was under review because of the Swiss government's dissatisfaction with PISA (international standardised test) results—confirming that even long traditions of direct democracy in educational practice are under siege within the homogenising policy effects of the managerialist state (Dehli 1996).

Simon suggests that democracy should be understood 'as a way of life, as an ethical conception, and hence always about the democracy *still to come*' (citing Dewey 2001: 13, italics added). Schooling is inevitably about the 'still to come' and has traditionally been perceived as a primary vehicle for preparing citizens for participation in democratic societies. While the rhetoric of democratic citizenship is evident in formal policy statements that accompany massive restructuring of education in the three Canadian provinces in this study—Ontario, Alberta, and British Columbia—many of the conditions for ensuring that practices in schools support its realisation in curriculum, pedagogy, and governance are not (Wallace 2004). If restructuring efforts that limit possibilities for democratic practice are to be resisted, the concept of and possibilities for democracy need to be clearly articulated so that they are understood and practiced knowledgeably by school administrators in formal roles of authority.

In this chapter, I will explore three areas of inquiry with a view to enabling a more rigorous understanding of democratic practices in schools and the challenges of implementing them to school administrators working within the constraints of 'the new managerialism' (Ball 1998: 122). First I will explore how democratic purposes of public education are shaped within current policies and practices in Anglo-American democracies. I will then examine the discursive positioning of neoliberalism within a continuum of political discourses. Finally, I will identify the tensions and omissions that are revealed in the 'walk and talk' of school administrators in school democratic practices.

## CONCEPTUAL FRAMEWORK AND RESEARCH APPROACH

Key tenets of democracy (Portelli and Solomon 2001) provided a conceptual framework for analysing the findings from a qualitative research project in which thirty male and female school administrators were interviewed in Ontario, British Columbia, and Alberta. In addition, policy documents were examined and open-ended follow-up interviews were conducted, promoting focussed responses but allowing for individual differences, with key personnel in teachers' and principals' associations in each province. Themes were identified using a constant iterative process among all the data, documents, and emergent policy developments as reported by popular media, professional associations, and formal policy documents. In this chapter, I will draw primarily on interview data as they relate to participants' mis/understanding of democratic practices in schools that were produced by state governance practices characterised as the 'new managerialism' (Ball 1998: 122).

## DEMOCRACY + RESTRUCTURING = DEMOCRATIC PURPOSES OF PUBLIC EDUCATION AT RISK

Portelli and Solomon identify characteristics that are common to conceptions of democracy: 'critical thinking, dialogue and discussion, tolerance, free and reasoned choices, and public participation . . . [and are] associated with equity, community, creativity, and taking difference seriously' (2001: 17). These key tenets contrast sharply with ascendant instrumental purposes of public education (Wallace 2004). As Manzer argues, economic restructuring has been a strong influence on educational purposes for public schooling in Anglo-American democracies (Australia, Canada, New Zealand, UK, and US), causing shifts between an emphasis on preparing students for citizenship in a democratic community to 'reforming public schools to serve industrial efficiency' (2003: 312).

Labaree (1997) extends Manzer's discussion by delineating shifts in educational purpose from a public to a private good. The traditional purpose of public schooling, he argues, is democratic equality—schools focussing on training citizens and ensuring conditions for each child to have an equal opportunity to become an actively engaged citizen—a public good. In contrast, social efficiency—schools focussing on training workers and an education that stratifies educational opportunities to prepare students for hierarchically arranged corporate needs—is both a public and a private good. Manzer (2003) documents the ways in which expansionist economic agendas and the challenges of addressing the needs of increasingly diverse populations in Anglo-American capitalist democracies following World War II provided an impetus for welfarist policies, including progressivist education policy, which brought changes in curriculum and school organisation more closely resembling Labaree's notion of democratic equality.[1]

Both Manzer and Labaree argue, however, that postindustrialisation and the concomitant forces of global capitalism in the late twentieth century have precipitated significant shifts in values, attitudes, and beliefs that have pushed purposes of public education toward the private good of social mobility—the belief that schools should prepare individuals for social positions based on class privilege and increased status. Doing so, Labaree argues, 'has elevated the pursuit of credentials over the acquisition of knowledge' (1997: 39). The phenomenon of commodified schooling he describes has been repeated across Anglo-American capitalist democracies (Harrison and Kachur 1999; Blackmore and Sachs 2007) and is represented within neoliberalism as a rational response to the imperatives of globalised capital.

## THE ROOTS OF NEOLIBERAL IDEOLOGY IN EDUCATION

Having identified the social and economic shifts that moved educational purposes away from democratic citizenship as a public good and toward instrumental economic ends as a private good, I will now turn to the ideological roots of neoliberalism: the key political discourse of managerialism that is reshaping the purposes of public education and its governance practices. The enactment of these practices is embedded in ideologies (Frazer and Lacey 1993: 17–20) which Marxists conceptualise as 'false consciousness' at the service of dominant capitalist interests. Post-structuralists have challenged this position as reductionist because it implies the existence of 'a true consciousness accessible via "correct" theory and practice' (Hall 1985). Instead, drawing on postmodern feminist cultural critic Ebert's (1988: 23) definition of ideology, I argue that ideological positions produce and reproduce discursive positions that are enacted in the lived experience of social subjects working within dominant historical arrangements of power that change over time. Understood in this way, I can trace a trajectory of discursive pressures on school administrators' practices within the ideological

*Table 14.1*   Political Ideologies

| | Socialist Liberalism | Liberal Humanism | Classic Liberalism | Liberal Conservatism | Traditional Conservatism |
|---|---|---|---|---|---|
| *Social/ Economic Benefits Distribution* | systemic inequality | meritocracy/ rights | meritocracy | 'natural' inequality | 'natural' inequality |
| *State Role* | state should be employed on behalf of exploited and disadvantaged and provide protection from privileged classes | acceptance of an activist (welfare) state to ensure equality of individual opportunity | laissez faire --interference only to the extent of ensuring individual's right to pursue personal well-being | welfare state tolerated as liberal status quo but conservative beliefs about human nature, order, stability, change, and 'natural' inequality | favour a strong but relatively inactive state to maintain social order (ideally dealt with by community/social norms) |
| *View of Good Society/ Person* | all humans are equal and have an essentially social or communal nature | shift from emphasising freedom from state to greater equality in enjoyment of liberty | 'natural' state of individuals free and equal but need to relinquish some freedom in interests of 'civil' state | noblesse oblige requires tolerance of need for social relief in order to maintain social order | idealised hierarchical society in which differing individual capacities are essential for community survival |
| *Power Distribution* | democratic and reformist; supportive of collective action | extension of franchise to increasingly broad constituency; expansion of rights claims of individuals | not totally comfortable with fully participatory democracy; some limits, checks and balances on participation | 'limited' democracy | traditional authority and power sources (e.g., God monarchy); less state power with democratic/ representative government |
| *Market Role* | capitalist market economy source of class inequities, therefore state should assume control and apportion capitalis social benefits equitably | abandonment of laissez faire economic policies | no regulation of private economic transactions of individuals | reform of market economy to enhance individual opportunities ad to improve collective (but unequal) good of society | markets serve the good of the community (premised on 'natural' inequality) |

*(continued)*

*Table 14.1*  Political Ideologies (continued)

|  | Socialist Liberalism | Liberal Humanism | Classic Liberalism | Liberal Conservatism | Traditional Conservatism |
|---|---|---|---|---|---|
| Key Philosophical Position | collectivism | rationalism | rationalism | rationalism/ traditionalism | traditionalism |
| Characteristics of Social Relationships | accept legitimacy of opposition and inevitability of pluralism | pluralism | limited tolerance of religious and moral difference | traditional social, moral, and religious beliefs ascendent; pluralism tolerated | little tolerance; traditional moral, social, and religious beliefs entrenched |

positions shaping those discourses. More specifically, I will explore how political ideologies shape the discursive space within which schools might engage in 'critical thinking, dialogue and discussion, tolerance, free and reasoned choices, and public participation,' particularly around issues 'associated with equity, community, creativity, and taking difference seriously' (Portelli and Solomon 2001: 17).

Table 14.1 identifies political ideologies that have informed the formation of the managerialist state within the conditions of globalisation. In addition, it introduces two continua that locate tentative ideological positions for the liberalism/communitarianism debate, and notions of negative and positive liberty that situate my discussion of managerialism later in this chapter. The categories used to describe political ideologies may be read as responding to the key tenets of democracy outlined by Portelli and Solomon (2001), although they do not correspond exactly. For example, distribution of social and economic benefits corresponds to equity and taking difference seriously, while the role of the state and the market designate possibilities for critical thinking, dialogue and discussion, and free and reasoned choices.

## THE LIBERAL-COMMUNITARIAN DEBATE

Liberalism has been the dominant political ideology in the modern age (Phillips 1993; Johnston 1997), affecting policy and practice in at least three ways. First, liberal democracies see society as a collection of individuals who are equally free moral agents. However, while each citizen is believed to be 'naturally' free, they relinquish some rights to the state in exchange for personal goods such as security. Second, within liberal ideology the role of the state in effecting a common good is limited to what Berlin characterises as 'negative liberty.' That is, liberty is conceived of as 'the freedom of individuals to pursue their own private interests with minimal interference from the state' (Carr and Hartnett 1996: 27). Olssen, however, suggests that communitarianism challenges liberalism in a number of ways—the most relevant to understanding the shifts in educational policy and practice within the managerialist state are: '(1) social ontology: the priority of the collective good over individual rights or utilities; and (2) a recognition of the social nature of the self' (1998: 71).

A communitarian ideology gives priority to the 'common good,' determined by shared community values defined through democratic processes. Communitarianism, unlike the liberal conception of the presocial 'natural' self (social action motivated by self-interest), 'maintains that the nature of the self is social in the sense of being "embedded in", "constituted by", and "dependent upon" the community' (Olssen 1998: 72). Policy, informed by a liberal utilitarian view of the common good, provides for limited intervention by the state to check the expression of unbridled self-interest that infringes on the rights of others, but such an approach is seen by communitarians as an impoverished view of self and society. Instead, a communitarian perspective of the common good includes policy that enables provision for humanist values such as:

> physical and mental well-being, material sustenance, the exercise and realization of human capacities and potentialities, for individual development in accordance with choice and reason, for action in accord with virtue, for friendship (*philia*) and interpersonal relations, and for pleasure. (Olssen 1998: 73)

Communitarianism will not serve the interests of citizens within state institutions, such as education, however, if 'the common good' ignores normative power relations and allows for systemic prejudice around class, race, gender, and other forms of exclusion. *Exclusive communitarianism,* characteristic of traditional conservatism, accepts traditional hierarchies of power as good because individuals within the community are sorted along these markers of difference to serve the common good efficiently. Critical theorists have long argued that public schooling has done just that—efficiently sorted students according to class in preparation to take on their class-based role in society (e.g., Apple 2000; Bowles and Gintis 1976; Labaree 1997)—but such practices clearly compromise democratic possibilities for schooling.

Another model of communitarianism, which I will call *inclusive communitarianism,* is associated with socialist liberalism. It makes room for a critical analysis of the prejudices that shape social relations and public policy—a key tenet of democracy. Inclusive communitarians would argue that liberals who see the state as a neutral arbiter of social benefits based on rational utilitarianism badly misrepresent the profoundly complex context of political action in which social and economic benefits are distributed. Rather, when particular socioeconomic forces, such as capitalism, racism, and so on, interfere with the ability of some citizens to fully participate in a more broadly conceived common good, the state has an obligation to intervene in order to ensure substantive equality for all citizens. Thus, from an inclusive communitarian perspective, individual rights exist 'in relation to the [common] good and not prior to it' (Olssen 1998: 73) and therefore can be altered in the give-and-take of social and political practices.

Although traditional liberals believe that the state should interfere only to the extent necessary in order for individuals to safely pursue their own interests, as capitalism flourished and disparities between classes threatened the civil state security, many modern liberal democracies shifted from 'negative liberty' to a more activist humanitarian position by instituting welfare measures and rights-based legislation to mitigate the effects of unequal access to social and economic benefits. However, liberalism in all of its guises has remained more or less committed to limited interference with a market economy and individual property ownership, and a belief in the state as a rational and neutral distributor of social benefits and merit-based employment opportunities, except as they interfere with individual rights. An inclusive communitarian position, on the other hand, is centred in a notion of the individual as essentially equal within a collective social experience. Inclusive communitarians advocate an active role for the state in order to ensure that its actions are based on a collective understanding of the common good derived from consultation with representatives of a wide range of social and cultural positions, not just traditional positions of power and privilege.

An inclusive communitarian position expands the *polis* in which public discussion is premised on the need for transforming dominant understandings of 'the other' in order to come to an inclusive understanding of 'the good society.' In contrast to liberalism, inclusive communitarianism proposes moving beyond individual notions of welfare and rights-based intervention to state-initiated reform and even replacement of capitalist mechanisms. However, in doing so, political actors must be aware of the fine line between *transforming* and *coercing* in attempts to move public debate and action away from traditional relations of power towards more equitable distribution of social benefits—including those distributed through the practices of schooling.

## THE EMERGENCE OF NEOLIBERALISM
## AND THE MANAGERIALIST STATE

Conservatism, as the etymological roots of its name imply, is predisposed to conserve what exists, to resist change, and to support the community or societal traditional ways. Somewhat paradoxically, because liberalism has been the dominant ideological position through much of modern political history in Canada, conservatism, in acting to maintain the status quo, may actually preserve classic liberalism. This may explain why an increasingly pervasive political hybrid comprised of *neoliberalism,* arguing for capitalism

unfettered by the state, and *neoconservatism,* touting the merits of traditional values of exclusive communitarianism, has emerged in recent years.
For example, Hall, commenting on the emergence of this phenomenon in
England during Margaret Thatcher's political leadership, suggested that
Thatcherite populism 'combined the resonant themes of organic Toryism
[neoconservatism]—nation, family, duty, authority, standards, traditional-
ism—with the aggressive themes of a revived neo-liberalism—self-interest,
competitive individualism, anti-statism' (1988: 48). These same themes have
reappeared, with only slightly differing emphases, in the current policies of
Republican US president George W. Bush, former Democrat US president
Bill Clinton, current Conservative Canadian prime minister Stephen Harper,
and Liberal Canadian prime ministers Jean Chretien and Paul Martin. Even
neosocialist leaders such as former Ontario premier, Bob Rae[2], and the newly
retired long-term prime minister of England, Tony Blair, adopted market-
driven neoliberal policy positions in response to globalisation. Thus, parties
that once held recognisably differing ideological views now hold positions
increasingly indistinguishable from one another, except in emphasis. Notably, none strongly espouse the key tenets of democracy.

Media commentary refers to this hybrid as 'The Third Way.' Academics,
such as Frazer and Lacey (1993) and Giddens (1994), have explored the
limitations of uncritical allegiance to political ideologies of the left and right
in light of globalisation challenges, computer technology's virtualisation of
time and space, and the restructuring of wealth in the hands of a larger and
more autonomous corporate market economy. These forces blur not only
the lines between political ideologies, but also existing nation states (Giddens 2001; Morgan 2006). As cultural communities (sometimes literally)
fight to preserve their physical and ideological borders, and transnational
corporations fight to increase their market share by circumventing state
interference, a postmodern *Jihad vs. McWorld* (Barber 1996) has emerged
with frightening consequences for democracy.

Education policies in the three Canadian provinces in this study have
responded to middle class voters who fear that not only they but their children will lose out in a competitive global economy (Ball 2002). Each province's response has included restructuring initiatives prompted by similar
political ideologies that limit opportunities for democratic practice. While
provincial school documents espouse some form of democratic practice,
such as dialogue and discussion in 'professional learning communities' (as
understood by Alberta boards), neoliberal ideology is challenging the ability
of each province's education system to nourish the potential of the democratic ideals described by Portelli and Solomon (2001). Schools that nourish democratic ideals 'have at their core ideals of inquiry and discourse,
equity and justice, authenticity and caring, shared leadership, and service
to community (O'Hair et al. 2000; Sergiovanni 1992; 1996; Starratt 1991)'
(Pounder, Reitzug and Young 2002: 270). However, British Columbia's
educational restructuring, following on the heels of Alberta's and Ontario's

(Harrison and Kachur 1999), mirrors 'the new consensus' for policy in public institutions, such as educational systems (Avis et al. 1996 in Ball 1998). Ball contends that there are five imperatives for this consensus. The first is *neoliberalism*—policy informed by marketplace ideology. The second is the new institutional economics that 'involves the use of a combination of devolution, targets and incentives to bring about institutional redesign . . . In education, the impact of such ideas is evident in the myriad of "site-based management" initiatives' (1998: 122). The third influence is a social phenomenon connected to the first two: performativity, 'a principle of governance which establishes strictly functional relations between a state and its inside and outside environments' (Yeatman 1994: 111). Performative measures are the quantifiable 'sign systems which "represent" education in a self-referential and reified form for consumption' (Ball 1998: 123). Public choice theory is the fourth imperative of the new consensus, while the 'new managerialism'—the cult of excellence coupled with efficiency in public sector institutions—is the fifth.

The question these political practices raise, then, is how does the new managerialism, which characterises public education policy and is shaping restructuring in jurisdictions across Anglo-American democracies, challenge democratic practices in school administration? In particular, how are the elements that characterise democracy—'critical thinking, dialogue and discussion, tolerance, free and reasoned choices, and public participation . . . associated with equity, community, creativity, and taking difference seriously' (Portelli and Solomon 2001: 17)—compromised by managerialist policies? The first concern for school administrators that I will turn to is the capture of democratic educational purposes by the marketisation that has compromised equitable educational opportunities within communities of difference.

## EDUCATION FROM PUBLIC GOOD TO EDUCATIONAL MARKETPLACE

The room for democratic engagement by each province's citizenry was compromised in the last half of the 1990s by majority governments with neoliberal ideologies that appeared to offer opportunities for public debate but, regrettably, limited opportunities for critical thinking, discussion, and debate. For example, Premier Ralph Klein's Conservative government[3] was notorious for holding legislative sittings for the minimum days required and limiting public debate. When Harris' Conservative majority was in power in Ontario, it quickly dismantled all equity legislation and reshaped almost every aspect of education in response to the new consensus with very little public input. Premier Campbell's Liberals (Conservatives by inclination if not by name) in British Columbia encountered more resistance to their neoliberal agenda but, because they had a large majority government, were able to move ahead with significant educational policy changes while limiting public input.

Each of these provinces manifests the new consensus of managerialism in a way that is unique to their economic and political history. Ontario, Canada's largest and most heavily industrialised province, experienced the greatest economic downturn from postindustrial restructuring of the workforce. Harris' 'common sense' platform in the mid 1990s appealed to a large majority of Ontarians frightened by the ways in which their lifestyle was challenged by forces they could not see or fully comprehend. Harris's message was simple—Ontario needs a more competitive workforce and a balanced budget—and it appealed to a broad spectrum of voters who elected the Conservatives in a landslide victory. British Columbia and Alberta are both resource rich provinces and are, therefore, economically dependent on the global marketplace for natural resource revenues. Alberta, with a long history of Conservative majority governments, is rich in oil and gas and its economic well-being is largely dependent on world oil prices that have resulted in Alberta's remarkable wealth. The multilateral agreements protecting Alberta's oil revenues, however, are not as advantageous to the natural resource industries of other provinces, like British Columbia's lumbering, mining, and fishing. Until Campbell's election, BC's fickle electorate was more suspicious of globalisation mantras than Alberta. Despite their differences, however, all three governments achieved wide appeal because of their 'new consensus' message of fiscal conservatism, global competitiveness, managerialism, and performative forms of accountability.

Each province's statements of educational purpose shifted from an emphasis on democratic equality and social efficiency in the 1970s and early 80s to one focussed almost entirely on social efficiency goals in the 1980s and 90s. Current prescriptive curriculum not only emphasises preparation for the workplace but also arguably exacerbates the stratification mechanisms preserving the effects of privilege while decreasing learning support, that is, social mobility. This shift is troubling in that it is driven by accountability measures tied to efficiency as measured by the 'bottom line' rather than more complex definitions of efficiency that include equity measures (McKenzie and Scheurich 2004)—a key tenet of democracy. Indeed, as competitive advantage in a globalised marketplace becomes a dominant 'common sense' social value, parents are portrayed in public discourse as demanding that schooling demonstrate positional advantage through standardised measures. Doing so, however, creates even deeper divisions between children from different socioeconomic strata more deeply inscribed by language, race, gender and other markers of difference. As Labaree argues, 'education can only promote social mobility (and simultaneously preserve the positional advantage of the privileged) to the extent that it prevents most students from reaching the top of the educational pyramid' (1997: 65).

Alberta was the first to choose a school-based management model, where school principals are required to develop business plans, outside polling services adjudicate community satisfaction with schools, and entrepreneurial strategies are encouraged that attract enough students to keep budgets viable.Both Ontario and British Columbia have implemented policies that encourage more competition between schools and devolve responsibility to the local level while maintaining rigid fiscal power at the provincial governance level. In Ontario, while citizens have pushed back against legislation that gave tax credits to parents who wish to send their children to private schools, high-stakes standardised tests remain the primary measure of 'success' for students and teachers. Therefore, neoliberal managerialist discourses drive a market-driven publicly funded education system that competes for its 'clients' based on performance indicators. Principals from Edmonton, Alberta, confirmed that schools openly compete for students by marketing their particular advantages (special programs in sports, arts, academics, etc.) on web pages, sign boards, newspaper advertisements, and through other enticements like highly organised open houses. One junior high principal, for example, noted, 'The competitiveness is really hard and I believe . . . that it takes away from some of our opportunity to just be good instructional leaders. And some dishonourable behaviour happens from some colleagues.'

## LIMITING DEMOCRATIC ENGAGEMENT IN PUBLIC EDUCATION

Educational governance systems in all three provinces have been restructured based on the imperatives of 'the new consensus' that limits the possibility of practicing democracy in any deep sense (Barber 1996). Boards of education have been 'rationalised' by redrawing their boundaries into much larger geographic areas and implementing provincial control of education taxes, thus limiting the role of local community representatives as well as their power to respond to local needs. At the same time that fiscal and governance power have been 'uploaded' to the province, responsibility for the day-to-day operations of schools has been 'downloaded' to the local level. Alberta and British Columbia principals are responsible for developing 'business plans' for their schools that must meet provincial approval and submit themselves and their schools to 'satisfaction surveys' distributed to the community their school serves. The result is the appearance of more democratic leadership—but only in the sense of particular forms of mandated accountability to 'stakeholders' (Taylor 2001)—without any meaningful control over resources at the local level. The complexity of competing discourses of stronger central control and devolvement of responsibility to the local school is particularly evident in Alberta. Principals who were interviewed expressed varying levels of comfort with mandated team building, 'visioning,' and providing a competitive instructional focus in their school, yet expressed a markedly higher sense of agency than their counterparts in Ontario and BC, where a more muted form of school-based management was introduced. Alberta principals felt that they had some control over school resource allocations and internal operations to support instructional goals and were able to respond to local needs and internal politics in a more nuanced and flexible way than is possible from a centralised office. One secondary school principal described how he allocated resources to meet instructional goals this way:

> The basic thing that drives the decisions in this school is students' results. So if, for example, one of the core areas is getting superb results, that may be an area where we may say, 'OK we're not going to deploy as many resources, either time or books or computers or whatever, in that area because they are doing really well right now, and we have just a finite amount of resources ... Eleven years ago, our social studies results were the worst in this district. So that was an area where we did deploy more resources. We also did a little more heightened accountability. But we put some extra stuff in there to build that core area up and it's now one of our leading areas.

While the language he uses to describe the resource allocation process is characteristic of the new managerialism, he is able to focus on instructional needs because of the school-level autonomy that he enjoys.

Most principals in Alberta welcomed the freedom to develop an instructional focus for their schools based on their own notions of instructional excellence, the particular needs of their students, and the desires of the school community. A principal whose school is well known for its innovative programs commented:

> I can't imagine a centralised system. I haven't worked within one and I like being able to decide along with my school community what our staffing needs to look like, what our instructional focus will be, what programming strategies we use. You know, with the [special programme], for example, people said, oh did you have to go to board? No, I didn't have to go to board; it's a strategy we're using. The school community wanted it; I was able to do it ... Decentralised systems look so different and from my understanding, [my board] still remains at one of the highest levels internationally in regards to what we're doing, what we're responsible for at school level.

The entrepreneurial discourse used by each of these principals is imbued with the language of the new consensus—'student results,' 'deploy resources,' 'being able to decide'—that are emblematic of the post-Keynesian shift in public educational policy discourses away from the tenets of democratic ideals. They reflect, instead, neoliberal perceptions that

> view bureaucratic control systems as unwieldy, counterproductive and repressive of the 'enterprising spirit' of all employees. Its notion of the

route to competitive success is to loosen formal systems of control . . . and to stress instead the value of motivating people to produce 'quality' and strive for 'excellence' themselves. Managers become leaders, rather than controllers, providing the visions and inspirations which generate a collective or corporate commitment to 'being the best.' (Clarke and Newman 1995: 15)

When one views the practices of these principals through the lens of democratic tenets outlined by Portelli and Solomon, the diminishment of possibilities for democratic practice becomes clear. Room for 'critical thinking, dialogue and discussion, tolerance, free and reasoned choices, and public participation' is diminished when pedagogical success is measured by standardised tests and participation by measurable satisfaction surveys. 'Equity, community, creativity, and taking difference seriously' is constrained when principals must become entrepreneurs to ensure that their school remains competitive and, therefore, open in an education marketplace.

## DEMOCRACY FROM THE 'TOP DOWN' AND THE 'BOTTOM UP'

Based on the discussion thus far, one might conclude that conditions at all levels of public school practice and governance seem to be working against creating conditions for 'the long-standing purpose of schools to prepare students *for* democracy while functioning *as* democracies' (O'Hair et al. 2000). Yet, as Barber (1996) argues, democracy is a public discursive space that emerges from the bottom up and can seldom be imposed successfully from the top down. In other words, as noted earlier in Dewey's concept of democracy as 'not yet,' democracy is lived, experienced and evolves; it cannot be imposed and mandated successfully by managerial imperatives—nor can the ideology of managerialism. Thus, despite the rather bleak picture that my research reveals when looking at policies that are being imposed from the top down in educational hierarchies, I also found examples of resistant practices that increased opportunities for democratic practices emerging 'from the bottom up.' For example, some inner-city principals reported working together as a collective in order to resist the competitive model of practice that was results-driven at the expense of a vulnerable community. Others reported strategies for carving out people-focused time by reworking or challenging central office demands so that they could work collaboratively with staff to meet the needs of a wider range of students. Some spoke about their struggles to address equity issues in their schools around race, ethnicity, language, gender, sexual orientation and other markers of discrimination that affect students' educational opportunities.

These examples were somewhat sporadic and muted articulations of democratic leadership values, but they exist. However, many principals could not articulate democratic ideals of leadership, even when asked directly. For example, when I asked one principal of a large secondary school in Alberta what she saw as the role of public schooling in Alberta society, her response danced between the poles of individualism and communitarianism, democratic equality and social efficiency. Her ambivalence, in terms of democratic practice, is revealing and, arguably, hopeful:

> I think the role of public schooling is to provide an educational and, I think, a social experience for students, and I'm going to help them to be good functioning citizens in our world. And I think what I like about public school is they don't decide which kids get to be the citizens and which kids don't get to be . . . And so for us in public education I think it's about taking those kids and knowing that somewhere along the line they're going to be 18, 19, 20, 21 years old and they're going to be out in our society. So what can we do to help them to be successful in that? . . . They need to be able to get along with their neighbours, get along with the people that they work with, contribute to our society, look out for people that are maybe less fortunate than they are, contribute to their community through community service and volunteerism . . . for the betterment of our entire society. I think if you only look at economics then you become very selfish, selfish and very self-centred. It's about me and my money and getting ahead, right? . . . So no, they need to have the skills to go out and get a job to earn a living to support a family . . . But I also think that within that is learning how to get along with all of the people that you live with, in your family, in the community.

The principal's words, although deeply imbued with liberal norms of equally free moral agents, also contain the seeds of hope for moving toward democratic administrative practice. She wavers between communitarian values and the constraints of managerialist policies but is not fully conscious of their ideological base. As a professor of educational administration, it has become my goal to enable future administrators to clearly understand their own political ideology as well as that of the policies shaping their practice—not to proselytise but to bring them to consciousness so that informed choices for practice can be made. The response above suggests that many graduate students who are or aspire to be school administrators may have a muted sense of the possibilities for democratic practice in reshaping purposes of public education and relations in the school, but their understanding is limited by the ceaseless rhetoric of managerialism in an educational marketplace. Umpleby suggests, however, that a critical awareness of 'the democracy still to come' (2002) is possible:

> Administrators can make a difference as we struggle to preserve public education. An ethical administrator can work effectively within a

dysfunctional system if s/he is knowledgeable about the restraints to positive interpersonal relationships that are in place. The principal must be a stalwart optimist whose faith is predicated upon an understanding of the political and educational realities and an utter belief in the possibilities of creating a school culture based on participatory and democratic ideals.

In order to do so, it is essential that administrators are able to trace the ideological roots of the political position from which their practice is shaped so that they are able to articulate and re/capture democratic practices in schools.

## NOTES

1. One example is *The Report of the Provincial Committee on Aims and Objectives of Education in the Schools of Ontario* (1968), another is *The Hall-Dennis Report,* after its authors, Justice E. M. Hall and Lloyd Dennis. It was highly influential across Canada and in many other parts of the world, capturing the *zeitgeist* of the 1960s by advocating for public education that enhanced self-realisation, offered individualised timetables based on student choice rather than required courses, and based its policy on progressivist ideals of democratic engagement.
2. Interestingly, Bob Rae revealed his more traditional liberal interpretation of socialist liberalism not only in policies introduced during his rather brief tenure as the leader of the National Democratic Party (Canada's socialist democratic party at the provincial and federal level) in Ontario's provincial legislature, but more explicitly in his recent attempt to become leader of the federal Liberal Party in Canada.
3. I reference newly retired Ralph Klein because it was under his government's lengthy watch that most neoliberal reforms were implemented. The new premier, Ed Stelmach, is, according to Conservative public announcements, attempting to demonstrate a more active interaction with citizens and opposition parties. The evidence suggests a kinder, gentler version of the same political ideology—including encouraging public/private partnerships for building public institutions such as schools and highways.

## REFERENCES

Apple, M. (2000) *Official Knowledge: Democratic Education in a Conservative Age,* 2nd edn, New York: Routledge.

Avis, J. et al. (1996) *Knowledge and Nationhood: Education, Politics, and Work,* London: Cassell.

Ball, S. (1998) 'Big policies/small world: an introduction to international perspectives in education policy,' *Comparative Education,* 34, 2: 119–30.

———, (2002) *Class Strategies and the Education Market: The Middle Classes and Social Advantage.* London: RoutledgeFalmer.

Barber, B. (1996) *Jihad vs. McWorld,* New York: Ballantine Books.

Blackmore, J. and Sachs, J. (2007) *Performing and Reforming Leaders: Gender, Educational Restructuring, and Organizational Change,* Albany: SUNY Press.

Bowles, S. and Gintis, H. (1976) *Schooling in Capitalist America: Educational Reform and the Contradictions of Economic Life,* New York: Basic Books.

Carr, W. and Hartnett, A. (1996) *Education and the Struggle for Democracy: The Politics of Educational Ideas*, Buckingham: Open University Press.

Clarke, J. and Newman, J. 'Managing to survive: dilemmas of changing organizational forms in the public service,' paper presented at Social Policy Association Conference, University of Nottingham, July 1992.

Dehli, K. (1996) 'Travelling tales: education reform and parental "choice" in postmodern times,' *Journal of Education Policy*, 11, 1: 75–88.

Dufour, R. (2005) *On Common Ground: The Power of Learning Communities*, Bloomington: National Education Service.

Ebert, T. *(1988) 'The romance of patriarchy: ideology, subjectivity and postmodern feminist cultural theory,'* Cultural Critique, 10: 19–58.

Frazer, E. and Lacey, N. (1993) *The Politics of Community: A Feminist Critique of the Liberal-Communitarian Debate*, Toronto: University of Toronto Press.

Giddens, A. (1994) *Beyond Left and Right: The Future of Radical Politics*, Stanford: Stanford University Press.

——, (2001) 'Dimensions of globalisation,' in S. Seidman and J. Alexander (eds) *The New Social Theory Reader*, London: Routledge.

Greene, M. (1988) *The Dialectic of Freedom*, New York: Teachers' College Press.

Hall, S. (1985) 'Signification, representation, ideology: Althusser and the poststructuralist debates,' *Critical Studies in Mass Communication*, 2, 2: 91–114.

——, (1988) *The Hard Road to Renewal: Thatcherism and the Crisis of the Left*, London: Verso.

Harrison, T. and Kachur, J. (eds) (1999) *Contested Classrooms: Education, Gobalization, and Democracy in Alberta*, Edmonton: University of Alberta Press/Parkland Institute.

Johnston, L. (1997) *Politics: An Introduction to the Modern Democratic State*, Peterborough: Broadview Press.

Labaree, D. (1997) 'Public goods, private goods: the American struggle over educational goals,' *American Educational Research Journal*, 34, 1: 39–81.

Manzer, R. (2003) *Educational Regimes and Anglo-American Democracy*, Toronoto: University of Toronto Press.

McKenzie, K. and Scheurich, J. (2004) 'Equity traps: a useful construct for preparing principals to lead schools that are successful with racially diverse students,' *Educational Administration Quarterly*, 40, 5: 601–32.

Morgan, G. (2006) *Images of Organization*, Thousand Oaks: Sage.

O'Hair, M. J., McLaughlin, J. and Reitzug, U. C. (2000) *Foundations of Democratic Education*, Belmont: Wadsworth.

Olssen, M. (1998) 'Education policy, the cold war, and the liberal-communitarian debate,' *Journal of Education Policy*, 13, 1: 63–90.

Phillips, A. (1993) *Democracy and Difference*, University Park: Pennsylvania State University Press.

Portelli, J. and Solomon, P. (2001) *The Erosion of Democracy in Education*, Calgary: Detselig Press.

Pounder, D., Reitzug, U. and Young, M. (2002) 'Recasting the development of school leaders,' in J. Murphy (ed.) *The Educational Leadership Challenge: Redefining Leadership for the 21st Century*, Chicago: NSSE.

Sergiovanni, T. (1992) *Moral Leadership: Getting to the Heart of School Improvement*, San Francisco: Jossey-Bass.

——, (1996) *Leadership for the Schoolhouse*, San Francisco: Jossey-Bass.

Simon, R. (2001) 'Now's the time: foreword,' in J. Portelli and P. Solomon (eds) *The Erosion of Democracy in Education*, Calgary: Detselig Press.

Starratt, R. J. (1991) 'Building an ethical school: a theory for practice in educational leadership,' *Educational Administration Quarterly*, 27, 2: 185–202.

Taylor, A. (2001) 'Education, business and the "knowledge economy"', in J. Portelli and P. Solomon (eds) *The Erosion of Democracy in Education,* Calgary: Detselig Press.

Umpleby, S. 'Whither the principal in a restructured BC educational system?' Paper presented at the annual meeting of the Congress of Social Sciences and Humanities, CSSE/CASEA, University of Toronto, 2002.

Wallace, J. (2004) 'Educational *purposes economicus:* globalization and the reshaping of educational purpose in three Canadian provinces,' *Canadian and International Education,* 33, 1: 99–123.

Yeatman, A. (1994) *Postmodern Revisionings of the Political,* New York: Routledge.

# 15 Listening to Student Voice in the Democratisation of Schooling

*John Smyth*

This chapter[1] deals with the theme of the democratisation of educational organisations through the lens of student engagement from a 'critical practice' (Vibert, Portelli, Shields and LaRocque 2002) perspective. A centrepiece of the discussion will be the place of student voice in the democratisation of schooling. Discussion will move beyond what McMahon and Portelli label 'popular discourses of student engagement' (2004: 59), especially around some current infatuations with 'student voice,' towards a more robust politicised and democratised view of schooling. As well as drawing from the Canadian work of Vibert, Portelli, Shields, LaRocque and McMahon on Emily Carr Elementary School, the chapter also discusses an Australian school I investigated called Plainsville School (Smyth and McInerney 2007a; 2007b).

The place of student voice in the democratisation of schooling is explored theoretically and practically in terms of how student voice was conceived and enacted in these two schools. In both instances, these schools were studied over a three-year period as part of larger, multisited ethnographies. In the case of Emily Carr, with a student population of 350 and a staff of 25, the school was located in a middle class suburban area, but its clientele were drawn from the poorest areas of this community, with the majority of families suffering the multiple effects of poverty. What made this school distinctive from the others studied by these Canadian researchers was its commitment to 'on-going school and classroom discussions about the working of power' (Vibert et al. 2002: 97). Plainsville School, a reception to grade eight school of 300 students and some 30 staff, on the deindustrialised fringes of a large Australian city, had roughly the same socioeconomic features as its Canadian counterpart and in every sense of the wording the school found itself daily living up to its motto of 'living on the edge' (Smyth and McInerney 2007b: 1132), as distressed families handled the crises that came with multiple and interacting forms of financial hardship and family dysfunction, including low income, high levels of (often inter-generational) unemployment, high levels of transience, protracted health problems, and low levels of parental education.

But before I come to the practical aspects of democratisation in more detail in these two schools, there are some philosophical and theoretical issues to be explored.

## WHY STUDENT VOICE?

In a recent themed issue of the *International Journal of Leadership in Education,* on the topic 'educational leadership that fosters student voice' (Smyth 2006), Fielding argued that:

> There is a 'new wave' of what many now call 'student voice' ranging over a huge vista of activities encouraging the involvement of young people which echoes the energy, if not the aspirations, of the 1960s and 1970s. (2006: 299)

Furthermore, according to Fielding, there is 'mounting evidence from a wide range of countries . . . that consulting young people about their experience of schooling is moving from the periphery towards the centre of government attention' (2006: 299). In respect of this trend, Fielding warns of the dangers accompanying the so-called 'high performance learning organization,' much vaunted in the educational management literature, in which there is an exploitative use of young people in a thinly disguised 'totalitarian' purpose of 'perpetual performance' towards 'targets, a usurious discourse of "user" engagement, and an "emotionally intelligent" articulation of economic purposes.' This version of student voice needs to be robustly 'exposed and opposed' (2006: 300). In contrast, Fielding argues that a very different mode of encounter and a more compellingly attractive alternative conceptualisation of student voice resides in a 'person-centred learning community' that articulates and aspires to reclaiming

> a commitment to education as a holistic undertaking, but also an alternative account of wider human flourishing in a democratic society. Here, student voice is essentially dialogic and, in its most exploratory mode, challenging of boundaries and demarcations. (2006: 300)

The essence of Fielding's argument resides in a four-fold typology of what he calls 'interpersonal orientations' within schools that present quite different levels of authenticity and commitment to the involvement of students in the life of the school. The first, the 'impersonal' school, is a predominantly 'mechanistic organization' committed to efficiency, in which relationships between students and school leaders are restricted to student voice of a formal consultative kind, the 'making [of] current arrangements more efficient' (2006: 302) and then, only in respect of designated matters. Students within this scheme relate to school leaders only through the formal consultative hierarchy of the school. In the second orientation, 'affective communities' are more inclusive, with student voice being given expression through the warmth of relationships of teachers to students in a genuine desire to help students learn and provide young people with opportunities to avail themselves of a variety of learning activities in the formal curriculum and 'other activities driven by student enthusiasm and interest' (303). In affective learning communities, student voice is characterised by 'ambient listening fostering closer understanding of those involved' (302). The third category is the school as 'high performing organization' in which success is measured purely in terms of outcomes and according to 'instrumental purposes within the context of the market-place' (305). Any sense of caring for young people is evacuated or 'hollowed out' (304) and replaced by the claim that performativity will deliver long-term benefits for students. The touchstone here is compliance. Student voice takes the form of 'wide-ranging formal and informal consultation to make current arrangements even more effective' (302). In Fielding's words, this archetype epitomises the 'new totalitarianism' (303). Finally, there are schools as 'person-centred learning communities' in which there is a pervasive commitment to a fundamentally different set of relationships within schools. For example, this involves 'an eradication or diminution of hierarchies' and its replacement by educative arrangements that are 'deeply dialogic in their modes of engagement' (307). This might take various forms, including different institutional architecture of 'schools-within-schools' (307) and 'student-led approaches to learning' (307). Here, student voice is the means to more democratic and authentic ends with 'wide-ranging formal and informal engagement to enhance the development of wise persons' (302). Issues of power and hierarchy are made more transparent here with student voice tending to be

> student-driven, staff supported and often a genuine joint venture. Whilst not eradicating either hierarchy or power, the centrality of negotiation, the foregrounding of values and the willingness to work through their consequences in an iterative way, the explicitly exploratory nature of what is undertaken, and the tolerance of ambiguity and unpredictability do a great deal to address both hierarchy and power in a recursive, on-going way. (2006: 307–8)

## THE PROBLEM FOR DEMOCRATISATION AROUND INFATUATIONS WITH STUDENT VOICE

Rudduck and Fielding are right to ring alarm bells about the 'rapid popularisation [of] schools interested in introducing student voice' (2006: 219). As they say, while it might seem eminently reasonable, on the surface, to argue for students having a greater say about the conditions of their learning, what is likely to get missed is that student voice becomes yet another educational fashion accessory—employed for all of the wrong reasons. As they put it, 'current popularity of student voice can lead to surface compliance—to a quick response that focuses on "how to do it" rather than on a reflective view of "why we might want to do it"' (2006: 219). The risk, as Rudduck and Fielding identify it, is that student voice becomes yet another form of educational commodification in the inexorable co-option process of politically driven school improvement. In respect of what is happening in the UK, they say:

> Today, government support for student voice and participation in schools is strong but it seems to have been fuelled by concerns other than the making of democratic communities. Familiarity with the principles of democratic governance is considered important but presented as something to be taught rather then experienced in the daily life of the school. (2006: 223)

What is being lost here is the understanding that there is 'more to this than recognizing that students might have things to say about improving their experiences in school' (221). Clearly, as Rudduck and Fielding argue, young people having a greater say about their schooling is important, but 'the implications of "finding a voice" are greater' (224). Far more profound is the capacity that student voice has to 'mak[e] spaces where [students can] develop their own identities and interests' (221). Here Rudduck and Fielding invoke the important work of Ranson (2000), and in what follows I unashamedly draw on Ranson's crucial thinking on these matters.

Ranson argues that in the increasingly fractured, detached and divisive societies in which we live, the 'twin tasks of urban regeneration and social inclusion will require [nothing less than] a renaissance in learning' (2000: 263). In Ranson's view, the nature of the profound challenge is to develop the 'capabilities' referred to by writers like Nussbaum and Sen (1994; Sen 1985; 1990), and 'finding a voice' is 'the core capability' (2000: 266) required to do this. The alternative Ranson alludes to lies in the ideas of 'active capability' and the pedagogy of voice in the radical remaking of learning communities. The wider social discourse Ranson draws from is that of 'social exclusion' and its concomitant 'inadequate social participation, lack of social integration and lack of power' (263)—all of which can apply to students in schools as social institutions as well as in their connection to the wider society. At the core of what Ranson argues for is whether or not people have the ability or are excluded from the opportunity 'to participate effectively in economic, social, political and cultural life' (264). In other words, social exclusion refers to the marginalisation and disconnection of people from relational as well as social and economic participation.

The relevance of this line of argument for student voice is that it provides a much closer linkage between the notions of 'the school as a democratic community, the confidence that young people can develop in such a setting and their community and their agency in helping improve the conditions of their learning' (Rudduck and Fielding 2006: 223). The important effect, according to Ranson, is that young people thus 'learn how to enter into a dialogue with others to transform practice' (2000: 266).

A 'pedagogy of capability' envisaged and argued for by Ranson is, therefore, inextricably linked to notions of citizenship and social power around four major points, that:

- reconnect learning to living through preparation for active citizenship, enhancing the capacity for participation in dialogue;
- understand all the needs of the learner, particularly emotional wellbeing;
- enrich our understanding of human capability and potential;
- promote active learning for developing responsible as well as reflective learners. (2000: 267)

The flow-on effect of an 'emergent pedagogy of capability' (267) in the interests of a more democratised view of schooling, is that learning becomes a more inclusive process, in which motivation

> grows out of a sense of purpose, of wanting to learn. This is likely to be stimulated [through] engaging the interests of the learner, and will be enduring when the learner, in wanting to do well and improve on previous performance, is self-motivated to learn more about the skills, qualities and virtues which lead to developing capability. (2000: 267)

In other words, learning is regarded as a process of growth, enhancing self-respect, discovering capability, and an intrinsic desire to improve performance through collaborative and co-operative endeavours. This view is markedly at odds with the 'narrow instrumentalism of much educational policy about learning over the past two decades' (Ranson 2000: 267) that has had a commitment to consumerist forms of 'new capitalism' (Sennett 2006) and the accompanying policy ensembles of performativity (i.e., the creation of a culture of performance indicators), competition, choice, accountability, and compliance through punishment and retribution.

All of this is by way of marshalling the argument that notions of 'active capability' and 'finding a voice' in schools and communities are about identity formation around capacities to:

- listen as well as express and communicate beliefs, feeling and claims;
- enter a conversation with others which leads to develop[ing] understanding and reflection in contexts of different views;
- discriminate and form judgements;
- choose and decide for oneself and with others;

• imagine and create a possible future. (Ranson 2000: 268)

In short, being a citizen in a school and in society, is, therefore, framed around a set of beliefs in relation to 'the capability to find a voice which asserts one's claims, and enables the learner to enter a dialogue with others, to reach shared understanding and agreement about how to resolve problems which are common to all in the public sphere' (Ranson 2000: 268). In a word, it is about creating schooling with a democratic intent.

I want to turn now to a brief discussion of two schools—one Canadian, the other Australian—that exemplify something of a move towards enacting democratic intent in the way they permitted and promoted authentic student voice.

## WHOSE RESPONSIBILITY IS DEMOCRATIC EDUCATION AND CAN SCHOOLS PROVIDE LEADERSHIP?

Biesta, in a recent paper entitled 'Education and the democratic person: towards a political conception of democratic education' (2007), argued that it is not the sole role of schools to necessarily produce democratic citizens, even though that might be a praiseworthy ideal. He does not see it as necessary for schools to have formal student parliaments or similar structures, nor for them to have a curriculum on democratic citizenship. It is more important, Biesta says, that schools be places that provide opportunities and spaces in which students can be 'subjects' in the sense of asking questions and having agency over their learning and lives more generally. 'Schools and educators . . . have an important role to play in inviting and supporting reflection on those situations in which action [is] possible and, perhaps even more importantly, those situations in which action [is] *not* possible' (2007: 763). In theoretical terms: 'What schools can do—or at least should try to do—is to make action possible, and hence create conditions for children and students to *be* subjects, to experience what it is and means to be a subject' (Biesta 2007: 764–5). To be clear about this, Biesta is not saddling schools with the awesome responsibility of producing democratic citizens, but rather he is 'put[ting] the question about responsibility for democratic education back where it actually belongs, namely in society at large' (2007: 765). He sees a much more modest, realistic and feasible role for schools in this regard of 'helping children and students learn about and reflect upon the fragile conditions under which people can act, and under which people can be a subject' (765).

To put some practical substance to this discussion, I return to the two schools mentioned at the start and, in particular, begin to examine the place of student voice in these two schools.

Vibert et al., in their analysis of Emily Carr, which they propose as an exemplar of a 'critical practice model' (2002: 93), take this to mean a situation in which educators take seriously a number of concerns:

The democratic purposes of schooling; the inevitability of the political dimensions of education and teaching; the importance of dealing explicitly with issues of race, class, gender, sexuality and all embodiments of social difference as a concern for social justice; the centrality of the notion of 'praxis' (Freire, 1998); and the inter-connectedness of voice, community, and curriculum. (2002: 95)

This perspective was not only given practical expression at Emily Carr through the way the school foregrounded issues of how power worked in the school and the wider community, but in the process it was illustrative of a place that did not shy away from asking questions about the forces that produced the 'shattering conditions of many of their students' lives' (98). The school was unprepared to regard these as matters to be deferred until after caring conditions of 'safety, comfort, emotional support and warmth' (98) had been created, essential though these might be. Rather, such matters were seen as educative candidates in and of themselves for students. For example:

When a newspaper article on Emily Carr Elementary identified it as a high-poverty school, middle-class community members wrote letters objecting. Instead of treating the incident as a public relations issue, some administrators and teachers brought articles and letters into the classroom and undertook with students a study of the social construction of poverty. Critical teaching requires courage. (Vibert et al. 2002: 104)

What was being actively pursued here, in the vein of democratic intent, was giving the children the experience of 'critical reflection' in ways that provoked them to 'raise questions about knowledge and experience and the connections between them' (104). Students were thus enabled to move beyond seeing poverty as 'the fault of poor people' (104), and to see it instead in terms of how the conditions of some people's lives were constructed through forces in a broader social context.

Another illustration of how Emily Carr was actively pursuing a 'curriculum of life' that was embedded in the lives of the children was the instance of a grade six maths teacher who captured the learning moment, as reflected in the following incident:

[She] addressed percentages and graphing (the official math curriculum) when students in her class organized, conducted and graphed a survey of differences between girls' and boys' responses to sexist language, growing out of an incident in which one boy told another not to be 'such a girl' (the actual curriculum). (Vibert et al. 2002: 104)

What is at issue and clearly on display here goes to the very heart of student voice and democratic intent. What is being enacted is the notion of 'respect,' not in the liberal humanist meaning of deferential regard, consideration or acting in a polite way to others, but a much more politicised view. As Vibert et al. put it, within the kind of critical context being pursued at Emily Carr

> 'respect' comes to mean more than listening to others and responding politely. A critical curriculum explicitly raises and deals with political issues including the question 'in whose interests is this account of things?' Such a curriculum introduces the 'impolite' (in the sense of uncomfortable) into public discourse, so that 'respect' comes to mean dealing with difficult and sensitive issues openly and compassionately. (2002: 104)

Relationships between people and big ideas flowed through and into the experiential relationships at Emily Carr. As Vibert et al. noted, student voice within the context of critical pedagogy at Emily Carr meant 'more than the representation of students' cultures in the public spaces of the school and more than the play of student choices within a pre-determined curriculum' (2002: 109). The very notion of what the school meant by 'community' was central to all that happened at Emily Carr: 'Rather than the smooth working relations grounded in shared norms and visions . . . such a community would centre on a dialogic process through which differences, disagreements and conflicts are expressed, exchanged and negotiated (2002: 110). It seemed the school conveyed the feeling of being more like 'a family' than an institution:

> What happened at this school was a sort of de-institutionalizing of relations. Normal routines of in-school relations did not entirely hold . . . Relations . . . appeared characterized by ordinary (and therefore extraordinary) humanity, not dictated by position and role. (2002: 111)

Emily Carr was a 'school *as* community' as well as a 'school *in* community' (109). The significance and meaning of this became evident in a number of respects:

> [the] flattening of the normal hierarchies; the de-institutionalized relationships to the extent that people were frank and open with each other in a substantive way; the degree of participation of all members of the school community; the shared projects in the world beyond the school . . . ; the discussions and activities on issues of real concern . . . ; [and] the focus on questions of how to live well together. (2002: 111)

What appeared central to how Emily Carr operated was their difficulty in speaking of the 'school as separate from community' (111). As the researchers put it:

> The community was in the school, involved in decisions of substance (e.g., drafting discipline policies, writing funding applications, establishing and

running a preschool and after school literacy program), and the relationship between the school and community was participatory. (2002: 111)

Without overromanticising things, it was not that decisions were always consensual, harmonious, or unanimous, but rather the case that when conflicts and disagreements occurred, as we would expect, 'they were the subject of dialogue and negotiation' (111). In other words, what community meant at Emily Carr 'was produced by the openness with which conflict among members was approached' (111).

In many respects, while it was distinctive in the particular way it was pursuing its democratic project, Plainsville School shared many similarities with Emily Carr. Located in a community ravaged by deindustrialisation, Plainsville had the damage marks to show it. Many parents had low levels of education, many failed to complete schooling, and there was difficulty in seeing the value of an education in a context where the rewards for education were not evident, and where two or three generations of unemployment were the norm.

The starting point for turning around the circumstances at Plainsville was a preparedness by the school to acknowledge the stark reality that the overall undemocratic context in which schooling operated was clearly impacting badly on a disadvantaged community already suffering from the tilted playing field. A radically different approach was required. What were needed were an elevation of expectations and the creation of a sense of worth in a community that had been repeatedly 'done to' so often that failure and exclusion were normal expectations. The axis for change was around the idea that schooling could be a rewarding experience for these children, that they could succeed, and that this would benefit the whole community.

The centrepiece for the transformation from 'old world' (their nomenclature for the system that was aggravating, alienating, dispiriting and disempowering) to the 'new world,' in which they had dignity, pride, success and power over their lives, was around the idea of '*student-initiated curriculum.*' Student-initiated curriculum was Plainsville's code for a set of educative experiences in which students had power over what they learned, where, how and with whom. Students developed *learning plans* or individual blueprints, with the assistance of adults in the school setting who helped them pursue meaningful learning. This learning was not only of interest to students but also helped put them on worthwhile career pathways.

Learning at Plainsville thus occurred in a context in which students were taught how to ascertain what was worth learning, how to access and marshal the human and material resources of the school to enable learning to occur, how to establish a particular focus on understanding their own community, how it came to be that way, how it could be different, and what students collectively might do to change that. Accountability was to students' immediate peers in daily meetings called 'talking circles,' and through 'individual learning meetings' with adults. Standards and curriculum frameworks were not regarded as mindless and punitive external impositions to be slavishly followed, but seen rather as places within which to create exciting learning challenges around students' interests. Learning was not seen as solely an individual activity, but a sophisticated social practice that involved bonding and participating with others as integral partners in learning decisions at all levels in the school. The general approach was one of avoiding deficit labels, regarding students as powerful learners capable of drawing upon and contributing back to and strengthening ties with the community.

The short description of how Plainsville positioned itself as an actual instance of working towards democracy, might be encapsulated as follows:

> (1)giving students significant ownership of their learning in other than tokenistic ways; (2) supporting teachers and schools in giving up some control and handing it over to students; (3) fostering an environment in which people are treated with respect and trust rather than fear and threats of retribution; (4) pursuing a curriculum that is relevant and that connects to young lives; (5) endorsing forms of reporting and assessment that are authentic to learning; (6) cultivating an atmosphere of care around relationships; (7) promoting a flexible pedagogy that acknowledges the diversity of young lives; and (8) celebrating school cultures that are open to and welcoming of students' lives and backgrounds regardless of the problems or where they come from. (Smyth and McInerney 2007b: 1163)

As we put it:

> [I]f there were two simple words that underscored what was unique, it would be the dynamic duo of courage and leadership. By this we mean, the courage to admit that schools are not working for the increasing numbers of disadvantaged children, especially those who do not fit the middle-class model of schooling . . . [T]his meant a preparedness to think outside the square and to literally put every aspect of the school under scrutiny regarding how it was serving students and their lives and futures . . . [I]t also meant having an abundance of the leadership skills to be able to envisage an alternative, and the passion to convince others of the indispensability of student inclusiveness in their reworked vision of schooling—and to carry all constituents along with that idea in practice over a sustained period of time. (Smyth and McInerney 2007b: 1163–4)

If indeed it is even possible to put a last word on something as complex as trying to describe the democratic intent underway at Plainsville, it might include something like this:

> This school was prepared to put a negotiated set of common understandings about children and how they learn at the center of everything

they did, and continually subject those ideas to interrogation, dialogue, and debate. It was unprepared to stand by and blithely accept an untenable neoliberal view of school reform that in effect blames students and their families, backgrounds, and cultures for a lack of educational success. (Smyth and McInerney 2007b: 1164)

## CONCLUSION

This chapter seeks to trace out some of the theoretical and practical complexities and underpinnings that come with the territory when discussing the democratisation of schooling in educational organisations. The chapter takes the current vogue term of student voice and shows that the ideal of engaging students from disadvantaged backgrounds in their learning can be a powerful force for good. It is a term that can be co-opted and hijacked to advance systems imperatives. The challenge is to ensure transparency in respect of whose interests are being served when the rhetoric of student voice is invoked. Drawing upon case studies of two disadvantaged schools, one in Canada and the other in Australia, this chapter pursues the more general issue of the politics of educational administration and leadership, and how this was given expression as these two schools sought to reinvent themselves around notions of active democratic intent. The fundamental point to be taken from the study of these two fascinating and courageously led schools is that schools are highly political entities—always serving some interests while denying or marginalising others. In the end, the challenge lies in the extent to which those least served by the dominant values can create, access and inhabit spaces within which they can construct an alternative life that is more equitable and just than the one offered to them under the status quo.

## NOTES

1. The author gratefully acknowledges the support of the Australian Research Council for two grants that made this chapter possible: 'Individual, institutional and community "capacity building" in a cluster of disadvantaged schools and their community' (Discovery Grant with L. Angus); and 'School and community linkages for enhanced school retention in regional/rural Western Australia' (Linkage Grant with B. Down). Grateful appreciation to Peter McInerney for his assistance on both these projects.

## REFERENCES

Biesta, G. (2007) 'Education and the democratic person: towards a political conception of democratic education,' *Teachers College Record,* 109, 3: 740–69.
Fielding, M. (2006) 'Leadership, radical student engagement and the necessity of person-centred education,' *International Journal of Leadership in Education,* 9, 4: 299–314.

McMahon, B. and Portelli, J. (2004) 'Engagement for what? Beyond popular discourses of student engagement,' *Leadership and Policy in Schools*, 3, 1: 59–76.

Nussbaum, M. and Sen, A. (eds) (1994) *The Quality of Life*, Oxford: Clarendon Press.

Ranson, S. (2000) 'Recognising the pedagogy of voice in a learning community,' *Educational Management and Administration*, 28, 3: 263–79.

Rudduck, J. and Fielding, M. (2006) 'Student voice and the perils of popularity,' *Educational Review*, 58, 2: 219–31.

Sen, A. (1985) *Commodities and Capabilities*, Amsterdam: North-Holland.

——, (1990) 'Individual freedom as a social commitment,' *The New York Review*, 14 June, 49–54.

Sennett, R. (2006) *The Culture of the New Capitalism*, New Haven: Yale University Press.

Smyth, J. (2006) '"When students have power": student engagement, student voice, and the possibilities for school reform around "dropping out" of school,' *International Journal of Leadership in Education*, 9, 4: 285-98.

Smyth, J. and McInerney, P. (2007a ) *Teachers in the Middle: Reclaiming the Wasteland of the Adolescent Years of Schooling*, New York: Peter Lang Publishing.

——, (2007b) '"Living on the edge": a case of school reform working for disadvantaged adolescents,' *Teachers College Record*, 109, 5: 1123–70.

Vibert, A., Portelli, J., Shields, C. and Larocque, L. (2002) 'Critical practice in elementary schools: voice, community, and a curriculum for life,' *Journal of Educational Change*, 3, 2: 93–116.

# 16 The New McCarthyism
## The Right Wing's Assault on American Academic Thought

*Fenwick W. English*

McCarthyism has been reborn in America. President Harry Truman defined McCarthyism this way:

> It is the corruption of truth, the abandonment of the due process of law. It is the use of the big lie and the unfounded accusation against any citizen in the name of Americanism or security. It is the rise to power of the demagogue who lives on untruth; it is the spreading of fear and the destruction of faith in every level of our society. (Oshinsky 2005: 349)

The new intellectual witch hunt of the twenty-first century involves a broad neoconservative attack across a wide spectrum of personnel at American colleges and universities, fostered by right-wing think tanks and paid political assassins who have rekindled public fear about new conspiracies being hatched among Muslim scholars, feminists, homosexuals, and the old reliable tirade against Marxists and former communists who reside in American academia.

The point man, but by no means the only right wing critic, is David Horowitz, a former left-wing Marxist, anti-Vietnam war protestor and secretary of the Black Panther party, who now repudiates his former views and actions and attacks those he believes are in his former camp as dangerous and corruptors of the true purpose of higher education. Horowitz has not only attempted to blacklist academics whom he believes conspire to undermine patriotism, and who are un-American and oppose the Iraq war and the Bush Administration specifically, but he has launched a legislative effort to rid the university of its alleged liberal 'bias,' exposing liberal professors who lean to the left. He founded an Internet web site called *RateMyProfessors.com* where students are invited to expose professors they believe are too liberal or biased towards the political left. The result is that at least in one state, Pennsylvania, a state representative decided to hold hearings to determine if such bias was indeed present in the state's colleges and universities (Jacobson 2006a). Mr. Horowitz is also behind organising students to fight liberal bias in the nation's elementary and secondary schools (Cavanagh 2006).

Schrecker insists that the contemporary assault on American higher education is 'more serious' than those of the McCarthy era. She points out that, 'Horowitz and his allies want to impose outside political controls over core educational functions like personnel decisions, curricula, and teaching methods' (2006: B20). And while Joe McCarthy attacked 'Communist professors' he also conceded that 'universities were also filled with "crackpots" and "screwballs" who posed no real threat to the nation's security' (Oshinsky 2005: 466). Schrecker indicates that Horowitz's campaign is aimed at depicting 'the entire field of Middle Eastern studies as radical, one-sided, and hostile to Israel and the United States.' She indicates that these charges 'have become so widely accepted that Congress has considered imposing constraints on federally financed area-study centers' (2006: B20).

## THE FIRST MISTAKE: NOT TAKING HIM SERIOUSLY

The first mistake many current academics make is to not take these attacks seriously and to underestimate their popular appeal. For example, Michael Berube (Jacobson 2006b), an English professor at Penn State and one of Horowitz's 'most wanted' academics, has some fun in doing an interview in which he responds to the question 'What makes you so dangerous?' with 'My slap shot [in hockey]' (Jacobson 2006b: A6). There is a tendency for some to look at Horowitz as a poseur. But Horowitz clearly understands what he is about. The battle is not to be won or lost in academia, but in the public mind—for as Conrad Russell opines, 'The big threat here does not come from Government: it comes from public opinion . . . The itch to be intolerant of something is very deep indeed . . . ' (1993: 24).

Loehr sees in such attacks the dark shadow of fascism in America, remarking that, 'Fascism is . . . a kind of colonization' the goal of which is 'to take people's stories away, and assign them supportive roles in stories that empower others at their expense' (2005: 88). Hedges places the drive to submerge those same voices and perspectives as a form of Christian reconstructionism called 'dominionism' which traces its roots to radical Calvinism. In contemporary American politics, 'dominionism' professes 'a belief in magic along with leadership adoration and a strident call for moral and physical supremacy of a master race, in this case American Christians' (2006: 11).

In his prescient *Fascists,* Michael Mann noted that fascism '[was] not a mere sideshow in the development of modern society' (2004: 1) and that 'fascist ideology must be taken seriously, in its own terms. It must not be dismissed as crazy, contradictory or vague' (2004: 2). He quotes Zeev Sternhell (1986) when he observed that fascism possessed 'a body of doctrine no less solid or logically indefensible than that of any other political movement' (2004: 2) and defines 'fascism' as 'the pursuit of a transcendent and cleansing nation-statism through paramilitarism' (2004: 13). As this chapter attempts to show, the current right-wing attack on the academy and their charges against those espousing ideas they find threatening and repugnant represent such a 'transcendent and cleansing nation-statism through paramilitarism' (2004: 13).

Mann also credits fascists with offering 'plausible solutions to modern social problems [that] . . . got mass electoral support, and intense emotional commitment from militants' (2004: 2):

> [M]ost fascists . . . believed in certain things. They were not people of peculiar character, sadists or psychopaths, or people with a 'rag-bag' of half-understood dogmas and slogans flitting through their heads . . . Fascism was a movement of high ideals, able to persuade a substantial part of two generations of young people (especially the highly educated) that it could bring about a more harmonious social order. (Mann 2004: 3)

The key to understanding fascists, according to Mann, is that 'the core fascist constituency enjoyed particularly close relations to the sacred icon of fascism, the nation-state. We must reconstruct that nation-state-loving constituency in order to see what kinds of people might be tempted toward fascism' (2004: 3). This chapter points out how right-wing critics of the academy are most agitated by those within it who raise questions and threaten the American nation state and its global moral and military supremacy. The chapter focusses on Horowitz's *The Professors: The 101 Most Dangerous Academics in America* (2006), which is part of a larger effort to discredit academics who write, speak, and teach contrary perspectives and values that criticise the nation state and those narratives it embodies in an ideal, purified condition. Thus, Horowitz and others rant about so-called 'left-wing' causes and the politicisation of the academy by their presence. For Horowitz, these ideas are pollutants, contaminants to the true purpose of higher education, which is to be 'a temple to the intellect' (2006: x) and 'dedicated to the disinterested pursuit of knowledge' (2006: xi).

Mann notes that fascists 'saw politics as unlimited activism to achieve moral absolutes' (2004: 8):

> Fascism saw itself as a crusade. Fascists did not view evil as a tendency of human nature. Fascists, like some Marxists, believed that evil was embedded in particular social institutions and so could be shed. The nation was perfectible if organic and cleansed. (2004: 8)

So the right-wing assault on some forms of thought within the academy represent an attempt to create a higher moral order by cleansing it of its perceived 'corruption' and 'intellectual debasement' in whatever forms and however shrouded in high-sounding rhetoric they may be packaged.

> Cultural studies, peace studies, whiteness studies, post-colonial studies, and global studies—even social justice studies—came into being

as interdisciplinary fields shaped by narrow, one-sided political agendas. Some of these programs attacked American foreign policy and the American military, others America's self-image and national identity. (Horowitz 2006: x–xi)

Indeed, on Horowitz's list of 101 dangerous academics there are sixteen directors of university centres or programmes for peace studies, global studies, conflict studies, women's studies, American and Jewish studies, human rights studies, Mexican-American studies, Marxist studies, African-American studies, cultural studies, and ethnic studies: '. . . never before in the history of the modern research university have entire departments and fields been devoted to purely ideological pursuits. Nor has overt propagandizing had such a respected and prominent place in university classrooms' (2006: xxxiii).

The list of professors 'subversive' to Horowitz's 'academic standards' include three former presidents of the Middle East Studies Association (Joel Beinin, Laurie Brand, Juan Cole), former presidents of the National Ethnic Studies Association (Larry Estrada), the American Sociological Association (Joe Feagin), the American Historical Association (Eric Foner), the American Philosophical Association (Alison Jagger), and the past chairman of the US Civil Rights Commission (Mary Frances Barry). Profiles of the 101 professors and their 'dangerous views' are detailed in Table 16.1.

While Horowitz concedes that some professors on his list are 'at the forefront of their professions . . . authors of books widely used as texts in their fields . . . funded by prestigious foundations and awarded the highest professional honors in their fields,' he accuses them of being 'capable of making disturbingly shallow intellectual judgments and expressing alarmingly crude political opinions' (2006: xxx–xxxi). He is exceedingly critical of those who allegedly lack scholarly qualifications and are therefore academically unsuited to teach the courses they do or express the kinds of political opinions he deplores as antithetical to the statism he enjoins. However, Horowitz never reveals his own scholarly qualifications enabling him to second guess the judgments of hundreds of others who have approved of his academic pariahs' appointments or any of his 'researchers' who have cherry picked his background data comprising his profiles.

Indeed, there is no serious discussion of the real intellectual issues at all in his book. When he lays out the agenda of those he criticises as politically motivated, they are consistently juxtaposed against his own 'approved' political positions. Often they are apologia for the agenda he finds objectionable. And it is often in these binary expositions that one finds the actual right-wing agenda he supports. Despite the disingenuous distinctions, what he really objects to is not so much 'teaching about' content he finds politicised, but 'teaching for commitment' (Horowitz 2006: xxvi). One finds on his list of dangerous professors *not a single* pro Republican, pro President George Bush, pro Iraq war, pro heterosexual marriage, pro capitalist or pro war academic. While Horowitz admits that Republican and conservative

*Table 16.1*   A Profile of David Horowitz's *101 Most Dangerous Academics in America*

Male 71%

Female 29%

Professors of Color 23%

Professors in the Humanities (English, Philosophy, History, Language, Black Studies, Women's Studies, Islamic Studies, etc.) 45%

Professors in the Social Sciences (Economics, Political Science, Psychology, Anthropology, Sociology, etc.) 33%

Professors in Other Fields (Journalism, Communication, Music, Law, Education, Engineering, Criminal Justice, etc.) 22%

(NB: there were no professors in the hard or 'bench' sciences. Only one in biology)

Major 'Dangerous' Perspectives Shared by the 101 Professors

-Anti-Iraq war (31%)

-Marxist in orientation or advocated or used Marxist writings or perspectives (28%)

-Anti-Israel (opposed to Israeli actions or treatment of Palestinians or to the State of Israel) (28%)

-Anti-American or Anti-American policies (19%)

-Anti George W. Bush (19%)

-Embraced feminist/lesbian programs, critical race theory, queer theory or homosexuality (18%)

-Anti-Capitalism (9%)

-Generally anti-war (7%)

-Anti-Semitic (6%)

-Pro-Palestinian (6%)

-Pro Cuba (5%)

-Anti Vietnam War (5%)

professors are a minority on most US campuses (Horowitz 2006: xxxv), it can't be that there aren't any in the academy. The lack of a single entry from the conservative side either means that all of them never 'teach for commitment' and maintain a strict kind of 'academic neutrality,' or Horowitz doesn't know of any transgressions because he isn't interested.

The latter is more likely the actual case. For example, Harvard history professor Stephan Thernstrom and his wife Abigail Thernstrom are long-time opponents of affirmative action, an advocacy view shared by Horowitz.

They are quoted on Horowitz's book jacket as saying of their fellow academics, 'They will hate this scathing critique, but will be hard-pressed to answer his charges.' Abigail Thernstrom is a senior fellow at the right-wing-funded Manhattan Institute, a Republican, and coauthor of *America in Black and White* (1997), wherein she ostensibly vented her anger because she was unable to obtain tenure (Brock 2004: 48). She and her husband coauthored the book *No Excuses: Closing the Racial Gap in Learning* (2003).

However, some black students at Harvard accused Stephan of racial insensitivity (Wiener 2005), and he participated in a public television broadcast, *Uncommon Knowledge*, where he attacked affirmative action ('A House Divided' 1997). Horowitz does not list Stephan Thernstrom for his views, writings, and public utterances, not because they are not radical, but because he agrees with them.

Another case is that of Francis Fukuyama, a distinguished professor of international political economy and director of the International Development Program at the School of Advanced International Studies at Johns Hopkins University. According to David Brock, Fukuyama and others have long been supported by 'subsidized sinecures within the right-wing think tank network. The think tanks paid the authors' salaries, awarded research grants, provided support staff, and established marketing and public relations funds to supplement the budgets of commercial publishers' (2004: 351). Fukuyama is not listed, even though in his latest book, *America at the Crossroads: Democracy, Power, and the Neoconservative Legacy*, he is critical of the Iraq war and the Bush administration and insightfully observed, 'By the time the war began, America's European allies came to be increasingly demonized as anti-American, anti-Semitic, or somehow imperfectly democratic' (2006: 64). Like the 31 per cent of the 'radical leftists' who oppose the Iraq war and the 19 per cent who are anti-Bush on Horowitz's 'subversive' roster, Fukuyama qualifies to be listed but is nowhere to be found.

Still another hiatus in the Horowitz 'most dangerous professors' list is the case of Glenn Loury. Dr. Loury was 'the youngest black professor of economics ever tenured at Harvard University' (Wikipedia 2006a). Loury had been a longtime African-American icon for neoconservatives. He opposed affirmative action and worked at the American Enterprise Institute, a right-wing think tank that supported the work of Dinesh D'Souza, Charles Murray, and William Bennett. However, as a result of changes in his personal life he did an about-face when he found that books by Dinesh D'Souza and Charles Murray were intellectually flawed. Hernstein and Murray's *The Bell Curve* (1994) contained 'sweeping conclusions based on poor science' (Higgins 2002), and Stephan and Abigail Thernstrom's *America in Black and White* (1997) contained 'intellectual lapses and racist assumptions' (Higgins 2002). Loury now resides at Brown University, where he is a professor of economics affiliated with the Population Studies and Training Center and Africana Studies (Wikipedia 2006a). Glenn Loury is not on Horowitz's list of 'dangerous academics' either.

This fundamental lack of balance makes Horowitz's claims for the 'debasement' of the university a not so thinly veiled partisan political attack. His objection is not that the university has become 'political,' but that prominent academics have embraced the wrong end of the political spectrum. And he wants them purged because they are anti-American, anti-Iraq war, anti-patriotic, anti-George Bush, anti-Republican, anti-capitalist, anti-heterosexual normativity, and anti-Israel or anti-Semitic. The purging, however, excludes those who are or have been political fellow travellers in the neoconservative movement.

## SO WHO IS HOROWITZ AND WHY DOES IT MATTER?

David Horowitz was born in 1939 in Forest Hills, New York, the son of Jewish parents who were school teachers and members of the Communist party (Wikipedia 2006b). He became a believer and activist on the radical left. His political about-face is a familiar narrative to those who have studied many of the intellectual leaders of the far right. As Dorrien observed in *The Neoconservative Mind,* 'The forerunners of neo-conservatism began their careers as communists' (1993: 19). He defines neoconservatism as: 'An intellectual movement originated by former leftists that promotes militant anticommunism, capitalist economics, a minimal welfare state, the rule of traditional elites, and a return to traditional culture values' (1993: 8).

Horowitz was editor of a leftist journal called *Ramparts,* in which he admitted that he published classified government information (2001: 1). He also authored *The Free World Colossus: A Critique of American Foreign Policy in the Cold War* (1965), in which he attacked US foreign policy (Brock 2004: 101).

When *Ramparts* folded, Horowitz joined the Black Panthers, becoming a writer for the organisation's newspaper. He remained part of the movement until a female friend of his was murdered, coming to believe that the Panthers were responsible for her demise (2003). He underwent a painful reconsideration of his views and work (Sherman 2000). When he reemerged, he began authoring caustic attacks on his former friends and perspectives. His book with Peter Collier, *Destructive Generation: Second Thoughts about the Sixties* (1990), was one example of his conversion to the far right. His shift from left to right, so very common among prominent right-wing speakers, rests on their common outlook regarding the state, the individual, and the role of dissent common to both camps.

Longshoreman philosopher Eric Hoffer observed that in the creation of mass movements there were not infrequent instances of converts—among even the most zealous—shifting allegiance from one to the other (1951: 25). Hoffer quotes Hitler, who allegedly said, 'The petit bourgeois Social-Democrat and the trade-union boss will never make a National Socialist, but the Communist always will' (Rauschning 1940: 134). Nazi leader Ernst Rohm ostensibly boasted that he could turn the reddest Communist into a glowing nationalist in four weeks (Heiden 1944: 30).

Horowitz began work in the Reagan administration, writing speeches for Senate leader Bob Dole in the 1988 presidential race (Brock 2004: 101). Eventually, he came into the circle of Bush advisor Carl Rove. With funds from right-wing financiers Schaife and Bradley, he directs the Center for the Study of Popular Culture in Los Angeles (Brock 2004: 101). There, according to Brock, he attacks 'political correctness' and affirmative action (2004: 102). His centre supports his web magazine *FrontPageMag,* in which he attacks Democrats and American colleges and universities, calling for a 'Campaign for Fairness and Inclusion in Higher Education' to be conducted by university administrators to 'implement inquiries into political bias in the hiring process . . . the selection of commencement speakers . . . allocation of student program funds . . . a zero tolerance policy towards the obstruction of campus speakers . . . and a code of conduct for faculty that ensures that classrooms will welcome diverse viewpoints and not be used for political indoctrination' (Horowitz 2002: 3–4). A significant number of the citations Horowitz (2006) employs to support his allegations against his 'dangerous professors' come from his own web journal.

In his study of fascists and their historical intellectual leaders, Mann notes that most were 'initially nonmaterialist leftists who embraced organic nationalism' (2004: 6). This meant that they were 'collectivists' and saw the state as transcendent only if it could be purged of impurities. They were contemptuous of 'bourgeois democracy' and did not believe that 'markets, parties, elections or classes could . . . generate morality. This must come from the community, the nation' (2004: 7).

This attitude was perhaps most poignantly expressed by Hilton Kramer, the former art critic of the *New York Times,* who spoke at the second conference of neoconservatives sponsored by the Bradley and Olin Foundations and partly organised by David Horowitz. Kramer scolded Horowitz and others as former leftists for not being sufficiently repentant for the damage they had done because they were failing to face 'the drug culture, the rock culture, the sexual revolution, the assault on the family and the middle class, the assault on high culture and the aggrandizement of popular culture, the devastation of the universities as the centers of cultural and intellectual life' (Dorrien 1993: 365). Apparently Horowitz had sufficiently 'repented' when he wrote:

> If I have one regret from my radical views, it is that this country was too tolerant toward the treason of its enemies within. If patriotic Americans had been more vigilant in the defense of their country, if they had called things by their right names, if they had confronted us with the seriousness of our attacks, they might have caught the attention of those of us who were well-meaning but utterly misguided . . . I appeal to those of you who are attacking your country, full of self-righteousness, who, like me, may live to regret what you have done. (2001: 2)

This tactic is a familiar one from the McCarthy era. It was employed by Louis Budenz, a witness for McCarthy, whose trajectory took him from Catholicism to Marxism and back. The tack was to say 'I am right now because I was wrong then. Only the ex-Communist can understand Communism. Trust me to lead you aright because I tried to lead you astray. My intelligence has been vindicated in that it made an all-out commitment to error' (Oshinsky 2005: 149).

Horowitz directs some of his wrath at campus antiwar groups, which, he claims, are embedded with individuals promoting 'the culture of Islamic terrorism and its anti-Western, anti-Israel and anti-American agendas' (2003: 2). While he says that he separates the right of free speech from those opinions expressed in the classroom, in practice many of his illustrations about the 'radical threat' on the nation's campuses come from students and professors exercising free speech either in on-campus rallies or off-campus presentations.

Why Horowitz (2006) represents a threat to the integrity and independence of the university system in America is that the battle for 'ideological power' of society lies in the balance. Foucault (1980) pointed out that knowledge is never neutral—it always comes packaged in systems of power; it benefits some people and works to the disadvantage of others. Horowitz's lament that the university has lost some sort of elevated 'sacred ground' that is nonpolitical is pure mythology. It enables him to attack the 'impurities' of the institution while leaving his own biases untouched and unexamined.

## INVESTIGATING CHARGES OF ANTI-SEMITISM AND ANTI-ISRAELI SENTIMENT

In Horowitz's adumbrated sketches of dangerous academics, at least 28 per cent are accused of being anti-Israel and 6 per cent with eliciting anti-Semitic comments/remarks/writings or sentiments from public utterances or in their writings. Many of the alleged remarks are very difficult to verify since the sources are other right-wing commentators or texts. Horowitz makes it a practice of referring to his own website journal *FrontPageMag* or to other right-wing blogs or websites as 'verification' of the prejudices of his cited academics.

Leaving aside for the moment the authenticity of comments he includes in his polemical vignettes, the connection between the dangerous professors and Israel and anti-Semitism may strike some readers as odd. In *With God on Their Side,* Kaplan explains that fundamentalist Christians believe that the formation of Israel and the Jews' resettling of the Holy Land is a sign 'that millennial prophecies about Christ's return were beginning to unfold' (2004: 24). Kaplan quotes Rabbi Yechiel Ekstein, who began the International Fellowship of Christians and Jews in 1983, which by 2002 had contributed '$20 million to projects in Israel and millions more to support Jewish resettlement to Israel' (2004: 25). Indeed, Christian Zionists take 'a hard-line, pro-Israel stance' (2004: 24) and they are extremely active in lobbying Congress for support for Israel and are estimated to be more influential and active than AIPAC (American Israel Public Affairs Committee) (2004: 24). When President Bush revealed his road map to peace in 2003, evangelical Christian leaders signed a letter to the president insisting that it would be 'morally reprehensible for the United States to be even handed between democratic Israel and the terrorist infested Palestinian infrastructure' (Kaplan 2004: 29).

## A TYPOLOGY OF THE RIGHT WING: 'STYLES OF THOUGHT' ON THE RIGHT

Eatwell has developed a typology of right-wing perspectives as 'styles of thought,' classifying them as: (1) the reactionary right; (2) the moderate right; (3) the radical right; (4) the extreme right; and (5) the new right (1989: 63). The reactionary right emerged after the French Revolution. According to Eatwell, it was 'aristocratic, religious and authoritarian' (1989: 63). The view of those on the reactionary right was that 'man was complex and had great capacity for evil—a trait which was often given religious form in the doctrine of the fall and original sin' (1989: 64).

The 'moderate right' had its spokesperson in Edmund Burke who espoused the view of limited government. Eatwell summarised this perspective as follows, 'The moderate right rejected liberal philosophy in four main areas: liberalism's individualism; its universalism; its rationalism; and its contractual and utilitarian principles' (1989: 67).

The 'radical right' is much more modern. Eatwell indicates that it was a response to socialism as opposed to liberalism, and decidedly activist as opposed to passivist. In echoes of Horowitz's criticisms of academe:

> The radical right took up the idea of salvation through politics. The stress on activism meant that programmes were seen as relatively unimportant . . . The result was a tendency to dwell in a romantic, uncorrupted past . . . The present was seen as decadent; there was nothing to conserve . . . The left was strongly attacked for its rationalism, for its failure to see that a true community could not be founded on class politics preached by the extreme left. (Eatwell 1989: 69)

Eatwell does not believe that the radical right embraced mainstream anti-Semitism, but that there were linkages. The 'extreme right' is the camp to which Horowitz and others belong. This style of thought includes a critical view of the left and,

> Communism in particular is attacked . . . These arguments are usually presented in crude form; indeed, a defining characteristic of the extreme

right is the paucity of its intellectual tradition. The reactionary, moderate and radical rights have produced significant political theorists. The extreme right has tended more to produce propagandists, indeed telling people what to think rather than how to think, and lacking originality. The radical right was genuinely interested in how to achieve the good citizen; the extreme right has been more manipulative, paranoid. (1989: 71)

A telling point in identifying extreme right arguments is the presence of conspiracy theory, that is, there are hidden groups plotting to undermine what the extreme right supports. Interestingly, various groups can be substituted for those who are the conspirators. Historically, the Jews have been positioned as conspirators. For the extreme right in America it has been the Communists. This was a key element in Joseph McCarthy's attacks on academics and government employees (Eatwell 1989: 1). Eatwell indicates that conspiracy theory is a manifestation of political myth: 'Mythology in its extreme right-wing form involves a particular set of views: these centre mainly around nationalism and racism, which can involve mobilizing, integrating and simplistic-explicatory myths' (1989: 72). Conspiracy theory invoked by the extreme right is used to explain the failure of the current political regime.

> Deep-laid plots offer a more congenial explanation for failure than the admission that the inherent intolerant and anti-democratic views of the extreme right are seen as illegitimate by most citizens. Conspiracy theory also helps provide a common sense of identity through the revelation of having seen the dark forces which run the world in their 'true light.' (Eatwell 1989: 72)

The 'new right' rejects Judaeo-Christian teaching and both left and right perspectives. Marxism is seen as a form of secular Christianity. Perhaps the best exemplar of 'new right' thinking is Thatcherism in Britain (O'Sullivan 1989: 183).

## HOROWITZ AS A 'STYLE OF THINKING' OF THE EXTREME RIGHT

Billig asserts that extreme-right perspectives are often fascist and distinguished by three criteria: they are nationalistic and racist, anti-Marxist and anticommunist, and antidemocratic (1989: 147). The fascist sees the nation and/or the race as the prime political unit. Horowitz's ultranationalism is a case in point. Professors who question American policy as he once did, or professors who criticise American actions and Republican Party dogma are seen as enemies. Extreme right perspectives reject the Marxist claim that classes are the basic unit of society, and the Marxist stress on equality is specifically rejected. Billig indicates that 'the ideology of the extreme right is avowedly elitist' (1989: 147). Horowitz's rejection of affirmative action, or the idea that African Americans as a class should be recognised as having been historically treated differently, attests to his elitist perspectives. Finally, according to Billig, 'The principles of elitism and nationalism will be formulated in such a way that democratic rights and liberties will be threatened' (1989: 147). Thus we have Horowitz's attack on those in the academy who contribute to the other side of the positions on issues he attacks. By characterising academics who represent the policies he opposes as 'dangerous' he is seeking to silence or ostracise them.

## HOROWITZ'S GAMBIT: ERASING THE NEED FOR ACADEMIC FREEDOM

In chess, a 'gambit' is a strategy in which one player loses a piece in order to gain a strategic advantage on the opponent later in the game. Horowitz's objective is to silence or eliminate from academia views he considers politically dangerous. To gain this advantage, Horowitz forfeits a large chunk of history in American higher education, by erasing it and substituting a new and mythical vantage point where professors in academia 'always' maintained a kind of strict neutrality about their politics. Thus, when he foments about the 'takeover' of universities by tenured radicals, Communists and other misfits and Mountebanks, the portrait that emerges is one in which the once 'pure' halls of academic thought are now awash in dreadful partisanship and political posturing which is antimainstream thought. In his words ' . . . the last few decades mark the first time in their history that America's institutions of higher learning have become a haven for extremists' (2006: xxxiii). By signalling that this change is 'the first time in history,' Horowitz does not have to deal with why the concept of academic freedom was put in place and what academic freedom really means. Academic freedom is the ability of professors to 'question and test received wisdom, and to put forward new ideas and controversial or unpopular opinions without placing themselves in jeopardy of losing their jobs or privileges they may have at their institution' (Russell 1993). By erasing the long history of controversy and contestation that has been the wellspring of academic work on American campuses, the need for academic freedom, that is, the right to speak out on unpopular ideas or causes is never raised.

Horowitz continually sketches out his mythical land of 'objective thought' when he criticises professor Melissa Gilbert of Temple University as one who specialises in 'feminist geography' and says, 'it is hard to imagine that her votes will encourage intellectual diversity or disinterested academic inquiry in her field' (2006: 193); or when he says of Todd Gitlin of Columbia that in his classes 'he immerses students in the obscurantist texts of leftist icons like Jürgen Habermas so that they can understand the oppressive nature of capitalist media' (2006: 194); or when he criticizes George Wolfe of Ball State and director of the Center for Peace and Conflict Studies because 'The center's website explains that "It is the mission of the Center for Peace and Conflict Studies to promote nonviolent alternatives to conflict resolution." This is a political vocation, not an academic pursuit' (2006: 21).

Even a cursory look at American higher education will reveal a very different picture than the ethereal intellectual nirvana that existed at some point in the past according to Horowitz. For example, Benjamin Rush (1745–1813), a physician, signer of the Declaration of Independence, and professor of chemistry at the College of Philadelphia, spoke out against slavery in the colonies and suffered from criticism and a loss of patients. For this reason he declined to publish his support for American independence and instead urged his friend Tom Paine to write it (Liell 2003: 55). Later, James Cannon, also affiliated with the College of Philadelphia, spoke out publicly against Paine's best seller *Common Sense,* which did urge American independence from Great Britain (Liell 2003: 91). Undoubtedly, Rush would be listed as one of Horowitz's 'dangerous professors' were he alive today and America still a part of the British Empire.

Still another example involves Harvey Cushing, America's pioneer in the medical practice of neurosurgery, who, when attending Yale University in the 1890s, confronted a notorious 'liberal' professor named William Graham Sumner (1840–1910). Sumner, an economist and sociologist, was an ardent champion of social Darwinism and free trade. Cushing's biographer, Michael Bliss, noted that, 'Cushing found himself indifferent to William Graham Sumner's lectures on political economy, which touched too often on free trade ideas to suit his Republican tastes' (2005: 46). Sumner was also an advocate of civil service reform and an opponent of regulation of business by the government and socialism (Merriam-Webster 1983: 961). It is clear that Sumner used his classroom to expound his views on the political issues of the day.

It would be nearly impossible, and certainly undesirable, to create a sterile environment in which the issues of the day were not part of classroom academic discourse. Fredrick Jackson Turner (1861–1932), considered the dean of generations of American academic historians, once wrote, ' beneath political issues, run the great ocean currents of economic and social life, shaping and reshaping political forms to the changes of this great sea, which changes continuously' (Billington 1973: 101).

But when professors do engage their students in the issues of the day they always run risks and these are not 'new' to academic life. For example, Richard Ely (1854–1943), an American economist who taught at Johns Hopkins and the University of Wisconsin, Madison, founded the Institute for Research in Land Economics and was a leader in the Progressive movement, stood accused in 1894 of 'favoring strikes, aiding strikers, and advocating 'utopian, impractical and pernicious doctrines' in his books and classroom' (Billington 1973: 147). Frederick Jackson Turner himself was denied a position at

Princeton University in 1896 because 'he was a dangerous religious radical—a Unitarian' (Billington 1973: 152). The president of Princeton, none other than Woodrow Wilson, wrote Turner, 'I am, probably at this writing the most chagrined fellow on the Continent' (Billington 1973: 152).

It was also Frederick Jackson Turner, an open advocate of Republican candidates for president (he voted for William McKinley in 1896 and 1900 and later Theodore Roosevelt), who said that all of the social sciences were part of a whole and used all of them in his teaching. Horowitz often rails against professors speaking out of their disciplines on the grounds that they are unprepared or unqualified to render opinions for which they were 'not trained.' For example, he says of Frederick Jameson, a long-time distinguished scholar of comparative literature at Duke University, 'In other words, a person with no formal training in history, under the smokescreen of a "literature" course, is teaching a primitive Marxist history of the western world' (2006: 231).

It was Frederick Jackson Turner who would have defended Jameson when he advocated that 'data drawn from studies of literature and art, politics, economics, sociology, psychology, biology and physiology, all must be used' [because]

> 'without the combined effort of allied sciences we shall reach no such results in the study of social development as have been achieved in the physical world by the attack on problems of natural science by the combined forces of physics, chemistry, and mathematics.' (Billington 1973: 495)

Ray Allen Billington, Turner's biographer, tells the story of a student who once left one of Turner's Harvard lectures saying aloud that while his class 'might be all right, . . . it wasn't history' (1973: 494). This transgression might certainly be registered on Horowitz's website, *RateMyProfessors. com*, today as another example of the 'liberal bias' rife within the academy. Turner would answer now as he did then: 'I don't particularly care what name I bear. I am one of those who believes in breaking fences, even at the risk of arrest for trespass, or disclosure of being an amateur, or something worse, breaking into the professional's game' (Billington 1973: 494).

And it ought to be pointed out that Horowitz feels free to attack many respected academic works on the grounds that they are not serious 'scholarly contributions.' This is a criticism he levels against Angela Davis, author of six books, some, such as her 1981 work *Women, Race, and Class,* widely used on college campuses. Such texts are merely political tracts penned by 'a political apparatchik through and through' (2006: 119).

Horowitz's real intention is to erase the idea that academic freedom is not necessary to protect professors who espouse views which at the moment appear absurd, outdated, obscure, or unpopular. Horowitz's judges are not on the bench, but in popular American mainstream thought, epitomised by George Bush's 'political base.' That core is religiously conservative, antigay, anti-Communist, anti–affirmative action, antifeminist, pro-Iraq war and anti-Muslim. Horowitz is attempting to politically assassinate professors who are critical of George Bush, the Republican Party, capitalism, racism, the Iraq and/or Vietnam wars, homophobia, the US policy towards Cuba, the US military and US militarism, US/Israeli relationships and/or Israeli militarism. His reasons for calling professors 'dangerous' have to be envisioned against a backdrop of how individuals whose views are not especially popular in academe have been attacked over a longer period by vested interests also represented in political power. Conrad Russell perhaps summed it up appropriately when he remarked, 'The silencing of an opponent sounds alarmingly like an admission that we cannot answer him' (1993: 44).

Horowitz's attacks on American higher education have resulted in calls for legislative censure of a wide range of academic traditions and the long-cherished concept of academic freedom. Like Joe McCarthy, Horowitz identifies 'names, documents, and statistics—in short, the *appearance* of research ... but his critics were right: he never uncovered a Communist' (Oshinsky 2005: 507). Similarly, Horowitz has never uncovered a political plot by liberal professors to bring politics into the classroom which discriminates 'against their conservative and Christian students' (Schrecker 2006: B20). In an apocryphal story a reporter once told about having lunch with Joe McCarthy he recalled, 'We pressed him about his information. I remember his words well. He said: "I've got a sockful of shit and I know how to use it." But he didn't give us a thing—not a damned thing' (Oshinsky 2005: 111).

## REFERENCES

A House Divided (1997) Transcript of Uncommon Knowledge. Online. Available HTTP: <http://www.hoover.org/publications/uk/342081.html> (accessed 24 September 2006).

Billig, M. (1989) 'The extreme right: continuities in anti-semitic conspiracy theory in post-war Europe,' in R. Eatwell and N. O'Sullivan (eds) *The Nature of the Right: American and European Politics and Political Thought Since 1789*, Boston: Twayne Publishers.

Billington, R. (1973) *Frederick Jackson Turner*, New York: Oxford University Press.

Bliss, M. (2005) *Harvey Cushing: A Life in Surgery*, Oxford: Oxford University.

Brock, D. (2004) *The Republican Noise Machine: Right-Wing Media and How It Corrupts Democracy*, New York: Three Rivers Press.

Cavanagh, S. (2006) 'Campaign targets perceived liberal bias in schools,' *Education Week*, 25: 5, 18.

Collier, P. and Horowitz, D. (1990) *Destructive Generation: Second Thoughts about the 60s*, New York: Summit Books.

Conason, J. (2003) *Big Lies*, New York: St. Martin's Griffin.

Davis, A. (1981) *Women, Race, and Class*, New York: Random House.

Dorrien, G. (1993) *The Neoconservative Mind: Politics, Culture, and the War of Ideology*, Philadelphia: Temple University Press.

Eatwell, R. (1989) 'The nature of the right, 2: the right as a variety of "styles of thought"', in R. Eatwell and N. O'Sullivan (eds) *The Nature of the Right: American and European Politics and Political Thought Since 1789*, Boston: Twayne Publishers.

Foucault, M. (1980) *Power/Knowledge*, New York: Pantheon Books.

Fukuyama, F. (2006) *America at the Crossroads: Democracy, Power, and the Neoconservative Legacy,* New Haven: Yale University Press.

Hedges, C. (2006) *American Fascists: The Christian Right and the War on America,* New York: The Free Press.

Heiden, K. (1944) *Der Fuehrer,* Boston: Houghton Mifflin Company.

Hernstein, R. and Murray, C. (1994) *The Bell Curve: Intelligence, and Class Structure in American Life,* New York: The Free Press.

Higgins, R. (2002) 'Breaking ranks: Glenn Loury's change of heart—and mind—the anatomy of racial inequality,' *Christian Century.* Online. Available HTTP: <http://,findarticles.com/p/articles/mi_m1058/is_26_119/ai?96195200> (accessed 25 September 2006).

Hoffer, E. (1951) *The True Believer: Thoughts on the Nature of Mass Movements,* New York: Harper & Row, Publishers.

Horowitz, D. (2001) 'I know a thing or two about college protests—and this time the students are dead wrong.' Online. Available HTTP: <http://www.jewishworldreview.com/cols/horowitz100101.asp> (accessed 12 September 2006).

——, (2002) 'The problem with america's colleges—and the solution.' Online. Available HTTP: <http://jewishworldreview.com.cols.horowitz090402.asp> (accessed 12 September 2006).

——, (2003) 'As a former "radical" I see the threat of militant Islam on American campuses.' Online. Available HTTP: <http://jewishworldreview.com/cols.horowitz040803.asp> (accessed 12 September 2006).

——, (2006) *The Professors: The 101 Most Dangerous Academics in America,* Washington DC: Regnery Publishing.

Jacobson, J. (2006a) 'Tilting at academe,' *The Chronicle of Higher Education,* 52, 29: A25–27.

——, (2006b) 'Dangerous minds: interview with Michael Berube,' *The Chronicle of Higher Education,* 52, 24: A6.

Kaplan, E. (2004) *With God on Their Side: How Christian Fundamentalists Tramped Science, Policy, and Democracy in George W. Bush's White House,* New York: The New Press.

Liell, S. (2003) *46 Pages: Thomas Paine, Common Sense, and the Turning Point of Independence,* Philadelphia: Running Press.

Loehr, D. (2005) *America, Fascism and God: Sermons from a Heretical Preacher,* White River Junction: Chelsea Green Publishing Company.

Mann, M. (2004) *Fascists,* Cambridge: Cambridge University Press.

Merriam-Webster (1983) *Webster's New Biographical Dictionary,* Springfield: Merriam-Webster.

Oshinsky, D. M. (2005) *A Conspiracy So Immense: The World of Joe McCarthy,* New York: Oxford University Press.

O'Sullivan, N. (1976) *Conservatism,* London: Dent.

Rauschning, H. (1940) *Hitler Speaks,* New York: G. P. Putnam's Sons.

Russell, C. (1993) *Academic Freedom,* London: Routledge.

Schrecker, E. (2006) 'Worse than McCarthy,' *The Chronicle of Higher Education,* 52, 23: B20.

Sherman, S. (2000) 'David Horowitz's long march,' *The Nation* as cited in Brock, D. (2004) *The Republican Noise Machine: Right-Wing Media and How it Corrupts Democracy,* New York: Three Rivers Press.

Sternhell, Z. (1986) *Neither Right Nor Left: Fascist Ideology in France,* Berkeley: University of California Press.

Thernstrom, A. (1997) *America in Black and White: One Nation, Indivisible,* New York: Simon and Schuster.

——, and Thernstrom, S. (2003) *No Excuses: Closing the Racial Gap in Learning,* New York: Simon and Schuster.

Wiener, J. (2005) 'What Jon Wiener says in his new book. historians in trouble: plagiarism, fraud, and politics in the ivory tower.' Online. Available HTTP: <http://64.233.161.104/search?q=cache:tcfgEWahyaUJ:hnn.us/articles/9216. html> (accessed 24 September, 2006).

*Wikipedia* (2006a) 'Glenn Loury.' Online. Available HTTP: <http://en.wikipedia. org/wiki/Glen_Loury> (accessed 25 September 2006).

——, (2006b) 'David Horowitz.' Online. Available HTTP: <http://en.wikipedia. org/wiki/David_Horowitz> (accessed 25 September 2006).

# 17 Supranational Organisations and their Impact upon Nation State Education

## The Case of the International Monetary Fund

*Michael Bottery*

Educational performance can be attributed to a variety of factors. The performance of members of particular social classes and cultures can be ascribed to qualities or deficiencies within the individuals or cultures concerned. Alternatively, it can be ascribed to the positions of particular groups within society as a whole, some in more advantageous positions, others in positions where inegalitarian and structurally unjust attitudes, behaviours and policies are imposed, normally by dominant societal groups. Performance can also be attributed to 'providers': criticism, for instance, has been directed at the teaching professions of many different countries (Levin 2001), leading to calls for a 'reprofessionalisation' of teaching forces, and consequently to greater control, surveillance, and direction of their work, and much greater specification and testing of pupils. Of course, such arguments can and have been turned round (e.g., Ball 1994; Bottery 2004): for if governments exhibit a 'discourse of derision,' with low trust in their work forces, this may lead to the lowering of esteem and morale within the profession, creating widespread disaffection, affecting performance in the classroom, exacerbated by boring curricula and stress-inducing government testing imposed on pupils. In this scenario, then, it is the low trust, high control attitudes of governments that generate the problems.

If these are individual, local and national levels at which causation for educational performances can be located, another, the global level, has increasingly been recognised. Writers like Apple (2000), Burbules and Torres (2000), and Olsen et al. (2004) argue that educational changes globally are moving increasingly towards a practical and ideological convergence, derived from 'travelling policies,' based upon neoliberal agendas of education for more economically competitive workforces and the greater privatisation of educational activity. Part of the evidence for such assertions, as Rizvi points out, must lie in describing 'the processes through which convergence is achieved,' and these processes should 'be viewed as the work of human actors and institutions, constituted by everyday practices' (2004: 26, 29). Part of such a convergence is achieved through the activities of organisations created by a complex of nation states, whose functions are intended to transcend that of any particular nation state. Some of these, like the UN, are predominantly political in nature; others, like the World Health Organisation, have more social concerns. Yet probably the greatest influence upon educational activity has been through the targeting by supranational organisations of the economic functioning of nation states. Since the 1940s, organisations like the World Trade Organisation (WTO), the World Bank, and the International Monetary Fund have had great influence upon nation states' economic functioning, and thereby education. This chapter, then, traces such effects by examining the activities of one particular supranational organisation, the International Monetary Fund (IMF). The IMF works beyond the control of any one particular nation state, yet is underpinned by economic and political ideologies that have particular effects upon nation state educational activity. Its current underpinning ideology is also shared by other supranational organisations, leading to a global power consensus favouring the developed world and disfavouring poorer countries, with particular impact upon the public provision of social goods, including that of education.

## DEFINING 'SUPRANATIONAL'

Before describing the origins and functions of the IMF, and its sister supranational economic organisations, it should be recognised that the term 'supranational' is not without dispute. Much of this is centred on the degree of independence, and ultimately power, of such bodies over nation states. Etzioni (2001) argues that central to the notion of supranational bodies is that government bodies are legally obligated to comply with their decisions; a defining characteristic of such organisations, then, is that nation states cede power to them, thus reducing their power to act independently. Such a definition may, however, be too restrictive for two reasons. First, there is very good evidence to suggest that organisations conforming to such a definition have not in fact managed to remain independent of the influence of rich and powerful nations. Secondly, even where nation states have supposedly entered into cooperative agreements over things like loans, there is good evidence that these are not necessarily freely entered into, either because of the parlous state of their economy, or because of the enormous political pressure being brought to bear. This chapter therefore argues that supranational organisations should be defined as those working at the international level, not owned by any one nation, but which through legislation, contractual agreements, or through political influence, are able to have an impact upon nation state policies. Because the IMF imposes conditions upon nations after they have entered into loan agreements with it, and because these loan conditions have substantive impact upon national education activities, the IMF is therefore a very appropriate choice for this chapter.

## ORIGIN AND FUNCTIONS

The origin of the IMF is part of the story of the rebuilding of the industrialised countries at the end of World War II, and of attempts at preventing the reoccurrence of the global economic instabilities of the 1930s. The IMF, then, along with the World Bank and the World Trade Organisation, had their origins on July 22, 1944, in New Hampshire in the US, when forty-four countries signed the 'Bretton Woods Agreements,' establishing the International Monetary Fund and the International Bank for Reconstruction and Development (now known as the World Bank). The original function of the IMF was some considerable distance from its present high profile activity of involvement, through financial loans, in the economic programmes of developing countries. Instead, its original role was to maintain pegged but adjustable exchange rates, largely with respect to the industrialised countries of Western Europe and the US. Paradoxically, given its current market-driven ideology, the IMF was based on the belief that markets did not work well, and that some kind of collective global action was needed to remediate their irregularities. As Vreeland points out, 'the IMF is itself a non-market solution to a market failure' (2007: 114). The World Bank, meanwhile, was given the task of promoting economic development in war-torn Western Europe. At the same Bretton Woods meetings, a process was also begun that later developed into the General Agreement on Tariffs and Trade, later to become known as the World Trade Organisation, designed specifically to promote free trade among countries.

All three of these organisations, and many others working at the supranational level, have tended to be controlled, and some would argue run, in the interests of rich and powerful nations. The World Bank's president, for example, is nominated by the US president. The head of the IMF is invariably a Western European. The G8 is an invited group of the rich and powerful nations—and does not yet include in its ranks China and India. The secretary general of the UN may be selected from a developing country, but real power lies with the permanent members of the Security Council, who have the ability to veto any substantive resolution. The most explicit admission of such domination is probably seen in the description of the Organisation for Economic Cooperation and Development (OECD) of itself as 'a club of like-minded countries . . . It is rich, in that OECD countries produce two thirds of the world's goods and services . . . essentially membership is limited only by a country's commitment to a market economy and a pluralistic democracy' (OECD 1997).

Any examination of the composition of such bodies reveals that they are largely controlled by the developed nations of the US, Canada, and Western

Europe. As we shall see, they have not always responded well to the needs of those requiring the most assistance and development. Part of this neglect springs from a strong element of self-interest, seen in George Bush's response to the issue of greenhouse gases that 'we will not do anything that harms our economy, because first things first are the people who live in America' (in Singer 2004: 1). However, part is also due to an adherence to neoliberal beliefs of the 'Washington Consensus'—that fiscal austerity, privatisation, and market liberalisation are necessary remedies for the economic problems of the developing world. It is time to look in more detail at how the IMF, and its underpinning ideology, work in practice.

## THE INTERNATIONAL MONETARY FUND

As already mentioned, the IMF's original function was concerned with the maintenance of international exchange rates. However, with the abandonment of adjustable pegged exchange rates in the early 1970s, this function became irrelevant and the IMF developed its current role—that of an international credit union, whose purpose is to loan money to countries that are experiencing balance of payments problems. The IMF is supported by subscriptions from its members, who may draw on loans from it in times of economic difficulty. Of course, drawing on loans can lead to 'moral hazard'—being able to draw on such a loan may actually reduce a government's incentive to avoid such problems in the future, and thereby induce the continuation of practices that got it into trouble in the first place. This is the reason why the IMF imposes 'conditionalities': a series of actions and policies that governments are required to take if loans are to be renewed. Yet, whilst the existence of a global organisation with such functions may make good sense, there are a number of issues associated with the IMF that have provoked considerable criticism. These boil down to the following questions, which will be examined in turn:

(a) Who controls the IMF?
(b) What kinds of conditions are attached to loans?
(c) What is the track record of the IMF on major indicators of its success?

## Who controls the IMF?

The IMF exists through the subscriptions of its members, with the size of the subscriptions varying with countries' size of donations. Economically powerful countries, then, have considerably more than their weaker brethren who receive loans, the conditions imposed upon the loans, and judgements and actions made about compliance with loans. Currently, the countries with the largest quota of votes are the US at 17.4 per cent, Japan at 6.24 per cent, Germany at 6.09 per cent, and the UK and France at 5.03 per cent (Vreeland 2007). Each member country contributes to the IMF's Board of Governors, but as it meets only once a year, day-to-day operations are delegated to a small Executive Board—which perhaps unsurprisingly, is currently made up of the United States, Japan, Germany, France, and the UK. While the IMF normally functions by gaining consensus on an issue rather than by formal voting, either way facilitates outcomes that favour the most powerful, though how exactly decisions are reached has historically been extremely problematic, due to the IMF's renowned secrecy in decision-making. IMF accountability—or its absence—is a long standing issue.

The most powerful nation in the IMF is the US, and while it has less than 20 per cent of total votes, and the managing director is normally European, it does have the largest quota of votes by some distance. Moreover, it has always been a pivotal member of the Executive Board, having veto power over the managing director's appointment and reappointment. In addition, there is a strong literature (e.g., Thacker 1999; Dreher, Sturm and Vreeland 2006) describing how the US has used the IMF for strategic political purposes over the years. It has, for instance, granted larger loans, with more lenient conditions, and pressured for less stringent judgements when compliance with conditionality is assessed, to those nations which support it on key votes in the UN.

Influence within the IMF does not rest just with powerful nation states, however. Private international financial institutions have a vested interest in supporting IMF lending in countries where they have strong financial involvement, as the IMF's ability to bail out such countries provides these banks with reassurance on the safety of their investments. Gould (2003) has found a close correlation between banks' investments in countries and IMF involvement. Moreover, in addition to loaning money, the IMF negotiates with such banks to provide supplemental loans; and these banks are encouraged to do so because of the conditionalities imposed by the IMF, as well as the likelihood of further IMF financial assistance if a country's economic situation deteriorates. Such private financial institutions, then, both through formal agreements and through the intimate contacts which exist between them and the IMF, are able to put pressure on the IMF not only in terms of granting loans to countries in which they wish to invest, but also in terms of the loan conditions imposed. It is clear, then, that a combination of economic and political power, private institutional interest, and secrecy have led to accusations of the IMF's partiality in a variety of quarters. Such criticism is not helped by the conditionality of IMF loans over the years. It is to this issue that we now turn.

## What kinds of conditions are attached to loans?

The purpose of IMF loans is to help countries experiencing balance of payments problems, and by attaching policy conditions to a loan, the IMF specifies what kinds of practices it feels need to be changed for the problems to be eliminated. The IMF assumes that basic problems stem from too great a consumption of imported goods, viewed by the IMF as stemming from a country importing more goods than it is exporting. The purpose of the loan is then to allow the country to service foreign loans, while at the same time engaging in reforms that will ensure that demand for imports and foreign financing is reduced. Such demand reduction can be achieved in a number of ways—by devaluing the currency, by raising interest rates, limiting credit, or by raising taxes, or cutting public spending. The elimination of 'excess' consumption has therefore been a primary objective, and in so doing, the IMF has become involved in the domestic policies of nations requiring loans, though the degree and nature of that involvement has varied over time. Thus, in its early years, the IMF practiced what has been called 'macroconditionality,' which normally involved three specific policies: reducing government deficit budgets by raising taxes and cutting spending; reducing the money supply by raising central bank interest rates; and, occasionally, devaluing national currencies. At this level of conditionality, considerable room is left for national politicians to choose specific policies to achieve these objectives. Yet, when most South American countries in the 1980s lurched further into economic problems, even though all of them had received IMF loans previously, the IMF did not conclude that the wrong conditionalities had been imposed: it argued instead that these policies had not gone far enough, and that what was needed was the specification of deeper and more intrusive policies, beginning a period of *microconditionality.*

It was also at this stage that neoliberal ideology really took hold, and by moving from macro- to microconditionality, the IMF could now call specifically for neoliberal policies of privatisation and deregulation, in the belief that markets of their very nature produced greater efficiencies. Microconditionality came under strong attack, however, particularly after the East Asian financial crisis of the late 1990s, and the subsequent collapse of the Argentine economy in 2001. A common criticism was that such microconditionality allowed little contextualisation by governments. Even subsequent responses by the IMF to involve countries more in the ownership of such policy programs have still not changed its view that the fundamental problem is one of excessive government spending, and/or the failure of such governments to properly implement its stipulated measures. Nothing within the IMF mindset currently suggests that the problem may lie with the policies themselves. This, however, leads to the third question.

### What is the track record of the IMF on major indicators of its success?

In a detailed examination of the literature on the successes and failures of the IMF, Vreeland (2007), while acknowledging the problems in measuring such complex phenomena, comes to fairly negative conclusions on its performance over the years. These findings can be divided into five areas: balance of payment issues; inflation; economic growth; social spending; and finally, income distribution. The IMF's primary role has been ameliorating the first of these, balance of payments, and here the evidence suggests that IMF loans have generally had a beneficial effect. In terms of controlling inflation, however, the evidence is mixed, with Vreeland (2007) concluding that existing studies suggest at best a neutral effect. The evidence on economic growth is more critical, for while the IMF acknowledges this as a primary objective, since growth would help reduce balance of payments problems by raising the quantity of exports to offset problems with imports, the evidence suggests that IMF programmes have a largely negative effect. Indeed, Hutchinson and Noy (2003) argue that the worst economic growth is associated with precisely those countries 'successfully' completing IMF programmes. Finally, if there is some variation in results of the above indices, those on social spending and income distribution are unequivocally negative: IMF programmes reduce social spending and exacerbate income inequality. Under IMF programmes, then, public expenditure on health and education tend to be cut as part of a strategy for reducing balance of payments problems, widening the gap between rich and poor. The implications for public sector education are clear—IMF policies in developing countries damage its development.

Overall, then, while there is evidence that balance of payments problems are ameliorated, with mixed results on inflation, there is strong evidence that IMF policies have negative effects on economic growth, public services and on the incomes of the poor. This is a worrying record, given the time, opportunity, and money that the IMF has had to address these issues. One clearly needs to ask why there are such negative results. This chapter suggests that the reasons are those shared with other supranational organisations involved in global economic activity at the present time, and have much to do with their underpinning ideologies.

## HOW ARE THESE NEGATIVE RESULTS TO BE EXPLAINED?

Imre Lakatos (1970), in his study of the development of scientific theories, described how proponents of paradigms do not normally surrender them when contradictory evidence is produced. They are more likely to suggest that there are problems with the generation of negative instances, or that there are other ways of interpreting the findings, or that negative instances don't affect the inner core of the paradigm, and they therefore generate new paradigm layers to explain negative instances. The result, suggests Lakatos, is that paradigms are never proved or disproved in some ultimate sense— they become either more 'progressive' or more 'degenerative' in terms of the perception of their 'truth' or importance, until in cases of multiple negative instances, they will be supported by only a hard core of believers, while the rest of the scientific community, and the public at large, embrace other paradigms with fewer problems.

Such 'ideological' commitment to particular positions is perhaps even more evident with economic theories, as they support not just particular academic positions, but can entail huge financial gains for those who espouse and implement policies based upon them. This certainly applies to many who have supported the theoretical underpinnings of the IMF. These are examined shortly, but we begin by looking at less critical explanations for these deficiencies.

The explanation normally offered by less radical critics is that the fault lies not with the policies themselves, but must be jointly shared between the recipient countries, who fail to fully comply with loan conditions, and by the IMF itself for failing to make them comply (e.g., Meltzer 2000). In a situation where the government of a country fails to fully implement the 'medicine' prescribed by the IMF, the loan has the opposite effect of its original intention: it subsidises the policies that led the government to ask for a loan in the first place, and so actually exacerbates the situation. Negative performances, according to this explanation, are to be found in the behaviour of the recipient country and compliance failures by the IMF.

There is a certain plausibility to this argument, in that not all governments seek IMF loans simply to address economic issues. They could, for instance, be managing their economy badly and seek a loan in order to blame the IMF for their own poor economic performance. Lack of compliance, if hidden sufficiently from the citizens of a country, may actually help in pinning the blame for poor performance on IMF policies. Even when committed to such policies, governments may also use the IMF as a means of pushing through electorally unpopular measures: IMF policies might benefit them and their supporters, at the expense of others within the community. These different sets of circumstances suggest that it would be simplistic to assume that all governments willingly sign up to IMF policies, and that they always attempt to implement them fully. There may be many different reasons for loan applications and similarly diverse reasons for degrees of implementation.

## THE IMF AS THE PROBLEM RATHER THAN THE SOLUTION

However, even if it is too simplistic to blame everything on the IMF, it is also too simplistic to blame government deficiencies for the economic woes of a country. Developing countries blame the IMF, along with sister organisations like the WTO and the World Bank, for putting immense pressure on them to eliminate trade barriers, while doing little about the developed world keeping their own barriers raised. In so doing, infant industries in the developing world are exposed to full-blown competition from the developed world before they are robust enough to survive. Moreover, they point out that many rich countries resist importing their agricultural exports, thereby depriving them of much needed export income, and exacerbating balance of payments problems.

There could be a number of explanations for such IMF behaviour. One explanation is that it is so controlled by countries in the developed world, that instead of acting like a true supranational organisation, it is more their political puppet. The way it is constituted, and the way decisions are made, lend credence to such an hypothesis. A second explanation is that, while essentially of good intentions, the IMF has utilised economic policies that have unwittingly had the opposite effects to those intended—the danger of ideological fundamentalism. A third and darker explanation is that the IMF, under the direction of developed countries, has selected and employed economic theories that maintain their own economic and political dominance. It is therefore necessary to examine these underpinning economic assumptions, and particularly the dominant role that markets play in the IMF's prescriptions to nation states.

As noted earlier, this central role for market solutions was not an original intention when the IMF was first set up, for the IMF was originally founded largely because of market failures in the 1930s. Yet there has been an almost religious conviction in the IMF, the World Bank and the World Trade Organisation, as well as the OECD (see Singer 2004; Rizvi and Lingard 2006; and Robertson, Bonal and Dale 2006) over the last two decades that markets, left to themselves, will solve the economic problems of countries.

How does such belief manifest itself? As mentioned above, the Washington Consensus—accepted by virtually all supranational economic organisations since the early 1980s—assumes that fiscal austerity, the privatisation of national assets, and the liberalisation of markets will resolve a country's problems, as it is believed that markets will eliminate the inefficiencies governments have created. Such assumptions were implemented in the first instance in response to the fiscal policies of many South American governments in the 1980s, which had managed to combine very large deficits with inefficient public institutions, and maintained private firms insulated against international competition. One of the aims of the Washington Consensus, then, was to bring a measure of fiscal discipline to such countries, resulting in: the reduction of government deficits by raising taxes and cutting spending; the reduction of the money supply and the raising of central bank interest rates; and, in some cases, the devaluation of national currencies. Yet, despite the belief that markets would 'naturally' replace jobs lost in the public sector because of reduced government financing, this did not happen, as high interest rates depressed the replacement of such jobs. The consequent high unemployment rates are particularly problematic for the poor of developing countries where there is little or no unemployment insurance and little health and education public funding. This, then, exacerbated a situation where governments were already told to cut public spending. Given such a set of IMF-driven circumstances, it is hardly surprising that the result was widespread violence and rioting. Yet the IMF, focussing purely on the economic situation, failed to take into account the social consequences of its policies, or, if it was aware of these, chose to ignore them. Indeed, the third—and darker—explanation of IMF policies might well be invoked here, particularly as the developed world does not normally follow IMF prescriptions in the same situations, but instead embarks upon expansionary rather than contractionary policies. When the US, for instance, faced a recession in 2001, it didn't take the medicine it prescribed for developing countries, but instead initiated a number of expansionary policies that have subsequently led to massive public and private debt (see Phillips 2007). Little wonder, then, that IMF policies of austerity are viewed by some critics not as simply misguided, but as deliberately pernicious.

If those instituting policies of fiscal austerity need to appreciate the consequences for those least able to fend off their negative effects, the application of privatisation similarly needs to be nuanced by an appreciation of the problems of unfettered markets. Even if it is agreed that some activities are better run by the private than the public sector, there is no hard and fast rule here. Circumstances may make government involvement absolutely essential if an activity is to survive, simply because it is not true that markets will 'naturally' spring up when governments withdraw. Moreover, there is a literature (e.g., Grace 1989; Bottery 2000) that strongly argues that some goods—because they are 'public goods' essential to citizenship development—need to be supplied by the public rather the private sector. Yet over the last two decades the IMF has adopted the simplistic perception that government involvement in economic activity is bad, and market activity is good—the true sign of what George Soros (1998) calls 'market fundamentalism.' A more realistic position is that both government and markets have their roles to play in the economic management of a country. It seems clear that *if* privatization is regarded as the best option, then, as Stiglitz argues, it 'needs to be part of a more comprehensive program, which entails creating jobs *in tandem with* the inevitable job destruction that privatization entails' (2002: 57). If it is not, large-scale unemployment and violence consequent upon such policies may be seen time and time again.

Finally, belief in trade liberalisation—the mantra not only of the IMF, but the World Bank and the WTO—that exposure to the efficiencies of global competition will benefit developing countries in the long run has been the standard reason why these organisations have pressured developing countries into eliminating trade barriers. Yet, as with so many principles, these need to be nuanced in practice. If fledgling industries are exposed to global competition before they are robust enough to survive, little good is done. Indeed, it has been argued (Chang 2007) that the economic success of the developed world is explained historically by the gradual rather than instant exposure to global markets encouraged by the IMF—and which led to such catastrophic results in Russia in the 1990s. Moreover, and as noted above, many richer countries still erect trade barriers, impeding the import of agricultural products from developing nations. It is then easy to see why darker explanations for such practices are invoked.

## THE IMPACT OF THE IMF ON EDUCATION

The IMF *does* affect education, yet it is more indirect than direct. It is sometimes easier to trace the effects on education of other economic supranational organisations like the World Bank, with its loans specifically for education, or the OECD, with its gathering and distribution of comparative information on educational performance. Yet this section argues that such indirect effects can be just as far reaching as those that are more explicit and obvious. It will also suggest that these effects are very different between developed and developing countries.

The effects on developed countries may at first glance appear to be slight, in part because most do not need to draw on IMF loans. They are therefore not subject to its conditionalities: demands for reduced public spending, higher tax rates, and reduced spending and borrowing. Indeed, to the extent that they largely control and direct the policies of the IMF, it might be said that they have more impact on the IMF than it does on them. This, however, would be too simplistic. While the IMF may not have direct impact, it is one of a set of supranational organisations advocating the implementation of neoliberal policies globally. Of course, nation states do not react to such advocacy in a monolithic manner, for they contain within them different strands of political thought about educational provision. While neoliberal approaches to educational provision have dominated the English-speaking world for the last two decades, they are not held by all within any one country, and it remains a minority view in most continental European countries. There is, then, a body of criticism arguing that neoliberal policies are detrimental, not only to developing countries but to developed countries as well. Barber, for instance, argues that privatisation reduces education in damaging ways, particularly by suggesting that education is little more than a consumer good, restricting recipients of education to only speaking 'the elementary rhetoric of "me",' preventing them from becoming the citizens who 'invent the common language of "we"' (1996: 243). Grace makes a similar point when he argues that education needs to be seen as a public rather than a private good 'because it seeks to develop in all citizens a moral sense, a sense of social and fraternal responsibility for others, and a disposition to act in a rational and cooperative manner' (1989: 214).

Privatisation and close links to business and economic theory lead to the danger that education becomes little more than their handmaiden. In so doing, it deprives those receiving an education from a wider view not only of the possibilities of education, but of their own existence. Moreover, by tying education so closely to national economic imperatives, the individual is prevented from developing an awareness of education as a good in itself, or a critical social instrument highlighting societal and global inequities, thus playing a crucial part in their remediation. Education becomes narrowly functionalist, acting as a conservative brake on change rather than an emancipatory potential to change societies for the better.

These kinds of criticisms apply to neoliberal policies in both developed and developing countries. While the IMF may have its most direct impact in developing countries because it embraces the same ideology as other supranationals, its influence on developed countries should not be discounted. Nevertheless, its effect is most pronounced within developing countries, as it is these which normally require its loans and need to embrace its neoliberal conditionalities.

Such conditionalities, as we have seen, have emphasised the privatisation of educational services, the imposition of higher interest rates for borrowing, as well as a general reduction in public spending. The effects have not only resulted in spending reductions on public services, on education in particular, especially in African and South American countries, but have also led in many cases to increased unemployment of both public and private sector workers, as such reductions have cut the number of jobs available. As documented by Vreeland (2007), they have also had the less intended effects of poor economic growth and heightened income inequalities. Of course, the degree to which such supranational policies have influenced particular nation states has depended upon a number of factors, particularly the degree to which countries have embraced and implemented conditionalities within a thorough-going neoliberal perspective, as well as the degree of microconditionality imposed by the IMF. So any impact needs to be nuanced by such considerations. Nevertheless, for populations on the receiving end of such general conditionalities, reduced public sector spending has generated predictable educational trends: less spending on public schooling, larger class sizes, less investment in equipment, and lower wages or greater unemployment for the teaching profession. Moreover, due to increased unemployment and greater social inequality, another predictable trend is more social problems in the homes of pupils. These may be termed indirect effects, but they are substantial, nevertheless, and need to be included in any overall assessment.


## DISCUSSION AND CONCLUSIONS

The IMF is a supranational institution whose policies are normally imposed at a distance through government economic policies as part of loan conditionalities. It is these conditions which then affect education, however, they may be too distant for their impact to be fully appreciated by the average citizen or educator. Even in the case where the IMF has demanded 'cost recovery' programmes for elementary education (Stiglitz 2002)—basically entailing parents paying for their children—the origins of such demands may not always be obvious. This paper, therefore, traces the economic assumptions, the functioning, the control and the conditions imposed by the IMF, and its track record, before looking at educational impacts, because any judgements made about the IMF's effects upon education need to be underpinned by a clear understanding of these other issues. Now that these have been uncovered, it seems that a number of conclusions can be reached.

First, the IMF is an example of a supranational institution guided by an economic fundamentalism that has benefited neither the developed nor the developing world. Economic fundamentalism of any kind ignores context, as it refuses to believe that there are instances which demand its modification; its beliefs then ride rough-shod over singularities, and in so doing, invariably damage that which they aim to improve. The evidence suggests that the IMF has been guilty of this in its devotion to the effectiveness of fiscal austerity, to the merits of privatisation, and to trade liberalisation, for fiscal austerity, if blindly applied, can damage the provision of public education; privatisation, if not performed gradually, can fail to heal the damage caused by reduced public provision. It can, moreover, pervert the 'public good' function of education, and so damage its ultimate purposes (see Bottery 2004). Finally, trade liberalisation, if performed too quickly, or not engaged in fully by all parties, can damage developing countries' economies. The result is that for two decades the IMF has worked with a fundamentalism which has done more harm than good to educational provision in developing countries.

Second, while the evidence for the IMF's performance in developing countries is not a cause for celebration, it would still be too easy to blame its policies for all educational problems faced by many developing countries. This paper began by suggesting that educational performance can be attributed to factors at a number of different levels, and that in each instance it is a combination of factors that produces particular results. The innate abilities of cohorts of children, as well as their health and education, the quality of the professionals, the equipment and infrastructure, the personalities of those involved, the nature of national policies as well as the effects of supranational organisational policies, all have a part to play. While the IMF seems to have contributed to as many problems as it has solved, many other contextual factors may be involved—one therefore needs to investigate all of these, and where problematic, address each of them rather than simply blame one.

Third, and most disturbingly, there is evidence to suggest that the IMF, far from being the even-handed transnational institution one might hope for, may instead be an example of Western global political and economic supremacy since WWII. The influence of the developed world generally, the evidence of favouritism of those countries supporting the US, and the covert nature of its decision-making all tend to support this version of events. If economic and political power in this century shifts towards Asia, it will be interesting to see how the balance of power within such an organisation develops. Certainly, it seems likely that if the power of the West declines, so will the influence of the neoliberal model of economic functioning. The recognition of a country's social context will also likely be enhanced, as will the role of government in economic management. To the extent that these are recognised, and neoliberal models de-emphasised, the outlook for governmental spending on education may improve.

Nevertheless, while such factors may be greatly emphasised, there must be debate over whether the IMF should become a more open and equitable global institution, or whether its influence should simply be shared out among a new group at the top table. If it is merely the latter, then one can expect no more than a different set of favouritisms and inequalities globally. If, however, the IMF is to become more equitable, then there need to be reforms at two levels. At the organisational level, there needs to be greater functional transparency, as currently it is not clear how decisions are made or on what basis. More debate is also required about its rules of governance, as there remains considerable distance between the functioning of its Executive Board, its accountability to its Board of Governors, and, ultimately, to the nations which finance it. At the functional level, serious attention needs to be paid to the issue of conditionality—not only in terms of the conditions themselves and the details of their specification, but also the length of such conditions and measurement of how accurately they have been met. So far, the IMF has not responded to calls for refocusing and reform with much enthusiasm.

One final optimistic thought may be allowed here. We live in an age when issues of global warming have begun to make even the most reluctant realise that this is a problem requiring genuine cooperation by rich and poor countries alike. If this is to happen, it is just possible that transnational organisations like the IMF might be recast in a more cooperative mould, rather than, as seems currently, an institution run by the few largely in their own interests. Global problems require global responses: the current partiality of the IMF is probably more of a hindrance than a help at the present time.

## REFERENCES

Apple, M. (2000) 'Between neoliberalism and neoconservatism: education and conservatism in a global age,' in N. Burbules and C. Torres (eds) *Globalization and Education: Critical Perspectives*, London: Routledge.

Ball, S. (1994) *Education Reform: A Critical and Post-Structuralist Approach*, Buckingham: Open University Press.

Barber, B. (1996) *Jihad vs. McWorld*, New York: Ballantine Books.

Bottery, M. (2000) *Education, Policy and Ethics*, London: Continuum.

——, (2004) *The Challenges of Educational Leadership*, London: Paul Chapman.

Burbules N. and Torres C. (2000) *Globalization and Education: Critical Perspectives*, London: Routledge.

Chang, H.-J. (2007) 'Protecting the global poor,' *Prospect*, 136: 26–40.

Dreher, A., Sturm, J. and Vreeland, J. (2006) 'Does membership on the UN Security Council influence IMF decisions? evidence from the panel data,'

CESifo Working Paper Series No. 1808. Online. Available HTTP: <http://papers.ssrn.com/sol3/papers.cfm?abstract_id=938371> (accessed 6 August 2007).

Etzioni, A. (2001) *Political Unification Revisited: On Building Supranational Communities*, Lanham: Lexington Books.

Gould, E. (2003) 'Money talks: supplementary financiers and international monetary fund conditionality,' *International Organization,* 57, 3: 551–86.

Grace, G. (1989) 'Education: commodity or public good?' *British Journal of Educational* Studies, 37, 3: 207–21.

Hutchinson, M. and Noy, I. (2003) 'Macroeconomic effects of IMF-sponsored programs in Latin America,' *Journal of International Money and Finance,* 22, 7: 91–114.

Lakatos, I. (1970) 'Falsification and the methodology of scientific research programmes,' in I. Lakatos and A. Musgrave (eds) *Criticism and the Growth of Knowledge,* Cambridge: Cambridge University Press.

Levin, B. (2001) *Reforming Education,* London: RoutledgeFalmer.

Meltzer, A. (2000) 'Report of the International Financial Institution Advisory Commission to the US Congress (The Meltzer Commission).' Online. Available HTTP: <http://www.house.gov/jec/imf/meltzer.pdf> (accessed 6 August 2007).

OECD (1997) *Education at a Glance: OECD Indicators,* Paris: OECD.

Olsen, M., Codd, J. and O'Neil, A. (2004) *Education Policy: Globalization, Citizenship and Democracy,* London: Sage.

Phillips, K. (2007) *American Theocracy,* New York: Penguin.

Rizvi, F. (2004) 'Theorizing the convergence of educational restructuring,' in S. Lindblad and T. Popkewitz (eds) *Educational Restructuring: International Perspectives on Traveling Policies,* Connecticut: Information Age Publishing.

———, and Lingard, R. (2006) 'Globalization and the changing nature of the OECD's educational work,' in H. Lauder, P. Brown, J. Dillabough and A. H. Halsey (eds) *Education, Globalization and Social Change,* Oxford: Oxford University Press.

Robertson, S., Bonal, X. and Dale, R. (2006) 'GATS and the education service industry: the politics of scale and global reterritorialization,' in H. Lauder, P. Brown, J. Dillabough and A. H. Halsey (eds) *Education, Globalization and Social Change,* Oxford: Oxford University Press.

Singer, P. (2004) *One World: The Ethics of Globalization,* New Haven: Yale University Press.

Soros, G. (1998) *The Crisis of Global Capitalism,* Boston: Little, Brown.

Stiglitz, J. (2002) *Globalization and its Discontents,* London: Penguin.

Thacker, S. (1999) 'The high politics of IMF lending,' *World Politics,* 52, 1: 38–75.

Vreeland, J. (2007) *The International Monetary Fund,* London: Routledge.

Williamson, J. (2000) 'What should the World Bank think about the Washington Consensus?' *The World Bank Research Observer,* 15, 2: 251–64.

# Contributors

**Lawrence Angus** is Professor of Education and Head of the School of Education at the University of Ballarat in Australia. He has a strong record of using ethnographic research to pursue questions about the embeddedness of social and cultural norms and equity relations in institutional structures, social attitudes, and conventional practices. The common thread is a focus on issues of equity and disadvantage within social contexts, the nature of community, and the nature of participation, identity, and change. He emphasises the interactive processes by which institutional and community norms are constructed, contested and transformed. Recent publications include 'Educational Leadership and the Imperative of Including Student Voices, Student Interests, and Students' Lives in the Mainstream' (*International Journal of Leadership in Education* 2006), 'Globalisation and the Reshaping of Teacher Professional Culture: Do We Train Competent Technicians or Informed Players in the Policy Process?' (in T. Townsend and R. Bates (eds) *Handbook of Teacher Education: Globalization, Standards and Professionalism in Times of Change,* Springer 2006), 'Transcending Educational Inequalities across Multiple Divides: Schools and Communities Building Equitable and Literate Futures' (*Learning Communities: International Journal of Learning in Social Contexts* 2006), 'New Methodologies and the Politics of Research: Re-visiting the Lessons of Critical Ethnography' (in G. Walford and G. Troman (eds) *New Debates and Developments in Ethnographic Methodology* 2005), and 'Globalization and Educational Change: Bringing about the Reshaping and Re-norming of Practice' (*Journal of Education Policy* 2005).

**Richard Bates** is Professor of Social and Administrative Studies in the Faculty of Education, Deakin University, Australia. His international reputation rests primarily on his contributions to the debate over the New Sociology of Education, on his work in developing an alternative 'cultural' tradition in Educational Administration and on his contributions to Teacher Education. He has published some seventy papers and books as well as being on the editorial boards of numerous journals. Some of his recent publications are: 'Public Education, Social Justice and Teacher Education'

(*Asia-Pacific Journal of Teacher Education* 2006), *Handbook of Teacher Education* (with Tony Townsend, Springer 2006), *Aesthetic Dimensions of Educational Administration and Leadership* (with E. A. Samier (eds), Routledge 2006), 'Educational Administration and Social Justice' (*Education, Citizenship and Social Justice* 2006), 'Culture and Leadership in Educational Administration' (*Journal of Educational Administration and History* 2006), 'An Anarchy of Cultures' (*Asia-Pacific Journal of Teacher Education* 2005), 'On the Future of Teacher Education' (*Journal of Education for Teaching* 2005), 'Can We Live Together: Towards a Global Curriculum' (*Arts and Humanities in Higher Education* 2005), *The Bird that Sets Itself on Fire: Thom Greenfield and the Renewal of Educational Administration* (Althouse Press 2003), and 'Morals and Markets: Adam Smith's Moral Philosophy as a Foundation for Administrative Ethics' ( in E. A. Samier (ed.) *Ethical Foundations for Educational Administration,* Routledge 2003). He is past president of the Australian Association for Educational Research, the Australian Council of Deans of Education and the Australian Teacher Education Association, and is a Fellow of the Australian Council for Educational Leaders and the Australian College of Educators.

**Michael Bottery** is currently Professor of Education and Director of Research degrees in the Institute of Education at Hull University, having formerly been Head of the Centre for Educational Studies at the same university. He has at one time or another been Visiting Lecturer at the University of Saskatchewan, Noted Scholar at the University of British Columbia, and Invited Professor at the University of Seattle Pacific. Currently he is Advisory Professor the Hong Kong Institute of Education, 2006–2009, having formerly been Visiting Scholar at the Institute. He was been Chair of the UK Standing Conference for Research into Education, Leadership and Management for 2004–2006. He has published six single-authored, and one jointly authored book, as well as numerous journal articles. His latest book, *The Challenges of Educational Leadership* (Paul Chapman 2004), argued that the global context of educational leadership leads to both a greater control and fragmentation of the work of educational professionals, and poses particular issues for them in terms of meaning, identity, and trust. His current research is an empirical examination of the impact of such global changes upon the day-to-day work of head teachers in England and Hong Kong.

**Read M. Diket** is Professor of Art and Education and Director of the Center for Creative Scholars at William Carey University in Mississippi. Her research interests include cognitive functioning, gifted education, semiotics, and the relationship of art to teaching and leadership practice. In 2006, she was named Distinguished Fellow by the National Art Education Association. She was 2003 Barkan awardee for manuscript of the year in art education and in the same year was named National Higher Education Educator of the Year by the National Art Education Association. She provided leadership and vision to the Department of Education–funded secondary analysis of the 1997 NAEP data for the visual arts. She recently served as the Southeastern Regional Higher Education Director for the National Art Education Association and as President of the Brain, Neurosciences, and Education Special Interest Group of the American Education Research Association. She is a charter member of the International Mind, Brain, and Education Society (IMBES). Dr. Diket worked on the joint National Association of Gifted Children and Council of Exceptional Children preparation of NCATE initial and advanced standards for teacher preparation programs in gifted education. She is author of 'Creating Artful Leadership' (with S. Klein, *International Journal of Leadership in Education* 1999) and was an editor and author of an international book, *Trends in Art Education from Diverse Cultures* (with Kauppenin National Art Education Association 1995). In 2006, Dr. Diket served on the advisory board of the Lauren Rogers Museum in Mississippi. She was named as a trustee of the Eastman Memorial Foundation in 2007.

**Fenwick W. English** is the R. Wendell Eaves Distinguished Professor of Educational Leadership at the University of North Carolina at Chapel Hill. Formerly he served as a program coordinator, Department Chair, Dean, and Vice-chancellor of Academic Affairs, the latter two positions in the Purdue University system. As a K–12 practitioner, he has been a superintendent of schools in New York, an assistant superintendent of schools in Florida, and a middle school principal in California. He also had a stint as an associate executive director of AASA and served as principal (partner) in Peat, Marwick, Main & Co. (now KPMG Peat Marwick), where he was national practice director for elementary and secondary education, North America. Dr. English has written over twenty books and one hundred journal articles. He recently served as editor of the SAGE *Handbook of Educational Leadership* (2005) and the SAGE General Editor of the *Encyclopedia of Educational Leadership and Administration* (2006), and is author of *The Postmodern Challenge to the Theory and Practice of Educational Administration* (C. C. Thomas 2003), a collection of papers given at Division A of AERA and UCEA over a decade. He is currently serving a second term as a member of the UCEA Executive Committee and is President of that organisation.

**Charles J. Fazzaro** is a member of the Division of Education Leadership and Policy Studies at the University of Missouri-St. Louis. His specialty is education policy, law, and Critical Enquiry, a project of research that uses post-structural and postmodern frameworks to examine the effects of education policies and practices in furthering democratic ideals. Recent publications include: 'Freedom of Speech, American Public Education, and Standardized Tests: A Critical Enquiry' (*Journal of Thought* 2006), 'Evil, Modern Thought, and Schooling Practices: Susan Neiman and Michel Foucault' (*The Journal of Philosophy & History of Education* 2005), and 'Schools for Democracy: Lyotard, Dissensus, and Education Policy' (*International Journal of Leadership in Education: Theory & Practice* 2002).

**Peter Gronn** is Chair in Public Service, Educational Leadership and Management of the University of Glasgow. Previously, he was Professor of Education in the Faculty of Education, Monash University, where he held a personal chair appointment. His research interests cover all aspects of leadership, including distributed leadership, leadership formation and the development of leaders, leadership models and types, and the connection between organisational culture, and leadership and organisational learning. The major focus of his most recent research has been leadership succession and principal recruitment, for which he received Australian Research Council (ARC) Discovery Project funding during 2004–2005. Peter is a member of a number of leading journal editorial boards, and has published a number of articles on recent developments in leadership in the *Leadership Quarterly, Educational Management & Administration, Leadership & Policy in Schools* and the *Journal of School Leadership*. His recent publications include *The Making of Educational Leaders* (Cassell 1999) and *The New Work of Educational Leaders* (Sage 2003).

**Carol E. Harris,** Professor Emeritus of Leadership Studies at the University of Victoria, BC, began her career in adult education and music. Until her recent retirement, she taught organisation theory, philosophy of leadership, and policy studies. In 1991, her dissertation 'Administering School Music in Three Canadian Settings: Philosophy, Action and Educational Policy' received the T. B. Greenfield Dissertation Award from the Canadian Association for the Study of Educational Administration. Her book, *A Sense of Themselves: Elizabeth Murray's Leadership in School and Community* (Fernwood Press 1998), reflects her research interest in arts at the intersection of school and adult education. Her articles appear in national publications of the *Canadian Journal of Education,* the *Canadian Journal for the Study of Adult Education, Educational Administration and Foundations,* and the *Canadian Music University Review,* and in international journals such as *Educational Administration Quarterly, Educational Management, Administration and Leadership,* and *Arts Education Policy Review.* She has also contributed chapters to eight books exploring philosophical and theoretical foundations for educational leadership and administration, including one on Heidegger in *Ethical Foundations for Educational Administration* (Routledge 2003), and on Collingwood in *Aesthetic Dimensions of Educational Administration and Leadership* (Routledge 2006).

**Gerardo R. López** is Associate Professor of Educational Leadership at Indiana University, where he teaches courses in school-community relations, critical difference/s in educational leadership, and inquiry methodology. His areas of interest are critical race theory, migrant education, and parental involvement. The majority of his publications directly challenge the taken-for-granted assumptions surrounding the role of parents in educational matters, and more specifically, how Latina/o home-based knowledges and practices redefine the terrain of involvement activity. His work has been published in *Educational Administration Quarterly, American Educational Research Journal, Harvard Educational Review, Journal of School Leadership, Journal of School Public Relations,* and *International Journal of Qualitative Studies in Education,* among other scholarly outlets. He is currently working on a book (with Maria Pabón López) on the education of undocumented children.

**Stephanie Mackler** is Assistant Professor of Education at Cornell College in Mount Vernon, Iowa. She received her PhD in Philosophy and Education from Teachers College of Columbia University and was awarded a Spencer Dissertation Fellowship for her dissertation research. Her current scholarly work involves research in philosophical hermeneutics, the philosophy of higher education, and philosophy as a way of living. Her most recent article is 'Educating for Meaning in an Era of Banality' (*Philosophy of Education* 2007). She has also published in *Educational Theory, Teachers College Record, Education Review, Philosophy of Education, Encyclopedia of Education and Human Development* (M. E. Sharpe 2005), and has an article forthcoming in *Policy Futures in Education.*

**Andrea Migone** is a Lecturer in the Political Science Department at Simon Fraser University, where he received his PhD. His research interests and publications are in the areas of public administration, global economics, and public policy, and he has both worked and conducted research in the area of historical public administration. He has authored 'Hedonistic Consumerism: Patterns of Consumption in Modern Capitalism'(*Review of Radical Political Economics* 2007), 'Dimensions of Globalization: The Cultural and Institutional Novelties of the Global System' (in S. McBride et al. (eds) *Global Turbulences: Instability in National and International Political Economy,* Kluwer Academic 2003), 'Professioni e Associazioni Mediche in un Sistema di Common Law' and 'Bar Associations e Law Societies: L'Avvocatura in Nord America' (in M. Bonanni (ed.) *L'Ordine Inutile? Gli Ordini Professionali in Italia,* Franco Angeli 1998). He was coauthor with R. Campbell and L. Pal of 'Air Farce: Airline Policy in a Deregulatory Environment' and 'Speaking Loudly and Using a Very Large

Stick: Hardball Politics and Softwood Lumber' (in R. Campbell and L. Pal (eds) *The Real World of Canadian Politics*, Broadview Press 2004). He is the cofounder and coeditor of *World Political Science Review.*

**Peter Milley** holds a PhD in Leadership Studies from the University of Victoria, BC. He is a Senior Advisor in Curriculum and Leadership at the Canada School of Public Service in Ottawa, where he conducts research on public administration, leadership, and management, and provides advice nationally and internationally to senior public officials on how to encourage leadership and learning in their organisations. He is author of 'Aesthetic Experience as Resistance to the "Iron Cage" of Dominative Administrative Rationality' (in E. A. Samier and R. Bates (eds) *Aesthetic Dimensions of Educational Administration and Leadership*, Routledge 2006) and 'Imagining Good Organisations: Moral Orders or Moral Communities' (*Journal of Educational Management & Administration* 2002), and has presented numerous papers at the Canadian Society for Studies in Education and the American Educational Research Association conferences.

**Eugénie A. Samier** is Associate Professor of Educational Leadership at Simon Fraser University. Her research and writing interests are in administrative philosophy and theory, Weberian foundations of administration, theories and models of educational leadership, and comparative educational administration. She currently holds a Guest Researcher position at the Humboldt University of Berlin during research semesters from Simon Fraser University, was Visiting Professor in the Department of Administrative Studies at the University of Tartu, Estonia (2003) and has been a guest lecturer at universities and institutes in Germany, Estonia, Russia, and Finland. Her publications include 'Demandarinisation in the New Public Management: Examining Changing Administrative Authority from a Weberian Perspective' (in E. Hanke and W. Mommsen (eds) *Max Webers Herrschaftssoziologie. Studien zu Entstehung und Wirkung*, Mohr/Siebeck 2001), 'The Capitalist Ethic and the Spirit of Intellectualism: The Rationalized Administration of Education' (in *L'éthique Protestante de Max Weber et L'esprit de la Modernité*, Editions de la Maison des Sciences de l'Homme 1997), and several articles on organisational culture and values, the New Public Management, the role of history and biography in educational administration, the role of humanities in administration (including aesthetic and literary analysis), and Weberian foundations of administrative theory and ethics in *Educational Management & Administration, Journal of Educational Administration, Educational Administration Quarterly,* the *Journal of Educational Administration and History, Halduskultuur,* and in a book series published by Peter Lang on vocational education. She is a founding board member of the international, multilanguage and interdisciplinary journal *Halduskultuur: Administrative Culture. Административная* культураю. *Verwaltungskultur. Hallintokulttuuri* and is editor, with a contribution on Kantian Ethics, of *Ethical Foundations for Educational Administration* (Routledge 2003) and principal editor (with Richard Bates) of *Aesthetic Dimensions of Educational Administration and Leadership* (Routledge 2006) with contributions on Kantian aesthetics, Romanticism (coauthored), and the aesthetics of charisma.

**Michèle Schmidt** is Assistant Professor, Coordinator of the Masters programme in Educational Leadership, and the Associate Director of Graduate Programs in the Faculty of Education at Simon Fraser University. Her research interests and publications are in the areas of the emotions of teaching and leading, leadership within a context of educational change and accountability, and sociocultural perspectives of education that focus on the implications of capital on children's school experiences. She received her PhD at OISE/University of Toronto and completed postdoctoral studies at Johns Hopkins University. Previously she was a department head and high school teacher in Ontario. Her most recent publications include: 'Sustaining Resilience' (in B. Davis (ed.) *Leading the Strategically Focused School,* Sage 2007), *Does School Size Matter? A Social Capital Perspective* (International Study Association for Teachers and Teaching 2006), 'Teachers' Sense-making about Comprehensive School Reform: The Influence of Emotions' (*Teaching and Teacher Education* 2005), and 'Risky Business: Leading the School System in British Columbia' (in K. Anderson (ed.) *An Educational Leadership Compendium: Emerging Canadian Scholars in Education* (University of Calgary Press forthcoming).

**John Smyth** is currently Research Professor, School of Education, University of Ballarat, Australia. He is also Emeritus Professor, Flinders University, Australia, Senior Research Fellow, Wilf Malcolm Institute of Educational Research, University of Waikato, New Zealand, and Graduate Adjunct Faculty Professor, College of Education, Texas State University-San Marcos. Formerly, he held the Roy F. & Joann Cole Mitte Endowed Chair in School Improvement at Texas State University-San Marcos, Research Professor at Edith Cowan University, and Foundation Chair of Teacher Education and Founding Director of the Flinders Institute for the Study of Teaching, Flinders University. For six years he was the Associate Dean of Research, School of Education, Flinders University. His scholarship has been recognised by a Senior Fulbright Research Scholar Award (1991), one of the rare ones awarded to Education in Australia, and he was the first non-American to receive the Palmer O. Johnson Award from the American Educational Research Association (1993) for outstanding published educational research. He is the author and editor of fifteen books with international publishers, and has authored over two hundred articles and book chapters. Recent books include: *Teachers in the Middle: Reclaiming the Wasteland of the Adolescent Years of*

*Schooling* (with P. McInerney, Peter Lang 2007), *'Dropping Out', Drifting Off, Being Excluded: Becoming Somebody Without School* (with R. Hattam et al., Peter Lang 2004), *Critical Politics of Teachers' Work: An Australian Perspective* (Peter Lang 2001); *Teachers' Work in a Globalizing Economy* (with A. Dow et al., Falmer Press 2000), *Schooling for a Fair Go* (with R. Hattam and M. Lawson, Federation Press 1998), *Remaking Teaching: Ideology, Policy and Practice* (with G. Shacklock, Routledge 1998), *Being Reflexive: Critical Approaches to Social and Educational Research* (with G. Shacklock (eds), Falmer Press 1998). He is currently a member of the following editorial boards: *British Journal of Sociology of Education, International Journal of Leadership in Education, Teacher Development, London Review of Education,* and *Journal of Learning Communities.* His research interests are in the areas of policy sociology of teachers' work, critical policy analysis, social justice and educational disadvantage, and the policy impact of educational reform on teachers and students.

**Adam G. Stanley's** research and writing centres around the validity of literature as a source for educational leadership and public administration and the need to embrace the art and craft of teaching as a humanities discipline. He has taught and conducted research in North America, the UK, Japan, Germany, and Russia, including a public lecture and follow-up seminar on the literary critique of Canadian public administration at the Humboldt-Universität zu Berlin and cotaught a guest class on the Canadian administrative tradition at the Institute for USA and Canada (Moscow). His publications include 'Stone Angels and Paper Airplanes: Literary Representations of Canadian Public Administration,' coauthored with E. Samier and published in *Representations of Canada: Cross-Cultural Reflections on Canadian Society* (joint annual publication of the Ministry of Education for the Russian Federation, Volgograd State University and Centre for American Studies Pennsylvania Canadian Studies Consortium 2007), contributions on the literary critique of educational administration and romantic philosophy and educational administration in *Aesthetic Dimensions of Educational Administration and Leadership* (RoutledgeFalmer 2006), and is coeditor of the *Journal of Educational Administration and Foundations* Special Issue on Aesthetics of Educational Administration and Leadership (in press).

**Janice Wallace** is Associate Professor in the Department of Educational Policy Studies, the University of Alberta, Edmonton, Alberta. She received her PhD at OISE/University of Toronto in 2000 and was awarded the Thomas B. Greenfield Award by the Canadian Association for the Study of Educational Administration for her dissertation exploring the phenomenon of resistance to gender equity employment policy in Ontario. Her scholarship focuses on equity issues in educational organisations and the particular effects of globalisation on the work of administrators. She was a faculty member at the University of Western Ontario, has been a visiting lecturer at the University of Victoria, and was an invited Visiting Scholar at the University of British Columbia. She was coinvestigator of a large SSHRC-funded story project on women educators. Publications include 'Assuming Leadership: Women Superintendents in 20th Century Ontario' (in R. Coulter and H. Harper (eds) *History is Hers: Women Teachers in Twentieth Century Ontario,* Detselig 2005), 'Running the Race: The Work of Principals in Restructured Educational Systems' (in H. Armstrong (ed.) *Examining the Practice of School Administration in Canada,* Detselig 2005), and 'Seeing Beyond Difference: Women Administrators in Canada and Israel' (in I. Oplatka and R. Hertz-Lazarowitz (eds) *Women Principals in a Multicultural Society: New Insights into Feminist Educational Leadership,* Sense 2006). She has also published in the *Journal of Educational Administration and Foundations, Oral History Forum, Educational Management Administration and Leadership,* and *Canadian and International Education.* She is guest editor of a special edition on women and education for the *Canadian Journal of Education* (2008 forthcoming).

**Michelle D. Young** is the Executive Director of the University Council for Educational Administration and an associate professor in Educational Leadership and Policy at the University of Texas, Austin. Dr. Young received her PhD in Educational Policy and Planning and then served as an assistant professor at the University of Iowa and an associate professor of Research at the University of Missouri. Dr. Young serves on the editorial board of the *Educational Administration Quarterly, Educational Administration Abstracts, Journal of Cases in Educational Leadership* and *Education and Urban Society.* She also serves on the National Advisory Board for ERIC, the Wallace Foundation's Education Advisory Committee, the National Policy Board for Educational Administration, and the National Commission for the Advancement of Educational Leadership Preparation. Her scholarship focuses on how school leaders and school policies can ensure equitable and quality experiences for all students and adults who learn and work in schools. Dr. Young is the recipient of the William J. Davis award for the most outstanding article published in a volume of the *Educational Administration Quarterly.* Her work has also been published in the *Review of Educational Research,* the *Educational Researcher,* the *American Educational Research Journal,* the *Journal of School Leadership,* the *International Journal of Qualitative Studies in Education,* and *Leadership and Policy in Schools,* among other publications.

# Name Index

# Subject Index